Black
Cultural
Mythology

Black Cultural Mythology

Christel N. Temple

Cover image: "Protection," from the series *Movement I: The Unknown World*, 2008. Mixed media, 48" × 42", by Joseph Holston.

Published by State University of New York Press, Albany

© 2020 State University of New York

All rights reserved

No part of this book may be used or reproduced in any manner whatsoever without written permission. No part of this book may be stored in a retrieval system or transmitted in any form or by any means including electronic, electrostatic, magnetic tape, mechanical, photocopying, recording, or otherwise without the prior permission in writing of the publisher.

For information, contact State University of New York Press, Albany, NY
www.sunypress.edu

Library of Congress Cataloging-in-Publication Data

Names: Temple, Christel N., author. | Lamousé-Smith, W. Bediako, writer of foreword.
Title: Black cultural mythology / Christel N. Temple ; foreword by Willie Bediako Lamousé-Smith.
Description: Albany : SUNY Press, [2020] | Includes bibliographical references and index.
Identifiers: LCCN 2019015193 | ISBN 9781438477879 (hardcover : alk. paper) | ISBN 9781438477886 (pbk. : alk. paper) | ISBN 9781438477893 (ebook)
Subjects: LCSH: American literature—African American authors—History and criticism. | African Americans—Intellectual life—20th century.
Classification: LCC PS153.N5 T43 2020 | DDC 810.9/896073—dc23
LC record available at https://lccn.loc.gov/2019015193

10 9 8 7 6 5 4 3 2 1

For
Tyler Temple Giles
and
the generations who shall always know

In memory of
Toni Morrison

Contents

Foreword	ix
Preface	xiii
Acknowledgments	xxi
Introduction	1
Chapter One Intellectual Foundations of Black Cultural Mythology	23
Chapter Two Commemoration Intervention	91
Chapter Three Harriet Tubman and Aesthetic Memorialization	137
Chapter Four Haiti as Diaspora-Wide Mythology	155
Chapter Five Richard Wright's Navigation of the Antihero	183
Chapter Six Mythical Malcolm in an Age of Marable	199
Chapter Seven Imaginative Rights	215

CONCLUSION
Introducing Africana Cultural Memory Studies					253

NOTES					263

BIBLIOGRAPHY					297

INDEX					315

Foreword

Willie Bediako Lamousé-Smith

Standing on the shoulders of Black literary and history giants, Christel N. Temple has produced a tour de force on Africana mythology. This book is the outcome of more than a decade of painstaking research of original data and comparative studies. It also offers a coherent framework for studying Africana memory and memorialization of heroes and heroic feats that have grown into mythologies.

From Temple's keen study and sharp analyses of heroics in Black mythology, it is incontrovertible that renewal of remembrance, commemoration, and celebration assure immortality for Africana heroes. Mythology keeps them alive among the living. However, for heroes to stay in memory, they must be talked about often. Stories of their adventures and achievements must constantly be resuscitated for the living lest they die. Heroes, just like spirits, die when they are not remembered and celebrated. Remembrance does not rely solely on public statues to sustain immortality. Transmission of memory by the spoken word in stories, tales, fables, songs, and riddles sustains immortality. And there have been Black preservers and refreshers of the remembrance: from the writings of Maria W. Stewart in the nineteenth century, through Shirley Graham Du Bois, John Henrik Clarke, Derek Walcott, and Ntozake Shange in the twentieth century, to contemporary writers such as Toni Morrison.

This outstanding book was completed in the quadricentennial year of the arrival of the first kidnapped African captives at Point Comfort in the Christian English colony of Virginia. In 1619 the English made their first sale of an African on the mainland of what became the United States of America. The first African to suffer this disconsolate fate was a Mbundu man from Angola. Although the wicked horrors on slave ships during the transatlantic crossings have been exposed a lot in recent decades, American selective public memory does not guarantee enshrinement of this memory. Brutalities and treatments of inhumanity meted out on land to those guiltless captives who survived the "Middle Passage" were no less horrifying. Heroes emerged in every phase of the enslaved Africans existence and, on behalf of all, fought not only to survive but also to be free. In the midst of being physically maimed and terrorized so that the victims would submit to unremittingly heinous exploitations, memories were being laid and stored by the Africans thus enslaved. Out of these hellish conditions arose individuals who would later be garlanded with the crown of mythology. They went through the phases through which heroes pass: from self-denial with single-minded devotion and commitment, they apply their uncommon talents to defeating powerful evil forces, becoming legendary in their lifetime, lauded in songs, fables, and tales, and entering the permanent mythic realm. Through intergenerational communication, their names and deeds were transmitted, not to be forgotten, memory was laid, maintained, and kept being resuscitated.

Among the heroes who sacrificed themselves to go through dangers in their attempts to liberate their consanguineous fellows were battlefield warriors such as Nat Turner, Toussaint Louverture, and Harriet Tubman. There were heroes who did not bear arms in their drive to free the oppressed descendants of Africa in the Americas: Marcus Garvey, Martin Luther King Jr., and Malcolm X are examples. There were intellectual heroes who ensured that memory did not drain away amid hostile distortions. Among them were Frederick Douglass, W. E. B. Du Bois, Booker T. Washington, Carter Woodson, Lorenzo Johnston Greene, Shirley Graham Du Bois, C. L. R. James, Frantz Fanon, Nathan Huggins, Molefi Kete Asante, and others. Literary heroes include Richard Wright, James Baldwin, Toni Morrison, Ntozake Shange, and Ralph Ellison. All these streams of Africana heroes and heroines have been, and continue to be, the fountain that feeds Africana mythology. Temple brilliantly brings out the heroics in all those named here, and others too numerous for space to be mentioned. She manages to distil their individual complexities into a framework for studying, analyzing, understanding, appreciating, and enjoying knowledge in Africana mythology. The power embedded in Africana mythology is made explicit.

The power of mythology has moved and enabled cultures to achieve prosperity and greatness and endure. Universally, every community and every culture has its own body of mythologies. The heroic is celebrated and honored for selflessness in redeeming the community. The heroic act needs not be physical or martial. It may be intellectual. With the publication of Temple's book, scholars of mythology may more readily begin to acknowledge the contributions of Africana mythology for other fields of the academic and intellectual enterprise.

In this outstanding work, Temple has opened a novel path for studies by scholars and all researchers with interest in the African diaspora experience in the Americas. This book has laid a living foundation on which others with considerable interest and curiosity in the subject of Africana mythology can build upon.

Preface

Black cultural mythology offers a new way of understanding the culture of the post-European enslavement African diaspora as a *sacred inheritance*. This new perspective provides a framework for itemizing not only processes of cultural survival but also the memorialization practices that support the broad narrative of this survival in literature, art, history, and folk culture. A hallmark of this mythology is its heroics, recalled in collective recognition of the culture's hearty legacy of historical figures whose acts of self-preservation and prowess in surviving incredible odds are the source of rich cultural remembrance and inspiration.

Several recent symbolic phenomena remind us of the range of the African American heroic, in particular in contemporary consciousness and discourses. African American womanist heroics are reenergized by the commemorative and memorial impact of Harriet Tubman's image, which is scheduled to appear on a future twenty-dollar bill. The US Senate's 2016 bill aimed at properly commemorating the milestone reached in 2019, of four hundred years of African life in the English colonies and the United States as "one of the greatest survival stories rarely told and not fully understood," set the stage, along with visionary nationwide community and scholarly activism, to assess in vibrant new terms how society should honor and recall the dimensions of African survival in the diaspora.[1] *Black Panther* (2018), as a dedicated feature film that brought to life the long-endeared, quintessentially royal, heroic, and technologically superior comic book world of Wakanda, made an international impact. First, it gave a twenty-first century push for Pan-Africanism and Black internationalism with its Africana-diverse cast of Black actors representing African America, Guyana, Trinidad and Tobago, Kenya, Zimbabwe, Benin, South Africa, Ivory Coast, as well as Afro-British and Afro-German populations. Second, it presented the image of powerful

Black women in more diverse filmic roles such as queen, princess, scientist, warrior, and superhero. The international and cultural ego-boosting impact of the film *Black Panther* is but one dimension of the era's characteristics for people of African descent who, unfortunately, still share a narrative about ongoing forces that challenge Africana freedom and survival.

While we celebrate the prowess of the Black Panther, T'Challa, plus the unexpected and enduring images of womanist determination, genius, and heroics that appear in *Black Panther*, we also lament too many instances of diaspora women such as African American Sandra Bland and Afro-Brazilian Marielle Franco emerging as part of a contemporary set of Black martyrs, whose activism in the face of death is a unique type of heroic. The era has given us other martyrs, like Trayvon Martin, who is a contemporary parallel to Emmett Till, both of whose lives were taken in the prime of youth, before they had an opportunity to fulfill their destinies of living potentially acclaimed and heroic lives. The responding activism—the civil rights movement mobilization in memory of Emmett Till and the Black Lives Matter movement in memory of Trayvon Martin—helps to ensure survival as brave men and women mobilize to resist dehumanization. Black men have been the most traditionally and publicly acknowledged icons who are the heroic and symbolic faces of assassination and death, and Black women have also been legacy leaders and heroic partners stabilizing the culture's mythological structure.

A remarkable social fissure appeared primarily in the African American press and in Black social media in late 2018 as a timely public discourse to immediately precede the publication of this study on *Black Cultural Mythology*, which has been in development for over ten years. Again, it is associated with the *Black Panther* phenomenon. In early October 2018, the magazine *Vanity Fair* released an excerpt from its forthcoming November 2018 issue's interview with Michael B. Jordan, the *Black Panther* actor who plays Erik B. Killmonger, the hero's nemesis. The community respects Jordan as a culturally informed actor because of his role as "Wallace" in the urban Baltimore cable television series *The Wire* and his performance as the heir—"Adonis Johnson"—of the slain Black contender Apollo Creed (from the third installment of the *Rocky* boxing film franchise) in the film and sequel, *Creed* and *Creed II*. The Black community credits him with an additional African-centered consciousness because of the dying words of his character, Killmonger, in the film *Black Panther*. He says, "Bury me in the ocean with my ancestors who jumped from the ships because they knew death was better than bondage." In the *Vanity Fair* interview, Jordan entered the realm of cultural criticism when he observed, "We don't have any mythology, black mythology, or folklore." He explains, "Creating our own mythology is very important because it helps dream . . . You help people dream."² This incidental, off-the-cuff, yet sincere remark summarized Jordan's earlier discourse in the interview where he highlighted Black heroes Fred Hampton (murdered martyr of the Black Panther Party) and Mansa Musa (wealthy fourteenth-century emperor of the West African kingdom of Mali) whose stories, like that of the fictional *Black Panther* hero, could be the source material for a greater balance of culturally heroic feature films.

Jordan did not mention any women in his short list of notable cultural heroes, yet this comprehensive study on Black cultural mythology is careful to present a balanced narrative of a wholistic vision of myth, memory, mythology, and heroics. It presents layers of both Black women's and men's contributions and critical idea formation. Prominent enslavement revolts (Gabriel Prosser, Denmark Vesey, Nat Turner), a nation-state revolution (in Haiti led by Toussaint Louverture), and nationwide activism that ended with public assassinations (Malcolm X, Martin Luther King Jr.) stimulate a legacy of public remembrance of honorable Black men as diasporic heroes. Yet, Black women also sustain Black cultural mythology through activist heroics (Harriet Tubman and Maria W. Stewart); deliberate heroic or gender-balancing storytelling (biographer Shirley Graham Du Bois, poet Laini Mataka, dramatist May Miller, and prose writers Toni Morrison, Gayl Jones, and Edwidge Danticat); and a vibrant trove of cultural and literary criticism.

The philosophical framework of Black cultural mythology prioritizes the cognitive, intergenerational, and memorial processes at work in cultural memory. Its concern is the cyclical transmission of chronicles of heroic narrative and collective ideas about memory. These serve a culturally preservationist function in diasporic worldviews. Whether in literature or in critical thought, the repertoire of mythological storytelling revitalizes our memory of real, authentically pioneered legacies of African diasporic resistance and survival.

Theorizing the practices and behaviors inspired by these legacies of survival by itemizing a set of over a dozen attributes that characterize the philosophical framework's processes is an organic intellectual feat that helps define diasporic mythology on its own terms. The objectives of this theoretical intervention of Black cultural mythology framed as sacred cultural inheritance are to claim diasporic legacies as mythology, to promote deeper reflective and meditative inquiries into the humanistic vitality of the cultural logic that African descendants generated in the diaspora, and to introduce a set of stable critical terminologies useful for both academic and popular engagements of diaspora heritage. The African American experience frames much of the inaugural case study for how Africana resistance behaviors and cultural activism are responsible for an organic, identifiable cultural mythology in an environment beyond the shores of Africa. The final product is a methodology of surveying, naming, and organizing the numerous isolated and informal contributions to African American and diasporic ideas and scholarship on myth, mythology, memory, and heroics. This is an effort to systematically theorize and formally institutionalize Black cultural mythology and a broader field of Africana cultural memory studies.

The Haitian Revolution is foundational in the creative legacies of diasporic mythological structure for being the pinnacle accomplishment of a shared and inspirational hemispheric fervor of collective African resistance. However, the US-based Africana experience requires further critical mining because a collective cultural mythology has been more difficult to institutionalize in a nation-within-a-nation predicament that silences and obscures discourses on the radical norms of Black heroics in the public domain.

Prioritizing conceptual innovation on the broad topics of myth, mythology, memory, and heroics, this book is an invitation for scholars from all critical vantage points that feature topics such as amnesia, enslavement memory, rememory, and more to participate in the philosophical and applied intervention. The uniformity promises to enhance the collectivity of an Africana cultural memory pursuit.

Also, this study *reorders* and *stylizes* the study of myth, mythology, memory, heroics, and African American and diaspora *survivalist* activity. Its timeline begins with the enslavement period, which forced Africans to *begin again* and to manage the processes of engraving identity on new soil in the diaspora. Its cultural-historical reference points are a host of original African worldviews and aggregate conceptual and memorial beacons reflected in diaspora people's broad memories. In broad cultural awareness, African Americans as diaspora people carry a memory, though sometimes blurred or nonexact, of a former geography whose wholeness and normalcy—where African people were free to live, behave, and commemorate on their own terms—were natural and embedded in firm geo-cultural identities. In that pre-enslavement existence, memory practices and legacy tools did not need to be excavated, reconceptualized, and catalogued from a comprehensive study of hundreds of years of history, achievement, feats of freedom, and self-actualization in a country the ancestors did not choose.

Black cultural mythology appears as an intervention with a new language that better equips us to treat the intersections of history and memory with cultural precision. Its key concepts relate to a philosophy of survival culled from interdisciplinary paths of African American and Caribbean sociopolitical thought, cultural theory, and creative production. We can, therefore, trace the conceptual antecedents of Black cultural mythology to nineteenth-century abolitionist-era ideas about cultural ascendancy and stability in prefreedom and postfreedom visions, to visionary preoccupations with the broad public history project, to an African-centered worldview and cultural theorizations from the Black Arts Movement, and to the best practices for African-centered well-being addressed in Black psychology views on mythological structure. As Black cultural mythology signifies on history, folk culture, and literature, it allows an expansion of the culture's sense of its own mythology as a self-reflexive narrative process of managing the corpus of actual legendary prowess. These efforts give it categorical power to stabilize and then cue the next generation of inquiries into uncovering how culturally organic processes and behaviors emerged to sustain survival in unimagined, new, and hostile environments.

Black cultural mythology formally announces a new intellectual tradition to enhance the study of the culture's philosophy of heroism. Its critical richness is the interplay between attributes of hero dynamics, ancestor acknowledgment, historical reenactment of worldview, resistance-based cognitive survival, hyperheroic impulses, epic intuitive conduct, immortalization sensibility, sacred observance, ritual remembrance, commemoration philosophy, mythological structure, sacrificial inheritance, aesthetic memorialization, reconciliation and renewal, and antiheroics. In the Black cultural mythology conceptual framework, antiheroics describes an individual, group, institution, or system that creative and historical narrators symbolically name as an opponent of Black agency.

Civic and readerly response to the legacy of diasporic experiences is enriched and best honored when it includes an itemization of the epic and the heroic—the *mythological*—elements and narratives of cognitive, behavioral, and conceptual survival, which are transmitted in the culture's rhetorical and symbolic creative production. It would be unwieldy to presume that any aesthetic artifact that produces a mythology-related discourse of the African American experience would actualize every attribute of Black cultural mythology. Nonetheless, in the pages that follow, I present an ambitious topical reckoning of ways to operationalize Black cultural mythology and its critical priorities as applied conceptual tools for explicating cultural phenomena.

The exemplars whose organic ideas help to frame Black cultural mythology's formal intellectual tradition have been identified through a decadelong immersive close reading of history and sources reflecting African American sociopolitical thought and cultural theory, as well as a search for seminal and sustained scholarship on dimensions of African American myth. This painstaking excavation is responsible for the bibliographic depth and examples introduced in the book's critical narratives. This inaugural book-length study prioritizes subjects (people and events) that have had high mythological and popular visibility in the African American experience of history and letters. This begins with a survey of commemoration, including the symbolism, ritual, and sacredness of collectively conscious memorial practices related to the year 1619 and to Emancipation Proclamation reflections. It also features the legacy of Harriet Tubman beyond historical norms to survey her extended potential in the realm of popular culture and the cycles of persona narrative that society receives in juvenile to adult experiences. With her ascendancy as the first African American women whose image is scheduled to appear on US paper currency, the challenge is to manage a more accurate perception of her persona and the dimensions of her symbolism. Next, the mythological view addresses twentieth-century to early twenty-first century neglect of the traditional honor and celebration due to the Republic of Haiti. Several perspectives reinforce the need to recast (for those who do not know) the nation of Haiti into its proper mythological structure, elucidating how the nation's revolutionary feat suffers from a double jeopardy of victimization and memory mismanagement.

Literary considerations eventually take the lead in this volume's revisionist efforts. A key priority is to extend the discussion of literature's role in Black cultural mythology through a biographical-literary engagement with the philosophies of Richard Wright and his repertoire, including the famed novel *Native Son* (1940). Exploring a balance of intellectual genealogy and literary criticism presents an opportunity to expand Black cultural mythology's vision for deconstructing the parameters of antiheroics in Wright's celebrated text. Genre becomes important for Black cultural mythology as well, particularly the need to disentangle much of what we presume about the negotiations between the art of autobiography and biography, particularly in the dueling of memory politics on Malcolm X, between the Alex Haley-assisted *Autobiography* and Manning Marable's *A Life of Reinvention*. As Black cultural mythology inevitably celebrates the function of the writer as a steady narrator of the culture's cycles of heroics and memory, this book ends with a dedicated reflection on African American literary history. It explores how Black Arts Movement orientations to an emergent philosophy of cultural mythology get redirected in contemporary fictive and dramatic prototypes of Black cultural mythology offered by Charles Johnson, Robert O'Hara, and Colson Whitehead. A shift toward modeling Black cultural mythology as literary criticism demonstrates the relevance and flexibility of the attributes to sustain critical discourses not only of cultural theory but also of literary history and narrative developments. Inevitably, the examination of the major superlative (e.g., *the first, the best known, the most remembered*, and so forth), symbolic and popular subjects ranging from 1619 to Tubman to Haiti to Wright and Malcolm, and an inaugural application to literary history demonstrates the vitality of Black cultural mythology's organic shift related to idea formation on myth, mythology, memory, and heroics. This activity becomes a catalyst for dynamic new conversations for the twenty-first century.

Acknowledgments

Completing this book is one of the most rewarding events of my career. It has taken over ten years for the core ideas to ferment into this final presentation. I expected the project to come to fruition at a faster pace, yet with each postponement of progress (job relocation, new motherhood, service as department chair), I had the opportunity to teach a different version of a course on the topic. These pedagogical immersions—in the end, four courses, at two different universities since 2008—were explorations and excavations of the topics that now make up this book. This pacing enabled me to delve more deeply into ponderings and research that led the topic into unexpected areas. I am forever honored that Joanne V. Gabbin from James Madison University so graciously welcomed my paper on "We Are African and Malcolm in an Ancestor" for the 2004 Furious Flower Conference. Charles E. Jones, then president of the National Council of Black Studies (NCBS) and Terry Kershaw (ancestor), who was then editor of the organization's *International Journal of Black Studies*, were kind and supportive mentors when Charles heard part two of the Furious Flower paper, "Malcolm X and Black Cultural Mythology," at the 2006 NCBS conference and recommended that I submit it to the *International Journal of African Studies*. The ideas were exploratory then, and Jones and Kershaw guided me toward John Henrik Clarke's and Michael Eric Dyson's works on Malcolm's mythology.

I thank the editors of *Journal of Black Studies* for publishing one of my early essays, "Rescuing the Literary" (2006), which introduced Black cultural mythology as a form of literary criticism. Mark Christian (now at Lehman University) arranged this special issue of the journal through a symposium at Miami University of Ohio that gave me the intellectual challenge and the public forum from which to share the new developments.

I placed a chapter on "Black Cultural Mythology" in my 2007 critical anthology *Literary Spaces: Introduction to Comparative Black Literature*, and I am grateful to the editors of Carolina Academic Press whose book series on African American Studies was a fruitful placement for my anthology. As I recall, the editors saw a reference to this in-progress anthology on my CV and courted it for publication, which gave me the opportunity to share an early ideation of Black cultural mythology much earlier than expected. I extend thanks to James L. Conyers Jr. of the University of Houston for the spark that challenged me to do a study of "Literary Malcolm X: The Making of an African American Ancestor" for his collection, *Malcolm X: A Historical Reader* (2008). The research for that chapter took me to Accra, Ghana, where my friend and colleague Barbara Eleanor Adams (ancestor) so graciously served as my Ghanaian travel mentor and guide. We searched for J. H. Kwabena Nketia at the University of Ghana, Legon, and for a funeral dirge ceremony to witness that would illuminate the communal celebration and memorialization structurally chronicled in his *Funeral Dirges of the Akan* (1955). There, I encountered phenomena that were bridges between my first wave of research on diasporan Africans as involuntary exiles due to enslavement, and the new project of cultural memory and mythology. The film festival at the National Theater, the Ali Mazrui lecture at the W. E. B. Du Bois Center, the visit to Cape Coast, and a fixation on Maya Angelou's ex-pat observations from *All God's Children Need Traveling Shoes* (1986) imprinted on my research directions. It was not until recently that I understood fully how the topic of diasporan Africans as exiles and the conceptual commitment to tracing Black cultural mythology are part of the same project: articulating what seemed like an overwhelming cultural loss into a more accurate quantification of our success at surviving.

I extend a special thanks to Ama Mazama of Temple University who invited me to participate in the Asante at 65 Conference in 2007. This was in the early stages of my Black cultural mythology research, and I kept discovering morsels of idea formation in Molefi Kete Asante's scholarship that caused me to fear that my notion of Black cultural mythology might have been already addressed. This invitation provided the perfect stimulus for me to undertake a content analysis of Asante's entire corpus of scholarship to mine his existing contributions to African American myth. I was shocked to discover a full repertoire of ideas. I thank Ama Mazama for positioning me for this challenge, which allowed me an audience with Asante as well as with Maulana Karenga who offered helpful suggestions and points of information. I am grateful to the organizers of the 2008 Richard Wright

Centennial Conference in Paris, where I presented "Richard Wright and Black Cultural Mythology," which evolved as chapter 5, tackling Wright's investment in cultural antiheroics. It was there that I encountered the Haitian-French rapper Kery James's music video for the song "L'Ombre de Show Business" that modeled the power of transnational revolutionary heroics. The video appeared on network television in my hotel several times per day, and it presented thoughtful and sustained likenesses of Malcolm X and Angela Davis to make a statement on Pan-Africanism and Black internationalism that, as an academic tourist, I embraced. This song and the possibilities of shared, transnational heroics was my contribution to the second biannual conference on Afroeuropeans: Cultures and Identities in Leon, Spain in 2008. The conveners have always been so welcoming and engaging, which benefited my research, as the collaborations helped me to enhance my theorization of transnational heroics. In the fourth biannual conference in 2012 in London, I was grateful for yet another opportunity to test my hypothesis on the extended cultural memory meaning of sacred Africana sites on European soil. This topic highlighted the pilgrimages that Haitians and other people of African descent were making to Toussaint Louverture's final resting place in Fort de Joux, France, and I am grateful to my colleagues in that session who helped me refine my thesis.

As always, the members of College Language Association have been tremendous in their support and nurturing as well as in their instigation of new ideas with each year's theme. I am grateful for multiple opportunities with the College Language Association. At the 2013 conference in Lexington, Kentucky, I was fortunate to have a highly engaged panel of co-presenters and an audience that offered important ideas to help fine-tune my path toward further exploring Haiti's identity as the first diaspora-wide mythology. This was a turning point for the ideas I eventually address in chapter 4. The College Language Association also thematically presented the opportunity to consider the function of text-to-film adaptation studies, which inspired my chapter in *Transcendence and the Africana Literary Enterprise* (2017) on "Autobiography and Documentary Forms of Paul Robeson's *Here I Stand* as Black Cultural Mythology." The support of the Cheikh Anta Diop International Conference (held annually in Philadelphia) and NCBS have been foundational because I developed six of the book's core themes among these two professional organizations. Another key opportunity was the invitation from V. P. Franklin to present at the 2012 NCBS conference on a panel responding to Manning Marable's newly released book on Malcolm X—*A Life of Reinvention* (2011). This presentation on "Living History, Biography, and the Challenge of Heroic Memory" evolved into chapter 6. In particular for the *Reinvention* panel, the data I was able to generate on Malcom X from a case study on the first wave of book reviews on *Reinvention* verified the book-worthy discursive possibilities for a theorization of Black cultural mythology. I am not certain that I would have selected to research the mythological structure of Malcolm in Marable's *Reinvention* if it had not been for this invitation. Among these, I am exceptionally grateful for the opportunity to give the Awards Luncheon Keynote at the 2015 Diop Conference where I negotiated key ideas about the commemorative value of Martin Luther King Jr., Harriet Tubman, and the 1619–2019 Quadricentennial in my address on "Narrative Agency in the Public Domain." These two opportunities have been the most important defining moments of this project.

I have had significant opportunities to present on Black cultural mythology and gather feedback from peers from two key events at the University of Pittsburgh. The first is the Center for Race and Social Problems' Brown Bag Speaker Series where I first introduced my usage of Amos Wilson's mythological structure as a part of the Black cultural mythology project. I thank Lara Putnam of the History Department for her insightful feedback. The second event was the Provost's forum on "American Memorials in the 21st Century," where I received feedback and affirmation for my project from colleagues Kirk Savage, Laurence Glasco, and Deane Root, as well as Andrew Masich of the Heinz History Center.

The most sustained expression of thanks goes to Willie Lamousé-Smith, professor emeritus of the University of Maryland Baltimore County. He has provided layers of feedback, insight, and wisdom that have improved my ideas. Over the years, he did not know the precise process of germination that my ideas on an Africana conceptual and philosophical framework of mythology were undergoing. Yet he was supportive from afar by gifting me *The Ultimate Encyclopedia of Mythology*, DVDs on religious mythology, Michael Wood's documentary *In Search of Myths and Heroes*, and two sources by Joseph Campbell—the book *The Hero with a Thousand Faces* and the documentary *Joseph Campbell and the Power of Myth*. I am grateful for your understanding that I needed to qualify and explore my organic ideas about a mythology born of my intellectual experience, for your encouragement about the possibilities of this book as a midcareer opus, and for your faith that I would find my own intellectual voice without a premature reliance on non-Africana sources that so many people incorrectly assume are central to the Africana inquiry into cultural memory and myth. I look forward to our future conversations about the global intersections of myth and mythology.

Acknowledgments

xxv

I cannot but acknowledge one of the most fascinating and informative email conversations that I have ever had, which was with early Black Arts Movement theorist Maulana Karenga. Your assistance in helping me locate obscure archival sources on the movement's mythology theorizations has allowed me to accurately represent the mythology foundations on which this work builds. A note of thanks goes to my good friend Acklyn Lynch who indulged my probing about the topic of Haiti, African independence strategies, and the Berlin Conference's view of Haiti as a threat. I am honored to have been a guest lecturer—twice—at Wisson West's Gallery Serengeti in Capitol Heights, Maryland, in 2011 and 2013, to discuss topics of commemoration and Black cultural mythology in the contexts of Black art. I discovered Maryland artist Joseph Holston in this gallery and fell in love with the painting and the etching of "Protection: Movement I: The Unknown World" from the *Color of Freedom* (2008) series. I extend heartfelt appreciation to Joseph Holston and his wife Sharon for allowing me to use the image on the book cover.

I own a brown, fine Italian leather notebook that a former student, Shawnisha Hester, gifted to me as a souvenir from a research trip in Italy. For a year, I admired the pristine book sitting on my bookshelf, unwilling to use it for mundane scribbling and choosing, instead, to preserve it for the right inspired research project. In 2007, I first began to use this beautiful notebook to chronicle every obscure, monumental, or historiographical reference on myth, mythology, heroics, and memory that I encountered for the next ten years. In 2017, when I finally began to write the manuscript with the vigor and focus to see it through to publication, I carefully wove this leather notebook's references into a narrative that I hope will be a gift to generations to come.

At the top of the list of the inheritors of an amazing Africana tradition of survival is my son, Tyler, who had to share his mommy for the past two years with this book project. Thank you, my darling, for your sweet spirit and understanding. I also thank my parents, who I hope found solace in the fact that their adult daughter still views the family homestead as a nurturing site where she can comfortably "zone" to engage in hours and hours of research and writing, sometimes even nestled in stolen moments between intergenerational vacations and family holiday gatherings. Thank you for respecting my research and my work ethic, and for loving me enough to not let my preoccupations put a damper on family time.

Finally, I thank my original SUNY Press editor, Beth Bouloukos, for sharing in my vision for this project, and, especially, Rebecca Colesworthy for investing in this inherited project with enthusiasm and constant support. This book is more readable and refined because of the unselfish critical commitment of a total of four readers and the efforts of a wonderfully skilled production and copyediting team. Finally, I acknowledge support from the Richard D. and Mary Jane Edwards Endowed Publication Fund.

Thank you all for your contributions to *Black Cultural Mythology*.

Any omissions in this work are pardonable, I hope, because they will inspire others to expand the meaning, logic, and applications of Black cultural mythology and Africana cultural memory studies through refined future research.

Introduction

Mythology is not necessarily a culture's fabricated origin or creation stories. An additional understanding of mythology is storytelling and symbolism that narratively utilize the core factual variables of an event, phenomenon, or persona and assume license to enhance the story's dimensions with benign or innocuous embellishment. Along these lines, Black cultural mythology is a framework of analysis and categorization that is attentive to the infusion of hero dynamics, legacy tools, heritage practices, and ancestor acknowledgment in Black literature and cultural behaviors. This is an important perspective, particularly in regions where Black legacy and heritage practices are marginalized because Blacks represent fewer numbers in the population, or because regions have national histories of enslavement that have led to institutionalized patterns of *selective memory*. Black cultural mythology is vital in regions where Black history and heritage are contested, overlooked, undermined, neglected, ignored, and deemed invisible. However, sustaining the visibility of this heritage, Black writers have demonstrated an imaginative, almost archaeological, search-and-rescue success in continuing to use Black historical figures, heroic episodes, and legendary folk images as content for their work. Black cultural mythology aims to create a greater collective cultural self-awareness of the imperatives of hero dynamics, legacy tools, heritage practices, and ancestral knowledge that inspire a reawakening of the cycles of oral-to-written-to-oral narrative. It accounts for antiheroics in its many forms and is a critical tool that is innovatively attentive to the theoretical and philosophical matters of cultural memory and its practice.

    As an introduction to a new theoretical approach, this volume is an invitation to scholars working in diverse orientations to cultural memory studies to consider new contexts and catalysts for comparative discourses about African diasporic survival and legacies. Reflecting history, cultural theory, critical thought, and aesthetics, this book explores an African American *mythology* defined as epic and hyperheroic post–Middle Passage survivalist behaviors and feats that suggest collective practices and sensibilities that are dynamic, functional, and culturally defining enough to be recycled in narrative form as sacred heritage artifacts. Black cultural mythology's intellectual genealogy is historical, theoretical, and aesthetic. It is interpreted from the cues found in a host of formative activist worldviews, observations, and scholarship that reflect diverse aspects of Africana sacred remembrance and heritage. Black cultural mythology is a framework that harmonizes the *narrative memorial* of African American culture. It negotiates a vision of what African diaspora communities lost in specificity during the enslavement period yet gained in organic survivalist behaviors and practices. Salamishah Tillet's warning about the snares of civic myths and of the myth of the African diaspora do not apply to Black cultural mythology's emphasis on diaspora agency in remembering the feats of survival and elevating mnemonic cues of heroic legacy on its own terms. It shares Tillet's concern for how American "civic myths mandate the exclusion of colonialism and slavery from the national memory," which is a challenge neutralized by Black cultural mythology's conceptually mature set of organic critical attributes.[1] Rejecting the over-re-membrance of "slavery" managed as an American and Western historical narrative preoccupation framed in terms of bondage and oppression, the attributes ensure that diaspora memorial and factually mythic discourses evolve along a path defined by their own nonhegemonic, self-determined, and even self-defensive survivalist needs.

The field of cultural memory studies is already quite nuanced in its approach to the effects of *enslavement* on African/a identity, collective memory, and amnesia. Even though Black cultural mythology emerges from a different disciplinary logic and functionality, all the discourses participate in a broad project of Africana cultural memory studies. Key cultural memory and collective memory sources offer little about theorizations of myth and mythology, amid their other compelling observations about the nature of remembering. In *The Collective Memory* (1968) sociologist Maurice Halbwachs's orientation to processes of engraving identity on new soil is a foundational gem on which Black cultural mythology draws, and it is adjacent to Molefi Kete Asante's revisionist chronological marker of "beginning again."[2] Halbwachs reflects on how people "engrave their form in some way upon the soil and retrieve their collective remembrances within the spatial frameworks thus defined."[3] Asante's concept of "beginning again" is the conceptual affirmation of reinvented Africanness on American soil, which is centered on survival and emphasizes conceptually reconstructing the narrative of African American historical experiences for optimum agency. In Africana literary studies, Carol P. Marsh-Lockett and Elizabeth West treat this phenomenon in terms of survival plus memory:

> More than their bodies came with displaced Africans who survived the Middle Passage, and more than bodies remained for those who escaped capture but endured the legacy of colonialism on their homelands. Africans who crossed the Atlantic brought with them cosmology, a will to survive, and an enduring presence rooted in memory and all of which, across the centuries, has left a distinct philosophical and cultural imprint throughout the diaspora.[4]

As cosmology informs one aspect of engraving identity on new soil, literary critic and cultural theorist Saidiya Hartman redirects our interest in and exposure to outright acts of violence more toward instances of "the terror of the mundane and quotidian."[5] As if to precisely describe and remember the existence that Africans were surviving and to account for the holistic identities of Africans before encounters with the diaspora, Hartman describes Africans as "unwilling and coerced migrants who created a new culture in the hostile world of the Americas and who fashioned themselves again, making possibility out of dispossession."[6] She then interrogates readers' and society's responses as "witnesses" or "voyeurs" and questions our motivation for "self-reflection" particularly in view of the pain and suffering from the enslavement era.[7] Black cultural mythology's compatible interest is in this phenomenon, but as a *meditation* on how the culture has immortalized itself in the diaspora, particularly through philosophies on survival and commemoration and in structured literatures, both fiction and nonfiction. Hartman writes of "the uncertain line between witness and spectator," which is also a demarcation of interest to Black cultural mythology. Witnesses offer a testimony of remembrance. A spectator watches with an unaffectedness and distance that allows a greater level of disengagement. Black cultural mythology strives to jolt the reader-spectator out of this gaze by alerting him or her to the resistance-based cognitive survival and the hyperheroics of historical actors whom Hartman describes as "self-made." To Hartman, self-making is "a central tenet of democratic individuality" tied to the body, labor, and the ability to become a self-made man or woman.[8] In Black cultural mythology terms, there is another dimension to this process of self-definition—the grit and the force responsible for resistance and achievement. The attributes and properties reveal continuity and serve as core critical guideposts to describe cultural heroics that have been mined from traditions of Africana sociopolitical thought and cultural theory. The attributes equip us with the tools to explore with deeper precision the phenomena of surviving and witnessing.

Studies on trauma have provided key discourses on cultural memory phenomena and have well documented diasporan literature reflecting enslavement-based experiences. Ron Eyerman in *Cultural Trauma: Slavery and the Formation of African American Identity* (2001) has a primary interest in identity as he views enslavement as a "trauma." Specifically, "as a cultural process, trauma is mediated through various forms of representation and linked to the reformation of cultural identity and the reworking of collective memory."[9] His focus is more on loss than empowerment through memory, namely "a dramatic loss of identity and meaning, a tear in the social fabric, affecting a group of people that has achieved some degree of cohesion."[10] Black cultural mythology favors an adaptation philosophy over Eyerman's premises of loss, disruption, fragmentation, victimization, fracture, and social crisis; and it prioritizes narratives on resistance efforts that are more consistent with liberation discourses.

Nancy Peterson in *Against Amnesia: Contemporary Women Writers and the Crises of Historical Memory* (2001) suggests that "literary texts can produce a desire for historical memory."[11] Specifically, "readers will become implicated in the historical events and traumas surrounding the texts they read. This investment in the text, then, creates the possibility of transferring historical memory to a community of readers, as a community with the potential to construct and nurture collective memory."[12] In her study of Toni Morrison's *Song of Solomon* (1977), she introduces how a writer "uses mythic sources to conceive of the past as dynamic and not fixed; myth allows the development of a historical consciousness that is not only factual or objective but constructive and fictional."[13] Peterson allows for the factual premise of myth/mythology instigated by fictive texts, and distances her approach from the rigidity of the field of history's skepticism about myth. She writes that "mainstream American history is so relentlessly optimistic and teleological that it has become painfully difficult to articulate counterhistories that do not share these values," as its "postmodern culture works against the sustained engagement with memory."[14] Mack Freeman's reaction to Peterson's ideas suggests a space and justification for a Black cultural mythology methodology: "Indeed, as Peterson implies, the sort of postmodern playfulness one finds in a good deal of contemporary fiction can serve as an accomplice to a kind of amnesia. The task, therefore, is precisely to *remember*, but to do so in a way that moves beyond the facile modes of historicizing that too often distort or obscure the lived reality of human suffering."[15] Chapter 7 presents a view of a new literary history of Black cultural mythology that comparatively features writers such as Robert O'Hara whose historical play *Insurrection: Holding History* (2004) can certainly be categorized as postmodern yet also as surmounting facile modes of historicizing when subjected to a Black cultural mythology reading. However, Peterson's concern for trauma, restated by Freeman as human suffering, is limited in its own way, especially from a disciplinary Africana point of view that insists on fully extending remembrances of oppression, trauma, disruption, and suffering to a more complete narrative about modes of resistance, survival, and futurism.

In *Amnesia and Redress in Contemporary African American Fiction: Counterhistory* (2011) Marni Gauthier researches many of the same variables within a set of multiethnic literatures, including the African American contribution of Toni Morrison's *Paradise* (1997). She does not consider mythology as a variable, but her ideas about amnesia and truth-telling in different cultural contexts are adjacent to those of Peterson as she, too, relies on historical fiction to mark the impact that literature can have on history. Black cultural mythology's interest is not in amnesia but in a forward-looking, pragmatic, yet also sacred ways of delving more deeply into the processes involved in the remembrance of survival. Scholars mention survival often but frequently as a brief item among lists of cultural concerns or achievement. Extending its analysis and theorization better prioritizes survival as a concept with vitality. This critical act challenges society's often static expectations of how fruitfully history can bloom into functionality and relevance when provided with a new lens from which to gaze at cultural phenomena.

Because of Toni Morrison's critical discourses related to memory that affirm her novels' commitment to exploring ways communities manage local histories and collective memory, critics cover much of her repertoire in cultural memory criticism. A. Timothy Spaulding's *Re-Forming the Past: History, the Fantastic, and the Postmodern Slave Narrative* (2005) is a study of not just Morrison's work as the African American sample in a multiethnic literary comparison, but of several of the most active African American novelists whose works reflect an aspect of cultural memory. Exploring additional works by Octavia Butler, Ishmael Reed, Charles Johnson, Jewelle Gomez, Samuel Delany, and Edward Jones, Spaulding chronicles novels that present a "retelling of slavery." Spaulding's contribution is identifying this nearly two-decade corpus of postmodern novels "as an epoch of sorts within the African American literary response to the history of slavery."[16] Spaulding's work is an adjacent discourse, but Black cultural mythology provides tools for itemizing the critical dimensions of how African people heroically responded to and behaved within histories of not only enslavement but also during the entire diaspora experience. Its conceptual tools inspire a more uniform critical process that shares with Spaulding a goal for society to "interrogate our past" but also to honor the sacred survival beyond enslavement with guideposts that reinforce a psychologically and sociologically relevant awareness of the culture's mythological structure.[17]

In a broader view of cultural memory studies, a survey of how Astrid Erll and Ansgar Nünning's volume *A Companion to Cultural Memory Studies* (2010) intersects with Black cultural mythology is philosophically informative. The topic of mythology weaves its way through discourses on European and American cultural memory. In the volume, contributors regard enslavement as a trauma addressed in discussions of collective memory. Cultural markers such as the terms "Africa," "Black," and "slavery" are not indexed in the volume, but several essays are informative. Jan Assman's contribution articulates core human concepts tied to memory as he defines the history of cultural memory in a culturally neutral way. He views it as "the connection between time, identity, and memory in their three dimensions of the personal, the social, and the cultural."[18] Specifically, he asserts, "Cultural memory is a kind of institute. It is exteriorized, objectified, and stored away in symbolic forms that, unlike the sounds of words or the sight of gestures, are stable and situation transcendent: They may be transferred from one situation to another and transmitted from one generation to another."[19] Assman and Eyerman discuss traditional aspects of collective memory and cultural memory in depth, but Black cultural mythology pivots from many of these theses with a new lens to consider what it looks like to merge cultural memory with cultural heroics to yield cultural mythology. Assman, in particular, uses terms such as "mythical history," which is at the intersection of cultural memory and time.[20] In a discussion of time, he clarifies, "The cultural memory is based on fixed points in the past. Even in the cultural memory, the past is not preserved as such but is cast in symbols as they are continually illuminating a changing present. In the context of cultural memory, the distinction between myth and memory vanishes."[21] Assman's final observation defends the legitimacy of a group's privilege to rearticulate the parameters of myth, memory, mythology, and heroics on its own terms without the burden to justify its culturally centered symbolism and meaning for its unique intellectual enterprise.

Jeffrey K. Olick's contribution to collective memory and the sociology of the mnemonic demonstrates the depth we can anticipate as Black cultural mythology discourses join the conversations related to social memory:

> Work emphasizing the genuinely collective nature of social memory has demonstrated that there are long-term structures to what societies remember or commemorate that are stubbornly impervious to the efforts of individuals to escape them; powerful institutions, moreover, clearly support some histories more than others, provide narrative patterns and exemplars of how individuals can and should remember, and stimulate public memory in ways and for reasons that have little to do with the individual or aggregate neurological records. Without such a collectivist perspective, after all, it is difficult to provide good explanations of mythology, tradition, and heritage, among other long-term symbolic patterns.[22]

Black cultural mythology could indeed be what Olick extrapolates from criteria from Halbwachs and Émile Durkheim, that "groups themselves also share publicly *articulated images of collective pasts*."[23] Specifically,

> Durkheim developed a sociological approach to what he called "collective representations," symbols and meanings that are properties of the group whether or not any particular individual or even particular number of individuals shares them. In this sense, very few people may be able to identify key figures or events of the Civil War, but those figures or events may nonetheless be important elements of American collective memory. Whereas survey researchers may conclude that a particular image or event not remembered by very many people is no longer a part of the collective memory, for a true Durkheimian, culture is not reducible to what is in people's heads.[24]

Olick's presentation of such conceptual flexibility gives complete license to phenomenology experts (e.g., Africana phenomenology) to do the critical work of discerning what is usable or remarkable from historical, literary, or other artistic narratives and artifacts, as signposts of sustaining cultural value. Black cultural mythology's attributes function in this way, as a revisionist offering to a public hungry for a stabilizing and preservationist logic that defends its core heritage from "traumas" of contemporary neglect and belittlement.

Finally, Renate Lachmann's essay in *A Companion to Cultural Memory Studies* (2010) approaches literary specificity and application that relates to Black cultural mythology's interest in the self-awareness and deliberateness in which authors participate in cultural memory. She suggests that "authors of literary texts like to explicate their own memory concepts. Some develop intricate mythopoetic theories which betray the assumption of philosophy or literary theory."[25] It has been refreshing for writers such as Charles Johnson, Toni Morrison, and Suzan-Lori Parks to share their theoretical orientations to myth and memory, particularly to exonerate cultural and literary critics from overimposing a lens of historical relevance onto an often fictive literary text. For example, Colson Whitehead's basic description of his novel *John Henry Days* (2001)—a central model of Black cultural mythology possibilities in literature explored in chapter 7—as an "anxiety myth" gives readers less of a critical roadmap from which to draw assumptions about his craft and storytelling.[26] Yet authors who infuse their texts with historical sensibilities invite cultural memory explication.

Critic Herman Beavers evaluates the writerly process concerned with these goals in the work of novelist Charles Johnson, another writer featured in chapter 7. He observes that "the assertion of memory is so important to the emergence of new literatures, so heavily associated with acts of breaking silence and bearing witness."[27] Johnson, himself, is concerned with exploring Africana survival through his corpus of black philosophical fiction. He writes, "Black experience becomes a pure field of appearances with two important poles: consciousness and the objects, others, to which it is related intentionally. We describe *how* these appear, and note that Black subjectivity (memory, desire, anticipation, will) stain them with a particular sense."[28]

Trudier Harris shares with Beavers an interest in writers' motives in constructing narratives reflecting memory, myth, and heroics, and her book *Martin Luther King Jr., Heroism, and African American Literature* (2014) is notable for the author's thoughtful deciphering of the processes of African American heroism. Her introduction on "The Ambiguous Nature of African American Heroism" emerges as an important clarification about African American perceptions of the relationships between folk heroics and legendary iconic lives such as King's. She narrates ambiguity primarily in a sense that, even to African Americans, King is a hero and, related to Black cultural mythology's itemization, possibly also an antihero. Her measures of the potential for African American heroics to be abstract, flexible, and revealed through "sustained reflection" are discerning, and her goal is to account for the role of the writer in managing heroics.[29] She explains:

> First, each of these writers recognizes King as a heroic figure, whether they applaud that heroism or deride it. Second, the heroic traits that ensure King's transcendence of the ordinary to extraordinary inclusion in literary works is based, in part, on African American folk traditions; thus, several of these works showcase occasions in which the folk imagination and cultural patterns drawn from folklore help to shape African American literature. Third, the inherent ambiguity of African American heroic folk traits makes for political as well as literary entanglements that call into question the life of King as incorporated into the literature as well as the intentions of the writers in preserving, tainting, reclaiming, or elevating King's historical legacy.[30]

Harris's investigation into the writer's motive is broadly folkloric and generalized, yet she captures the collective process. She itemizes the impulses:

> Together, these seemingly contradictory conditions indicate that African American heroes are embraced, shaped, defined, and redefined to coincide with cultural needs, to highlight long-standing cultural patterns, and to emphasize that ambiguity in heroic construction—or, indeed, suspicious or questionable actions in heroic construction—provide opportunities for continuing celebration, instead of rejection, of cultural heroes. Consequently, the very act of writing about such figures is evidence of celebration, even if the portraits depicted are less than complimentary.[31]

Harris's qualification mirrors historians' necessity to distinguish between truth and fabrication:

> Placing Martin Luther King Jr. in the African American folk and literary heroic tradition is not to suggest that either aspect equals his life. The act is an exercise in claiming and perception, not in absolute truth. . . . In the African American imagination, folk narratives carry equal weight to researched narratives, for indeed the masses seldom read the latter. People nonetheless have extensive perceptions of their heroic historical figures. Folk

stories, literary creations, and biographies all have their kernels of truth—and those kernels carry weight in proportion to those creating and putting them forth. They all carry *a* truth that, perhaps collectively, yields a substantial portion of *the* truth.[32]

Harris's study shares with Black cultural mythology an interest in "the impact of historical heroic creation on artistic heroic creation," and her study on King is a discourse in Africana cultural memory studies that affirms how literature is a "site of reclamation" of African American heroics.[33] Harris addresses myth briefly, but her conclusion's itemization of topics such as immortality, the institutionalization of the King holiday, how his assassination is a part of African American traumatic cultural memory, and the national King Memorial in Washington, DC, further suggests how her study aligns with Black cultural mythology and African cultural memory studies. While Harris is not consistently measuring cultural memory, one of her final comments is relevant: "While time may diminish memory, literature may refresh it because literary portrayals shape and reshape with the times."[34] Harris announces the early twenty-first century as "a time when African American writers can take even the most revered of their historical figures and, trusting in their creativity, produce works about them that, without excessive derision or undue veneration, are engaging, provocative, and well crafted."[35] Approaching remembrance as survivalist mythology with even more attributes than heroics, myth, cultural memory, and immortality is a dynamic, forward-moving engagement. It expands theorization and application to literature, holidays, monuments, and commemoration in a more comprehensive way that extends the impact of the seeds Harris plants in her literary study of King's legacy, which, through the book's dedication, indicates her respect for "the sacred."

This demarcation between Black cultural mythology and the ebb and flow of cultural memory and collective memory discourses is celebrated for the synthesis and synergy it reveals among cross-disciplinary divisions of intellectual labor. The new orientations to the worldview of diasporic memory in a Black cultural mythology theorization are not for the faint of heart, but the path along a new map of idea formation, which reflects on ways myth and mythology emerges from latency in cultural memory discourses, will be rewarding.

In the field of history, there is a tension between history and memory. Milton C. Sernett, in *Harriet Tubman: Myth, Memory, and History* (2007), conveys this in a dialectic that pursues balance or a leveling that does not discredit or marginalize memory in the field of history's hierarchy of the two and its processes of selectivity. " 'History' and 'memory' jostle together in confusing fashion in the public mind. While professional historians explore the past with the intent of discovering 'the way it really was,' none have been totally successful in extracting themselves from 'the politics of memory.' "[36] He further explains that "the historian nevertheless analyzes the past with a critical—and . . . more secular eye than the keepers of 'memory.' "[37] Sernett quotes Civil War historian David W. Blight's argument that memory

> "is often treated as a sacred set of potentially absolute meanings and stories, possessed as the heritage of a community. Memory is often owned; history, interpreted. Memory is passed down through generations; history is revised. Memory often coalesces in objects, sacred sites, and monuments; history seeks to understand context and the complexity of cause and effect. History asserts the authority of academic training and recognized canons of evidence; memory carries the often powerful authority of community membership and experience."[38]

Then, he features much of Michael Kammen's approach to memory from *Mystic Chords of Memory: The Transformation of Tradition in American Culture* (1993):

> "Memory," it is said, is a "social construction" to suit the needs of individuals and groups of one kind or another. "Memory" selectively gleans the past for what is useable in the day-to-day struggles of various segments of society for a place at the national table where goods and services are distributed. Since the past cannot be remembered in its totality, individuals and groups create their histories out of selective memories, conflating and confusing the analytical categories of "memory" and "history" about which the scholars talk. . . . "What history and memory have in common is that both merit our mistrust, yet both must be nevertheless nourished."[39]

The historian's practice of taking exception to memory is duly noted, and Sernett eventually confesses that " 'History' often sets itself in judgment over 'memory.' "[40] For a book such as his *Harriet Tubman: Myth, Memory, and History*, Sernett has the unenviable task of convincing historians that memory is also a relevant trove. His approach paves the way for a more nuanced exploration of memory that does not place traditional and newer disciplines in a hierarchy. The linkages between Black cultural mythology and Sernett's step beyond the boundaries of the historian's craft to construct a volume that prioritizes myth and memory are delightful and reveal great possibilities for collaboration across disciplines for the benefit of a robust field of Africana cultural memory studies. There is a shared interest in stories, fabrications, legend, elaborations, mythmakers, the symbolic, icons, "dreamed up" testaments, hagiography, mythologizers, and folklore in assessing the "durability" of memory of historical actors.[41]

From Geneviève Fabre and Robert O'Meally's classic collection on the study of memory in African American historical and cultural studies, the final, anchor essay by Pierre Nora also reinforces the hierarchy, and since *History and Memory in African-American Culture* (1994) is the first text that comes to mind upon the mention of African American cultural memory, it must be addressed and even *decentered* as a central text for Africana-based idea formation regarding myth, memory, mythology, and heroics. The ideas about memory in the Fabre and O'Meally volume are not necessarily representative of the most contemporary points of view. The volume has a diversity of contributors, but the collection's final essay, "Between Memory and History: *Les Lieux de Mémoire*" by Pierre Nora, heavy-handedly differentiates myth from history. His essay favors the methodology of professionally trained historians in deciding the final word about the value (or limited value) of myth and memory orientations to the past. Significant for its closing argument to the volume, it manages to blur the rights of newer disciplines to conceptualize myth and memory in frameworks that may compete with those of the traditional discipline of history.[42]

Also, it is not too bold to assert that Black cultural mythology is a twenty-first century inheritor of Carter G. Woodson's motives, which sustained the early twentieth-century formation of Black history practices. According to historian Pero Dagbovie in *The Early Black History Movement: Carter G. Woodson and Lorenzo Johnston Greene* (2007), the early Black history movement is responsible for "the first significant body of scientific historical scholarship" on the diaspora population of African Americans.[43] In his study of the roles of Carter G. Woodson and Lorenzo Johnston Greene as key agents whose commitments pioneered the field that ensured the institutionalization of the "black historical professions," Dagbovie highlights their success in "popularizing black history."[44] Just as Dagbovie emphasizes Woodson and Greene as "two of the most important figures in the early black history movement," as both "forerunners" and "figureheads" based on how they were "willing to sacrifice" and how they advanced their goals as a "life-and-death struggle," the theorization of Black cultural mythology also has key figures, addressed here as *exemplars*.[45] There is no need to include Woodson as an exemplar of Black cultural mythology because his craft served a prerequisite calling, to preserve and advance the actual historical narrative of African Americans. Instead, his work in popularizing Black history is that of a methodological forefather. His method of "taking black history to the masses, the working class, and the youth throughout the nation" as a "source of pride" was successful and is the foundation of the now stable "black historical enterprise."[46] The contemporary generation has scarcely known a time when we did not have ready access to annals and narratives of Black history. But in contemporary generalist Black history and Black History Month practices, especially in the public domain, the masses' engagement with history is at times rote, disengaged, and unimaginative. Black cultural mythology blooms as an inheritor of early Black history activity to energize behaviors toward history by introducing a new, compelling *logic* for legacy practices that celebrates the heroism and impulses of survival and that challenges us to meditate on the tactics for survival embedded in our history's epics and mythologies. Woodson's *African Myths and Folktales* (1928) and *African Heroes and Heroines* (1939) share the language of myths and heroics. The former is a collection of legends and folk tales aimed at youth audiences. The latter is

> a biographical treatment of [continental African] heroes and heroines intended to show the possibilities of the field. These leaders of a despised people measure up to the full stature of the heroic in the histories of other nations. With their record the youth in quest of the dramatic in history may read with unusual interest these exploits of an all but forgotten people. The curriculum can hereby be enriched with this racial heritage which will broaden the minds of the youth and make for better citizenship in the modern world.[47]

Woodson's stated audience for *African Heroes and Heroines* is junior and senior high school students, and he issued the second edition of the book to meet the post–World War II demand for "literature on the background and the present status of Africa and Africans."[48] In dedicating the book to "My Uncle George Woodson who in captivity in America manifested the

African spirit of resistance to slavery and died fighting the institution," Woodson affirms his respect and honor for his family's survival sustained by the heroic legacy of fighters such as his uncle.

Aligned with Woodson's Black history enterprise, Black cultural mythology is the organic effort to begin to map, label, categorize, and formalize the heretofore random, yet consistently illuminated, ideations of myth, memory, mythology, and heroics. The metaphor of *constellations* is appropriate for the seeds and fragments planted in the traditions of sociopolitical, cultural theory, and aesthetic discourses on the broad aspects of African American mythology. Again, borrowing from Dagbovie's exploration of the early Black history movement, the matter at hand is "infrastructure"—specifically, what is the infrastructure of the field's organization of knowledge related to myth, memory, mythology, and heroics?[49]

Black cultural mythology isolates the matter of popularizing Black history that Woodson and Greene inaugurated in the early Black history movement by redirecting historical inquiry more toward exploring the dimensions of myth, memory, mythology, and heroics in society's expectations of and uses of history in memory practices and as legacy tools. Burnis R. Morris, in *History, the Black Press, and Public Relations* (2017) follows this line of inquiry as well, emphasizing Woodson's Black history "public-education program" and "campaign."[50] In fact, the language he uses to describe Woodson's work aligns even more with Black cultural mythology. He writes of Woodson's goal "to honor a subject whose past was clouded by misinformation and contempt," its goal "to save the black race from extinction," and the way Woodson's program sought to be an "antidote" to "low self-esteem."[51] This framing is compatible with chapter 1's discussion of the field of Black psychology's priorities of maintaining African American mythological structure.

Inevitably, Woodson would smile upon the innovative efforts of Black cultural mythology as an applied version of many of his objectives. Dagbovie observes that Woodson "foreshadowed modern Black studies scholars in stressing that the study of African descendants be scholarly, sound, creative, restorative, and directly relevant to the black community."[52] The differences, or sometimes *tensions*, between how disciplines and subfields approach the study of myth, memory, mythology, and heroics do not interfere with the organic idea formation of Black cultural mythology. Instead, the comparisons reinforce uniqueness and disciplinary specificity. Comparing the historians' views of memory and myth to the approaches of the exemplars discussed in chapter 1 further delineates how Black cultural mythology is forging a new intellectual tradition.

As a theoretical work, this volume responds to Houston A. Baker's approach to keeping intellectual creativity grounded. In a warning to beware of when and if one truly is creating something new, Baker's checklist highlights the role of theory to explain, to adequately predict, to order understanding, and to help us to better appreciate the depth of phenomena, particularly in terms of going "beyond the tangible in search of metalevels of explanation . . . in intellectual discourse."[53] Baker's description of African American origins is one of many cultural-literary indications of the mental, psychic, and emotional character, disposition, and worldview of Africans. As a response to the dislocation from Africa to the Americas, he corroborates that Africans "were compelled not only to maintain their cultural heritage at a meta (as opposed to material) level but also to apprehend the operative metaphysics of various alien cultures. Primary to their survival was the work of consciousness, of nonmaterial counterintelligence."[54] Heroic and biographical literatures help to "inscribe a unique personhood in what appeared to be a blank and uncertain environment"[55] that has defined the continuum of Africana experience and its intellectual traditions that reflect survivalist impulses from the grit of these experiences. Baker notes, "Our intellectual history privileges the unseen and intangibly personal. The trajectory of this process is from what might be called the workings of a distinctly syncretic spirit to autobiographical inscriptions of spirit work."[56] Black cultural mythology extrapolates from Baker's layering of the narratives and heroic recollections of African American survival.

As an inquiry into historical theory, defined by Alison Moore in her discussion of cultural historiography as "a model of theoretical criticism [that] engages both descriptive and prescriptive readings of historiographic practices, with a view to evaluating their epistemological value,"[57] Black cultural mythology emerges as an *organic* response to Africana survivalist priorities emanating from its own genealogies. Valuing how literature appropriates the historical to influence identity and memory extends Black cultural mythology's relevance to cultural history. Africana cultural memory finds itself on the margins of discourses within the field of cultural memory studies, within a subject area loop of topics of enslavement memory in fiction and the history of enslavement memorials and commemoration. Moore describes this difference and its processes in terms of how "we each reinvent historiographic innovations for ourselves in parallel fashion, and without reference to examples in other places."[58] This is consistent with Cilas Kemadjiv's sense of invention/reinvention, where he suggests, "The mythification of postcolonial heroism arises from the effort to understand one of the decisive questions for the future of postcolonial peoples: how to invent functional identities that allow them to mark their presence in the world, how to be part of the world without the risk of breaking apart."[59] As such a reinvention, Black cultural mythology is a conceptualization that indicates a rupture and a shift away from relying wholeheartedly on models immersed in other disciplines' priorities and orientations.

Black cultural mythology directs our interest toward the *forces* responsible for diasporan survival, fortitude, and memory practices cultivated and maintained during and after the dehumanizing and threatening, fight-or-flight conditions that have always accompanied African life in the United States, in the Caribbean, and in Afro-Latin America. The framework intersects with cultural criticism and history, yet also significantly with literature and aesthetics, as Black writers have been the most consistent storytellers compelled to revive and recycle the culture's archive in creative, spiritual, and embellished ways with attention to a folkloric inquiry into African diasporic bravery, courage, valor, superhuman feats, boldness, fearlessness, daring, audacity, gallantry, chivalry, nobility, guts, spunk, and grit.

African American historical and cultural studies reflect an understandable preoccupation with what is heroic in the experiences of African people on US soil. Whether referencing African precolonial exploration of North America, feats of freedom along the Middle Passage, revolts, the creation of maroon societies, or broad African resistance responses to the perils of enslavement and postenslavement, African people whose relocations have sustained the diaspora have experienced an inordinate set of conditions that foster the emergence of acts and sensibilities that compel heroism for survival.

Africans arrived in North America culturally whole and with knowledge, skills, histories of achievement, and survivalist resilience from which they drew to endure the hostilities of a new environment and socio-legal status. The heritage of most enslaved Africans is broadly West African, and a cultural point of reference for this inquiry is embodied in the observations of writers such as Isidore Okpewho, who reorients Western academic assumptions toward a more culturally relevant philosophical understanding of precisely what is *epic*. African narratives such as the feats of Sundiata of Mali, the tales of Yaa Asantewaa's fight against the British, and the valor of Usman dan Fodio and others who opposed the European assault on Africa are central to African pre-enslavement cultural memory that is a shared transatlantic feature of diasporic African remembrance. This study does not linger on the historiography of African ethical and moral contexts of heroism, but they are parts of the origin narrative and cultural etymology of consciousness for African people transplanted to the US and the broader diaspora through the disruption of enslavement. However, Ngugi wa Thiong'o's *Something Torn and New: An African Renaissance* (2009) stands out as a profound treatise on frameworks of "disremembering," "re-membering," and "memory, restoration, and African renaissance" that Ngugi offers to address his early twenty-first century "thinking on the decolonization of African memory."[60] Ngugi contemplates memory concerns for both Africa and the diaspora:

> Here then is the major difference between the continental African and the diasporic African. Forced into a crypt, the African in the diaspora tries to break out of the crypt, and grasps whatever African memory he can reach, to invent a new reality. On the continent, the reformed African tries to enter the crypt and store his inventions there.
>
> It seems to me that what is needed is to break out of the crypt. We have to confront the realities of our past and mourn the dead in a proper way. Zora Neale Hurston must have had such an idea when in 1945 she proposed to W. E. B. Dubois the purchase of a hundred acres for a "cemetery for the illustrious Negro dead," so that "no Negro celebrity, no matter what financial condition they might be in at death, lie in inconspicuous forgetfulness. We must assume the responsibility of their graves being known and honored." The lack of such "a tangible thing allows our people to forget, and their spirits evaporate."[61]

Ngugi's synthesis of African and African diaspora worldviews gives us much to consider, and his vision of a remedy for the problematic he and Hurston perceive is compatible with Black cultural mythology. He suggests something greater than

> a physical site for the remembrance of a few. It is a matter of re-membering the entirety of Pan-Africa. Every year across the continent and the entire diaspora there should be a month, a week, even just a day of collective mourning for the millions whose souls still cry out for proper burial and accordance of proper

mourning rites. And accompanying these formal performances should be works of art, music, literature, dance, and cinema that connect our past to our present as a basis for the future.[62]

Mourning and funeral rites are not specifically isolated variables in the theorization of Black cultural mythology, yet they are implied in the emphasis on sacred inheritance and ritual remembrance. Appreciative of Ngugi's framing of the transnational and intergenerational remembrance phenomena and standing on a collective African and Pan-African past that supports and intersects with the continuum of African culture that evolved in the diaspora, this study on Black cultural mythology is interested in a postenslavement, African-centered *philosophy of heroism*, defined organically from diasporic experiences with survivalist impact, achievement against the odds, and the extension of human capacity beyond the ordinary. While Ngugi speaks of diaspora populations reaching for African memory, the diaspora is additionally itemizing the memory practices that it has created on new soils, beyond the African homeland.

The disruption of enslavement requires a psychological deconstruction of what occurs cognitively to groups of people when they experience collective trauma. Such a speculation about African people and their traumas includes survivalist responses to capture in the West African terrain, to forced pedestrian travel across this terrain from familiar to unfamiliar continental regions, to imprisonment in dungeons, and to a terrifying nautical relocation journey. This also includes the survivalist camaraderie of the Middle Passage complicated by losses such as companion death, by the dispersal of captured communities of Africans at different ports and auction blocks, by anxieties of original and future family separation in the new environments, and more. In essence, new research on a comprehensive transgenerational Black psychology framework is needed to account for the psychology of Middle Passage survival as a prerequisite to understanding the psychology of chattel enslavement survival. Matters of geography, intergenerational familiarity with environments, and exponentially increasing diagnoses of European-American oppressors' pathology become part of the narrative of cognitive survival that contributes to an understanding of the depth of African American heroics and the culture's articulation of antiheroics. Antiheroics relay information and warnings about a culture's opponents and enemies against whom African people in the diaspora have and must continue to maneuver for survival.

Interdisciplinary nuances of topics of myth, memory, mythology, and heroics appear frequently in cultural studies scholarship about diasporic experiences, yet not in a considerably coherent way. Terminologies and ideas appear as overlapping constellations without a key or a map to guide interpretation. In response to this, Black cultural mythology represents a shift toward a more holistic study of the intersections of history with topics of myth, memory, and heroics that proceeds with a duality that accounts for multiple perspectives in healthy comparative engagement. First, Black cultural mythology captures idea formation and a mapping of the intellectual traditions from which a set of useful terminologies emerges to guide society's conversations about how to enhance present and future Black life with a more functional awareness of what is at stake when we choose to regard our mythologies as an active and ongoing process essential for cultural stability and self-esteem. Implementing the study of Black cultural mythology as an Africana curricular innovation is an exciting development. The second aspect accounts for a broader cross-disciplinary field of Africana cultural memory studies that prompts a collective push to layer related ideas about history, memory, amnesia, monuments, commemoration, museums, and heroics across the academy and community. This reinforces the understanding of how the disciplinary specificity of Black cultural mythology is one among many broad academic approaches to cultural memory studies. African historian Walter Hawthorne helps to recalibrate our understanding of the potential of theoretical work on memory and myth in his review of *Crossing Memories: Slavery and African Diaspora* (2011), a collection edited by Ana Lucia Araujo, Mariana P. Candido, and Paul E. Lovejoy. He calls for greater "logic" in approaches to memory studies that relies on "theoretical, methodological, and historiographical contribution[s]."[63] He also emphasizes the value of work "that forces a rethinking of the way historical memory is constructed."[64] Black cultural mythology is precisely this, a theoretical framework for conceptualizing postenslavement survivalist experience in the Americas. Formally, the theorization of Black cultural mythology proposes that in the African diaspora experience of beginning again and engraving identity on new soil, the logic and effect of memory practices can be itemized optimally when we equally prioritize the content and the function of what we recollect and retell. The function is to reinforce the culture's mythology as a transgenerational narrative map of survival maintained by an intellectual and aesthetic tradition concerned with immortalization and with the influence of heroics. An awareness that waves of ancestors, sociopolitical and cultural activists, writers, and artists, though underacknowledged, have had an intergenerational commitment to elevating Africans in the diaspora to heroic personhood despite predicaments of bondage and inequality, further enhances the culture's commemoration of itself and its ongoing philosophical capacity to sustain sacred cultural remembrance. A set of critical attributes emerges as a tool to manage discourses related to this cultural phenomenon.

Shifting away from the broad collectivity of discourses in cultural memory, history, and theory, the chapters examine specificities and microdiscourses of Black cultural mythology's more organic idea formation. Chapter 1 offers a survey of the casual ways ideas about myth, mythology, and memory appear in broad Africana discourses. The chapter's first priority is highlighting foundational sensibilities mined from activists and thinkers such as abolitionist Maria W. Stewart, writer and journalist Shirley Graham Du Bois, culturalist scholars Larry Neal and Maulana Karenga, Black psychologist Amos N. Wilson, and early "Black myth" scholar Molefi Kete Asante. Its second priority is to expand this renewed sense of a latent intellectual tradition, by featuring many of the key discourses on memory that have been sustained by writers and philosophers such as Toni Morrison and Audre Lorde. This survey of the intellectual genealogy and tradition of critical thought ends with the presentation of over a dozen critical attributes that are the working conceptual framework for Black cultural mythology. Chapter 2 is a study of the diverse meaning of commemoration in an intervention format that relays commemoration historiography, the significance of the 1619–2019 Quadricentennial, and contemporary developments in the enslavement memory industry. This chapter is also an analysis of commemoration methodologies mined from Black perspectives on the 1776–1976 US Bicentennial and the 1865–1965 Emancipation Proclamation centennial in the writings of A. Leon Higginbotham, Martin Luther King Jr., James Baldwin, Derrick Bell, and Gil Scott-Heron. The next two chapters merge cultural criticism and theory with literary models to carry the discourse to fruition. Chapter 3 responds to the announcement of plans to place Harriet Tubman's image on the US twenty-dollar bill and explores the nation's irregular racial-cultural pattern of managing her hero dynamic. Chapter 4 stabilizes Haiti, its revolution, and its heroes as the first diaspora-wide mythology of a Black revolutionary event, which gives Black cultural mythology an even more formal legacy into the eighteenth century. Chapter 5 is an exploration of Richard Wright's philosophies and literature that represent not only the pinnacle of antiheroics (through *Native Son*), but also a sensibility of the relationship of the writer to his or her culture's myths. Chapter 6 tackles the complexities of managing mythology in spite of the tensions between the autobiography of a historical figure—Malcolm X— and historian Manning Marable's revisionist, or *deconstructive*, contemporary biography. Finally, chapter 7 teases out the foundations of Black cultural mythology's literary history not only by revisiting the impact of the Black Arts Movement era literary philosophy of myth/mythology (per Larry Neal) but also by considering David Walker's *Appeal* (1829) as a foundational conceptual document of Black cultural mythology in the canon of African American structured writing—in this case, nonfiction. This chapter features critical studies on three remarkable literary texts—Charles Johnson's novel *Dreamer*, Colson Whitehead's novel *John Henry Days*, and Robert O'Hara's play *Insurrection: Holding History*. Formally extending the possibilities of Black cultural mythology concepts as tools of literary criticism—which is suggested in sections of earlier chapters that offer explications of literature by May Miller, Langston Hughes, Ntozake Shange, Laini Mataka, Edwidge Danticat, Ralph Ellison, Edouard Glissant, and Derek Walcott—this chapter is dedicated to thorough literary explication.

The balance, and even *layering*, of theoretical and applied approaches to Black cultural mythology supports rich possibilities for new critical analyses sustained by a comprehensive and original set of concepts that are logical and clarifying historical and culturally self-reflexive markers.

Chapter One

Intellectual Foundations of Black Cultural Mythology

Black cultural mythology is a renewed approach to stabilizing cultural memory that collectively ensures the preservation and recollection of African American and broader diasporan legacy using conceptual tools to actively engage the culturally relevant past. Historicizing the intellectual foundations of Black cultural mythology requires a survey of primary and secondary Africana survivalist ideas as well as a reorientation to African-centered worldviews that are at the core of cultural legacy practices and collective identity. This includes the inheritance of African continental traditional practices such as the funeral dirge, memorialization, and cosmological orientations to the meaning of ancestry. Classical African worldviews such as Ancient Egypt's Middle Kingdom's spiritual, philosophical, and architectural commitments to sacred remembrance are distant, yet relevant, origins of a broad mythological sensibility. Additionally, in the direct intergenerational cultural practices of West African societies from which formerly enslaved African American and Caribbean populations descend, there were numerous stable practices and orientations to remembrance, ancestry, and sacred inheritance.

The attempt to construct a philosophical framework of Black cultural mythology draws upon these premises and ideas as key intellectual discourses that stabilize related historical-cultural-literary analyses. The attributes of Black cultural mythology—hero dynamics, ancestor acknowledgment, historical reenactment of worldview, resistance-based cognitive survival, hyperheroic actions, epic intuitive conduct, immortalization sensibility, sacred observation, ritual remembrance, commemoration philosophy, mythological structure, sacrificial inheritance, aesthetic memorialization, reconciliation and renewal, and antiheroics—are culled from the intersection of and extended implications of these ideas and philosophies.

Numerous diasporan philosophers, historians, and activists have contributed ideas that reinforce the culture's orientations to its cultural mythology, and the short list of key contributors has emerged from a close study of sociopolitical thought, cultural theory, and myth studies. The key exemplars have newly uncovered models and ideas about beginning again and engraving identity on new soil. Collectively, their ideas contribute to the itemization of variables that coalesce in the critical mapping of Black cultural *mythology*. The ideas and philosophies of Maria W. Stewart, Shirley Graham Du Bois, Larry Neal, Maulana Karenga, Amos Wilson, and Molefi Kete Asante help frame the phenomenon in distinct ways that add to profound and influential works on *memory* pioneered by writer and philosopher Toni Morrison. There are many other diverse, though less sustained, perspectives that enrich the intellectual tradition and frame further idea formation surrounding this phenomenon. The exemplars have provided seminal or sustained ideas about a host of variables—immortalization, memory, biography, myth, mythology, and cultural mythology. The Black Arts Movement and the Black Aesthetic Movement introduced myth and mythology for Africana cultural discourse and planted the early seeds from which Black cultural mythology blooms.[1] This collective, intergenerational range of ideas has important precursory formations on which Black cultural mythology builds in the process of offering an expanded and applied philosophical and theoretical framework.

While the exemplars have ideas that lay a foundation for what emerges as the new logic of Black cultural mythology, there are even more thinkers who have also reflected on a broad range of cultural memory concerns that contribute to the intellectual tradition from which Black cultural mythology emerges. In a survey of sources on early Black consciousness, orientations to and models of the culture's heroic ethos abound. David Walker's *Appeal* (1829) blooms in a Black cultural mythology reading. It is a product of Walker's epic intuitive conduct that relies on cultural memory, inheritance, and illumination of antiheroics amid rhetorical strategies that attest to his activist identity, which is infused with hyperheroism and epic conduct.

Frederick Douglass's *The Heroic Slave* (1852) is certainly among the pioneering narratives of the Black cultural mythological literary craft as it creatively embellishes Madison Washington's rebellion aboard the vessel *Creole* in 1841.[2] By 1852 diaspora-wide mythological structure could claim to its credit numerous documented epic and heroic acts whose retelling and duplication systematically affirmed African cognitions of extreme resistance and survival. The Haitian Revolution of 1791–1804, Gabriel Prosser's revolt in Richmond, Virginia of 1800, Denmark Vesey's Charleston, South Carolina, revolt of 1822, and Nat Turner's Southampton, Virginia, revolt of 1831 were the "thrilling narratives"[3] of national and hemispheric Africana cultural discourses. Harriet Tubman self-emancipated in 1849 and led her first group of freedom-seekers out of the South in 1851. The events and timelines of most frequently renarrated epic African activity in the Americas dating from the Haitian Revolution to the bravery and courage of Harriet Tubman—roughly 1791 to 1851—are the first major triumphs of diasporan freedom that captured the broad survivalist and creative imaginings of Africana traditions on American soils. These stand as topics that attest to the fermenting of resistance and the creation and recycling of narratives that preserve this resistance. In effect, Black cultural mythology filters and itemizes the core substance of the collective historical and folk record related to memory.

As a new intellectual category, Black cultural mythology is an organic elaboration of nearly two and half centuries of ideations on Africana faith in and predictions about how to stabilize the integrity of cultural memory of African American and other diaspora populations as transplanted yet thriving groups. The conceptual seeds that thinkers and visionaries have planted are extraordinary. This inaugural survey aims to reorient the discourse and invite broader analysis of the phenomenon.

Maria W. Stewart and Immortalization

Abolitionist orator Maria W. Stewart (1803–79) is one of the earliest Black activist thinkers to promote immortalization as a collective cultural objective. Immortalization in the African American historical experience is the organic, deliberate, and intergenerational process of inscribing norms of reproducible greatness and the highest cultural acclaim. Stewart's legacy, though analyzed most frequently for her Black nationalism and evangelical fire, is a significant antecedent of Black cultural mythology.

Marilyn Richardson's edited collection *Maria W. Stewart, America's First Black Woman Political Writer: Essays and Speeches* (1987)[4] is the yeoman's source responsible for the groundwork that enables us to recount Stewart's legacy. Stewart contributed speeches to the abolitionist journal *The Liberator*, and Richardson credits her with being the first African American woman to "leave extant copies of her texts."[5] Her printed works include a political pamphlet from 1831, religious writings from 1832, as many as four public lectures from the years 1832 to 1833, an 1835 compilation of her works, and an 1879 edition of her collected works that included an autobiographical sketch as preface.[6] She also wrote a memoir entitled "Sufferings During the War" that exposes her life during the American Civil War.[7] Richardson notes that scholar Dorothy B. Porter first began the excavation of Stewart's legacy in the 1930s.[8] Richardson's summary of the "gaping spaces of lost or thinly documented years" of early Black women elevates the meaning of what we do possess on Stewart. Inevitably, from Richardson's summary we can identify variables that reveal the value and challenges of documentation and preservation of the organic ideas of women theorists like Stewart:[9]

> While her speeches and essays reveal a great deal about her intellectual and spiritual life, as yet no personal documents such as journals or letters which might tell us more about the daily realities of her existence have come to light. She affords us, however, a singular occasion to study not only the published thoughts and words of an influential early black female activist, but the unique opportunity to trace the sources of her arguments and beliefs to specific points of origin in the documents she studies and by which she herself was most influenced.[10]

Thus, an inquiry into the evolution of Stewart's ideas about immortalizing the Black experience in America forces us to be attentive to sources such as other abolitionist writings, *The Liberator*, Black nationalist texts, and the Bible, which all influenced her. Autobiography and other approaches to personal and life narrative such as memoir, biography, and even documentary film are also important genres for Black cultural mythology because they are rich storehouses of narrative that inspire heroic activity. Much of Stewart's legacy is contained in autobiographical sources, and this reveals that Stewart exhibited an early engagement of deliberate immortalization practices through her efforts to preserve her words and ideas through published pamphlets. Richardson's work on Stewart, in the form of critical biography with significant autobiographical reprint, contributes to the preservation needed to sustain practices of Black cultural mythology for future generations.

Interpreting a philosophy of immortalization from the ideas and activism of Stewart is a new critical treatment, and, in order to clarify this divergence, it is useful to review the multifaceted intellectual roles assigned to Stewart's legacy. Scholars reference and engage Stewart in conversations on rhetoric, print culture, feminism, abolitionism, prophecy, spiritual narrative, religious pamphleteering, ethical leadership, evangelism, spiritual authority, Black nationalism, and the middle class. Several studies on these topics survey aspects of Stewart's legacy that parallel features of Black cultural mythology.

Ebony A. Utley describes Stewart's writings as "irreplaceable artifacts heralding . . . rhetorical and political prowess."[11] Similarly, Jami Carlacio reveals how Richardson's compilation of Stewart's writings contributed to her process of placing Stewart in the field of "rhetorical theory as it relates to writing, oratorical practice, or in terms of the historical trajectory of theory itself."[12] Carlacio places Stewart in the traditions of rhetorical history, oratory, and writing, with implications for feminist rhetorical scholarship and "alternative rhetorical practices."[13] In a similar revisionist analysis Jennifer Rycenga comparatively places Stewart's work in the context of English and American women abolitionist's historiography.[14] Central to Rycenga's critique of Stewart and her white contemporaries is the assessment that "women who were activists in radical causes nurtured their critical faculties through religious questing, and in the process they questioned much more than the issues that immediately sparked them."[15] The term "questing" appropriately responds to Stewart's heroic activity, even as she emerges as increasingly meaningful to Black cultural mythology, and later examples demonstrate how inherent articulations of Black cultural mythology in Stewart's rhetoric and writing seemed to bloom from analytical spaces beyond her immediate religious anecdote or reference. Rycenga refers to this as the evolution of "transformative ideas and practices" as Stewart and her contemporaries freed their minds to "adopt rhetorical strategies in their writings that underline their logical social analyses with the urgency of religious emotion."[16] Stewart went beyond mere social analysis and into the sphere of prophecy and cosmological analysis, which are factors that support the introduction of a framework of immortalization credited to Stewart. Rycenga cites a compatible characteristic of Stewart's work, that it "claim[s] future and past legacies for women as thinkers and activists," and, indeed, legacy matters are central to Black cultural mythology.[17] Rycenga describes Stewart as "[a]n unwanted prophet in her own land,"[18] and Marcia Riggs also confirms this in *Can I Get a Witness? Prophetic Religious Voices of African American Women* (1997).[19]

There are many elements that link Black cultural mythology to several culturally centered studies on Stewart that consider the African cosmology and worldviews at work in nineteenth-century activism. Judylyn S. Ryan briefly outlines Stewart's "use of spirituality as a source of authority and as a counterhegemonic resource" wherein "authority is based not simply on the assertion of rights but also on the embrace of responsibility—responsibility to meet the spiritual, psychological, and material needs of the cultural community."[20] Kathy L. Glass critiques Stewart in the frameworks of "courting communities," "syncre-nationalism," and "eclectic resistance strategies."[21] For Glass, syncre-nationalism is the ideology that permits Stewart to engage in innovative cultural work based on a pursuit of imagined African-centered community ideals that sustain her activism for racial uplift.[22] "Stewart re-imagined the rationalist ideology of the national community . . . and created a context in which cultural transformation . . . could occur," Glass explains. "Cognizant of the fact that one must first envision change before experiencing it, Stewart's productions call for a new way of seeing the world."[23] Ida Young directly reinscribes Stewart's hero dynamic in light of Stewart's neglect by historians, and she emphasizes, "With her distinct rhetorical style, Stewart symbolically wove the ancestral fabric of the African foremother at a time when many looked away from Africa. Her lectures evoked an African past of pride and great achievement."[24] Black cultural mythology infuses the collective record of Stewart's legacy with a set of language and terminologies that reinforce the need for deliberate, intergenerational, spiritually reflective, and ritualistic practices to sustain cultural memory, and these elements are a priority for contemporary and future community-building.

Stewart's contribution begins in 1831 and sets the standard for the Black activist voice in maintaining cultural identity through (1) immortalization, (2) the Ebonic use of heroes, and (3) predictions of Black cultural mythology through the promotion of hero dynamics and ancestor acknowledgment. These three objectives are features of Stewart's contribution in addition to her process of deliberately immortalizing herself in the public and historical record. She did this by collecting the printed sources that documented her early activism, and she included these primary print sources in a volume of her writings and autobiography. These actions, viewed through a Black cultural mythology lens, are related to more spiritually preservationist ancient practices of tomb inscription, which is an evolutionary form of print culture, representing the earliest transcription technologies that permitted self-eulogy, legacy maintenance, and, in contemporary print practice, autobiography.

Stewart collected and printed her speeches, writings, and autobiography as a response to mistreatment and disregard by the Washington, D C, community that knew her only in her poverty-stricken and geographically isolated old age, rather than in her militant youth. After nearly forty-five years of a life of struggle and poverty in New York City, Baltimore, and, mostly, Washington D C, where Stewart lived out her final days, she made *legacy use* of print media to republish and preserve the intellectual accolades of her young adult career. She thus cemented her role in the turbulent abolitionist period of African American history.

One can speculate that Stewart knew that her days were numbered, and the fact that Stewart's Boston-based public speaking legacy survives today is testament to Stewart's success in deliberately immortalizing herself through the republication of her 1835 volume. Inevitably, Stewart's contribution to her hero dynamic includes her perpetuation of her own legacy through print media. Richardson's collection on Stewart confirms the historical methods of excavation and search-and-rescue that are needed to locate, preserve, and revive nineteenth-century print culture. While Stewart republicized her legacy through print, Richardson and others actively engage in the print culture tradition that modern technology and access permit us to take for granted. Nonetheless, the complete historiography of Stewart's legacy is one of using republication as a tool of print culture to preserve African American legacy.

There are several theoretical sources that support this treatment of Stewart's legacy. An early essay on myth written by Molefi K. Asante and Kariamu Welsh is central to the framework of Black cultural mythology because it cites nineteenth-century Black orators as the forefathers and foremothers of Black cultural speech-delivery devices that are also preserved in the printed record of the Black speech tradition.[25] Stewart is a recognized figure in nineteenth-century Black history, but recent sources have begun to better assess her legacy in the areas of religion, rhetoric, and, now, Black cultural mythology.

Stewart's primary focus was on Black women's experiences, but it was not exclusionary. During the early 1830s, when she was the only woman to speak to abolitionist audiences, her primary forums were among Black women. Her advocacy, though directed toward female audiences, is applicable to the Black community as a whole. A premise of immortalization credited to Stewart in this reading is an aggressive belief in the empowerment of Black women and an emphasis on their role as nurturers and educators in the home. This relates to traditional African-derived cultural use of the oral tradition in the home environment as a vehicle for the transmission of cultural values and education. In their conceptualization of African American myth, Asante and Welsh identify the "mother-earth" or "suckling" category of African American myth that "reduces everything to the motif of caring," and there may be an inclination to associate Stewart's focus on women with this category.[26] However, to Stewart's credit, she promoted a Black nationalism–influenced role for women in the mythmaking process, which inspired women's activism in spheres both in and beyond the home. Glass refers to this as "re-imagining the role of the female subject."[27]

According to Stewart, Black women carry the responsibility of raising their children in revolutionary ways that ensure the transmission of a cultural legacy. In "An Address Delivered before the Afric-American Female Intelligence Society of America," Stewarts proclaims, "O woman, woman! Upon you I call; for upon your exertions almost entirely depends whether the rising generation shall be anything more than we have been or not. O woman, woman! Your example is powerful, your influence great; it extends over your husbands and your children, and throughout the circle of your acquaintance."[28] Stewart challenged Black women to pursue supernatural and divine objectives for future generations of African Americans. In a printed tract on "Religion and the Pure Principles of Morality, the Sure Foundation on Which We Must Build" (1831), Stewart spoke directly to Black women about securing their legacy in the framework of maintaining a hero dynamic and as mythology for the race. She encourages the audience, saying, "O, ye daughters of Africa, awake! Awake! Arise! No longer sleep nor slumber, but distinguish yourselves. Show forth to the world that ye are endowed with noble and exalted faculties. O, ye daughters of Africa! *What have ye done to immortalize your names beyond the grave? What examples have ye set before the rising generation? What foundations have ye laid for generations yet unborn?*" (emphasis added).[29] This is a precise declaration of cultural legacy and heroic sensibility found in the early African American intellectual tradition in which a Black woman acknowledged the supernatural process of ancestor creation and the Black woman's role in this eternal effect. This statement is the foundation of Stewart's philosophy of immortalization, which she poses as a solution to the oppression of the era. Later in the essay, she reiterates in a prayer that God "grant that every daughter of Africa may consecrate her sons to thee from birth,"[30] which is another call for Blacks to take advantage of a divine relationship that has the potential to positively influence destiny and the broader future of Africans in the Americas. Stewart exhibits Black nationalism by using religion to divinely inspire pro-Black revolutionary behavior. Shirley Wilson Logan, in *"We Are Coming": The Persuasive Discourse of Nineteenth-Century Black Women* (1999), devotes a chapter to Stewart's attention to African origins and evaluates how studies on traditional Black usage of the biblical reference of Psalm 68:31—"Princes shall come out of Egypt, and Ethiopia shall soon stretch out her hands to God"—rarely mention the scripture's appearance in the writing and speeches of Black women like Stewart.[31]

An *Ebonic use of heroes* is sustained in the pantheon of heroic examples Stewart used, and her oratory craft relates to another thesis of Asante and Welsh. They suggest that "the myth is so embedded in the culture that its use is impossible to avoid if one is a frequent speaker. The real mythical essence of these heroes occurs with regularity in the discourse of the African American orator."[32] This is a liberating observation of how African American discourse innately reveals cultural location. In the 1830s, when Stewart spoke regularly to audiences, she pulled from the only examples available and transformed them into Black cultural hero dynamics. Ebonic use of heroes refers to how Stewart forced the only histories available—European/Eurocentric history, United States current events, biblical stories, and scattered realms of Black Ethiopianism[33]—to function toward inspirational freedom objectives. In essence, she transforms European women into models for Black progress without featuring their European-ness as a condition to be emulated.

Stewart best uses these devices in her "Farewell Address to Her Friends in the City of Boston" (1833). She offers a lengthy paragraph describing a remarkable young woman from thirteenth-century Bologna, Italy, who succeeded as student, funeral orator, doctor of laws, and public speaker at a time when society limited women's options. Stewart asks, "What if such women as are here described should rise among our sable race?"[34] Drawing from biblical examples, Stewart offers a roll call of biblical heroines to support the cause of Black women's freedom and rights to a public platform. She summons biblical women, namely Deborah, Esther, Mary Magdalene, and the woman of Samaria, as ancestors of the Black woman's cause. Remarkable in Stewart's craft is that she does not fall into the trap of viewing immortalization as primarily a Christian value aimed at a heavenly home. She uses Christianity toward a liberation theology and relies on the Bible as a significant source in her development and rhetoric. Rycenga describes this as "women's intellectual self-development through religion."[35]

In her speeches and writings, Stewart directly references Black hero dynamics consistent with Asante and Welsh's projection that African American myth will be inherently referenced by the Black orator. Stewart makes occasional references to Ethiopianism, invokes an example about Egyptian women,[36] and mentions activist David Walker, who was a personal friend before his murder. Rycenga refers to Walker as Stewart's "mentor" and questions the fact that "Stewart's speeches, which so effectively extended and enhanced Walker's voice, are rarely cited in relation to his acute analyses."[37] Walker's use of print culture and his strategic, covert maritime distribution of his *Appeal to the Coloured Citizens of the World* (1829) garnered him enemies; some believe he was killed because of his abolitionism and defense of Africans. Stewart's treatment of his memory indicates a hero dynamic as she regards him as an ancestor and powerfully invokes a reincarnation of his spirit of resistance in generations to come.[38] She writes, "But where is the man that has distinguished himself in these modern days by acting wholly in the defence of African rights and liberty? There was one, although he sleeps, his memory lives."[39] It is memory that sustains the hero dynamic, and in the context of charting the hero dynamic, Stewart's words represent a much more lasting phenomenon than that for which she is given credit. Stewart also acknowledges Haitian epic, hyperheroic, and resistance-based survival, saying, "And the Haytians, though they have not yet been acknowledged as a nation, yet their firmness of character, and independence of spirit have been greatly admired, and high applauded."[40]

Stewart predicts Black cultural mythology by calling for functional Black hero dynamics. In "An Address Delivered at the African Masonic Hall" (1833), Stewart laments, "When I cast my eyes on the long list of illustrious names that are enrolled on the bright annals of fame among the whites, I turn my eyes within, and ask my thoughts, 'Where are the names of our illustrious ones?' "[41] In this speech, Stewart further ponders, "Where can we find among ourselves the man of science, or a philosopher, or an able statesman, or a counsellor at law? Show me our fearless and brave, our noble and gallant ones. Where are our lecturers in natural history, and our critics in useful knowledge? There may be a few such men among us, but they are rare."[42] She acknowledges that enslavement has prevented the elevation of Black men and women to such rank, but her words summon these accolades into existence.

Much of what we know about Stewart is based on her decision to reprint *Meditations From the Pen of Mrs. Maria W. Stewart* in 1879 as an act of self-immortalization. Richardson says that Stewart, though poor, "came into a modest widow's pension which she immediately invested in a new edition of her collected works. By way of a preface to that 1879 volume she composed an autobiographical sketch which, through an inventive use of narrative technique, presents us with a significant and previously unexplored resource in the study of Black women's literary history."[43] Thus, Stewart's investment in Black cultural mythology is literal, as she allocated her financial windfall to model the importance of preserving her life story for future generations. In addition, her unique narrative devices have implications for the print culture of women's self-publishing and autobiography. Stewart is a heroic character in African American history, and she deserves even more accolade for the fact that she "transformed the Ladies' Department of the *Liberator* with her bold insights."[44]

Most historical sources on Stewart's Boston years refer to the fact that her career was short-lived because of opposition from the Black community, including Black women, as well as white abolitionist leaders. However, Rycenga makes an additional point that suggests that white abolitionist women's racism (except for Prudence Crandall) is a factor that directly reduced historical attention to Stewart's heroic abolitionist activity. "I despair that white female abolitionist readers of the *Liberator* must have been aware of Stewart yet did not cite her,"[45] Rycenga says, and quotes Jean Yellin from *Women and Sisters*, who writes that "apparently either racism or class bias—or both—prevented them from identifying with Stewart. Nor did they identify with [Fanny] Wright or [Ernestine] Rose. Their model was not the black Christian, the English-born libertarian, or the free-thinking Polish Jew."[46] The indictment of white racism as a barrier to the promotion of a Black person's contribution to the history of print culture represents a history of discrimination and exclusion and is additionally antiheroic in the framework of Black cultural mythology. In terms of her clarity regarding the race's opposition, Stewart also skillfully critiques and transposes the racist and condescending writings of an Englishman named John Adams, whose work appeared in Boston seventeen years after circulation in England.[47]

Stewart's *philosophy of immortalization* and her *Ebonic use of heroes* are part of the early history of Black cultural mythology and is made possible by her personal attention to capturing her legacy in print. Her legacy exists in religious and womanist contexts based on her speeches-turned-pamphlets, and in the contemporary era these historical documents have informed an early philosophical antecedent of Black cultural mythology.

This chapter introduces a series of interconnected events that inevitably enable us to begin to structure an early history of Black cultural mythology. Stewart's interpretive genius, fiery delivery, and culturally based political activism achieve permanence in the historical record through her published pamphlets and written or preserved speeches, which reflect the mythological power of oratory. Stewart's processes of legacy self-preservation also have implications for studies on the role of elders in influencing their eulogies and funeral dirges, which is another frame of reference in Black cultural mythology.[48] Without Stewart's agency to defy the gendered odds of the period and to preserve her legacy through written sources, we would not have access to her nineteenth-century ideas of immortalizing the race in spite of conditions of bondage and oppression. Thus, a cultural philosophy of immortalization is a profound early seed excavated in the conceptual framework of Black cultural mythology. Stewart reveals how to secure a legacy in a land that Africans initially did not voluntarily choose.

Stewart's ideas appear in unique forms among her contemporaries of nineteenth-century Black womanist critical thought as women continued to interrogate developments in African American progress, achievement, and personhood. Frances Ellen Watkins Harper (1825–1911) shared ideas about the race's moral development and Black women's roles ("enlightened motherhood") as nurturing and inspiring mothers. Harper's approach to heroism, survival, and cultural mythology is emphatic, but less fiery and transcendental than Stewart's. Among Harper's writings, we find assertions of achievement prowess, such as when she writes in the essay "A Factor in Human Progress" that

> we are living in the midst of a people who have in their veins the blood of some of the strongest nations on earth—nations who have been pioneers of civilization, macadamizers of paths untrod, masters of achievement, and we have need of the best educational influences of the home, school and church to prepare us to fill our places nobly and grandly in the arena of life; for this we need more than the training of the intellectual faculties.[49]

Harper frames the fight for emancipation as a "heroic struggle," and she grounds John Brown's legacy from the 1859 revolt at Harpers Ferry with the wish that "your martyr grave will be a sacred altar upon which men will record their vows of undying hatred to that system which tramples on man and bids defiance to God."[50] Harper also infuses discourses from her novel *Iola Leroy, Or, Shadows Uplifted* (1893) with ideas about cultural memory. The character Lucille Delany, the southern teacher who eventually marries Iola's brother Harry, says that

> instead of forgetting the past, I would have them hold in everlasting remembrance our great deliverance. Hitherto we have never had a country with tender, precious memories to fill our eyes with tears, or glad reminiscences to thrill our hearts with pride and joy. We have been aliens and outcasts in the land of our birth. But I want my pupils to do all in their power to make this country worthy of their deepest devotion and loftiest patriotism.[51]

The ideas of Anna Julia Cooper (1858–1964) also reveal threads of concern for these topics. In her essay, "What Are We Worth?" (1892), Cooper is precise in describing cultural inheritance. She suggests that the "quantum of resistance and mastery are the resultant forces which have been accumulating and gathering momentum for generations. So that, as one tersely expresses it, in order to reform a man, you must begin with his great grandmother."[52] The language of assessing African American resistance, mastery, and momentum is a powerful set of evaluative terms to add to the points of reference that Stewart and Harper offer. Cooper even suggests a path to "immortalize genius":

> Wealth must pave the way for learning. Intellect, whether of races or individuals, cannot soar to the consummation of those sublime products which immortalize genius, while the general mind is assaulted and burdened with "what shall we eat, what shall we drink, and wherever shall we be clothed." Work must first create wealth, and wealth leisure, before the untrammeled intellect of the Negro, or any other race, can truly vindicate its capabilities.[53]

Like Stewart, Cooper references a list of achievers in the "world's roll of honor"—"the Shakespeares and Miltons, the Newtons, Galileos and Darwins—Watts, Morse, Howe, Lincoln, Garrison, John Brown"—who set a standard for "having taken the world's bread and paid for it in immortal thoughts, invaluable inventions, new facilities, heroic deeds of loving self-sacrifice."[54] To her, these men "dignify the world for their having lived in it" and "the world will ever bow in grateful worship as its heroes and benefactors."[55] This type of Ebonic use of heroes (though in contemporary agency-driven scholarship some of the names would be struck from the list) functions as a norm from Cooper who then redirects her attention to the development of Africana achievement. She confirms that "it may not be ours to stamp our genius in enduring characters—but we can give what we are *at its best*."[56] She then highlights the accomplishments, heroism, and bravery of achievers such as the poet Phillis Wheatley; the Loiseaux brothers of South Carolina, who gained international prestige for their rosebush cultivation; sculptor Edmonia Lewis; the first and third regiments of African American troops of the Louisiana Native Guards, who fought bravely in the Civil War; and Booker T. Washington, founder of Tuskegee Institute. From these examples of cultural heroics, she emphasizes that "each is under a most sacred obligation not to squander the material committed to him, not to sap its strength in folly and vice, and to see at least that he delivers a product worthy the labor and cost which have been expended on him."[57]

With the foundations of the language of immortalization and heroics that Stewart's ideas and words provide, we gain a clearer vision of a critical lens for identifying discourses on cultural mythology, heroics, and cultural memory. Her fiery calls for immortalization and advancement of the race's heroic sensibilities and valuation of what is culturally sacred are profound early models that continue to be in conversation not only with Harper and Cooper but also with future traditions of Black critical thought.

Shirley Graham Du Bois's Biography Project

In spite of Shirley Graham Du Bois's extensive repertoire in numerous aesthetic genres, biographer Gerald Horne in *Race Woman: The Lives of Shirley Graham Du Bois* (2000) as well as other recent scholars have unfortunately had to preface their studies on Graham Du Bois with descriptions such as "cloaked in obscurity," "her star has faded despite her manifest accomplishments," "forgotten," "castigated," "suppressed," and "reclaim[ed] from obscurity."[58] Exploring Graham Du Bois's exemplary contribution to African American heroic biography is a much-needed corrective to literary history as well as to the intellectual tradition on which Black cultural mythology builds.

Graham Du Bois wrote eleven biographies on African American and nonwhite heroes between 1944 and 1978: *Dr. George Washington Carver, Scientist* (1944; twenty-second printing in 1964), *Paul Robeson: Citizen of the World* (1946), *There Once Was a Slave: Frederick Douglass* (1947), *Phillis Wheatley* (1949), *Your Most Humble Servant: Benjamin Banneker* (1949), *Pocahontas* (1953), *Jean Baptiste Pointe de Sable: Founder of Chicago* (1953), *Booker T. Washington* (1955), *Gamal Abdel Nasser* (1972), *Julius Nyerere: Teacher of Africa* (1975), and *W. E. B. Du Bois: Pictorial Biography* (1978). In 1947 she told the *Daily Worker* newspaper, "I came to feel that not only as a Negro must I do outstanding work but especially as a Negro woman."[59] Elsa Jane Dixler said of her, in a letter to Graham Du Bois's son David Du Bois, "It is not easy to be a woman—even less to be a very gifted woman—and less still to be a black woman—she had all three hurdles to clear."[60]

Graham Du Bois's role is seminal for her biographical work, which envisioned the global heroics of people of African descent. This transatlantic or Pan-African interest in storytelling models Black cultural mythology attributes of generating sources that invite society to consider nonfiction and fiction literatures that prioritize the culture's hero dynamics, cultural memory, heritage practices, legacy tools, ancestor acknowledgment, immortalization perspectives, commemoration, and historical storytelling. Graham Du Bois even treats antiheroics within a continuum of recalling African American intuitive epic conduct, hyperheroic activity, and resistance-based cognitive practices over the course of beginning again since 1619 and engraving identity on American soils. One example of this is her role in the 1938 Chicago Negro Unit's theater production on the Sambo figure for youth audiences. Jodi Van Der Horn-Gibson credits Graham Du Bois with an ability to "focus on fostering a self-defined identity and consciousness in the diaspora" and regards her as having an "African aesthetic" that helps her to deconstruct negative stereotypes associated with Africanity.[61]

It is significant to address the ways scholars recalibrate the legacy of Graham Du Bois's biography project in the record of cultural history. Horne's biography is essential, and Robert Dee Thompson Jr.'s study on socio-biography,[62] Julia Mickenberg's study of Graham Du Bois's legacy in the genre of juvenile Black biography,[63] and Alesia E. McFadden's archival survey[64] explore Graham Du Bois's multidisciplinary and multigenre legacies. The mythological value appears most in discourses related to the production of her biographical repertoire.

Scholars have comprehensively addressed Graham Du Bois's biographical project, yet there is room for an updated analysis of her contributions to broad African American mythology discourses. A conceptual framework of Black cultural mythology permits a reading of Graham Du Bois's interest in and execution of biography on methodological and theoretical levels of cultural productivity, within an intellectual genealogy of cultural memory and heroics.

Horne's early mention of the biographies is in an economic context: "In her spare time and in rapid succession she wrote a series of popular biographies. . . . Sales from these works finally put her on the road to prosperity, but as her economic fortunes rose, her personal fortunes declined."[65] This first mention in the context of "spare time" is inconsistent with the travel and immersion he describes earlier.[66] On the other hand, it also suggests Graham Du Bois's extensive familiarity with the heroic outlines of African American history. To produce eleven biographies in fourteen years suggests a dedication and acumen beyond the notion of "spare time," which Horne further clarifies as a process of "self-imposed isolation that allowed more time for writing the series of biographies that propelled her into the rarefied atmosphere of financial security" after her son Robert's death.⁶⁷ Horne also characterizes her renewed interest in mothering society for the creation of "a better world," which is related to a newspaper's description of her identity and role at the Open Door Community Center in Brooklyn as "combination mother, probation officer and kindergarten teacher."⁶⁸

Horne captures the achievement of Graham Du Bois's "invention of dialogue," and he notes, "Though some critics railed at her re-creations of dialogue, others found this aspect trailblazing, adding a new dimension to the recounting of history, postmodern in import."⁶⁹ Favorably, "they were reviewed in mainstream publications and consumed ravenously by hungry readers eager to acquire images of Negroes that contrasted with the dominant representations that too often portrayed them harshly."⁷⁰

Graham Du Bois's legacy provides a critical opportunity to further theorize Black women's life work. It is based on a Black cultural mythology reading of Graham Du Bois's biography project, which is a superlative example of historically reenacting worldview and of aesthetic memorialization. She was interested in the genre of biography that can be categorized as juvenile fiction, which is a credit to her interest in contributing to the cultural-historical awareness of African American schoolchildren as well as the nation's schoolchildren (her book on George Washington Carver was a selection of the Junior Literary Guild).⁷¹ Her biographies were flexible enough to be categorized as literary fiction in close proximity to the biographical novel, which armed adults, as well, with cultural narratives that had the potential to increase their historical consciousness of African American and African achievement and heroics. In turn, adults could presumably invigorate the storytelling they transmit to youth in routine socialization or in programming. Graham Du Bois's sheer productivity mostly as a single author reveals a devotion to chronicling the past in accessible and readable formats.

There are other biographers who have made biographical contributions, but their productivity is not as consistent as that of Graham Du Bois. In addition, her motives for writing are notably African-centered. In response to gaining permission to be Robeson's biographer she writes, "I had no words last night to express my feelings when you told me I might present you between the covers of a book to the men and women in whose hands lie the glorious task of building our 'new world.' "⁷² In fact, she describes her biography on Robeson as a "symphony on life."⁷³ The publishing house, Julian Messner Publishers, gave Graham Du Bois her first opportunity to pursue a biography—on George Washington Carver—but she embraced this project as her own and took full advantage of being employed, gainfully for once, for her writing skill, which her son David claimed came "easily" to her and was "therapeutic" at different periods in her life.[74]

Horne structures his study of Graham Du Bois with a categorization of her "many lives [that] present us with many lessons," and, similarly, this Black cultural mythology reading adds to Horne's litany an explicit category of lessons related to her life as a biographical novelist.[75] This addition is based on considering the theoretical and methodological practices she foregrounded as a precursor to Black cultural mythology. McFadden briefly references Graham Du Bois's biographies as a significant and emergent (over her writing career) body of work that "gave lessons in American history that chart the unfolding racial compact being shaped" throughout America's interactions with people of African descent that "memorialized" Black heroes.[76] She also suggests that Graham Du Bois's work was inspired by *Crisis* editor W. E. B. Du Bois's and Jessie Redmon Fauset's *The Brownies' Book*, which aligns her vision of aesthetic memorialization with the magazine's philosophies for empowering youth. *The Brownies' Book* managed numerous educational and racial esteem objectives for African American children. This included general heroics in the sense of familiarizing children with African American mythological structure, the antiheroics of racism, and an explicit impact of advertising other legacy sources such as Elizabeth Ross Haynes's book *Unsung Heroes* (1921)[77] that featured African American heroics.

The primary criticism of Graham Du Bois's biography project is the debates about imagined dialogue. However, this feature is precisely what makes her biographical project valuable. It places her within a continuum of Black women theorists and creative writers like Maria W. Stewart, May Miller, Helen Webb Harris, Ntozake Shange, Thulani Davis, Suzan-Lori Parks, and Laini Mataka (as well as Black men writers such as William Branch, Randolph Edmunds, Edgar White, Phillip Hayes Dean, Langston Hughes, Ralph Ellison, Charles Johnson, Edouard Glissant, Derek Walcott, Ron Milner, and Colson Whitehead) who dared to imagine—meditatively—dialogue primarily through creating dramatic texts that recycled African American mythologies and heroics (including actors in the Haitian Revolution).

Graham Du Bois's contribution to cultural mythology has been heretofore unacknowledged. Focusing on the interpretation of mythology that relies on *actual* historical activity as a basis for symbolic, metaphorical, allegorical, origin-based, and innocuously embellished storytelling that aims to inspire a cultural group and serve as a model for approaches to recycling memory, Graham Du Bois's imaginings of dialogue are profound. Of her Carver biography, Alain Locke noted that much of the volume was "important social documentation," and since Carver died in 1943, the volume has served multiple functions of commemoration and ancestor acknowledgment.[78] A Black cultural mythology theorization of Graham Du Bois's life work extols her contribution to heritage practices and is possible through this conceptual revision and revaluation that acknowledges her deliberate construction of memorable narratives aimed at sustaining African American cultural identity.

James Baldwin reviewed *There Once Was a Slave* (1947) in the *Nation*,[79] and he was not a fan of the volume. For him, Graham did not show enough of Douglass's flaws, and her volume did not promote "interracial understanding." He describes her approach as "breathless reverence and a high purpose" and of "wild-eyed adoration."[80] He fine-tunes his criticism of fictionalized biography, in particular, writing, "At best it usually manages to be simply a readable account of a historical figure: most often the validity of the characterization suffers in the degree that it is fictional. It is just not possible for a contemporary biographer to know what So-and-So said to his wife at the breakfast table in 1866, or how he felt walking through the woods, or his physiological reactions to heartbreak."[81] For Baldwin, this method functions to "inject an element of unreality. And the false intimacy vulgarizes the subject."[82] Black cultural mythology encourages creative artists to conduct character and methodology studies that reflect the recorded contributions of the cultural pantheon of historical actors within a conceptual framework that could produce inspiring agency-driven dialogue. Accounting for both layers of agency—the actual and the speculative—in the Black cultural mythology process is vital to encouraging greater appreciation of the processes of documentation, speculation, and imagination. Cultural philosophy and cultural memory are inextricably linked.

For Graham Du Bois, *process* is illuminating. Horne's volume gives history and context:

> She was now spending more time at home writing. Her first biography, *Dr. George Washington Carver, Scientist*, was published in 1944 to critical acclaim. She had been in the top ranks of playwrights, but this had not secured for her a suitable living. Her biographies—though at times criticized sharply for their inclusion of imagined dialogue—may not have been at the apex of the biographical art but, unlike her work on the stage, they did bring in a decent income.
>
> Actually the critics were a bit unfair, for Graham did conduct primary research for these works, scouring archives and

libraries. When she wrote a biography of Benjamin Banneker she excavated primary material from the Library of Congress and the Maryland Historical Society. To immerse herself in the details of her subject's life she would "[walk] up and down the streets where [the] person was." For her biography of George Washington Carver, she "went to Tuskegee, wandered about the countryside, grew to know the people he had served." For her award-winning biography of Frederick Douglass, she met with his descendants and others who knew him.

Still, her invention of dialogue for her biographies was an extension of her life, for if she could create—and unmake—details of her own life, why couldn't she do it for someone else? To be fair, Graham in her memoir characterized this genre as the "biographical novel," though this was not the impression provided to contemporary readers and critics. That these biographies were successful both critically and financially could only encourage her to continue reinventing her own autobiography.

As the day approached for publication of her Carver book, her excitement rose. "The publishers tell me that it is going to take some literary prize—a movie producer is waiting for the corrected galley sheets." She had written with a purpose in mind; "my Carver book is designed to melt the heart of the most ignorant 'cracker'—while at the same time offering no compromise."[83]

Graham Du Bois's later volume on the living Nasser clarified that "conversations in the book are based on fact and are an attempt to delineate character. They are not taken from records or tapes."[84] Methodologically, this indicates that she sought accuracy in her literary storytelling and that her work contributed to a realist, and not romantically fabricated, mythology. Horne describes her biography of Nyerere as "hagiographic," as it is accurate but overflowing with praise.[85] Even in this sense, it functions as innocuous mythology, whose literary embellishments are not ahistorical, even if one-sided.

Another methodological function of Graham Du Bois's biographical project is the reciprocity and parallel between her biographical narratives as texts (biographies) and as radio programs. This duality conforms to Black cultural mythology's interest in reinvigorating oral traditions in the process of storytelling that is inspired by the availability of and prevalence of African

American heroic narratives. The Carver and Wheatley biographies were also radio programs. The dramatist Graham Du Bois was adept at "imag[ining] the lives of famous personalities," and her vision linked the genres of drama, biographical fiction, and audio performance, with a one-time possibility of visual production in film.[86]

McFadden surmises an interesting methodology about Graham Du Bois's biography on Jean Baptist Point De Sable wherein she seems to merge her personal heritage with embellishments borrowed from the pioneering hero De Sable.[87] Black cultural mythology's itemization of ancestor acknowledgment includes elements of honor, praise, dirges, and eulogies, as well as naming. Graham Du Bois's apparent decision to link her Cheyenne-Potawatomi heritage with De Sable's established Potawatomi background is an understandable heritage practice enabled by cultural mythology and comparable to the philosophical intent of kinship and innocuous embellishment suggested by Alex Haley's personal interest in the *Roots* story.[88]

In preparation for her biographies Graham Du Bois conducted primary research at the Library of Congress and at state historical societies; went on walking tours of her subjects' cities, streets, and homes; and met with her subjects' descendants in order to learn from family recollections. After this ethnographic, archival, and visual research, she constructed hypothetical dialogues to enrich her storytelling. This procedural approach to biography, layered with her commitment to racial uplift, to social mothering, and to African American youth development is remarkable and an exemplary forbearing model for Black cultural mythology.

In addition, Graham Du Bois's contribution to a Pan-African vision of Black cultural mythology is not lost. Actors in the Haitian Revolution comprise the most embraced non–African American group whose heroics appear in the African American literary tradition. Graham expands this Pan-Africanism with texts on Nasser of Egypt and on Nyerere of Tanzania and can thus be credited with directing us toward a vision of global Black cultural mythology and the possibility of the types of shared heroics indicated by African Americans' valuation of Haiti's heroics. Graham Du Bois even coauthored a 1955 play on Haiti—*The Revolutionists*—with Selden Rodman. Domestically, it is suggested that her biography on Phillis Wheatley is a response to the heritage practice of so many YWCA branches across the country being named after Phillis Wheatley.[89]

Part of Graham Du Bois's pioneering as a foremother of Black cultural mythology is that she wrote during the era of virulent McCarthyism, and it appeared to hinder the agency of her critical voice in the biographies of Pocahontas and Washington.[90] Horne cites many instances when Graham

Du Bois proceeded with a political correctness, or "cautious lineaments."[91] He notes that she was subject to "enormous pressure . . . to conform to certain conservative norms, particularly when discussing the founding myths of the nation."[92] McFadden describes shifts from Graham Du Bois's methodology in the Carver biography (aligning blackness and whiteness in brotherhood) to her methodology in the Robeson biography (political incorrectness, global humanitarianism).[93]

Graham Du Bois expressed interest in the biographies of Colonel Charles Young, an African American of the highest rank in World War I, and in Emmett Till, even though these volumes never emerged. Black cultural mythology credits Graham Du Bois for groundwork in the biography genre, for the methodological aspects of her craft, and for her life's work in many different genres and even professions, which, collectively, is a model of foremothering what has emerged as Black cultural mythology.

Larry Neal, Maulana Karenga, and Black Arts/Black Aesthetic Philosophy of Mythology

Both Larry Neal and Maulana Karenga appear in the *Norton Anthology of African American Literature* in the section on "The Black Arts Era, 1960–1975" with their own entries that chronicle their major contributions. Neal is a theorist and a writer, with graduate training in folklore. Karenga is a theorist, organizer, and scholar. In the section's introductory essay, the authors provide an important clarification that reminds us how, in dutiful survey, rereading, and cyclically reanalyzing, the canon is part of the process of discovery and rediscovery from whence expanded idea formation blooms:

> Literary history is not exempt from "history" in general. Time moves; reassessments and revisions follow. As we navigate the new millennium, evidence and critique make it clear that we must revise our notions of the scope and personnel of the Black Arts movement. It is now clear that some writers who have been deemed successors of the Black Arts were, in fact, fellow travelers and, in some instances, pivotal sharers. Ideological fault lines and local controversies tend to occlude the finer lines of anxiety and influence during the "present" of any literary movement. In retrospect, however, history yields a more inclusive, sometimes precise, version of people and events. It is so with the Black Arts movement.[94]

In terms of chronicling mythology in African American literary history, Neal's 1968 essay "The Black Arts Movement" appears in the section before Karenga's excerpts, and the editors have added footnotes to extend clarity for sections of the essay that readers may not fully understand. They do not provide such a footnote for Neal's reference to Karenga's vision of culture, which is the most prominent reference to mythology in African American literary history. In *Call and Response: The Riverside Anthology of the African American Literary Tradition*, the editors only include the Neal essay, and more recent generations have begun to prioritize Neal's engagement with the topic of mythology more than Karenga's, whose corpus of ideas are equally, if not more, philosophical and clear treatises on the meaning and function of mythology in culture. This is a corrective priority for Black cultural mythology.

Neal's essay mentions mythology five times, including an excerpt from Karenga's view of culture for which mythology is the first of seven criteria. Neal's initial presentation of mythology's role in the Black Arts Movement is a proposal for "a separate symbolism, mythology, critique, and iconology."[95] Next, he celebrates Amiri Baraka's play *The Black Mass* because "it is informed by a mythology that is wholly the creation of the Afro-American sensibility."[96] The play's effect of applying the myth of Yacub results in what Neal describes as "we, the audience, come to understand that all history is merely someone's version of mythology."[97] Finally, he measures the legacy of the Harlem Renaissance based on his view of its ability to "address itself to the mythology and the life-styles of the Black community."[98]

In theoretically and broadly asserting an updated meaning of mythology for diaspora communities, Neal's, Karenga's, Baraka's, Charles Fuller's, and Etheridge Knight's 1960s and 1970s ideas, interpretations, and visions for the future of the arts specifically elicit such theorizations and elaborations on the key interventions of Black Arts Movement ideas. Neal quotes Knight early on in "The Black Arts Movement," linking a Black aesthetic to Knight's understanding that "the black artist must create new forms and new values, sing new songs (or purify old ones); and along with other Black authorities, he must create a new history, new symbols, myths and legends (and purify old ones by fire). And the Black artist, in creating his own aesthetic, must be accountable for it only to the Black people."[99] Neal gives these collective cultural directions a genealogy and heroic identity when he observes, "There is a tension throughout our communities. The ghosts of that tension are Nat Turner, Martin Delaney, Booker T. Washington, Frederick Douglass, Malcolm X, Marcus Garvey, [James] Monroe Trotter, DuBois, Fanon, and a whole panoply of mythical heroes from Brer Rabbit to Shine. These ghosts have left us with some very heavy questions about the realities of life for Black people in America."[100] This tension "resolves in recognizing the beauty and love within Black America itself."[101] He describes it as "a profound sense of a unique and beautiful culture" and adds that it "cannot be dealt with until certain political, social, and spiritual truths are understood by the oppressed themselves—inwardly understood."[102] He assigns the future tasks of analysis and expounding to "the "theoreticians among us [who] can break down its components."[103] Here, Neal speaks specifically to the literary enterprise, which is the most consistent in sustaining the mythological enterprise. Specifically, he stresses that "Black literature must become an integral part of the community's life-style" and "it must also be integral to the myths and experiences underlying the total history of black people."[104] He clarifies that "what we are asking for is a new synthesis; a new sense of literature as a living reality. . . . We must integrate with ourselves, understand that we have within us a great vision, revolutionary and spiritual in nature."[105] For Neal, this means that the culture should strive to advance "collective ritual," to "embellish the context" of art, maximize "collective experiences," and "understand and manipulate the collective myths of the race."[106] As a foundation for what emerges as Black cultural mythology, Neal's ideas continue to be fruitful seeds of inspiration.

Neal also offers usable terminologies and references to the culture's *private mythology* and *emotional history* or "common emotional history," which relate to his powerful explanation of Malcolm X's value. This explication is among the best articulations that help society understand why Malcolm is the prototype for deliberate, self-conscious, and intergenerational mythological iconography.[107] Neal describes Malcolm's death as a "psychological setback" to which the culture reacted with unprecedented cosmological unity.[108] He writes, "Never before had black artists entered into such a conscious spiritual union of goal and purpose. For the first time in history there existed a 'new' constellation of symbols and images around which to develop a group ethos."[109] Malcolm was at the center of these symbols and images, and Neal's writings are vital for understanding the psychic processes that reinforce contemporary Black cultural mythology. He writes, "All the development of our remembered and unremembered history began to weigh down on us. And the more of our memory that returned to us, the sharper, the more acute our pain became."[110] Neal's prose poem "The Summer After Malcolm" reiterates the meaning of Malcolm's death as a catalyst for the emergence of African American cultural rites, ritual, memorialization, dirges, and praise song poems. In African American poetry there is a strong legacy of biographical and memorial poems, but the conditions of Malcolm's life, death, and radical nationalist vitality energized new impulses in creative production. Neal itemizes "love memory" and "ancestral ghosts," confessing that "the Summer after Malcolm, I lost myself in a jet stream of mad words, acts, goading bits of love memory" and "I grappled with ancestral ghosts."[111] With such observations, even extending to a broad realization that "there was a concrete historical reason for everything that we felt," Neal emerged as a formidable agent in the intellectual foundations of Black cultural mythology.[112]

In his introduction to the Second Annual Larry Neal Writers Conference of 1983, Baraka reiterates Black Arts Movement goals from which contemporary Black cultural mythology responds. He writes of "an art that would educate and unify black people."[113] He admits that in real time, the Black Arts Movement was "not clear enough about our logical and spiritual antecedents" and adds that they "did not have the science at our disposal to transform rebellion into revolution" with institutions that could "carry and sustain it, create it, generation after generation at yet higher levels."[114] Baraka encourages the conference and future generations to take up "the black baton of our history" and "to spread and revive the power and relevance of Larry's art and political message."[115] Regarding a foundational exemplar of what is now Black cultural mythology, Baraka's words are prophetic. He writes, "Larry is an example for us. Read his work. Heed his example and imperatives. Understand why he was so hip. It is all critical and necessary. As we pass the baton from generation to generation . . . we need to preserve ourselves . . . by honoring his work and bringing into reality its demanding vision!!!"[116] Neal's legacy is a set of writings, though not fully developed, that tease out concepts that are meaningful to the emergent conceptualization of Black cultural mythology.

Charles Fuller provides the introduction to the section on Neal's poetry in the 1989 critical anthology *Visions of a Liberated Future*, and the context he offers nearly ten years after Neal's untimely death at forty-three years of age is an additional landmark that guides society's valuation of Neal. Fuller insists that we must "generate a desire for our tales in the bellies of our people."[117] He advises, "Create an entirely new world view!," and adds that "we have to see ourselves in another mode, seize our own reality and not flinch from the truth of it! Seize the history—retell it! Liberate it—from top to bottom."[118] This impassioned reflection is a follow-through to Fuller's 1967 philosophies from *Black Fire!* about the directions of literary criticism for Black art. Black cultural mythology invokes not only historiography but also cultural and literary criticism. In the essay "Black Writing Is Socio-Creative Art" (1967), Fuller notes, "When we address our own community, a new set of values created by the community takes over."[119] He elaborates that "only when Black writers relate their work to easily recognized symbols and ideas can any hope of a realistic dialogue between writer and community occur."[120] He defines socio-creative art as "a means of self-expression and artistic form born directly from the collective social situation in which the Afro-American found himself in this country."[121] Thus, it is not regressive to bypass contemporary literary criticism to restore our sensibilities to the philosophy and ideas of a critical artistic movement that imagined and predicted a critical framework such as Black cultural mythology. Fuller's historical sensibility is compatible with Asante's reclamation of 1619 as the culture's moment of "beginning again."

Larry Neal's contribution to the edited collection *The Black Aesthetic* (1971) is a four-page table that presents key concepts of his theorization in-progress. He warns, "This outline below is a rough overview of some categories and elements that constitute a 'Black Aesthetic' outlook. All of these categories need further elaboration, so I am working on a larger essay that will tie them all together."[122] It seems that Neal never finished an intended comprehensive essay in his lifetime, but his notes as well as his other shorter works that delve into brief mythology discourses are vital seeds that bloom in contemporary Black cultural mythology. He highlights categories and terminologies of mythology, neomythology, race memory, transmutation and synthesis, meaning and memory, and unitary myth. In this outline, he aligns mythology with a type of living spiritualism in which African religious worldviews, enslavement experience adaptations of this spirituality, ancestors, and the ways such spirit appears in human personalities compel a new critical format. His categories and premises rely on African diasporic music and dance as indicators of indigenous African and Middle Passage–derived influences on race memory.[123] Neal describes neomythology as diasporic and folk culture adaptations of his mythology classification's more original African orientation. In this description writers participate in Black Aesthetics as neomythologists, and literature as the spoken and written word functions as a process between African people, the blues, and meaning and memory.[124] Finally, what the framework of Black cultural mythology refers to as hero dynamics is "history as unitary myth" in Neal's outline, and this category includes a pantheon of heroes, achievers, and symbolic oral tradition and folk narrative characters.[125] Neal offers two conceptual ideas amid these lists that reveal the philosophical depth of his idea formation. He writes that "revolution is the operational mythology," and adds, "All of this links up with the transmutation of African styles and the revitalization of these styles in the West."[126] Drawing from Neal's groundwork here, the backward-gazing task of canvassing the tradition of cultural and literary idea formation that has sustained a mythological worldview since Africans' beginning again and engraving identity in the Americas is indeed a *revitalization*.

In *The African Aesthetic: Keeper of the Traditions* (1994), Molefi Kete Asante's essay on location theory and African aesthetics points readers in the direction of mythology:

> Only Larry Neal and Maulana Karenga endeavor to demonstrate an understanding of continuity with Africa in terms of philosophy and mythology. In doing this they do not deny the contextual immediacy of the African American aesthetic experience, but rather present the African American aesthetic in the tradition of its origin. For example, Neal expresses the view that mythology and neo-mythology, particularly as they relate to themes from Yoruba history, are connected through formal manifestations of African American aesthetics as demonstrated in oratory, blues, dance and poetry.[127]

Asante lyrically describes the desired effect of a philosophical framework such as Black cultural mythology, and in his discussion of the topic of "being cultured" Asante again refers readers to scholars whose works are compatible with the concerns of Black cultural mythology.[128] There is still a needed demarcation that diaspora mythology does not necessarily seek its core from the African past, but, instead, quantifies and itemizes legacy in terms of survivalist heroics. Asante's close reading of Black Arts Movement mythology discourses ensures that Karenga's contribution is not overshadowed: "The criteria for culture derived from the actual life of the African-American people are contained in Maulana Karenga's seven constituents: history, mythology, ethos, motif, social organization, political organization, and economic organization. Those criteria constitute what Dona Marimba Richards calls the *utaratibu wa kutizama*, African philosophy and worldview."[129]

As the other primary Black Arts Movement theorist whom we credit for planting the seeds of mythology in Africana cultural discourse, Maulana Karenga had written earlier, in "On Black Art," that "in terms of history, all we need at this point is heroic images."[130] In *The Norton Anthology of African American Literature* the editors present Karenga's essay, "Black Art:

Mute Matter Given Force and Function" (1968), based on its judged merit "as the clearest and most accessible statement of black aesthetics."[131] However, the essay does not mention mythology. Readers are left giving Neal virtual credit for the concept. Indeed, Neal makes strides in formulating a structural context for mythology, but it was left incomplete. Karenga articulated the scope of mythology in several key works that are not in easy circulation, but are central to understanding his role as an exemplar in the intellectual tradition of Black cultural mythology. In fact, Karenga presented mythology as the first of the seven criteria for culture as early as 1965, and the concepts appear in print in *The Quotable Karenga* (1967), one year before Neal's essay on Black Art.[132]

Karenga's fullest discussion of mythology appears in *Kawaida Theory: An Introductory Outline* (1980). In this text, Karenga has a full section on "Kawaida on Mythology" that defines mythology as

> the totality of secular and sacred assumptions and constructions which join the human and natural with the supernatural in an attempt to answer ultimate existential questions and validate behavior and institutions. Myth-making, Kawaida asserts, is also an art form and yields some of the most beautiful and inspiring poetry and prose. Sacred mythology is better known as religion; secular mythology is often considered heroic history.[133]

From this definition, Black cultural mythology aligns more with what Karenga describes as secular mythology and heroic history. Black cultural mythology does have room for the sacred in its theorization, but its conceptualization of the sacred is *not* paired with religion. Instead, Black cultural mythology's sacred attribute acknowledges honor, remembrance, psychic empowerment, and reverence for feats of survival against tremendous odds. Karenga's definition affirms literature's relationship to mythology in terms of aesthetic value.

In exploring Karenga's role as an exemplar in the idea formation that supports contemporary Black cultural mythology it is clarifying to reinforce his role as a corrective in the historiography on African American mythology. When Karenga writes of mythology again in "Overturning Ourselves: From Mystification to Meaningful Struggle" (1972), published in the *Black Scholar*, he clarifies mythology as "religion," though it is based on a very specific Kawaida philosophical interpretation of religion.[134] Specifically, he writes, "The essential character of a culture is determined by its values, for culture is simply that, a system of values reflecting ways of doing and looking at things on seven levels, i.e., in terms of mythology (religion), history, social organization, economic organization, political organization, creative motif (art, music, literature, and technology) and ethos."[135]

Karenga abandoned the language of mythology because the public too often embraced it as Judeo-Christian mythology. The term is barely traceable as a usable concept in his contemporary work, but he replaced it with other ideas about sacred cultural practices, ancestor acknowledgment, and memorialization. These are radical and profound contributions to Africana cultural memory, but there has not been uniformity about precisely what mythology means or implies for African American and other diaspora cultures. In the early 1990s we still see theorists, such as Pulitzer Prize–winning playwright August Wilson, recalling Karenga's emphasis on mythology, yet with revisions. In an interview, Wilson said, "If you look at the criteria of culture using Maulana Ron Karenga's criteria of mythology, history, religion—we had all those things. But the one thing which we did not have as black Americans—we didn't have a mythology. We had no origin myths."[136] This declaration is identical to what Michael B. Jordan exclaimed in his *Vanity Fair* interview, but it is apparent that Jordan's and Wilson's understandings of *mythology* are not equivalent. Mythology as an origin myth is not what thinkers such as Karenga and Neal had in mind when they painstakingly tried to tease out a formational logic to encapsulate what they witnessed in the culture's worldview and memory-making. In the first edition of *Introduction to Black Studies* (1982), Karenga links the Black Studies endeavor with Kawaida theory:

> Moreover, this conceptual framework is taken from Kawaida theory, a theory of cultural and social change which has as one of its main propositions, the contention that the solution to the problems of Black life demand critiques and correctives in the seven basic areas of culture (Karenga, 1980). These areas of culture are: mythology (religion), history, social organization, economic organization, political organization, creative motif, and ethos. The categories of mythology, creative motif, and ethos were changed to coincide with course titles, but the definition and analysis of these subject areas in this volume are essentially the same.[137]

In the second edition of *Introduction to Black Studies* (1993) this description appeared with revisions in which mythology was completely absent and in which the word "spirituality" replaced mythology:

Intellectual Foundations of Black Cultural Mythology   51

The seven basic subject areas of Black Studies then are: Black History; Black Religion; Black Social Organization; Black Politics; Black Economics; Black Creative Production (Black Art, Music and Literature) and Black Psychology.

This volume is structured around these subject areas for they represent core courses in most Black Studies programs and departments and thus serve as excellent foci for a survey course in Black Studies, i.e., a broad but substantive introduction to the discipline of Black Studies. Furthermore, this conceptual framework is taken from *Kawaida* theory, a theory of cultural and social change, which has as one of its main propositions the contention that the solution to the problems of Black life demand critiques and correctives in the seven basic areas of culture (Karenga, 1980). These areas of culture are: religion, history, social organization, economic organization, political organization, creative production and ethos. The categories spirituality, creative motif and ethos were changed to coincide with course titles, but the definition and analysis of these subject areas in this volume are essentially the same.[138]

This comparison answers the question of how mythology *disappeared* from contemporary Africana studies discourse. It is alive and well in the canonization of Neal's essay "The Black Arts Movement," but there is limited discussion on mythology as an active phenomenon. Paired with Neal's balance of ideas, which suggest a relationship between mythology and memory, the critical thought inherited from Black Arts and Black Aesthetic discourses has still managed to induce an interesting cycle of conceptual renewal. Black cultural mythology adds ideas about *survivalist philosophy* and *memorialization* to these core ideas, in the process of the seeds of the abandoned concept of mythology reappearing in full bloom. The renewed scope also sustains new "course titles," which was a measure of Karenga's decisions about inclusion.

Maulana Karenga: An Intellectual Portrait (2009) by Molefi Kete Asante translates Karenga's evolution beyond his early itemization of mythology. The intellectual biography reveals that in Karenga's contemporary and evolved cultural lens, there is a more anterior, ancient Egyptian philosophy from which we can draw to link African American ancestral and sacred practices with the diaspora's heritage philosophies and ideas. Asante writes, "Constantly in his writings Karenga highlights the idea of cultural reconstruction with stress on human dignity, social responsibility, and struggle. In this focus on *revivification* of a people and cultural construction, he parallels and emulates in one sense Malcolm's socio-religious concept of resurrection" (emphasis added).[139] Resurrection in this sense is a matter of regaining cultural, historical, and religious consciousness as a diaspora agent who is aware of his or her total inheritance.[140] This inheritance is based on African American and diasporic survival and genius beyond the shores of Africa, as well as on continental African legacies. Asante confirms this, noting that

> Karenga discovered in the Zulu example inspiration from the heroics of Dingiswayo, Shaka, Ceteshwayo, and the Zulu defeat of the British army at the Battle of Isandlwana on January 22, 1879. Indeed the story of the Zulu's defense of their homeland would become one of mythical proportions. Black people were not always victims and could assert independence and dignity. This is where the idea of dignity-affirming action becomes part of the Karengarean construction of a theory of agency and ethical action.[141]

The definition of revivification, in Karenga's own words, features Ancient Egyptian terms, including "*sedjeb*, restore to life; *min*, revive; *wehem ankh*, live again, be reborn; and *seankh*, which is truly polysemic and means make live, preserve, revive, nourish, feed, and perpetuate."[142] In fact, Karenga views mythology in a shifting trajectory toward religion, operationalized as *spirituality and ethics*. In this sense, his most contemporary scholarship, such as the seminal volume *Maat, the Moral Ideal in Ancient Egypt: A Study in Classical African Ethics* (2006) and *Odu Ifa: The Ethical Teachings* (1999), are advanced, deep cultural explorations beyond our limited assumptions that inform how we have traditionally encountered the word "mythology" in relation to Africana culture.[143]

Karenga's value as an exemplar and forerunner of Black cultural mythology and Africana cultural memory is also based on his value to what Keith Mayes describes as "commemoration nationalism." Commemoration nationalism includes the African American holiday tradition that Kwanzaa represents, even though the Kwanzaa holiday is a late blooming of an African American sense of its own celebratory calendar of distinct observances that have centered cultural meaning. Mayes's description of Karenga's profound and holistic approach to commemoration is worth quoting at length:

Karenga's approach to commemorating Malcolm X would slightly differ from east coast organizations. Karenga provided a rationale for Malcolm's commemorative legacy and underscored it with a Swahili name, "Dhabihu," meaning sacrifice. Dhabihu would become the official holiday name for Malcolm X's birthday in Los Angeles. The holiday name for the Swahili word sacrifice, Dhabihu, or Malcolm's martyrdom, immediately proved promising.[144]

Karenga's vision of what constitutes proper memorialization is remarkable, according to Mayes:

> Karenga would play a role in popularizing another Malcolm X observance—May 19—adding a second Malcolm commemoration to black America's growing protest calendar. . . . While black nationalist groups honored Malcolm X on his birthday, it was Karenga who pushed the idea of making the day a black American holiday with real commemorative import. First, Karenga attached a Swahili name to Malcolm's birthday calling it "Kuzaliwa." Second, Karenga desired more than the usual black nationalist organizations partaking in the holiday.[145]

In Asante's biography on Karenga, we learn about a parallel narrative that quantifies Malcolm X's heroic value to a young Karenga: "At twenty-four years of age Maulana Karenga saw as the answer to our collective problem the translating of Malcolm's philosophy into a ritual of resistance and transformation."[146] Karenga uses the word "heirs" to affirm that the African American community is an inheritor of Malcolm's legacy, and Karenga's response to Malcolm is a model of how progeny should honor and make use of the gifts an ancestor bequeaths. Asante describes how ancestors and their heroics compel us to *act* and to *behave* in ways that confirm our understanding of the function of our heroics, mythology, and inheritance. Viewing Karenga as a respondent to Malcolm, Asante observes that

> here is where Karenga took his opportunity to advance the rituals that had been proposed in Malcolm's thinking. Here is where he deconstructed the intellectual capacity to grasp the deeper meanings of Malcolm's rhetoric and logic of liberation, that

for him became a central resource. Retrieving Malcolm's legacy and developing it in the context of Kawaida was a project of great importance to Karenga. And he worked to discover him in all of the proper intellectual spaces, the obscure yet pregnant interstices that would yield a clearer and firmer grasp of society and the world.[147]

Karenga's meditation on Malcolm is a prototype for how diasporans should respond to the legacies of the culture's heroes. In this passage, we can discern all the key elements of Karenga's contributions. Indeed, mythology was a rather undeveloped terminology during the Black Arts era compared to how it evolved in Karenga's contemporary thought: concepts of revivification, heirship, inheritance, meditation, ritual, and a sense of the African American *sacred*. These have a cultural etymology that includes both the nineteenth-century Zulu resistance models as well as ancient ethical ideals related to concepts such as restoration and preservation, which are key concepts even in the historiography of Africana cultural memory.

This idea formation is not random. Instead, it is a manifestation of Karenga's Kawaida theory, "a communitarian African philosophy created in the context of the African American liberation struggle and developed as an ongoing synthesis of the best of African thought and practice in constant exchange with the world."[148] Cultural movements and literary anthologies as well as contemporary criticism that contextualize Black Power and Black Arts contributions to critical thought still quote Karenga's late 1960s seven criteria of culture—mythology, history, social organization, political organization, economic organization, creative motif, and ethos; but they do not update the more refined ideas that link Black Arts Karenga to contemporary Kawaida Karenga. Kawaida's "seven basic dual emphases" should be the second part of society's engagement with the Black Arts Movement, which is part of a continuum of living ideas about the depth and sacredness of Black culture. The seven criteria of culture get replaced by the seven dual emphases of Kawaida: "(1) philosophy and practice; (2) culture and community; (3) tradition and reason; (4) dialog and recovery; (5) language and logic; (6) critique and corrective; and (7) synthesis and exchange with the world."[149] As an exemplar of what has emerged as Black cultural mythology, Karenga demonstrates the process of cultural meditation that inspires us to consider the depths of our cultural heroes' values and legacies, useful for sustaining contemporary African American and diasporic survival, stability, agency, and cultural personhood. Ancestor acknowledgment is at the core of this process.

In "Us in the Tradition of Our Ancestors: Decades of Daring Distinction" (2006), Karenga shares his processes of sacred meditation:

> No matter how many times I am to write or speak at length on the Sixties and its significance for Us, as an organization and a people, and on our role in this decisive decade, I do not take it lightly. Nor do I let my first-hand active knowledge of this period of fierce passage and fundamental turning diminish my sense of obligation to always give it the careful and considered attention it deserves. And so I sit down in solemn meditation like a Maatian or Ifa priest before prayer, and I read and study the sacred words of the women and men who made me, our organization and the Movement possible. These include men and women like Malcolm X, Marcus Garvey and Sekou Toure; Anna Julia Cooper, Mary McLeod Bethune and Julius Nyerere; Messenger Elijah Muhammad, Fannie Lou Hamer and Frantz Fanon; Maria Stewart, Ida B. Wells, Frederick Douglass and countless others, as well as the writers and teachers of our sacred texts, the *Husia* and the *Odu Ifa*.[150]

These meditative and reflective sensibilities model for the diaspora how to practice cultural remembrance as sacred, and it functions like an African libation prayer. It also articulates the responsibilities for memory and memorialization. He continues, "We pause to pay due and depthful homage to our ancestors whose teachings and lives have informed, inspired, and guided us thru good and terrible times and whose awesome legacy we've tried our best to honor thru the terrible times and whose awesome legacy we've tried our best to honor thru the steadfast and worthy ways we understand and assert ourselves in the world."[151] This process further includes a testament of how the organization's members have "self-consciously walked and talked daily with our ancestors, reverently researched their thought and practice and used these findings as a foundation and framework for the intellectual and practical work we do."[152] Much like an African libation prayer, Karenga's postmythology ideas are sacred, culturally grounding, and relevant to an emergent Black cultural mythology.

Mayes includes a sense of Karenga's ethos that is worth sharing to summarize his sensibility that paves the way for Black cultural mythology. Karenga said, "It's a matter of intelligence and self-determination that everyone who claims to be free should determine . . . who should be the heroes and what days they should be honored."¹⁵³ As a forerunner for Black cultural mythology, Karenga's self-determination includes the right to look to the African heritage for inspiration. This includes linguistic parameters, such as taking Swahili names, and philosophical parameters, such as excavating and internalizing models of Ancient Egyptian ethical and moral ideals. The right to discern one's own cultural heroes, who may appear as villains or antagonists in Eurocentric narratives, is another foundational right of mythological behavior and consciousness. Karenga's and Neal's placement of the concept of mythology in Black nationalist consciousness and as part of a core cultural itemization are celebrated Black Power and Black Arts era contributions that serve as intellectual maps for future generations of scholars to consider in the pursuit of traditional foundations of new knowledge.

Amos N. Wilson and Black Psychological Dimensions of Cultural Mythology

In *The Developmental Psychology of the Black Child,* Amos N. Wilson evaluates the totality of black child development and conveys a secondary discourse on how cultural mythology functions in African American life and family dynamics. He describes mythological structure as the Black person's "explanatory system which seeks to explain how what he perceives as reality came about, what is his place and function and destiny in that reality."¹⁵⁴ Wilson even equates mythological structure with worldview. Wilson's terminologies and psychological explanations of the role and contexts of mythological structure are important because he itemizes how mythology has a deeper influence on and meaning within Black consciousness than society realizes. Wilson focuses on the problems of a negative Black world view frustrated by Black powerlessness at the hands of whites, but Black cultural mythology focuses on the positive Black worldview represented by Black historical activities of heroic resistance (as well as antiheroics). Instead of operating "at a cognitive, behavioral, motivational *deficit* in the context of white society" (emphasis added), Black cultural mythology identifies resistant and survivalist behaviors wherein Blacks operate at cognitive, behavioral, and motivational heights.¹⁵⁵

In the philosophy of Black cultural mythology, a discussion of antiheroics would best complement Wilson's approach to negative mythological structures. "To a marked degree the character and attendant mythological structure of black culture has developed out of the chronic frustration and powerlessness of black people."¹⁵⁶ While there are notable segments of the

Black community that exhibit "frustration" as a psychological life pattern than lends itself to ideas and behaviors that are counter-nationalistic and self-effacing, there is another angle to pursue regarding mythology—the survivalist view of Black cultural mythology. It is conversant with Wilson's focus on the cause-and-effect nature of intergenerational frustration. The refocus on the cause-and-effect nature of intergenerational *empowerment* is a solution to the problem that Wilson identifies, namely that "many of the characteristics of black cultural and individual behavior can be attributed to the reactions to frustration and the socialization of the black child by frustrated black parents."[157]

Wilson's evaluation of mythological structure and cultural mythology is largely about problem solving and resolutions. He suggests redirecting "the socialization practices of black parents and community leaders" and reiterates his study's concern with correcting "those factors which unnecessarily retard" Black well-being.[158] Wilson is one of a handful of scholars who uses the precise terminology of Black mythology, thus his approaches are part of the foundational scholarship upon which Black cultural mythology builds. Wilson's conclusion confirms that most Blacks in America "do not fit the foregoing descriptions" of dysfunction, and he mentions the "number of cases where blacks have maintained their identity, fought frustrating barriers and yet have fully realized their intellectual, cognitive, behavioral, emotional and social potentials."[159] He does not discuss the mythological structure of these conscious examples, and contemporary Black cultural mythology makes that leap.

Wilson is also responsible for offering a very usable language that further itemizes psychological and social-behavioral language related to Black cultural mythology. For example, he presents "organic historical-experiential events" as "symbols."[160] In language and in written texts, such as the models of Black literary texts that have helped to record, transmit, and enliven the Black mythological record, Wilson notes that these organic historical-experiential events "carry psychosomatic, personal and interpersonal, subjective and objective, conceptual and emotional, conscious and unconscious meanings."[161] A feature of Wilson's description of mythology is that it should "permit new points of view . . . lead to new discoveries, provoke new questions, create new problems that must be solved in new ways, [and] jolt the imagination."[162] Wilson orders these as part of a "mythological methodology" that can be "self-generating" and that is "inextricably tied to a particular geophysical, psychosocial situation." Furthermore, he contends there is "mutual interaction between method and situation. . . . Thus, the structure of the environment, including its potentials, will tend to limit and shape both mythology and methodology."[163]

In general, Wilson's volume on *The Developmental Psychology of the Black Child* encourages the cultivation of best practices for Black children's mental, emotional, social, and educational growth. He examines mythology in many frameworks as it pertains to socializing Black children for optimal consciousness. The contemporary, more expansive theorization of Black cultural mythology relates Wilson's ideas to the deliberate, intergenerational transmission of mythology through oral and written traditions that emphasize hero dynamics, ancestor acknowledgment, heritage practices, legacy tools, commemoration, immortalization ideas, cultural memory, and more. The processes inherent in Black cultural mythology seek to enhance the intergenerational survivalist and resistance tendencies in direct relationship to Wilson's observation that "the way a culture socializes its children is a function of the way it perceives the world at present and the world of its children. The world perception is a historical-experiential product of a people and a mythological structure is built upon that perception. The methods of childrearing, the values taught to the children, etc. are organically connected to the cultural mythology (or world view)."[164] Similar to Woodson's shorter texts on folk culture and African heroes, Wilson is committed to positive cultural reinforcement and socialization of Black children. The antithesis to this positivity is that a "distorted black cultural mythological structure" results in a "dysfunctional socialization process."[165]

Wilson's scholarship, from the lens of Black psychology, descriptively layers variations of cultural and mythology tendencies and symptoms, and these are useful contributions to a more expansive conceptual and philosophical theorization of cultural behavior. Black cultural mythology is configured based on Wilson's significant groundwork, including his discussion of how the lack of heroic images in a child's own ethnic group frustrates child's play from "what should be its natural goals of reality testing, broad environmental mastery, ego strengthening, integrating the self with social reality, [and] the facilitation of intellectual and thought development."[166]

The Black psychology component of cultural mythology is a measure of cultural well-being, because deficits in cultural mythology are unhealthy to diasporan populations. Wilson writes of African Americans who have a distorted or frustrated black *mythological structure* because their parents do not transmit sufficient cultural and survivalist data to stabilize, culturally, the child they are rearing. Of all the possibilities that a strong cultural mythology can reinforce, Wilson's suggestion of its capacity for "ego strengthening" is among the most hopeful manifestations of cultural memory. In addition, Wilson makes three critical observations that help ground the seriousness of Black cultural mythology. First, "mythologies create vocabularies, concepts, ways of thinking, perceiving, feeling and behaving" and "the linguistic, perceptual, affective, cognitive, behavioral patterns of that mythology [are] taught to their children and these grow up to be like their mentors (usually their parents)."[167] Here Wilson establishes the intergenerational impetus of mythology. This perspective is vital for informing the critical analysis of juvenile literature sources that intend to represent diaspora heroics yet fail miserably because of lack of nuance and historical perspective. The juvenile literature on Harriet Tubman contains many examples of these types of failures that Wilson identifies, which demonstrates the value of cultural, historical, and worldview specificity in heroic storytelling and imaging.

Wilson acknowledges the normalcy of cultural mythology, noting that "each culture develops a mythological structure—a structure which perceives the phenomenal and metaphysical worlds after a certain fashion and seeks to explain those worlds in terms of its perceptions. Out of this mythological structure come conceptual, evaluative, behavioral, motivational, cognitive systems and methods for dealing with the mythologized world."[168] Finally, he confirms that "the character of the mythological structure is determined by prevailing historical, geophysical, economical, psychosocial circumstances" and "cultural mythological structures guide cognition, percepts, affects and behavior."[169] All of these elements are documented in diaspora traditions of beginning again, engraving identity on new soil, and sustaining cultural memory practices and orientations. Basing the philosophy of Black cultural mythology on these psychological attributes reinforces its value and the urgency that it be critically itemized from within a vast tradition. Wilson's contribution also validates Black cultural mythology as a cognitive and behavioral matter.

Molefi Kete Asante and African American Myth

The critical ideas of this chapter's exemplars, activists, and theorists constitute the intellectual genealogy of Black cultural mythology. As an approach reflecting self-consciously African-centered points of view, Black cultural mythology advances discourses on memory and cultural identity uniquely from the treatments of African American myth in Americanist and Eurocentric formations. Many of these seem to center the priorities of myth and memory discourses within the traumatic legacy of enslavement with a limited applied framework wherein matters of myth, memory, and heroics are central to successful cultural living and empowered worldviews. Black cultural mythology reorients the lens toward critically analyzing the intricacies of past models of Black agency in the art of surviving that are inspirational cultural lifelines for future generations.

Molefi Kete Asante is the primary pioneer of an underacknowledged corpus of scholarship on African American myth studies. Society tends to credit him most for his more popular late twentieth-century work on Afrocentricity and for his contemporary work on continental African history and geopolitics. Black cultural mythology adds Asante's work on myth to the early pioneering foremothers and forefathers—Stewart's immortalization ideology, Graham Du Bois's Black biography work, Neal's and Karenga's nationalist work on cultural mythology, and Wilson's psychology-based analyses.

Asante's groundbreaking treatment of myth and mythoforms provides intellectual tools to define the worldview of the African identity that evolved on American soil. The framework of Black cultural mythology stands on the shoulders of a set of ideals, historical interpretations, and language that Asante offers as tools to encourage more concise definitions of the African American past. Groundbreaking essays, diverse treatments of the variables of myth, and procedural analyses of Black hero dynamics are central features that inform Black cultural mythology's revisioning of the agency of the African American past.

Asante's repertoire includes a central set of focused writings that celebrate proactive Black achievement without prioritizing and overemphasizing how oppression has interrupted organic processes of *being* and *becoming* as Africans adapted to American environments. In the worldview that sustains this process, African people have always been subjects of their own experience. Asante's formulae for acknowledging the myths that sustain Africana development in the Americas remind society that America's negatives (white supremacy, racist laws, discrimination, skin-color privilege, support of racial genocide) have never been the central features of Africana identity, self-concept, and worldview. It is important to chronologically examine Asante's contribution toward a conceptualization of mythology directly relevant to and functional for people of African descent in the Americas. These works include the groundbreaking essay with Kariamu Welsh, "Myth: The Communication Dimension to the African American Mind" (1981), which Asante reconstructs as "Rhetoric and Myth" (2006); his treatment of mythoforms and myth in *The Afrocentric Idea* (1987); and his procedural analysis of the Black hero dynamic through the model of Malcolm X in *Malcolm X as Cultural Hero and Other Afrocentric Essays* (1993). However, the chronological examination of his discourses on myth since 1969 reveals how these ideas evolve and meander over time.

Asante's *Rhetoric of Black Revolution* (1969) sets the stage for his evolving process of relating African American oratory, operationalized in this volume as *rhetoric*, to African American myth. In this text, he emphasizes the legacies of David Walker, Charles Lenox Remond, Frederick Douglass, Marcus Garvey, W. E. B. Du Bois, and Martin Luther King Jr. *Rhetoric of Black Revolution* is concerned with the "rhetorical situation that produces and sustains the rhetoric of black revolution" as well as its spokesmen and its themes.[170] Asante's next volume with Stephen Robb, *The Voice of Black Rhetoric* (1971), transitions his ideas about rhetoric and revolution into notions of rhetoric and *voice*.[171]

Asante first acknowledges the problem that the American school curriculum has marginalized and ignored the African heritage in its curriculum, and he describes the Black response to this problem as a goal to "re-indoctrinate."[172] Asante identifies the cultural corrective as a process of engaging the past in order to learn what the "black forefathers" knew.[173] Acknowledging the spirit of self-preservation that Africana forefathers possessed upon their arrival on America's shores, he honors the "illiterate and semi-literate blacks [who] told their children that times would be better" and who transmitted a resolve that enabled Africans to create adapted mythologies to sustain them and their progeny in a radically new, and severely hostile, environment.[174]

Asante addresses another angle of myth in the history of the rhetoric of the Black revolution, particularly concerning the Nation of Islam and its rhetoric of exaggeration:

> Black heritage and identity can be based on the true nature of African history without the obvious tall tales propagated by some nationalists and the Black Muslims. Elijah Muhammad taught his coterie of black nationalist preachers that a black scientist created the white man by mistake thousands of years ago. While the attempt by Muhammad's preachers to persuade the black masses never really succeeded, the exaggeration did teach the masses something about myth-making. Convinced that the white man had dominated other peoples of the world *because his myths were stronger*, the black rhetors saw an opportunity to re-direct and re-structure reality.[175] (emphasis added)

Asante presents this perspective as a response to the superstitions of racial dominance that continued to enslave Blacks, mentally, after Reconstruction and as one of the rhetorical methods to protect the community from the distorted self-images projected by racist myths of physical and intellectual inferiority.

Another strategy that Asante identifies that is related to myth is the term "mythication," which he defines as "employing language that suggests the sanction of supra-rational forces, the agitator creates a spiritual dynamism for his movement. Seizing on what is probably the rationale for black hope, the agitator often attempts to use religious symbolism in an effort to demonstrate the righteousness of his cause."[176] Mythication is linked to the religious supernatural in the context of Black revolution, and Asante also considers history to be an instrument of the processes of mythication to the extent that the Black revolutionary speaker "wants to demonstrate that his agitation is sanctioned by history because great agitations have sought to establish justice, create equality, and build dignity."[177] In this sense, mythication is the strategy that infuses an assurance of supernatural support and encourages the Black community to have faith in the possibilities of their imagination: "This strategy is primarily exhortative in the sense that it becomes a type of group self-congratulation by the agitator in order to inspire them to a greater dedication. It is identifiable in the written and oral discourse of the black revolutionists by appeals to God, posterity, history, the race, forefathers, destiny, and so forth."[178] Mythication inspires pride and self-esteem based on the legacies of the past and on supernatural cultural affirmations. We can view it as an aspect of the practice that sustains the mythological structure that Wilson spoke of.

The second half of Asante's *Rhetoric of Black Revolution* serves as a form of Black cultural mythology because Asante reprints speeches from the nineteenth and twentieth centuries to demonstrate how such legendary orators as Charles Lenox Remond, Frederick Douglass, Adam Clayton Powell, Franklin Florence, Eldridge Cleaver, and Bobby Seale used rhetoric and African American myth to connect to Black audiences for collective unity and empowerment. He relies on the same methodology in the biographical chapter on the rhetoric of Henry Highland Garnet in *Language, Communication, and Rhetoric in Black America*.[179] This model is inspirational for the conceptualization of Black cultural mythology, particularly how Asante emphasizes the role of nonfiction—the biography form. He offers a powerful example of Garnet's use of heroics in his speeches as he praises Denmark Vesey, Nathaniel Turner, Joseph Cinque, and Madison Washington, and calls forth Toussaint Louverture and others in heroic litany.

Asante is the leading theorist who identifies a linkage between oratory (rhetoric) and myth, whose natural progression is a relationship between oratory (rhetoric), myth, *plus* their visual representations using modern technology. There are numerous possibilities for how the visual arts, including film, painting, drawing, computer technologies, publishing, and other postmodern coded, symbolic, and digital forms, transmit myth.

Asante mines history with an intriguing interest in the culture's narratives, and he honors the craft of orality that the ancestors fashioned:

> Unable to read or write English and forbidden by law in most states to learn, the African in America early cultivated his natural fascination with *Nommo*, the word, and demonstrated a singular appreciation for the subtleties, pleasures, and potentials of the spoken word which has continued to enrich and embolden his history. Thus, in part because of strict antiliteracy laws during slavery, vocal communication became for a much greater proportion of blacks than whites the fundamental medium of communication.
>
> The study of black speeches, then, emphatically imposes itself upon any true investigation into black history. Bringing with them to America a fertile oral tradition augmented by the pervasiveness of *Nommo*, the generating and sustaining powers of the spoken word, the Africans' use of the word permeated every department of life.[180]

Black cultural mythology prioritizes the objective of returning to the orality of storytelling and other oral forms of cultural transmission, and Asante's groundwork is still relevant to contemporary and future cultural developments. Asante's early works on oratory pose an interesting warning that "the scholar, be he rhetorician or historian, who undertakes an analysis of the black past without recognizing the significance of vocal expression as a transforming agent is treading on intellectual quicksand."[181] Like Stewart, Asante engages in a type of heroic prompting through interrogation when he asks, "And how can black people regain their preslavery, indeed, pre-American heritage?"[182] Placed in comparison with Stewart's question about how the race can immortalize itself, we realize there is a push and pull, or a borrowing and trading, relationship going on between the past's vision for the future and the present's reliance on skills from the past. This is another critical attribute that Black cultural mythology aims to reconstruct in its interest in the *force*, or ethos, that enabled early African populations in the diaspora to manage a secure vision of personhood and collectivity worthy to be duplicated and sustained as a survivalist inheritance. Asante makes a case for the prevalence of Nommo in speech and music, as well, but stops short of delving into Nommo's forces in literature (beyond nonfiction).

Nearly twenty years after *Rhetoric of Black Revolution* Asante published his seminal construction of the meaning of mythoforms in *The Afrocentric Idea* (1987), and his approach to oratory was infused with the images and broader meanings of Black myth. *Afrocentricity: The Theory of Social Change* (1980), particularly the revised edition (1988), is also remarkable for its broad overviews of Black mythology that are more academically stated in *The Afrocentric Idea* as aspects of the formalized discipline of Black studies.

Asante's ideas on oratory (rhetoric) evolved into his conceptualizations of myth, and he began to address black responses to the "myth of white superiority" and to explain the heritage challenges facing blacks in the process of intercultural communication.[183] In his seminal work with Peter Andersen on transracial communication, the authors review and interpret studies that address levels of race consciousness in order to assess the social meaning of the Black image. They examine the role of symbols in their discussion of the problematic that, in the process of heritage practices, "the parents of young blacks are mostly assimilationists striving for integration but attempting to adopt 'white' cultural symbols."[184] This line of inquiry relates to levels of dysfunction that Amos Wilson noted in his study of the critical importance of a healthy mythological structure. The authors also address the power of heroic heritage naming (i.e., naming a black child "Chaka").[185]

In the volume *Afrocentricity* (1988) Asante features the significance of having "an ideology of heritage" whereby one has respect for "one's own prophets" such as Garvey, Du Bois, Fanon, Nkrumah, Muhammad, Malcolm, and Karenga.[186] Asante also writes of "symbols which will, in their completeness, transform the whole of the African world," an interpretation that is also similar to the theorizations of Black cultural mythology but differs from the meaning of symbols from an African American history perspective.[187]

Black cultural mythology embraces elements of Asante's introduction to Afrocentricity in which he itemizes the sacredness of iconic African places and heroic African American historical actors that is not dissimilar from Ana Lucia Araujo's contemporary studies on memorialization. The key difference is that although Araujo is the leading scholar in memorialization studies, her domain is sites of memorialization in the Atlantic enslavement trade. Asante's site memorialization goes beyond enslavement:

Afrocentrism teaches us to honor Jamestown where the first bloods truly destined touched the American earth; to honor Thebes, the most sacred city; to honor Oshogbo where the healing waters flow; to honor Lake Bosumtwi where the God of Africa dwells; to honor the sacred spot where Nat Turner planned his revolt in Virginia. We have within our own history the most sacred and holiest places on the earth. Afrocentrism directs us to visit them and meditate on the power of our ancestors.[188]

Asante calls for behavior and action that invoke sacred mythology. Unlike Karenga's approach, Asante's version of the sacred avoids an analysis of religion. Asante writes, "We have a formidable history, replete with the voice of god, the ancestors, and the prophets."[189] Asante also counters the historian's view that history and mythology are not compatible when he asserts that "Afrocentricity is the belief in the centrality of Africans in postmodern history. It is our history, our mythology, our creative motif, and our ethos exemplifying our collective will."[190] In the African experience with the West on American soil, the essence of this will has been to survive by being attentive to the empowerment transmitted in the history of legendary Black achievement. This focus on the survivalist legacy that African ancestors bequeathed as a type of sacrificial inheritance in inferred in Asante's contention that "you must always begin from where you are. . . . if you are African-American, begin with African-American history and mythology."[191]

In *Afrocentricity* Asante affirms the ancestral role of Black poets as guardians and transmitters of the mythology "for they have kept us always from losing ourselves." This parallels Black cultural mythology's acknowledgment of the role creative writers play in the processes of cultural memory, and is articulated by several other scholars such as Trudier Harris in her study on Martin Luther King Jr.[192] His affirmation of this process is noteworthy because he calls out names from the African and African American past:

> Our poets, the greatest ancestral voices among us, Guillen, Soyinka, Dunbar, Dumas, Bitek, ya Salaam, Karenga, Okai, Kariamu, Sonia, yes, Pathé, Hughes, Haki, and Baraka, know the truth of ancestral objects. They sing of coconuts and palm trees, Martin Luther King avenues and soul blues, Chaka, Dinizulu, Osei Tutu, Akhenaten, Piankhy, Taharka, Nzingha, Candace, Yaa Asantewa, Harriet, and Sojourner. Their words of soul spring forth from Shango; they know umbanda and can shout

with the Baluba in amazement at our deep spirits. This is not all they know or can do. By extension, they are in touch with every fiber of the image of a nation contained in our people.[193]

Asante also offers a lengthy overview of Black iconic leadership, referencing Booker T. Washington, Marcus Garvey, Elijah Muhammed, Martin Luther King, W. E. B. Du Bois, Malcolm X, and Maulana Karenga, and highlights Karenga's work on mythology:

> Mythology refers to a people's place in the universal scheme. Karenga correctly understood that we had to organize our mythology in order to give purpose, identity, and direction. All people have a mythology; Africans who have not given up their ethnic culture have their own mythologies that say how the world began and their place in it. African-Americans had not begun to systematize mythology until Elijah Muhammad and Maulana Karenga attempted to reconstruct our mythology. They both recognized the need for the creation of systematic national history and mythology; yet Karenga's understanding led him in a direction which personified his individual political genius and collective cultural insistence. Karenga became a cultural scientist who emphasized the structural realities of culture.[194]

This passage is one of the few indicators of a latent tradition of Black cultural mythology. While the critical framework prioritizes additional pioneers, Asante's early description is seminal. Thus, through Asante's detailed study and interpretation of mythology in *Afrocentricity*, his scholarship on the topic is an introductory map that highlights the intellectual routes to understanding factors of mythology. In fact, while we regard Asante as the father of Afrocentricity, we can also have a superlative in mind referencing Asante's intellectual role in conceptualizing African American mythology, a precursor to Black cultural mythology, which is now an even more distinctly defined theoretical discourse.

Finally, in *Afrocentricity*, Asante notes, "Despite the fact that a great many African-Americans know next to nothing about African life, Africa is the most prevailing symbol of African-American mythology."[195] This is one feature of Asante's scope of mythology that Black cultural mythology tempers in a redirection away from Africa and more toward the diaspora, even though Africa as a heritage and identity value remains central. Asante's inclusion, what he eventually refers to as confraternity, is a reminder of the Africa-to-diaspora cultural unity based on acknowledgment of a heritage homeland.[196] Black cultural mythology, as a conceptual framework for (re-)/integrating deliberate heritage practices into the diasporan experience, is a methodology for preserving and illuminating diasporan genius, capability, and triumph in new environments. Future studies can help to expand the more global implications of Black cultural mythology beyond this inaugural African American contextualization.

Related conversations on myth and mythology simultaneously appear in Asante's writings from the 1980s in which he addresses several topics related to contemporary Black cultural mythology. These include the role of television and media, Harriet Tubman as the prototype for African American myth, and issues of symbolism. Asante's approach to cultural mythology is universal, as he contextualizes global, not solely Afrocentric, patterns and meanings of mythologies:

> A cultural group's mythology provides the group with an understanding of its relationships, that is, the relationship of person to person, person to group, person to the environment, person to members of external groups, and person to supernatural forces. . . . When conflicting mythologies encounter each other, misunderstandings occur, unless the interactants are able to draw upon a common set of rules. . . . Mythology is significant because how we see ourselves (Newmark and Asante, 1975) and others dictates what responses we can expect; in fact, we get an idea of what responses ought to be made across cultures by understanding that mythology affects communication.[197]

In this context, wherein mythology is a topic in intercultural communication, Asante's objective is not necessarily to highlight a specifically Afrocentric aspect. Instead, he corroborates that diasporan Africans—in spite of the forced relocation to the US through enslavement—are entitled to an autonomous, centered, self-defined mythology that is not bound to imitate the mythology that emerges from non-diasporan experiences.

With respect to television and the media, Asante considers how television and even computer technology alter the "creation, presentation, and reception" of symbols and how television functions as a "mediator of symbolic messages."[198] It is an ideal companion piece to Amos Wilson's *The Developmental Psychology of the Black Child* (1987), which also includes a section on the role television plays in the choices of heroes and heroic models available to Black children. Wilson notes that overproduction of white heroes at the expense of black heroes on television can interrupt the social development of Black children.

Asante and Kariamu Welsh's study on "Myth: The Communication Dimension to the African American Mind" (1981) is the most powerful and direct treatise on African American myth and is a key methodological premise of Black cultural mythology. In this essay, the authors detail the uniqueness of the African American experience and how this distinction requires the culture's mythology to be articulated in metahistorical terms. The authors redirect the meaning of the "suffering genre" of African American myth to be "an acceptance of victory historically," which is an assumption that mythological behavior is motion toward sustaining a brighter past.[199] While Asante and Welsh feature the mythologies of Harriet Tubman, John Henry, Stagolee, John Jasper, and Malcolm X, they contend that "Harriet Tubman is the strongest mythical character in African American history":

> The Harriet Tubman myth manifests itself in how we relate the stories of the Bible to our everyday realities. Those stories are not real because of the lives of Moses and Jesus; they are real because the experience of Harriet Tubman lives within the heart of every African American person. That is why people find it difficult to accept the appellation "the Moses of her people" for her. She was more than Moses; she was life and love. She performed not out of duty to her people but out of love for them.[200]

Their deconstruction then centered reconstruction of Tubman's hero dynamic is groundbreaking, and their treatment concludes with a direct statement of the relationship of myth to Afrocentricity: "Myth in its Afrocentric reinterpretation may be used to elevate and sustain African Americans in the challenges ahead. A communicative experience, deriving from our own symbology, will add to the human capacity to speak clearly, directly and with propriety about the immensity of the crises in intercultural communication that we now share."[201]

Asante's interpretation of the relationship between rhetoric and symbolism is important for brokering space within the national and international fields of cultural memory studies for the framework of Black cultural mythology, which speaks to centered African diasporic experiences sustained by the ideas and worldviews of a uniquely Africana intellectual tradition.

"Even rhetorical discourse among Africans in the Western world is polluted, distorted and dismembered by the onslaught of European images and symbols," Asante writes. "Sharing of images is reasonable, valuable, and positive; image domination, however, is the same as other colonial conquests, vile, repressive, and negative."[202] Black cultural mythology counters Eurocentric image domination, and this domination is political. "Politics is the struggle for symbols, that is, the endeavor to secure some predetermined objective. Power is the ability to see those symbols materialized and the objective realized."[203] Asante acknowledges that "Europeans and Africans have such limited understanding of each other's essential mythologies and motifs," but too few sources explore the details that inform the *essential* cultural mythology that sustains African American culture.[204]

Asante's approach to mythology is deliberate; he poses the question, "What mythological bases exist in African culture?"[205] There is a small amount of scholarship on African mythology, which engages tales and beliefs, and there is even less on diasporan mythology. Ngugi wa Thiong'o's newer ideas about dis-membering and the relationship between memory and decolonization in *Something Torn and New: An African Renaissance* (2009) is a shift that scholars are beginning to take a closer theoretical look at the meaning of myth and memory beyond tales of magical realism and beliefs imbued with supernatural cosmologies. Black cultural mythology is distinguished as a primarily diasporan phenomenon that is in conversation with continental African views. Identical to Asante's description of the year 1619 as a "beginning again," Black cultural mythology's concern is the process of clarifying the parameters of a functional mythology for Africans who survived relocations and culturally evolved on their own terms in new and hostile environments.[206]

Asante's framing of the role of myth has implications for literature, specifically in his discourse on the relationships between symbolism and creativity: "To symbolize is to find representatives for our thoughts, ideas, values, and attitudes that teach us how to create and to enhance our creativity."[207] In the theorization of Black cultural mythology, live actors of the African American past are the symbols that transmit the culture's legacy through their hero dynamics (and even through their antihero dynamics). Thus, while Arna Bontemps wrote the novel *Black Thunder* (1936) to feature the legacy of Gabriel Prosser, and while Charles Johnson wrote the novel *Dreamer* (1998) to eternalize a vision of Martin Luther King Jr., the live actors are symbols that, like within the *mfundalai* rite, enhance cultural development.[208] The mfundalai rite that Asante mentions is an example of

Kariamu Welsh Asante's rite of passage for Black children. The component that requires "the child's recitation of the deeds, events, and personalities in our history" (based on *Njia: The Way*) is a practical application that resonates with the priorities of Black cultural mythology.[209]

Over the years, Asante has contributed original discussions and philosophical ideas on heritage practices that systematically treat the variables of rhetoric, symbolism, myth, identity, and ancestry as they relate to Africans in the American environment, and his treatment of these variables is a foundation on which the contemporary philosophy of Black cultural mythology stands. Asante's next set of theoretical writings on Afrocentricity systemically outlines the roles and functions of myth. Asante charts a unique role for the study of myth in later volumes on Afrocentric theory—*The Afrocentric Idea* (1987) and *Kemet, Afrocentricity and Knowledge* (1990). His presentation introduces effective vocabulary, synthesizes and revitalizes his earlier published ideas about myth and mythology, and inspires a new generation of scholars to advance his groundwork.

In *The Afrocentric Idea*, Asante's focused treatment of myth appears as a discussion of "mythoforms." He integrates ideas from his 1981 coedited essay on myth with Welsh and surveys Western interpretations of myth to demonstrate how the Afrocentric interpretation stakes its points of departure. Asante begins by introducing the perspective that "myth is an organizing principle in human symbolic discourse," but he goes further to relate myth to the concept of the mythoform.[210] "Myth is most pervasive as a mythoform, the all-encompassing deep generator of ideas and concepts in our living relationship with peers, friends, and ancestors," Asante explains. "A productive force, it creates discourse forms that enable speakers to use cultural sources effectively."[211] The similarity between this presentation of mythoform and his earlier concern for myth's effectiveness for the Black orator is clear. The goal of the new terminology is to present myth—often understood as a *basic* concept reflecting origin narratives of embellished truths found in legends—as a more remarkable and expanded conceptualization. The mythoform also relates to history in Asante's development of the new terminology as a distinct categorical inquiry.: "I have chosen to consider the evidence of African American culture alone, an Afrocentric view, to say that the context of the mythoform is such that it adapts to the circumstances of history. In this respect, the myths I examine have nothing to do with the general concept of universality. They represent the African's response in the Americas to a historic moment."[212] This clarification prepared us for Asante's diagnosis of what Wilson would describe as the mythological structure.

Asante explains the practicality of myth as a tool to deal with "questions of geographical and cultural alienation, conflict with a hostile society, and the separation of technology and nature. What is more significant is that myth is connected to life and its social functions."[213]

Asante's inquiry into the functionality of myth for African Americans goes deeper, and it is in the context of maintaining cultural memory that his groundwork informs Black cultural mythology. His contention that "one use of mythoforms is to preserve links to the past—that is cultural history" refers to the "ever-presence of the ancestors.... The dead are the agents who continue to energize the living. They assure us that the discourse of life will not be chaotic, and we take this, in whatever society we live, as a permanent expression of rebirth.... even in our modified form we see how ancestral myths are a part of our communicative sense."[214] Linking ancestor acknowledgment with cosmological worldviews and with cultural inheritances born of an earlier generation's sacrifice suggests a manifold reciprocity in the culture's cyclical relationships with the history and its memorial record. Similar to Jan Assman, Asante links myth (not memory) with time to reinforce memorial reciprocity between generations and the ancestry. He suggests that "the myth emerges as a story with a basis in historical or indefinite time, but in all cases the story is of triumphs and victories," the likes of which are remembered and recalled as cultural heroics maintained by ancestral heroes.[215]

In terms of memory and mythmaking as sociocultural activism, much like what Karenga did with the legacy of Malcolm X, Asante's logic is also a means of preventing African American agency and cultural memory from disappearing into the United States' questionable melting pot ideal. Under this ideal, nonwhite cultural accolade is subsumed under the description of "American," which, in the public domain, silences Black, Native American, Latino, and Asian cultures by daring them to unpatriotically reclaim the heroic as a cultural (and not as an "American") narrative. In the melting pot, diaspora heroics must negotiate whose identity and comfort they serve, as the nation constructs some heroics in order to stabilize a paternalistic or self-congratulatory white supremacist version of diversity. Asante condensed this notion as an objective of the Afrocentric approach to prevent cultural "invisibility."[216]

This chapter on the intellectual genealogy of Black cultural mythology reveals that the development of Black cultural mythology technically owes a debt to the substantial early corpus of work that Asante did on myth. In fact, even in the central categories that frame his later project on

Afrocentricity, myth continues to be a core attribute of his discourses and interventions. In defining the cosmological issues, Asante writes, "The place of African culture in the myths, legends, literatures and oratures of African people constitutes, at the mythological level, the cosmological issue within the Afrocentric enterprise."[217] While racial formation, culture, gender, and class are the central categories of the cosmological issue, myth is a key feature of only the culture category as Asante suggests a need to better understand "the fact that African Americans constitute the most heterogeneous group in the United States biologically but perhaps one of the most homogeneous socially."[218] His inquiry suggests a need to examine what cultural factors give African Americans such social unity, and myth is a possibility.

Asante's description of the epistemological issue presents the idea that "in Africalogy, language, myth, ancestral memory, dance-music-art, and science provide the sources of knowledge, the canons of proof and the structures of truth."[219] In the discussion of the epistemological issue, Asante's lengthiest description is on the consideration of myth:

> There is an idea of preconcept, prebelief based upon the particularity of the African experience in the world. I postulate that myth, especially the central myth of the next millennium in heterogeneous but hegemonically European societies, will be the resolution of ethnic conflict. All behavior will be rooted in experiential patterns played out in the intervention of ideas and feelings in the imposing movement of the European worldview.[220]

He also mentions mythoform in the broader discussion. This treatment of myth warns against a dysfunctional understanding of diversity as a cultural reduction in favor of a generic identity. W. E. B. Du Bois warned of a similar lure in 1960 on the verge of civil rights movement gains. He questioned whether African Americans would be duped into deracialization, which would make cultural mythology and memory irrelevant.[221] Asante's perspective predicts the US fascination with postracialism as well as fame-driven identity constructs. In such constructs, popular culture's artificial and media-instigated hero worship threatens to replace or overshadow the more traditional, legendary, and functional cultural heroics of legend that relied on the clarity of culture-based and race-based sociopolitical activism, community development, and worldview to self-stabilize.

Finally, while myth is not an itemized feature of the axiological issue it is suggested in the aesthetic issue's aspect of epic memory. Specifically, "Epic memory carries with it the idea that the art contains the historic memory that allows the artist and audience to participate in the same celebration of pathos."[222] Black poets' treatment of Harriet Tubman, Frederick Douglass, Malcolm X, Martin Luther King, and Rosa Parks, among others, suggests aspects of collective memory. Black cultural mythology's critical valuation of the concept of immortalization is attentive to "life after death," which is *the vitality of cultural legacy, achievement, and models of worldview and identity survival.* Here, Asante's ideas begin to engage with religion. He paraphrases Karenga's presentation of religion (as one of the seven constituents of culture) as interchangeable with mythology, thus in the context of the cultural/aesthetic classificatory aspects of Africalogy, he defines "religion or mythology [as] the ritualized manner in which a people present themselves to humanity."[223] It is interesting to map how key concepts of myth, memory, heroics, and mythology circulate within the intellectual tradition as the basis of contemporary Black cultural mythology theorization.

In the 1990s, after over two decades of scholarship on myth studies, intercultural communication, Afrocentricity, and an Africana disciplinary paradigm, Asante published a volume that directly addresses an iteration of *heroics, Malcolm X as Cultural Hero and Other Afrocentric Essays* (1993). A key essay on history and myth in the volume better explains how we should optimally appreciate the power of history without attempting to live in the past:

> Because we commit ourselves to our own historical tradition, that is, we choose what is recognizably our own sources of legitimacy, we are able to hear the voices of our ancestors. . . . The past is alive only to the degree that we capture it in our own depths. History allows us access to the living models of Afrocentricity. There was a time when Harriet Tubman walked this earth. Ausar and Auset did exist. By studying the past I can gain some access to their lives, to their histories, to their power. In practice, I can be judged by how deeply I go in appropriating my history for the present moment of living. This is the true meaning of an Afrocentric approach to our history.[224]

This articulation of Afrocentricity suggests an even deeper premise in a process of linking historical study with reverence for ancestral experience and inheritances, thus infusing an academic enterprise with a healthy sense of the sacred.

Asante's collective critique of Eurocentrism includes how many American observers fail to critically analyze how monuments and building structures in the US reaffirm multiple aspects of European mythology. To expand awareness of this as an active function of myth, he notes how "cultural motifs" are expressed "through the creation of buildings, monuments, and memorials."[225] He considers this to be "one of the highest forms of historical writing. . . . Because with one's own sense of art, aesthetics, image, and rhythm one can reinforce the values and views of generations of ancestors."[226] In response to society's assumptions that Western architecture is universal or its proclivity not to overanalyze structures in plain view, Asante suggests a response that epitomizes the logic of Black cultural mythology. He insists that "the African-American architect must stretch his or her imagination, must read African-American history, and African thought and mythology to be able to accomplish first-order creations out of the motifs of the culture."[227]

Asante envisions how Africana creativity should utilize heroic images to give optimum meaning to cultural spaces. He imagines, "What a joy to see a public building with the images of Tubman, Douglass, King, Malcolm, Garvey, and Sojourner Truth!," and laments, "I have never seen such a sight and yet for whites in the United States it is an everyday occurrence to see their history reflected in the architecture created by their architects."[228] In the deconstructionist approach suggested by the antihero dynamic, Asante makes an innovative contribution to an overlooked meaning of the allegedly *shared* physical space of American cities and structures. This can be considered an example of the Eurocentric "colonization of geography" that Asante explores in his discussion of the European Rosetta Stone mythology.[229] Inevitably, expanding functional cultural mythology practices equips Africana cultures with tools for image self-defense.[230] Asante claims victory against the media's distorted and imbalanced cultural projections, noting that "our particular heritage is rooted in the will of Harriet Tubman, David Walker, and Martin Delaney."[231]

This evaluation of the observations and practices of key African American activists, theorists, and scholars whose seminal ideas and works sustain the logic of Black cultural mythology as an orientation to Africana cultural memory studies is central to affirming an existing, though heretofore unacknowledged, intellectual tradition. The chapters that follow continue to weave a narrative of how the intellectual tradition layers with additional cultural and literary dimensions of cultural mythology and cultural memory. While Stewart, Graham Du Bois, Neal, Karenga, Wilson, and Asante have a larger repertoire of recorded ideas from which Black cultural mythology draws, there are many other writers, theorists, and scholars with sustained ideas, as well as visionary morsels of thought, who are also foundational to the intellectual tradition.

Ideas beyond the Exemplars

The exemplars are highlighted for their sustained contributions to an ethos that invokes, cultivates, and celebrates the survival and achievement of African Americans after beginning again and in the protracted and instinctual process of engraving identity and mythological sensibilities on American soil. Because scholarship has not itemized their contributions as part of a logic of cultural memory, they require a distinct introduction immersed within Black cultural mythology idea formation. Writer and activist John Oliver Killens describes these types of efforts as acts of a Black consciousness:

> It calls upon us to write our own history, create our own myths and legends. Washington and Jefferson do not belong to our children. They are not the founding fathers of black Americans; they are not our legendary heroes; they were our people's slavemasters. No amount of falsification of history can disguise this fact. Our legendary heroes are Nat Turner, Frederick Douglass, Denmark Vesey, Harriet Tubman, Sojourner Truth, white John Brown, and Red Sitting Bull. These and many more are our heroes, and most of us have never heard of them."[232]

Killens's sensibility from the mid-sixties is a historical and common-sense survey of the differential between white American and African American worldviews of legacy and inheritance, and later twentieth-century cultural philosophers have articulated brief, and often passing, nuances of a creative vernacular on memory that is an important part of the compilation and exploration of the many parts of a burgeoning contemporary discourse.

There are many constellations—the brief, sometimes obscure, yet nonetheless important cues, traces, and hints—of brilliant writers, theorists, and scholars who have contributed to the intellectual map that leads us to a more concentrated understanding of myth, mythology, and memory within the traditions of African American history, cultural theory, and literary criticism. These contributions are gifts—intriguing morsels of genius—bequeathed to present and future generations to decipher, utilize, and expand.

Toni Morrison's ideas and artistry are among the best known as she summons notions of memory and ancestors in two seminal works—"The Site of Memory" (1995) and "Rootedness: The Ancestor as Foundation" (1982). Literary critics have voraciously consumed her essays as the dominant African American reflection on cultural memory, and with good reason. In "The Site of Memory," Morrison explores how autobiography and the writerly imagination inform her creative processes. In this essay, she proffers two notable remarks about memory. Briefly, she teases readers to ponder a basic observation, that "the act of imagination is bound up with memory."[233] In the most substantial quote on memory, she writes:

> First of all, I must trust my own recollections. I must also depend on the recollections of others. Thus memory weighs heavily in what I write, in how I begin and in what I find to be significant. Zora Neale Hurston said, "Like the dead-seeming cold rocks, I have memories within that came out of that material that went to make me." These "memories within" are the soil of my work. But memories and recollections won't give me total access to the unwritten interior life of these people. Only the act of the imagination can help me.[234]

Morrison's meditations on the role of memory in the imagination speak to Black cultural mythology's requisite that we meditate on the ancestors' experiences in the past. The culture's engagement with the past and its actors is a routine worldview behavior and not part of an artistic process of creating a cultural artifact such as a novel or a play. But when it appears in literature, it reinforces the norms of having a healthy relationship with the past. This awareness or consciousness, as Killens describes it, is part of the process that writers maintain as a methodology, and it is, then, natural that writers are valued and revered in the theorization of Black cultural mythology for their ongoing artistic and visionary genius in sustaining hero dynamics and mythology. Like Morrison's revealing essay on the processes of her diasporan worldview, writers meditate on and engage with memory, which infuses their writing with clues and cues that keep the cultural readership grounded and connected to its heritage and legacy.

Because of her existing centrality to what society regards as African American cultural memory, I choose not to include her essays in the section on the *new* exemplars who represent an excavated and sometimes even organic, era-based logic that illuminates variables and nuances of mythology, exclusive of *memory* as its defining category. This categorization does not imply that Morrison's contributions are less important. "The Site of Memory" has been cited nearly a thousand times, yet a different, comprehensive essay directly on Africana myth—Asante and Welsh's "Myth as the Communication Dimension of the African American Mind"—has been cited less than two dozen times. This reflects the distance between popular literary ideas about memory and cultural memory *versus* a more archival, era-based, and movement-specific idea formation around the subjects of myth, mythology, immortalization, and heroics. The discovery of a dynamic circulation and overlap of ideas, concepts, compatible nuances, and applications enriches the tradition and intellectual genealogy of a continuum of diasporan ideas about the outcomes of beginning again and engraving identity on new soil.

In "Rootedness: The Ancestor as Foundation," Morrison shares her philosophy about how the genre of the novel functions in the African American experience. After identifying the function of music as a primary healer for Black people, Morrison suggests that the novel inherited the function of healing and cultural rites of passage after mainstream society's co-optation of Black music:

> It seems to me that the novel is needed by African-Americans now in a way that it was not needed before—and it's following along the lines of the function of novels everywhere. We don't live in places where we can hear those stories anymore; parents don't sit around and tell their children those classical, mythological archetypal stories that we heard years ago. But now information has got to get out, and there are several ways to do it. One is the novel.[235]

Morrison also mentions "the characteristics of Black Art" several times in this essay, which is Black Arts Movement language associated with Neal and Karenga. She is inherently working in the post–Black Arts Movement tradition, sharing language such as discussions of mythology, cosmology, and ancestors. In fact, she laments that the criticism of her work does not rely on a related vocabulary to capture such cultural characteristics woven through her work.

Morrison's detailed interpretation of the ancestor in African American fiction reinforces Black cultural mythology's itemization of ancestor acknowledgment. She writes, "It seems to me interesting to evaluate Black literature on what the writer does with the presence of an ancestor. . . . There is always an elder there. And these ancestors are not just parents, they are sort of timeless people whose relationships to the characters are benevolent, instructive, and protective, and they provide a certain kind of wisdom."[236] Black cultural mythology embraces this as well as the broader African-centered cosmology of reverence for the ancestral cycle and the interconnectedness that assures, comforts, bears witness, and is a source of empowerment for the future. The quest is to centralize these aspects of engaging with the ancestral for methodologies of survival, for knowledge of how populations in the diaspora oriented themselves toward conflict and problem solving, to celebrate what we learn from their past experiences, and to enhance this wealth of knowledge with the benefit of contemporary insights, developments, and tools of inquiry. Morrison reinforces it more concretely as an African-centered cosmology when she says that "the continuum in Black or African-American art" is a "deliberate effort, on the part of the artist."[237]

Indeed, there is much effort apparent in the craft and philosophy of writers to order cosmology, mythology, and ancestors, but the contribution of Black cultural mythology is its effort to formally combine and to further conceptualize these types of discourses found in sociopolitical thought, cultural theory, and aesthetics into a more traceable intellectual tradition that will bloom into even more critical tributaries. However, a demarcation is necessary for clarity. Black cultural mythology has infinite potential as an applied critical lens, but this inaugural analysis centers literary texts that reenvision precise legendary cultural heroics in innovative, comprehensive, and sustained narrative models of imaginative remembrance of historical actors. Subsequent chapters present a range of hero dynamics in literature, from Harriet Tubman to canonical Black men's and women's writings on the Haitian Revolution. The final, more concentrated literary chapter explores Johnson's novel, *Dreamer*, about Martin Luther King Jr.; Whitehead's novel, *John Henry Days*, about John Henry; and O'Hara's play, *Insurrection: Holding History*, about Nat Turner. Future waves of scholarship incorporating Black cultural mythology's critical lens will likely apply and mine the framework's critical attributes for their capacity to offer new readings on the mythologizing and memorializing effect initiated by writers who choose to create narratives that *signify* on a hero dynamic to produce an independent, nonhistorically based, imaginative story. These narratives rely on the reader's awareness of a sacred or epic event or historical actor to imbue the literature with memorial depth that must also be reconciled. Morrison's ideas about memory and ancestry plus edited collections such as *Toni Morrison: Memory and Meaning* (2014)[238] by Adrienne Lanier Seward and Justin Talley, which promote the language of "memory," may prompt readers to expect Morrison's novels such as *Beloved* (1987) to be explicated in chapter 7's application of the conceptual framework of Black cultural mythology as literary criticism. *Beloved* imagines a world inhabited by possibilities stemming from the social memory of the dramatically heroic act of Margaret Garner, the self-emancipating woman who killed one of her four children en route to freedom in Ohio in 1856 to prevent reenslavement. Morrison's creative signification on and imaginative speculation on a historical event is different from the types of texts selected for chapter 7's application of Black cultural mythology as literary criticism. Specifically, in chapter 7's inaugural models of literary criticism, *Dreamer*, *John Henry Days*, and *Insurrection: Holding History* are historically immersed literatures that offer *sustained* engagement with *specific historical events or actors*.

Two texts by Gayl Jones—*Corregidora* (1975) and *Song for Anninho* (1981)—also come to mind as texts that readers might expect to appear in an inaugural treatment of literary criticism applying Black cultural mythology because of Jones's genius approaches to cultural memory and heroics. However, these texts, though visionary and imaginative in their use of heroic referents, invoke a different type of critique that responds to tracing the power of historical referents rather than reflecting an immersive structure of memorializing legendary figures. In *Corregidora* there are brief but foundational textual references to Portuguese and Brazilian icons. Princess Isabel and her contribution as the regal advocate behind the 1888 Emancipation Law appear in the novel, as well as a model of the two-hundred-year living history of the Palmares maroon settlement. Jones mythologizes Palmares in the freedom dreams of a self-emancipating Black man who drowns in the process of fleeing capture. *Song for Anninho* is a lyrical and epic memorial conversation captured in poetry that reveals the spiritual communication and living memory of a pair of lovers separated after the 1697 Portuguese raid on Palmares. Relying on memory, on the protagonist Almeyda's African grandmother's philosophies about spiritual time, and on a medicine woman's prompts to Almeyda to commune spiritually with her missing warrior, Anninho, the narrative fuses the lovers' memory of Palmares as a noble historical site. The epic poem also provides brief literary eyewitness accounts of the leader Zumbi's immortalization even after capture and beheading as well as an articulation of the Portuguese as mythological antiheroes. Jones's rich narratives pose promising challenges to the future of Black cultural mythology literary criticism for a different type of critical mining of the heroic survivalist narrative.

Additionally, although it does not fit chapter 7's concentration on texts that embellish a famous and legendary persona, Octavia Butler's indirectly heroic and commemorative novel, *Kindred* (1979), is a masterful narrative that subtly and cleverly deconstructs society's assumptions about the impact of and the legacy-based meaning of the 1976 US Bicentennial. The episodes of Dana's time travel back to the antebellum South emerge as both a primer and a psychohistorical treatise on Black survival. The novel centers the symbolic, ancestral, and intuitive relationship that Dana Franklin, a Black woman with a contemporary white husband and with a needy and summoning antebellum white male ancestor, has with the 1976 US Bicentennial moment.[239]

In 1982, Audre Lorde subtitled her autobiographical work *Zami: A New Spelling of My Name* as a *biomythography*,[240] and this subtitle, which Lorde does not much define, has inspired a generation of scholars to interpret her intent. Some scholars decipher the term to be a stand-in for Lorde's accumulated identities, but Heather Russell, in her chapter on Lorde in *Legba's Crossing: Narratology in the African Atlantic* (2009), makes a case for Lorde's effect within the realm of the mythically spiritual. Russell's chapter digresses from the scope of Black cultural mythology yet would be suitable for the broader, collaborative, comparative, and cross-disciplinary field of Africana cultural memory studies. Russell describes the subtitle biomythography as "purposeful resistance to Western discursive hegemony."[241] In effect, Lorde's life story is "engendered by the collective consciousness of an African Caribbean cosmology. The guiding hand of Legba is at work everywhere in *Zami*, moving us analytically and discerningly through communal myths, histories, and memories that frame the trajectory of Lorde's discursive journey into a communally representative work."[242]

Russell draws on an intriguing set of epistemologies in ordering Lorde's autobiographical sensibility as a part of Legba divination. Invoking Africana philosophy—specifically Afro-Caribbean diasporic philosophy—per engagement with Paget Henry's ideas from *Caliban's Reason: Introducing Afro-Caribbean Philosophy* (2000), she mines new data on the topic of the mythic that further extends the discursive possibilities related to Black cultural mythology:

> In making the case against the ways in which Western philosophy tends to "caricature" the idea of myth, Paget Henry saliently argues that mythic thought primarily functions like modern Psychoanalysis. Both bodies of knowledge, Henry asserts, function to "discursively intervene" in the realm of subject formation,

providing a venue "where human agency confronts the conditions of possibility and impossibility."[243]

Lorde's contribution is challenging society to acknowledge the mythic in personal narrative. Mapping scholarly interest in and usage of her intervention reveals a trajectory of myth in discourses ranging from literature to philosophy.

Research on the topic of African American myth and mythology reveals varying sporadic references, and a brief survey of these serves to acquaint us with how a theorization of Black cultural mythology, relying on its critical attributes, can serve as an organizing principle. Playwright Suzan-Lori Parks addresses a craft centered on *disremembering* and *re-remembering*. In the essay, "Possession," which is part of the front matter of *The America Play and Other Works* (1995), she writes:

> The history of Literature is in question. And the history of History is in question too. A play is a blueprint of an event: a way of creating and rewriting history through the medium of literature. Since history is a recorded or remembered event, theatre, for me, is the perfect place to "make" history—that is, because so much of African-American history has been unrecorded, dismembered, washed out, one of my tasks as a playwright is to—through literature and the special strange relationship between theatre and real-life—locate the ancestral burial ground, dig for bones, hear the bones sing, write it down.
>
> The bones will tell us what was, is, will be; and because their song is a play—something that through a production *actually happens*—I'm working theatre like an incubator to create "new" historical events. I'm re-membering and staging historical events which, through their happening on stage, are ripe for inclusion in the canon of history. Theatre as an incubator for the creation of historical events.[244]

Effortlessly, Parks maneuvers through a dynamic and original sensibility of the interconnectedness of theater, history, memory, and the ancestors, and Black cultural mythology makes room for an invigorating analysis of the possibilities of her craft and its impact.

There are even more distant voices from the past that contribute to framing the contexts of Black cultural mythology. It responds to Richard Wright's contention that "an attitude of self-consciousness and self-criticism is far more likely to be a fruitful point of departure than a mere recounting of past achievements," and this suggests Black cultural mythology's power to reform heritage practices.²⁴⁵ Wrights adds that

> in the absence of fixed and nourishing forms of culture, the Negro has a folklore which embodies the memories and hope of his struggle for freedom. Not yet caught in paint or stone, and as yet but feebly depicted in the poem and novel, the Negroes' most powerful images of hope and despair still remain in the fluid state of daily speech. How many John Henrys have lived and died on the lips of these black people? How many mythical heroes in embryo have been allowed to perish for lack of husbanding by alert intelligence?²⁴⁶

Black cultural mythology aims to manage this "husbanding" and to prompt such "alert intelligence." Wright's perspective on theorizing culture is also useful. He writes, "Tradition is no longer a guide. . . . Surely this is the moment to ask questions, to theorize, to speculate, to wonder out of what materials can a human world be built."²⁴⁷ As a critical reorientation that recalculates the depth of adaptation and cultural formation on American soils, Black cultural mythology emerges from the practices that Wright described to account for emergent African diaspora culture.²⁴⁸ Also from Wright's era, Paul Robeson writes:

> The *power of the spirit* that our people have is intangible, but it is a great force that must be unleashed in the struggles of today. A spirit of steadfast determination, exaltation in the face of trials—it is the very soul of our people that has been formed through all the long and weary years of our march toward freedom. It is the deathless spirit of the great ones who have led our people in the past—Douglass, Tubman, and all the others.²⁴⁹

Surely his description of "deathless spirit" is an articulation related to the epic intuitive behaviors and hyperheroism of African cognitive survival in the diaspora.

Anecdotally, scattered ideas and reference to ancestors, heroics, mythologies, and more appear in African American traditions of sociopolitical thought, cultural theory, and aesthetics. Fannie Lou Hamer reminds us of the sacredness of survival when she writes, "Never forget where we came from and always praise the bridges that carried us."²⁵⁰ Liberian senator Hilary Teague's 1846 speech in Alice Dunbar's *Masterpieces of Negro Eloquence* references "longings after immortality."[251] Pauline Hopkins contributes to engraving identity with her primer and biographical sketches in the *Colored American*, which are deliberate acts of engaging hero dynamics, heritage practices, and legacy tools without using the word "mythology." Wilson Moses's *Afrotopia* (1998) references "historical contexts that have given rise to the peculiarities of African American mythologies."[252] Sandra G. Shannon's case study on August Wilson cites an Africanist perspective that "Afro-American mythology is not 'strange' but a common, natural part of life."[253] Cornel West writes of "conjuring up mythologies that put Afro-Americans on superior footing."[254] Historian George Yancy reflects on the school-aged children who "will be reading [European] mythology when they hand out the history books."[255] Literary critic Addison Gayle asserts that "the refusal to accept white American definitions of reality leads to a refusal to accept its definitions of such concepts as manhood, heroism, beauty, freedom, and humanism."[256] Novelist Sherley Anne Williams introduces *Dessa Rose* (1986) by observing, "I now know that slavery eliminated neither heroism nor love; it provided occasions for their expressions."[257] Dona Richards (now Marimba Ani) writes about how critical it is to "devote more of our energy to revealing the mythological, ideological, and value aspect of concepts like the ideas of progress, so that they can no longer be used to enslave African people psychologically and ideologically."[258]

This concentrated survey shows how iterations of myth and heroism exist unperceived and referenced but not *theorized*; in Africana cultural discourses, Black cultural mythology is the theoretical response that unifies ideas about myth, mythology, heroics, and memory. It is a promising catalyst for a more broad, diverse, and collaborative interdisciplinary subfield of Africana cultural memory studies. In the chapters that follow, superlative topics, such as 1619 as the *first* enslavement sale in English North America, Harriet Tubman as the *most* well-known African American hero who led the *most* clandestine trips into the South to rescue others from enslavement, Haiti as the *first* diaspora-wide mythology, Richard Wright as the author of the *first* best-selling African American novel, and Malcolm X as one of the *most* memorialized political actors in African American history, are interrogated for their symbolic value as key discourses in Black cultural mythology.

Defining the Attributes of Black Cultural Mythology

The detailed language, variables, and terminologies from the intellectual tradition of philosophies and ideas about immortalization, heroics, myth, mythology, memory, and the sacred support a comprehensive, itemized, and concept-driven critical framework of Black cultural mythology. The expectation is that the key concepts will invigorate discourses and prompt a greater appreciation of the multitude of conditions that African diasporans have had to navigate as they began again and engraved identity on new soil. It is an effort to empower society's cultural discourses with language that expresses optimum agency in narrating the past. Many of these terms or core ideas have appeared informally, already, in earlier chapters that frame the contexts and exemplars of Black cultural mythology, and the explicit survey of the attributes, or properties, of Black cultural mythology serves more as a glossary that supports how Black cultural mythology theorizations operate as tools for the critical analysis of later chapters. (See figure 1.1).

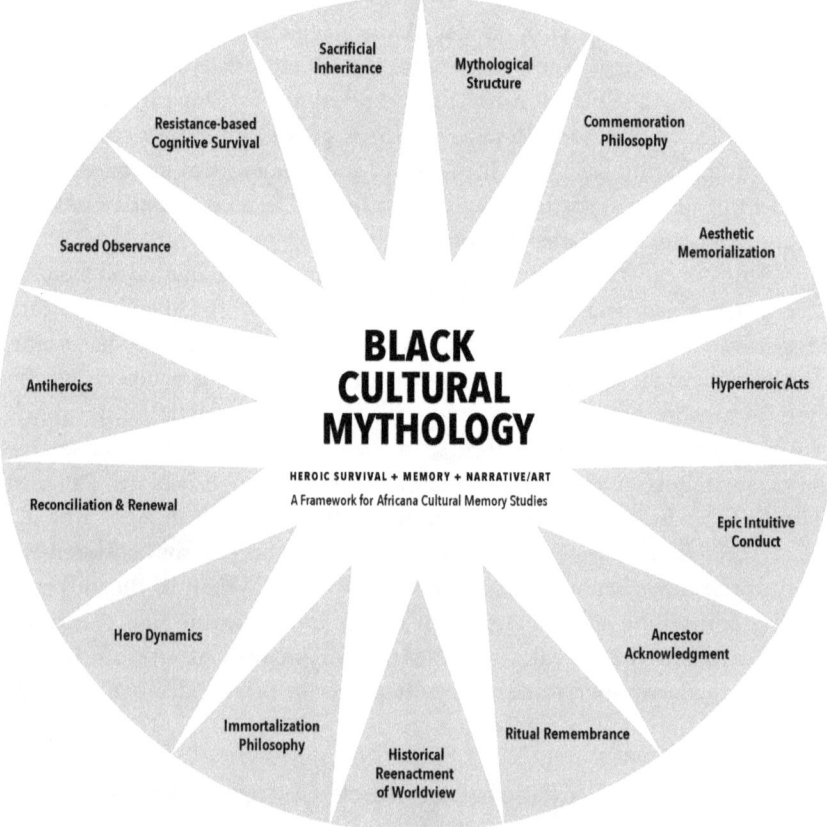

Figure 1.1. Black Cultural Mythology Conceptual Framework

The dimension of *hero dynamics* reflects both regional and transnational diasporic collective consciousness that emerges as culturally based opinions and points of view about the force and sustaining energies that support effective action in processes of change. Based mostly on individual or collaborative human prowess, these can be narrative, visual, or historical feats and accomplishments that stimulate an active and proud cultural worldview, recollected and valued as formal and informal models of courage, achievement, and nobility.

Human prowess, when remembered, celebrated, and itemized like a libation prayer or litany in ways that assume a traditional and practical African-centered existential reality constitutes *ancestor acknowledgment.* This is the most basic expression of a belief that first accepts as truth the validity of the ancestral cycle, which normalizes the layered consciousness that the living, the deceased, and the unborn are active and interrelated modes of existence. Second, it affirms that any life lived well deserves gratitude and appreciation. This requires familiarization with the historical narrative and geographical shifts such as enslavement from which some retain memories of both an African-based and an American-based version of Black heroic sensibilities.

Historical reenactment of worldview is an optimum, psychology-adjacent practice of speculative recollection that encourages the legacy reproduction of cultural episodes in order to most accurately achieve an understanding of ancestral experience. Popular African American museums' reproductions of the enslavement ship environment, as well as pedagogical reenactments of Middle Passage physical compartmentalization in the hull of vessels, accomplish this, to an extent. However, Black cultural mythology's theoretical interest in this is based on using descriptive historical data layered with practical human logic and emotion to consider ancestral reactions, responses, points of view, and probability of experience based on historical data and description.

Resistance-based cognitive survival is the process of using consciousness, especially in being aware of and alert to one's surroundings, and interpretation-based mental activity, such as perception, judgment, and reasoning, to preserve one's existence in hostile and life-threatening environments. Cognitive survival in the diasporan context relates specifically to a pioneered and remembered skill set of critical analysis and problem-solving toward protectionism in the Americas and in other sites of dispersal and migration beyond the continent of Africa. The urgency of this protectionism overrides emotional (feelings and moods) processes and is more intellectual than volitional (human will) processes.

Volitional processes reflect *hyperheroic acts and impulses* wherein human prowess is based on feats whose grandeur and success are hardly explicable and exist as phenomenal testaments of unusual endurance, perseverance, physical strength, grit, and emotional resilience. Hyperheroism is particularly valuable for its capacity to be effectively rendered as Africana superhuman ability in innocuously embellished cyclical storytelling. Over time the norms of the culture's archetypal and rhetorical practices of transmitting such remembrances and cyclically prophetic models of elevated prowess emerge as norms for *epic intuitive conduct*. These are behaviors based on layering cognitive survival with structural expectations of cause-and-effect outcomes found in detailed, documented, speculative, and adventurous accounts that are not only part of the culture's oral tradition but also are suggestions of successful behaviors to be used in identical encounters. The assumption is that feats elevated to storytelling become embedded remembrances that African diaspora people summon instinctively, on a psychic level of knowing, when their lived encounters and experiences mimic the conditions of a known hero dynamic.

This supports *immortalization philosophy and sensibility*, which occurs when cultural agents offer historical sentiments and cultural narratives to challenge the diasporan population to summon epic, intuitive, heroic, ethical, social, political, economic, and educational aspects of achievement, accomplishment, or progress to ensure the culture's stability and legacy. Immortalization is the Africana iteration of cultural eternal life, of never forgetting, and of never being defeated, and is characterized by ideas of perpetuity, immovability, and even life after death, figuratively. It is aligned with cognitive survival to the extent that it elevates what, in the past, was a contest for physical and freedom-based survival to a more rational, empirical, and statistically indisputable record of inspiring achievement and accomplishment. For many diasporan agents, their immortalization sensibility is layered with ancestor acknowledgment because there is an acceptance that the liberation conditions they seek may not manifest until after they have died and become ancestors, which is the idea of impermanent mortality.[259]

In returning Black cultural mythology discourse toward ancestry and cultural perceptions of the human relationship with the afterlife, the categories of *sacred observance* and *ritual remembrance* normalize diasporan cultural histories as indeed sacred. The central historical event—the European enslavement trade—that is responsible for African existence in the diaspora initiated a catastrophic and genocidal amount of suffering and loss of life. In addition, the material conditions of inequality, whether political neglect, assassination, poverty, police or mob brutality, health disparity, incarceration, gratuitous drug and undereducation epidemics, and casual social violence, have defined the diaspora as a site of morbidity and premature death. These losses, as part of sacred remembrance, have only recently begun to be memorialized properly, at least on a large scale through monuments and national museums. There is also a spirituality-aligned dimension of ceremony that is an effective formal solemn rite for fellowship, cultural communion, healing, remembrance, and empowerment. On an informal scale within the public domain society has not adequately integrated the word "sacred" into its conceptualization of Africana experience. Practices of mourning and healing from the grief of cultural losses are compatible with African oral, narrative, and ritually performative aesthetics such as the dirge and with diasporan models of odes, elegies, memorials, eulogy, and more.

Commemoration philosophy embodies many of the above attributes related to ancestry and remembrance and reflects diasporan approaches to annual and periodic remembering and celebrating, on its own terms, iconic events and cultural episodes. In many diaspora sites, communities contest Western holidays with their own African-centered philosophies and interpretations. Majority white Western nations assume universality in their approach to national holidays, which are incorrectly presumed to hold the same value to Africana populations as they do for European-derived populations. The act of engraving identity on new soil includes processes for the maturation of diaspora peoples' holidays, remembrances, and calendar or era periodization. In some instances, collectivity is challenged in the face of cultural versus patriotic nationalism and in terms of reconciling whether an annual or periodic (e.g., centennial) event is worthy of anniversary celebration, somber acknowledgment, lamentation, or private intracultural ritual. In conceptual and narrative approaches to commemoration, the culture also engages in speculative negation in the form of considering and hypothesizing worldview as if enslavement never occurred. Africana communities have not sufficiently dialogued on these types of questions with advanced conceptual markers, and Black cultural mythology creates discursive space for these types of inquiries and evaluations.

Mythological structure is a psychological aspect of the broad cultural memory enterprise. If a culture's and, more specifically, a nurturing family unit's mythological structure is intact, the greater the cultural well-being of its members and especially of its children. Cultural mythology and cultural memory are historically aligned, and when children and families develop within a culturally aware and culturally empowered environment, well-being is optimized as self-knowledge and cultural history inevitably transmit confidence, self-esteem, pride in the racial-cultural identity, and culturally protective and culturally stabilizing behavior and worldview. Mythological structure and cognitive survival are linked by the ego-building benefits of knowing the cultural dimensions of power and capacity from a lifetime of engaging with heroic and pedagogical historical narratives and viewing the world from an African-centered point of view that empowers.

Similar to a much-needed itemization of how the sacred is a far more important reality of diasporan cultural reflection, the notion of *sacrificial inheritance* also requires reintegration into cultural consciousness as a routine practice and itemized variable. It is a synthesis of inheritance and sacrifice. Heritage and legacy conversations often omit inheritance as an asset that indicates the processes of bequeathing wealth. Wealth of knowledge and awareness of one's history also have conceptual value as inheritances. Inheritance is accessible as an intangible possession, timelessly bestowed, that can be neither taken away nor exhausted. Too often diasporic inheritances are subsumed in assumptions that the enslavement experience bequeathed permanent stigma rather than a powerful narrative of victorious consciousness and ingenious survival (that naturally had costs). *Inheritance* is among the more abstract attributes of Black cultural mythology because its valuation can be articulated in many different contexts such as a survivalist cultural trait, likeness in features or appearance, behavioral or personality affinity to an exemplary life, communion with and guidance from an iconic ancestor, the perception of being spiritually blessed, prowess in liberational oratory or rhetoric, a routine tendency to achieve in the face of discriminatory odds, artistic visual symbolism, or conceptualizations of the gift of survival. Sacrifice is a companion attribute to inheritance. It simply represents a belief that current existence is the calculated and planned progressive outcome envisioned by those who endured ill will, trauma, and loss for the benefit of others and for future generations. It becomes theoretically empowering for the culture to itemize faith, hope, and positive outcomes of the investment of energy to claim future fulfillment and success.

The late twentieth century bore witness to increased African and Caribbean migration to the United States, and the groups' lack of acknowledgment of a genealogy of African American *sacrificial inheritance* has emerged as a source of significant breach in cross-cultural, Pan-African, or transnational fraternity. Couched in terms of a lack of respect for the gains made by domestic African Americans that inevitably benefitted immigrants of African descent, inevitably the conflict is more about the practical dimensions of cultural mythology rather than about newcomers benefiting disproportionately from diversity and affirmative action policies. The claim could be made in reverse based on incidents of African American exceptionalism or flippant tourism to African, Caribbean, Afro-Latino, and Afroeuropean sites while being oblivious to the nature of the Africana historical specificity and struggles for agency in these regions. Nonetheless, many of these attributes can be layered for a personal arsenal of *legacy tools*, which, though generalized, confirm a practical need for diaspora persons to be equipped with an effective conceptual and historical apparatus to maneuver in the world as people of African descent with a global collective consciousness. With these tools, diasporan populations achieve *heritage behavior* as a comprehensive and informed worldview of cultural standards that serve to proactively secure harmony and balance in the process of Africana living.

Aesthetic memorialization diverges from the conceptual aspects of cultural memory and mythology and poses a redirection to symbolic and tangible manifestations in literature and the arts, which covers the narrative, the visual, and music-dance-song. Creative literature sustains much of the narrative and symbolism derived from diaspora histories. However, music, the visual and material arts, naming, and monuments comprise a lasting and often institutionalized corpus of cultural memory indicators. The extent to which society itemizes these beacons as part of the mythology-memory continuum is questionable, but the philosophical approach of Black cultural mythology invites society to better categorize these types of structures and representations as part of a vibrant cultural context. *Reconciliation and renewal* emerges here and in other formations in which naming, physical cultural resemblance, monuments, and memorials invoke corrective or revisionist processes that also reflect cyclical remembrance or storytelling.

The final variable of Black cultural mythology is *antiheroics*, which is an oppositional and villainous *anti-Black antiheroic*. It is aligned with the conventional sense of the antihero, as a formidable oppositional individual or even system that lacks conventional morality and valor or a hero. Antiheroics describes a racialized opposition or even an agent of Black internalized self-hatred or counterproductivity. Awareness of antiheroics is a discernment that sustains cognitive survival. It compels diasporan actors to surveil and share covert cultural intelligence with a precise revelation of the individuals, collaborators, or institutions that behave as declared enemies of and antagonists to Africana well-being. It is a necessary inclusion on a list that identifies culturally intrinsic attributes for sustaining a worldview of cultural wholeness, but it is also a practical dimension that protects diaspora communities from misaligning their cultural legacy and priorities in detrimental ways that overstep into the realm of cultural nonnegotiables. Diversity, multiculturalism, colorblindness, patriotism, and other shared and intersectional sensibilities often leave little room for the specificity of racial-cultural experience, yet a discussion of antiheroics grounds the diaspora in delineating the sources of cultural opposition.

Black cultural mythology intervenes to restructure how we categorize and discuss cultural memory and living mythology based on an original *set* of attributes that serve as a unit of refined terminologies. As a lexical unit and as a glossary for the first unified, conceptual orientation to contemporary Black cultural mythology that ignites the field of cultural memory studies, the language initiates a more ordered engagement with the cultural artifacts that sustain remembrance and reflection. These key concepts, as well as the perspectives of the exemplars as forerunners, collectively frame the theoretical core of Black cultural mythology. The topical chapters that follow model the dexterity of the attributes for sustaining discourses that meander through superlative historical and literary conceptualizations for a range of critical possibilities of how myth, memory, mythology, heroics, and commemoration function in the African American diasporic experience.

Chapter Two

Commemoration Intervention

On August 1, 2014, in the forum *Yahoo! Answers*, a purported foreigner observing African American life and American possibilities for the immigrant posed the question, "Do African Americans feel lucky that their ancestors were slaves? If it didn't happen, 'African Americans' would be in Africa and maybe starving. Now they can get welfare, some medicare, and other benefits that most countries don't have, especially in Africa."[1] The nine respondents, from all types of American ethnic backgrounds who volunteered answers to this question, were mostly incensed. They even accused the writer of being a troll—an instigator. On October 6, 2012, Hillary Crosley, an African American journalist for *Root Magazine*, wrote an article on "Crazy Talk: 'Slavery Was a Blessing in Disguise.' "[2] In it, she reacts to Arkansas State Legislator Hubbard's observations from his self-published book *Letters to the Editor: Confessions of a Frustrated Conservative* (2009):

> He said, "slavery was a blessing in disguise" because Africans were eventually "rewarded with citizenship in the greatest nation ever established upon the face of the earth" (Hubbard 183–89). He claims Black lives are better than its members "ever would have enjoyed in Sub-Saharan Africa." Then he asks, "would life in enslavement have been any crueler than a life spent in Sub-Saharan Africa?"[3]

Previously, on March 22, 2008, in a diatribe titled "Buchanan to Obama" regarding presidential candidate Barack Obama's church membership under Reverend Jeremiah Wright, Pat Buchanan said, "America has been the best country on earth for black folk. It was here that 600,000 black people, brought from Africa in slave ships, grew into a community of 40 million, were introduced to Christian salvation, and reached the greatest level of freedom and prosperity blacks have ever known."[4]

These are the types of intentionally distorted narratives that Black cultural mythology counters. Many segments of US society have an interest in seeking ways to negate, erase, deconstruct, or renarrate the origin story of African life in the United States. The "insincere slogans" of postracial discourses that emerged in response to the campaign and election of Barack Obama to the US presidency are examples.[5] Commemorations introduce challenges for society's skills of interpreting the milestones of African existence and achievement in the Americas. Commemorating the year 1619 as the *first* enslavement sale in English North America has had symbolic and conceptual value not only in the nation's practices of framing its historical narratives but also in its commemoration practice. The year 1619 will always be a major chronological event that will continue to inspire critical reflection on not only commemoration but also on Africana narrative agency in the public domain's discourses on African American origins. Memories and recollections of the enslavement experience are not commemoration; instead, they are a cause for lamentation and memorialization. A commemoration is a ceremonious remembrance or celebration. A remembrance is a solemn act of memory, often reflecting on ancestors or on the deceased. Lamentation as commemoration catapults variables of ancestor acknowledgment, sacred ritual observance, and dynamics of memorialization to the forefront of both African American and national public discourse, including the implications for public policy.

Cultural memory enters the conversation about the impact of social policy because cultural memory is the worldview that determines the extent to which society regards "the sacred" as a point of consideration in its decision-making. The outcomes of these decisions are identity-driven, as citizens react, respond, and perceive truth from categories of identity that represent their worldviews. Worldviews and identities can be cultural, political, national, regional, and more, and historical narratives, including personal, familial, and ethnic or racial ones, in which there is a striver, an oppositional force or opponent, a victor and a loser, sustain citizen choice about worldview, and subsequently about public policy. Nathan Huggins's historical reflection that foregrounds the creative and mythic symbolism of US colonial politicians reveals the great length the US's founding personalities went to *create* dimensions of a mythic national identity, ordained by its own markers of a type of origin story, and that inevitably has sustained racialized patriotism embodied in whiteness.[6]

Social policy is often based on a dominant group's belief or embrace of a common narrative that policy should be based on the priorities of a historical narrative of the group, in this case, whites. It is optimistic to suggest that the public policy supported and produced by citizens who claim an identity and worldview of whiteness does not necessarily oppose other identities of color. Policy advocacy and public sentiment that ignore African American group realities related to policing, education, housing, health care, and more suggest that the nation oversimplifies or is unaware of the sacred and guiding depth of African American cultural memory. It is a narrative and recollection of the past and continued survival in what is often still a society of opposition with parallels to historical structures of inequality.

In discussing mythology as the culture's conceptualization and narration of its own epic achievement and systematic practices of remembrance, particularly in contested national and social spaces like the United States, where African Americans have always been smaller percentages of the population, one is bound to consider how environment shapes memory and celebration. The temporal and chronological variance of religious, spiritual, harvest, lunar, solar, astronomical, seasonal, environmental, social, political, and both individual and familial memorial acknowledgments also compels an interest in what African people regarded as worthy of remembrance, as cultural heroics, and as public ceremony prior to their experiences in the Americas. While these are comparatively chartable, this study is more attentive to how to conceptualize the practices and survivalist effort since people of African descent began creating strategies for living and surviving in the dramatically different worldview and experiences of life in the Americas. The interest is not necessarily in African American holidays, but in the ability and confidence of African Americans to articulate the value and constituent parts of their heritage memory, or their cultural mythology, which is an act of stabilization and of critical grounding.

There are multiple approaches to the philosophy of commemorative periodization. Commemoration introduces many historical questions. For example, in a Western context, we assume a commemoration structure based on numerical reasoning that prioritizes annual, decadal, midcentennial, and centennial/multicentennial acknowledgment. Western, media-driven culture is also attentive to historical and memorial reflections of major positive and infamous events and phenomena related to legendary figures. The Africana approach to memory is not necessarily concerned with these structures of commemoration but rather with how to manage memory practices and motives to create a more culturally reflective practice. The historiography of African American commemoration is embodied in several core works in which authors present their studies in terms of celebrations, festivals, and commemorations. They focus on periods of Emancipation, Reconstruction, and the Nadir (after Reconstruction through World War I), with even some modern points of reference.

While the philosophical and intellectual genealogy scope of Black cultural mythology is an intervention that shifts how we conceptualize, label, and categorize survivalist worldviews and behaviors, the historiography of commemoration is part of the broader interdisciplinary orientation to Africana cultural memory studies. To speak of commemoration intervention is to address how historical studies and the archive of commemoration practices better order and formalize the culture's academic research approach to myth, memory, mythology, and legacy. The process of forging Black cultural mythology includes identifying sources in the existing tradition that contribute to the newly categorized and theorized epistemological structuring.

William H. Wiggins Jr.'s *O Freedom! Afro-American Emancipation Celebrations* (1987) pioneers knowledge production in this area. "When I began my research into Afro-American freedom celebrations, there were no scholarly books in print on the subject," Wiggins explains. "Aside from a meager list of articles, such freedom observances had generated little interest within America's intellectual community."[7] In fact, he describes the condition as "scholarly lethargy toward the subject," and he acknowledges that in the two sources that, at first glance, seemed to be on the path to capture the history and nuances of this commemoration activity, "neither writer paid significant attention to Afro-Americans' reactions to freedom."[8] Within a contemporary reading, it is safe to surmise that Wiggins was indeed looking for documentation of African American agency and worldview. He found it; and his book is an empowering documentation of a lively African American collective personhood and commemoration philosophy. His study documents "dramatic proclamation readings, historical pageants, colorful parades, all-night barbecues, exciting ballgames" and other rituals and customs.[9] It is dynamic to read his account of African Americans proudly assessing the commemorative norms of their communities, in which January 1, Emancipation Day, was a stable culturally significant date, over a hundred years before the creation of the Kwanzaa holiday week, which culminates on January 1. Wiggins sensitively captures the voices and memories of African

Americans' endearment for various local calendars that set aside days, though not always the same dates in each community, to celebrate Emancipation and Juneteenth.

Wiggins's book is an essential text for Africana cultural memory studies. He documents the preservation and, in some cases, the demise of "symbolic rites of fellowship, worship, and entertainment" that take place in the community havens of the African American South.[10] His emphasis is on the recurrent positioning of rite and symbol. One example of this is how he links the power of the scent of open pit barbecuing (as "olfactory" symbol) with ancestry, which implies an even deeper potential and effect for the Black cultural mythology category of ancestor acknowledgment:

> The aroma of the pork drippings sizzling in the white-hot hickory ashes . . . conjures up in the minds of the older celebrants memories of past good times spent around similar pits with family members and friends, now deceased or absent. The distinctive smell of these slow-rising spirals of smoke also link celebrants with their slave ancestors who smelled the same aroma during their slave social gatherings and their initial freedom celebrations. In other words, celebration barbecuing allows each new generation of freedom celebrants to recreate in rite and symbol their ancestors' original observances of Emancipation.[11]

Wiggins's work is comprehensive and narrated with in-group awareness and with a lyricism that testifies to the legacy and value of such rites. Even though Wiggins's *O Freedom!* is a model of capturing cultural memory, he does not itemize memory as a central variable. Instead, memory is the conduit that stabilizes the structure and value of Emancipation celebrations, although in some communities the occasion is dying out as older generations transition.

The next important work on this topic prominently features memory, though it is in historical narrative rather than in theoretical conceptualization. Mitch Kachun's *Festivals of Freedom: Memory and Meaning in African American Emancipation Celebrations, 1808–1915* (2003) extends commemorative periodization farther into the past to include the earliest African American celebrations of the January 1, 1808 US law that prohibited the international enslavement trade, the celebrations of the Slavery Abolition Act that went into effect on August 1, 1834 in the British colonies, and the 1915 semicentennial of emancipation. He describes the study as "the first book-length historical analysis of nineteenth century Emancipation celebrations" yet with two correctives.[12] First, he stresses how celebrations functioned to allow African Americans to "congregate," "educate," and "agitate," and second, he introduces a long tradition of African American Freedom Day celebrations that predate Civil War era Emancipation by nearly two centuries.[13] He mines the seventeenth-century historical record for evidence of African festivals and gatherings such as Negro Election Day events and the Pinkster Festival, and details the precision, rigor, and routine of free, northern, African American communities that rallied around and celebrated major freedom events in the eighteenth and nineteenth centuries. Kachun's history introduces numerous topics that are operationalized in the broad conceptual and theoretically descriptive approach of Black cultural mythology. Like *O Freedom!*, Kachun's study is of primary importance to the broader, interdisciplinary subarea of Africana cultural memory studies.

As a contemporary work, *Festivals of Freedom* is conversant with matters such as how the internet introduces challenges to the academic maintenance of history. As a memory-aligned study, Kachun's analyses pivot on topics of collective history, the function of celebration, festive culture, collective memory, race pride, emulation of heroes, Black history, Black accomplishments, public memory, sacrifice, biracial public celebration, the Black heroic pantheon, cultural priorities, remembering vs. forgetting, the shame of the enslavement past, monument culture, symbolic resources, and commemoration traditions, rituals, calendars, transnationalism, and history.[14] A Black cultural mythology coding of Kachun's historical narrative is attentive to the language of memory and commemoration on which he relies to link the chronologies of Freedom Day, Emancipation Day, Decoration Day, and Juneteenth celebrations and festivals. The historical queries he frames around this language enrich *Festivals of Freedom* as a significant historical source for the study of Africana cultural memory. In particular, chapter 4, on "'Let Children's Children Never Forget': Remembrance and Amnesia, 1870–1910," is of seminal importance.

In this significant chapter on memory, Kachun's cumulative interest in the power of Black oratory is a historical narrative of what Black cultural mythology precursor Molefi Kete Asante theorized in his 1960s to 1980s work on the quality and content of mythic value in the Black utterances of oratory. Kachun touches on the debates over enslavement memory that the framework of Black cultural mythology aims to decentralize in favor of a more organic interest in the nature of African survival that does not overemphasize this status, which was a condition of an oppressive era. And, even though Kachun does not mention the immortalization ideas of Maria

W. Stewart, which are central to the theorizations of Black cultural mythology, he does highlight a formidable list of historical actors who advanced collective memory sensibilities. For example, he introduces Reverend Jeremiah B. Sanderson's emancipation speech of 1869 in Stockton, California. In the speech, Sanderson listed Africans of the Roman Empire and early Christian history, to emphasize that "the race that produced these was African. African blood and mind have contributed to the material and intellectual wealth of the nations in ages past. They will, one day re-assert the old power."[15] Kachun features an 1874 editorial from Benjamin Tanner that used the language of immortalization that Stewart had used approximately forty years earlier.[16] Tanner advocated for a conceptual view of the 1870s as a pioneering moment of African American infancy—a "heroic age"—similar to Asante's framing of 1619 as beginning again.[17]

An original contribution to commemoration discourse is Kachun's attention to the role of the Black press and its editors, such as T. Thomas Fortune, who advocated for the financing of African American monuments and emphatically corrected white racist dismissals of Black contributions that should be more highly regarded as the race's patriotism. Kachun's narration of the "monument craze" and "monument fever" of the 1860s to the 1910s features a pantheon of Black heroes and proven allies that the African American community sought to honor: Richard Allen, John Brown, Frederick Douglass, Harriet Tubman, Nat Turner, Crispus Attucks, John Mercer Langston, William C. Nell, Phillis Wheatley, George Washington Williams, and T. Thomas Fortune.[18]

Festivals of Freedom is a comprehensive history reflecting individual, community, regional, and institutional African American heritage practices. It expands our sense of how each community of free Blacks in the North had its own local activists and Black nationalist thinkers who articulated ideas about freedom and the African American saga. They also sustained a vitriolic critique of America's commemorative freedom hypocrisy (e.g., the meaning of the Fourth of July) that rivals and reiterates ideas that we tend to credit exclusively to more popular orators such as Frederick Douglass. Additionally, like Wiggins in *O Freedom!*, who itemizes fellowship (food and partying), worship (church services with a prominent speaker delivering a heritage keynote address), and entertainment (baseball games and youth achievement contests) as key structures of weekend-long Emancipation celebrations, Kachun also characterizes a standard structure of African American commemoration events that further reveals a traditional *template* for community heritage event organization. This suggests that the commemorative model of how the City of Hampton, Virginia, regularly plans events for its annual African Landing Day celebration and how the nation has approached the 1619–2019 commemoration are also part of a *programmatic* tradition.

Another significant text in the historiography of African American commemoration studies in Kathleen Ann Clark's *Defining Moments: African American Commemoration and Political Culture in the South, 1863–1913* (2005). Emerging two years after Kachun's comprehensive history, which demarcated how African Americans in the North had an earlier tradition of commemoration than that which occurred more routinely in the South after Emancipation, Clark focuses on the competition between white and Black worldviews of commemoration. These battles concerned rights to urban, southern space and rights to visibility in city centers and avenues of the public domain. She also makes contributions to commemoration discourse by narrating ways in which African Americans in the South were "emboldened" to commemorate on their own terms amid resistance from whites who rejected and derided their symbolic displays of freedom. This includes in-group, intergenerational differences about how to manage and regulate the pain of the history of enslavement in memory and commemoration.[19]

Clark offers compelling observations related to Black cultural mythology variables, beginning with her analysis of how Black southern leaders managed "the responsibility to shape the collective representation of African American interests and identities through public ceremonies."[20] She captures the critical decision-making process about heritage practices and the public domain's symbolic legacy events that Black actors in the post-Emancipation and post-Reconstruction South had to manage during an unprecedented time of social change and upheaval. This era-specific context of social change was one in which African Americans faced significant antiheroics as "most virulent white supremacists insisted on the impossibility of any form of African American achievement whatsoever."[21] While not directly a Black cultural mythology variable, Clark equates much of the heroic policy activity of Black southerners with a "collective demonstration of black citizenship," and this dimension of her study is compelling, possibly as an expansion of subvariables of a Black cultural mythology conceptual framework. In fact, Clark describes this in a way that could be compatible with Maria W. Stewart's clarion call for the race to actively immortalize itself. Clark suggests that "both the transformation of slaves into citizens and the reconstitution of the nation required cultural labor that rested, in part, on the ability to make history, that is to assert particular understandings of the past."[22] She adds that "looking to the future, they stressed the proven accomplishments of black men, whether in ancient Egypt or in American wars, as proof positive of their capacity for the full rights of citizenship, including suffrage."[23] In this politicized use of heroics, the audience is not the internal Black community using memory, narratives of epic-intuitive conduct, and hyperheroics for in-group reciprocal encouragement. Instead, Clark documents how heroics (not simply religious morality, hard work, and cleanliness) were put to vindicationist uses, to further convince the white power structure (an antiheroic institution) to respond favorably to African American achievement dynamics. Black antiheroics appear in Clark's discussion of those who questioned "the wisdom of remembering slavery," especially when resistance to white terror and agitation for equal commemorative space in the public domain were too costly and demoralizing.[24]

Clark also features an in-group gender-based antiheroic element of "the systematic construction of black history and progress in terms of male achievement and the persistent emphasis on female respectability and domesticity as a measure of freedom's successes."[25] This was a factor with which Maria W. Stewart contended, and even though Frances Ellen Watkins Harper and, later, Anna Julia Cooper incorporated ideas of achievement and heroics in their discourses, many of their accounts and interpretations of gendered versions of achievement had to maneuver through these imbalanced assumptions of "racial achievements [defined] almost exclusively in terms of male accomplishment."[26] One insightful example of male accomplishment is in Clark's discussion of the African Methodist Episcopal (AME) Church as a Black institutional model of commemoration. Her historicizing of the church in this manner layers nicely with Wiggins's more anthropological and folk cultural ethnography. Wiggins presents the Black church positively in southern cultural memory and mythology as a home place, a site of security, gossip, and entertaining sermons and pageants, a source of good food, and a site that reinforces the maintenance of formal protocols of respect for an elder-based hierarchy of kinship. In contrast, Clark reveals the church to be a site of debate, conflict, and a concerted effort to elevate masculine heroics. These include AME Church anniversaries, "calls to memory," official commemorative church histories, and reminders specifically of AME origin history—that the "denomination, which began as a religious rebellion, had evolved into a full-fledged institution."[27] Thus, in a Black cultural mythology reading of Clark's historical chronicle, there are examples of "rebellions" that serve the same purpose as historical memory of "revolts" and other types of individual and collective resistance. Clark's description of the narrative structure of how the AME Church routinely honored one of its pioneers—Richard Allen—is valuable for its narrative markers more than for its representation of masculine heroics:

> Spokesmen told and retold the story of Allen's departure from the white church in Philadelphia, the subsequent establishment of an independent black denomination, and the expansion of the AME Church throughout the North. Most clergymen drew a direct line from Richard Allen to Abraham Lincoln and from the founding of the AME denomination to the advent of freedom. And they argued that the church's past revealed the ascendancy of black manhood.[28]

Clark's *Defining Moments* makes new contributions to the historiography of African American commemoration.

Wiggins, Kachun, and Clark wrote important volumes that historicize and humanize African American agency in heritage practices. These narratives provide the stable historical grid from which we can ask different questions of the historical narrative, often related to capturing meta-analyses of cultural phenomena and models of agency that sustained survival and that have cosmological and ontological value for itemizing an Africana worldview. As a creative theoretical conceptualization that prioritizes organic diasporan idea formation, Black cultural mythology follows the trail of such interdisciplinary evidence to construct a narrative of cultural idea formation and logic from structurally unique yet parallel queries.

Kachun's *Festivals of Freedom* has an additional distinction for its documentation of the Jamestown Tercentennial, which supports this chapter's transition to exploring the commemorative fervor for the quadricentennial of African arrival in English North America in 1619. In his discussion of the 1915 Negro Historical and Industrial Exposition in Richmond, Virginia, aimed at celebrating the semicentennial of Emancipation, Kachun introduces Giles B. Jackson, "a former slave, a Richmond lawyer and entrepreneur" who "was also deeply involved in black commemorations in Virginia, having organized the Negro exhibit at the 1907 Jamestown Tercentennial and already beginning to plan the three hundredth anniversary of the first landing of Africans at Jamestown in 1619."[29] With Jackson's experience with organizing African American commemorations, one would expect him to have structured the African American point of view of 1919 in a similar format, but his activism lost momentum in the interim years.

African American historical commemoration is less uniform than it was just over 150 years ago in the community-based and African American institutional intoxication over Jubilee, Emancipation, and Juneteenth. Twentieth-century commemoration has been more academic (explored through conferences) and newsroom based, such as commemorations of the *Brown v. Board of Education* decision, civil rights legislation, and other celebrated and landmark legal and policy gains. In *Defining Moments*, Clark captures the processes of waning organized commemoration due to racialized contests over the rights to commemorate in public spaces, particularly as African Americans sought to take advantage of patriotic national holidays where workers were given the day off to enact and perform their own worldview of patriotism and pageantry to which whites took offense, particularly in the South.

The defining language of the historiography is not yet uniform, as these historiographical works are variably indexed with a mix of terms such as slaves, Emancipation, anniversaries, political culture, centennial celebrations, social life, and customs but not uniformly as *commemoration*. Wiggins and Kachun refer to African Americans as "celebrants," which is a festive rendering of purpose and worldview. These few studies that comprise the emergent historiography document the distant and recent past. The core of Wiggins's folk culture and anthropology research represents 1972–73 fieldwork and early 1980s debates about the merits of a Martin Luther King Jr. federal holiday. Kachun ends his 1808–1915 period study of the North by highlighting Wiggins's research. Clark's study of the 1863–1913 South is a view of a fifty-year struggle around Emancipation celebrations. Wiggins and Kachun expand the historical legacy of Emancipation celebrations into the topic of the African American holiday tradition.

Along these lines and adding to the historiography, Keith A. Mayes updates the scope of commemoration with *Kwanzaa: Black Power and the Making of the African-American Holiday Tradition* (2009). This study is a more focused scholarly treatment than Ishakamusa Barashango's two-volume study of *Afrikan People and European Holidays: A Mental Genocide* (2001), which explores the holidays of Thanksgiving, Christmas, and Kwanzaa (book 1) and the Fourth of July, Maroon Wars, and the Revolutionary War (book 2) in terms of African and African American history. He writes, "One of the things among the many we must examine is the celebration of European holidays. Black people must ever keep in mind that these holidays are tributes to Euro-American Nationalism, that is white nationalism."[30]

In contrast, Mayes researches the Black protest calendar, the culture's holiday traditions, the legitimacy of the African American cultural calendar, and the Kwanzaa holiday as a multilayered historicization of this lesser recognized feature of the Black Power movement. In comparison to Barashango, Mayes invokes a stunning demarcation between mainstream American and African American holiday traditions: "The black holiday tradition never existed on its own; it needed the American holiday tradition and its accompanied calendar to do its work of exclusion and marginalization."[31] His introduction pivots on the distance between Frederick Douglass's 1852 deconstruction of the relevance of the Fourth of July to mid-nineteenth-century Africans in America and Basir Mchawi who, much like Barashango, in 1974 called for African Americans to reject "crazy cracker celebrations."[32] Specifically, Mayes notes, "Douglass' and Mchawi's remarks were conceived by a kind of Jim Crow reality on the American calendar that rendered black participation in mainstream holiday observances minimal to nonexistent."[33] Mayes echoes Clark here, as she painstakingly demonstrates episode after episode of the African American fight to engage in public, cultural versions of America's holidays, especially the Fourth of July. Mayes extends the analysis, clarifying, "What emerged was the black protest calendar, providing African-American temporal space for their holidays and commemorations."[34] He also extends Clark's discussion of contested public spaces during holidays. Mayes notes that "most often, the mainstream black public sphere was not a safe political space for Kwanzaa to evolve and mature."[35] He then explores the capacity of the African American community to incubate its holidays in intimate cultural spaces he describes as "the secondary black counter-public of black independent schools, community-based organizations, community centers, and to some extent, the major arteries of a neighborhood."[36] The role of Black institutions—their funding, their role as space for gathering, and so forth—is an important logistic of cultural memory practices.

Mayes addresses a certain logic of commemoration that differs from the logic of Black cultural mythology, which asserts that meditations on hero dynamics, ancestry, hyperheroics, epic intuitive conduct, immortalization, commemoration, sacrificial inheritance, and more are *not* calendar based; they are daily and intrinsic, once introduced. Mayes researches "a certain logic in black holiday placement. Though the preoccupation of placing black holidays next to dominant American ones began with July Fifth celebrations in the nineteenth century, Kwanzaa remakes this tradition in the late twentieth century."[37]

Mayes's study has implications beyond the historiography that gives it greater parallels to Black cultural mythology theorization. In offering a formal history, he introduces rarely studied holidays such as July Fifth, Umoja Karamu (Black Thanksgiving), Black Solidarity Day (the day before Election Day in November), Black Love Day (instead of Valentine's Day), Ancestor Honor Day (versus Memorial Day), and African Holocaust Day (instead of Columbus Day) as well as Martin Luther King, Jr. Day and Kwanzaa.[38] His study also assesses elements of ancestral acknowledgment as well as ritual, through "mapping Kwanzaa and its ceremonial procedures."[39] With attention to these elements, Mayes's history is one of the most aligned with Black cultural mythology, and his study pivots on actors of Black Power. Because of the public's limited access to and awareness of Maulana Karenga's role in sustaining mythology discourses, Larry Neal is the central Black Power/Black Arts figure in assumptions about cultural mythology. This is not so in Mayes's study, which provides a detailed narrative of Karenga's leadership evolution and philosophical worldview.

Adding 1619 to the Historiography as a Commemorative Reference Point

In the historiography, Kachun is the only one to prominently mention 1619 as a commemoration opportunity, and the contemporary vision of Black local heritage sites and their adoring communities presents an opportunity to extend the historiography from a Black cultural mythology lens. A case study of the commemoration behaviors of citizens of Hampton, Virginia (which is the contemporary site of Point Comfort where the first Africans landed) reveals an active practice of living Black history in the city of Hampton since the late 1990s. What distinguishes Hampton's commemoration is its confidence that it is the geographical location of origin for African people in English North America. This narrative of origin is not mythology, but history. The City of Hampton's commemorative activism to stabilize its heritage and origin narrative is a Black cultural mythology behavior. The city catapulted its agency in the nation's commemorative history, building momentum for the quadricentennial a decade in advance. In the contemporary media-driven society, commemoration increases in value based on newer strategies the City of Hampton is using to demand a national critical discourse on its heritage, which is related to the heritage origin of the US nation, as well.

In an Africana worldview, the city of Hampton has value as a sacred geographical location based on its heritage as a site of diaspora origin during the colonial era. Unlike Emancipation and Juneteenth celebrations, which commemorate the achievement of *freedoms* and mark legal, physical, and conceptual shifts in the status of freedom, the City of Hampton's commemorations acknowledge a point of *encounter* that frames the geographical and environmental scope of the United States' diaspora narrative inherited from the English colonial era. A Black cultural mythology orientation to this event sharpens the historical gaze to consider not only the encounter of first contact memorialized by the City of Hampton but also the precursory encounters between Africa, the Caribbean, and Mexico that are equally important as a backstory to the 1619 commemoration. In the case of speculating on the worldview of the first Africans who landed at Point Comfort, Black cultural mythology compels a meditation that situates the African-centered memories, observations, and speculations not only of what it must have been like to disembark from a Middle Passage vessel onto the shore of the Virginia Colony, but also the experience of being accosted by the Portuguese in the Congo and Angola; being pirated twice en route to being shipped for sale to Vera Cruz, Mexico; being buccaneered en route to Vera Cruz by the *White Lion*, an English pirate ship; being rerouted to an enslavement port in the Bahamas; being sold to a Dutch ship bound for the eastern coast of the English colony of Virginia; and watching the ship head off to Bermuda to sell the remaining Africans whom the Virginia colonists did not purchase. Here, the speculation of how African mobility was objectified based on Portuguese, Spanish, and English colonial and maritime politics is an equally important history upon which contemporary generations who respect the African legacy in the diaspora must speculate and imagine with historical precision informing their remembrance.

Measuring the memorial and commemoration value of *beginning again* and *engraving identity* on new soil from the perspective of Hampton, Virginia, and its Black commemoratively activist citizenry is a significant starting point from which to begin the inquiry of how commemoration practices stabilize cultural memory and emerge as a priority for the theorization of Black cultural mythology.

The City of Hampton proclaimed August 20 as its annual African Landing Day, and the first commemoration day festival was in 2010. The event's rhetoric invited the community to "come help us REMEMBER the first arrival, and our ancestors who lost their lives through the Middle Passage, and endured 246 years of bondage."[40] The next featured description of the annual event describes its value as "a commemoration of the first Africans who arrived in America on English occupied territory at Point Comfort, today's Fort Monroe in Hampton."[41] The central priorities of the event from these descriptions are remembrance and commemoration, which a Black cultural mythological theorization enhances to include additional, more systematic, features of lamentation, ancestor acknowledgment, historical reenactment of worldview, and sacred observation.

Examining the commemoration philosophy of the African Landing Day Commemoration Festival as a case study deciphered through the Black cultural mythology theoretical lens is this chapter's first intervention. The case study does not aim to deconstruct the legitimacy of the work of the activists, historians, and communities who have pioneered and institutionalized the remembrance. Instead, a case study of the structure and commemorative choices for the annual event measures the theoretical and conceptual variables of the event. As an intervention, applying the organic set of Black cultural mythology parameters to the event demonstrates how its theorization can empower the community's legacy activism through supporting conceptual uniformity. Also, the event has traditional elements that Wiggins described as a fellowship-worship-entertainment structure and that Kachun encapsulated in terms of commemoration's function to allow African Americans to congregate-educate-agitate.

The 10th Annual African Landing Day Commemoration Festival took place on August 18–19, 2017 at several locations in the city of Hampton, ranging from its Coliseum to its parks. The Friday evening film festival showing of *American Denial* (2015) produced by Christine Herbes-Sommers, Llewellyn Smith, and Kelly Thomson—about the causes and legacy of racial bias—set the stage for Saturday's full day of events. The festival's sponsors were the Hampton, Virginia, 2019 Commemorative Commission, the National Juneteenth Observance Foundation, Project 1619, the National Parks Service, Roots to Glory Tours, and the Fort Monroe tourism commission. The day's events were a naming ceremony, a Pilgrimage Prayer, a libation prayer offered by Ekgbe Chiefs of Cameroon, African cultural dance and drumming performances, a formal ceremony acknowledging African arrival, local drum and dance performances, and an African American Heritage Jazz Concert.

Structurally, the events of the Festival represent a beginning, middle, and final placement of contemporary African American identity and worldview reinforcements (the film, local performers, and the closing jazz concert). These are primarily African-centered legacy behaviors that prioritize Black cultural mythology variables, without conceptually organizing them in ways that make formal Africana cultural memory practices recognizable as succinct, self-reflective diaspora behaviors. Memorial maturity and conceptual uniformity are the priorities of Black cultural mythology, and the intervention is appropriate for not only public domain celebrations such as African Landing Day and Black History Month but also for general, institutional, and communal African-centered education and pedagogy events.

The Festival's naming ceremony parallels Black cultural mythology priorities for ancestor acknowledgment, historical reenactment of worldview, and reconciliation and renewal. The Pilgrimage Prayer emphasized reconciliation and healing, which are aligned with priorities of cognitive survival and renewal. The actual ceremony of the Festival included a libation prayer, drumming, dancing, and honoring the arrival, which are heritage behaviors related to Black cultural mythology's categories of ancestor acknowledgment, immortalization sensibility, and sacred observance and ritual remembrance. This is reminiscent of one of the celebrants that Wiggins interviewed in *O Freedom!* who described the celebration's value in terms of retrospection, reappraisal, reassuring, and reminding—functions that ensure cultural preservation.[42] The Festival always includes participants from African countries such as Cameroon and Senegal as well as African embassies from countries such as Angola and Sierra Leone for the purpose of collective and mutual reconciliation of global Africanity and Pan-Africanism. In fact, even the film on racial bias is an inclusion associated with the category of antiheroics. The Festival's previous nine years had similar events, including the 2015 dedication of commemorative highway historical markers designating Point Comfort as the landing site of the first Africans.[43] This is a physical act of commemoration influenced not only by the activism of the city of Hampton's citizens but also representative of a compliant act of affirmation and respect from the Commonwealth of Virginia. Thus, the event's itineraries have reflected conceptual maturity as a practice of Black cultural mythology. As these concepts gain traction within the community's and the nation's formats for legacy practices, there should be a blooming of traditional confidence in Black nationalism-aligned modes of self-determination and group cultural actualization that stabilize collective consciousness through the use of common variables of applied cultural mythology and memory to this site, which activists refer to as hallowed ground.[44]

Another consideration is the programming of African Landing Day, which the Hampton 2019 Commemorative Commission and several founders of Project 1619 who have embraced a long-term commemoration mission work collaboratively to sustain. Virginia Wesleyan College is one of many local collaborators that structured programming related to the quadricentennial. Understanding the drive and philosophy behind these and other collaborations is essential to further framing the commonality of vision and activism that sustains community-based and organizational Black cultural mythology practices. Calvin Pearson is the primary activist responsible for the momentum for commemoration, which he began in 1994. His Project 1619 is a nonprofit organization with a drive to promote and commemorate the African history of Point Comfort.[45] His work is in opposition to antiheroics, particularly against the myth that the first Africans were brought to Jamestown, Virginia, rather than to Point Comfort. The Africans were later dispersed throughout the Virginia Colony, including to Jamestown. Pearson has been honored by the African Tourism Diaspora, a group that is a central topic of Ana Araujo's work on enslavement memory. Project 1619's objective is to "change the narrative of the arrival,"[46] which has been successful. Organizers also frame the narrative as a "perilous voyage," in terms of being the origin of the nation's "disparities," and a marker for the nation's "cultural manifest."[47]

The Hampton, Virginia, 2019 Commemorative Commission, which partners with local groups to plan and promote African Arrival events, has the following mission:

> Appointed by Hampton City Council in an effort to engage citizen experts and to bring awareness of the role that Hampton has played in the development of Virginia and the nation, the Commission will engage the public with educationally enriching and culturally relevant commemorative events and activities, accomplished through discourse, planning, promotion and implementation of commemoration activities that serve as opportunities to broadly engage public participation on local, national and international levels.
>
> We wish to engage school children and educators, to call their attention to Hampton's remarkable African American heritage, and encourage the teaching of this narrative, including it in curricula and SOLs [Standards of Learning]. We will accomplish this through:
>
> Discussions about the process for reconciliation and healing
>
> Support of legislation for a proposed welcome center in Fort Monroe

> Creation of a time capsule
>
> Co-sponsoring a maritime and military event with Langley AFB
>
> Develop commemorative historical markers
>
> Host signature events that commemorate the 2019 Arrival of Africans at Point Comfort
>
> Attract the attention of national entities, such as The Smithsonian
>
> Promote commemorative activities and educational materials to attract visitors to Hampton[48]

The commission inaugurated African Arrival Day with a 2016 event to launch awareness of the commemoration. It included events and activities similar to Project 1619's annual celebration. From a Black cultural mythology perspective, it met criteria for ancestor acknowledgment, sacrificial inheritance, reconciliation and renewal, sacred observance, and ritual remembrance by including a "William Tucker Cemetery Dedication" (for the firstborn child from among sold Angolans) and a commemorative ceremony with a Christian prayer, an African libation prayer, and "recognition of sacrifices and contributions of Africans to the early formation of this nation."[49] This part of the program also included an African naming ceremony, a pilgrimage prayer, and a prayer service. The event's scheduled historical tours met the Black cultural mythology criteria of historical reenactment of worldview and commemoration philosophy through offering narratives of the arrival and information about Antony and Isabell—the Angolan couple whose child was the first *documented* (when the colonists did not necessarily record African births) African birth in the colony. Also, the event publicized the new historical marker "First Africans in Virginia."[50] It is helpful to compare the narrative on the historical marker to the many historical and organizational descriptions of the event's gravity. It reads as follows:

> The first documented Africans in Virginia arrived in 1619 when a Dutch warship landed here at Point Comfort. The "twenty and odd" Africans, captured from the Spanish, were traded to the Virginia colonists in exchange for foodstuffs. Early Africans who lived here include Antony and Isabell, and their son, William, likely the first black child in present-day Hampton. They served Point Comfort commander William Tucker, but whether the

Africans were treated as servants or indentured slaves is uncertain. The institution of slavery evolved during the 17th century as the terms of service of Africans was extended for life. The U.S. abolished slavery in 1863.[51]

The activities and activism of the City of Hampton to properly recognize the worldview importance and the sacredness of the arrival of Angolans in 1619 is laudable, and explicating such heritage behaviors through the lens of Black cultural mythology serves public domain activism by helping citizens better conceptualize the structural processes that they are practicing in their fervent commemoration spirit. Action is enhanced when guided by conceptualization.

The Hampton Commission's commemoration was more African-centered, while another regional commemoration organization based just west of Hampton in Williamsburg, Virginia—the American Evolution project—examined 1619 for its layers of national diversity. Its informational narrative reveals a decentering of a meditation on African American experience in the quadricentennial, noting that "AMERICAN EVOLUTION™ commemorates the 400th anniversary of several key historical events that occurred in Virginia in 1619 that continue to influence America today. Featured events, programs, and legacy projects inspire local, national, and international engagement in the themes of democracy, diversity, and opportunity."[52] The next promotion tells why 1619 is important:

> 1619 was a pivotal year in the establishment of the first permanent English Colony in North America. It was the year of the first representative legislative assembly in the New World, the arrival of the first recorded Africans to English North America, the recruitment of English Women in significant numbers, the first official English Thanksgiving in North America, and the development of the Virginia colony's entrepreneurial and innovative spirit.[53]

The goals of the organization reflect Virginia's self-concept, namely, "The Commonwealth of Virginia, along with notable Virginia institutions and national partners, will launch a series of education programs, signature events, and legacy projects of national and international significance. These programs and events will build awareness of Virginia's role in the creation of the United States and reinforce Virginia's leadership in education, tourism, and economic development."⁵⁴ Finally, the organization advances a national (not culturally African American) view of the importance of commemoration:

> The commemoration of formative events in our nation's history is a core element of civics education. As a society, we need to fully understand the foundation of today's America. Learning about the challenges, successes, and inequities of the past enables a full appreciation of the difficult path our nation has taken to become what it is today. This honest historical perspective empowers and motivates both current and future generations to take an active role in shaping the course of our nation's future.⁵⁵

The structure of the discourse that the group AMERICAN EVOLUTION initiates reinforces a traditional contest between white American patriotic versions of history and African American sacred remembrance, along the same lines of the traditional contests noted in Kachun's and Clark's histories as well as in Asante's discourses. Only now, postracialism, diversity, multiculturalism, and color blindness work in tandem to shadow and reduce public domain discourse on Africana agency. Black cultural mythology intervenes here.

Conceptually, the African historical narrative in the Americas does not begin with 1619 but with a discussion of African identity before enslavement. African life in the early colonies and later in the US is a secondary narrative of engraving identity on new soil, which emphasizes creation and agency in surviving. African people, faced with death, abuse, exploitation, kidnapping, and all sorts of physical and psychological traumas and abominations against their humanity, mustered up practices and tactics for *epic survival* in the most heightened examples of human *survivalist creativity*. The ancestors were a culture that, under enslavement brutality, spent an inordinate amount of their existence in the condition of fight or flight. This expression describes a mechanism in the body that enables humans to mobilize a lot of energy and sensory ability rapidly in order to cope with threats to survival. It is an automatic response of the central nervous system. Most threats are false alarms, but it is reasonable to understand that African ancestors—faced with the unknowns and mysteries of the European enslavement trade, with bondage among Europeans in the Americas who treated them like animals, with beatings and regular humiliations and threats—existed for hundreds of years at a heightened survivalist alert system that is partly responsible for the conscious and subconscious transmission of skills and tools for cultural survival (communication and communicative body language, gazes, glances, movements, habits, and gestures).

Storytelling about negative experiences benefits from ending on a note of triumph because African survival is the testament of cultural victory over what the dominant ruling society had planned for Africans in the Americas. The ruling society takes cultural survival for granted; at a minimum, we have not theorized it comprehensively from an Africana worldview. One wonders whether the ruling society, in general, and African people, in particular, *meditate* on the encounters of our ancestors enough to render specific, itemized attention to the miracle-working, superhero, achievement-against-the-odds narratives of the culture's collective experience in the Americas. This attention helps us understand, honor, and even duplicate the *force* that sustained Africana survival. It is at the center of understandings of Black cultural mythology.

Mythology indicates a timeless, honored, and revered narrative of Africana culture's legendary impulses worthy of remembrance, celebration, and memorialization because it includes accounts of a *repertoire of survival* based on agency, resistance, and hyperheroic conduct. In considering the notion of beginning again within an African American legacy narrative since 1619, the key feature of this narrative is survival. Survival was practiced at such an elevated level that it yielded regular feats that can be described as superhuman and miraculous. The retelling of this history and heritage is worthy to be called "mythology" (the real-life behaviors worthy of being remembered and retold) and it is a *sacred inheritance* based on the maintenance, even if underacknowledged, of an accumulated aggressive approach to existence. Such a methodology for survival infuses the present with spirit, memory, life, gratitude for sacrifice, responsibility, and reciprocity, all to be transmitted to posterity.

Understanding 1619 is a multilayered critical engagement. There are two key matters. The first is understanding what 1619 means to people of African descent in what was originally English North America and is now the United States. The second is assessing what 1619 means to the nation in which people of African descent are now generations into citizenship. Black cultural mythology poses an opportunity to shift the nation's conversation and static assumptions about the African American past, even though the comparison of competing commemoration models in Hampton and Williamsburg, Virginia (Project 1619 versus AMERICAN EVOLUTION) reveals a contest in black versus mainstream commemoration groups' comfort level with engaging in an immersive, African-centered commemoration. Thus, the approach to reflecting and remembering this historical encounter first needs to be explicated with greater narrative accuracy, placing Mexico, piracy, and Angolan worldviews into optimum historical consciousness. The approach can be very Pan-African as we explore the possibilities of critical discourse on the meaning of 1619.

While 1619 is exceptional for activity that was foundational for English North America, another highlight for early commemorations of the African encounter with the Americas is the more ancient narrative of precolonial encounter from sources such as Ivan Van Sertima's *They Came before Columbus* (1976)—published, ironically, in the year of the US Bicentennial—but also the expansive enslavement history involving Spain's and Portugal's activity in South and Central America that predates the year 1619 by over one hundred years. These encounters are well documented, but they are not always properly narrated in commemoration historiography. Such a multilayered meditation on the meaning of 1619 would illuminate the conceptual and narrative differences in cultural memory between African and European descendants, whose views reveal distinct national versus cultural priorities of cultural memory. The pre-1619 encounters reveal evidence of ancient and precolonial African exploration of the Americas and include narratives of African agency as Africans manned ships in exploration and in encounters and were equals as they accompanied earlier European adventurers who voyaged to the Americas. A deeper study of this period of European colonial history includes an itemization of distinct European national aggressive behaviors (the Spanish, the Portuguese, the Dutch, the English) against Africans and of how, as Carter G. Woodson describes in the preface to *African Heroes and Heroines* (1939), Africans appear in European narratives within contexts of extreme bias.

Mainstream priorities in acknowledging the 1619 commemorative moment are focused on narratives of what happened *after* 1619, yet African-centered memorial narratives are attentive to narrating the historical moment to reflect a complete story of what transpired *before* 1619. Ana Lucia Araujo's *Shadows of the Slave Past: Memory, Heritage, and Slavery* (2014) poses this problem, as well, particularly the tendency of memorials and commemorations to selectively convey information based on "the needs that the prevailing groups have in the present moment."[56] These needs are often in competition between patriotic views and Africana worldviews. Kadiatu Kanneh describes such a problematic with the temporal uses of the Middle Passage in African American literature: "This dreaming of the Middle Passage as the unfixed yet eternal space from which an African-American origin can be traced makes the wide and uncertain journey *away* from shore, rather than to the reality of Africa's shore *itself*, into the founding moment of Black American consciousness."[57] Advancing commemoration relying on meditation from a cultural center is what Black cultural mythology empowers, and it helps reveal "a more complicated story" that is at stake as African Americans and diasporans become more conceptually vigilant in properly narrating the history's cultural meaning in both scholarship and in the public domain.[58]

To summarize the 1619 moment, readers learn that twenty Angolans were sold over and over again. They were exchanged for food. They were objectified by the Spanish asiento that contracted other nations (in this case Portugal) to supply its colonies with enslaved Africans. This basic narrative benefits from conceptual intervention.

The 1619 group initially embarked for a Mexican plantation owned by a Spaniard in Seville. They were on a ship bound to deliver forcibly captured Angolans from the Portuguese colony of Sao Paolo Loanda in Angola to Vera Cruz, New Spain (modern day Mexico). Once in the Virginia Colony, they were part of a group of twenty (or so) Africans in August 1619 that had increased to thirty-two by March 1620 (fifteen males, seventeen females). A few more Africans were brought to the colony with the second pirate ship that also sold Africans in Bermuda. The ship departed from Angola in 1619, and the Africans were in the hands of at least five different groups of Europeans along their journey: in the Angolan port (and likely earlier along the trek from Loanda), on the Portuguese vessel, on two English "piracy" ships whose merchants or sailors kidnapped a smaller group of Africans and separated them from the larger population that remained on the attacked Portuguese vessel, and at Point Comfort where there was an auction/sale (which further dispersed the Angolans to the Jamestown Colony and to other Virginia Colony settlements). This involuntary *mobility* is a discursive point that is lost in standard narratives about the Angolans who were sold in the Virginia Colony. The standard narratives convey that most likely

> they were captured from the nearby kingdom of Ndongo, where in 1618 and 1619 the governor of Angola, Luis Mendes de Vasconcelos, fighting alongside a ruthless African mercenary group called the Imbangala, led two campaigns against the kingdom's Kimbundu-speaking people. Thousands were captured and likely provided the cargo for six Portuguese slave ships from Angola that arrived in Vera Cruz between June 18, 1619 and June 21, 1620.[59]

The further details of this account reveal that the twenty or so Angolans who arrived at Point Comfort were a small group from six ships full of

Kimbundu-speaking people from Angola. These ships likely included close family, friends, and distant kin, whose bloodlines were dispersed throughout the Americas. These are the types of details that are important in a reconstructive memory project that should be better illuminated in the historiography of 1619 to ensure proper memorialization and commemoration, which is a transnational matter.

The underlying logic of Black cultural mythology is that geography, relocation, cultural identity, worldview, and detailed narratives of saga are vital details that equip us with knowledge from which to narrate a comprehensive history of survival and cultural memory. This type of theoretical intervention is a corrective that reorients the approach to conceptualizing the English colonial segments of the US past in which the 1619 African saga of *beginning again* developed. A commemorative remembrance of the 1619 encounter is a testament to layers of European antiheroic behaviors toward Africans. These include kidnapping, selling, victimization, separating from families, renaming, objectification, and cultural strangulation. It also includes Eurocentric mythologies because there are narrative loopholes in the archive's interpretation that Antony and Isabell willingly named their first-generation, Angolan-English (Angolan-American), indentured/enslaved baby "William Tucker," after a local English planter. From the cultural logic of an African-centered perspective, the story of William Tucker's birth as the first "recorded" African birth operates as a Eurocentric colonial myth. The myth has emerged in society's paraphrasing as the "first birth," which is incorrect. It works to silence the probability of the natural increase among at least two dozen women in the Virginia Colony who were captured in Angola in 1618–19 and traded and pirated throughout the Caribbean before arriving in the Virginia Colony in 1619. African women must have given birth in the five years between 1619 and 1624 when Antony and Isabell married and William Tucker was born in 1624. Inevitably, the value of the "first recorded" birth is ambiguous. It means that for five years, African children's births were unacknowledged in the colony's civil documentation. Then it suggests that Angolan-born Antony and Isabell forgot, forsook, or renegotiated the value of the names of their lineage and language to commemoratively favor an Englishman's name for their firstborn son. In cultural meditation and speculation, we strive to reconcile the absences in and the peculiarities of this myth/narrative. In its traditional presentation, it is not logical in an African-centered view of traumatic relocation, bondage, worldview, and family dynamics.

For the 1619–2019 commemoration we have witnessed the preservation of the national ego of US whiteness and European-American heritage in bland, watered-down, limited detail and through the lenses of American multiracial nationalism that dilute the year 1619's story of African experience and agency.

Many scholars have asked the right questions of this historical event. The "1619: The Making of America" conference in September 2013 in the Tidewater, Virginia region (Norfolk and Hampton) gathered scholars from a wide range of academic disciplines to begin to better define 1619 in anticipation of the quadricentennial and beyond; it took place in cooperation with Project 1619. The conference distinguished 1619 by describing it as the first African enslavement *sale*, which is a clearer assessment of its superlative in response to the disciplines of history, diaspora studies, and transnational critiques that seek to decenter the stereotyped popularity of the date 1619 by relying on important points of information that better contextualize the diversity of Africa-to-North America points of contact.[60]

The African experience in the region of English North America from which African Americans emerged is but one of many diaspora narratives. Approximately twenty thousand Africans already had been transferred to Mexico by 1619, which was the original destination of the over twenty Angolans who were pirated from that path and sold at Point Comfort.[61] The 1619 event is neither the first nor is it the most important episode of enslavement activity in North America and the Americas, even though it is historically and symbolically important to African American cultural memory and memorialization, especially in terms of survival, ancestral origins, and maintaining a continuous narrative about the US national origins of African experience. This national narrative begins in 1607 in Jamestown, Virginia with the point of contact with the land base that would become the United States.

The meeting's interest was in the "narrative portrayals" of 1619, "the essential role these narratives played in the formation of Atlantic world culture," and "the spirit of commemoration."[62] The scholars in attendance framed much of their discourse around the year 1619 in terms of its challenges of misunderstanding, misrepresentation, its complicatedness, the inconsistency of the narratives, the incompleteness of historical memory and "elisions," even as they affirmed its "ongoing narrative construction."[63] A Black cultural mythology approach to the memory and meaning of 1619 is compatible with the many thoughtful and revisionist observations that scholars have generated to begin to better frame what cultural memory should accomplish in 2019 and beyond. For example, Angola is an important part of this story, as "the captors of the Angolan slaves held the pen of African American history in their hands, representing a people who were rich in culture and history, yet were not allowed to represent themselves."[64] The "1619" conference had a balance of scholarly presentations representing history, legal studies, literature, and more, plus performances and song. Its content addressed hero dynamics and ancestor acknowledgment in presentations of the political maneuvering of Queen Nzingha of Angola during and after 1619, as well as her legacy and memory in Brazilian literature and art, which relates to the category of aesthetic memorialization.[65] A descendant of William Tucker, recorded as the firstborn child from this group of relocated Angolans, also demonstrated Black cultural mythology variables of ancestor acknowledgment, immortalization sensibility, and sacred observance with ritual remembrance as she "performed a West African water ritual and chant to invoke the spirits of ancestors and represent the continuation of African narrative."[66]

The heritage practices that complemented the conference's intellectual examinations also included a vocal performance of the song "How Come We Here Lord," which "evoked the emotional and spiritual transformations of African narrative as it entered into the domain of American slavery."[67] This performance exemplified Black cultural mythology's itemized category of reconciliation and renewal. The academic papers and discussions contributed to Black cultural mythology's tenet of historical reenactment of worldview, as presenters deliberated on the terms of this worldview, especially concerning debates about incorrectly describing the enslaved Angolans as already creolized, which "understated the effect of African culture on the formation of the African world."[68] The conference also captured elements related to Black cultural mythology's itemization of antiheroics linked simultaneously to the too often overlooked value and agency of Indigenous narratives. The participants challenged the privileging of Eurocentric narratives that ignore the deeper questions of African and Indigenous agency. The conference extended this aspect of antiheroics to deliberations on the relationships between colonial and contemporary law and systems that reinforce the criminalization of African Americans. A legal studies panel subtitled "From 1619 to Trayvon Martin" reinforced the need to take a long view of the African narrative in English North America.

More recently, historian Michael Guasco's interest in 1619 is in finding "the best place to begin a meaningful inquiry into the history of African people's in America."[69] He evaluates 1619's meaning in terms of "understanding slavery as an institution" and serving "to help us better grasp the complicated place of African peoples in the early Atlantic modern world."[70] This is a different objective than Black cultural mythology's approach to 1619 that reconsiders Guasco's contention that "as a historical signifier, 1619 may be more insidious than instructive." Instead, in a Black cultural mythology reading, 1619 has a conceptual value that instigates a truer form of historical meditation and even speculation. Guasco's observations on the topic of *agency* are more aligned with Black cultural mythology. For example, he redirects Winthrop Jordan's conjecture from *White over Black* (1968) on the European rhetorical thoughts about the encounters between the settlers and the enslaved to reinforce that Angolans had agency as "Africans as actors in their own right."[71] Guasco also addresses the topic of memory when he contends that attention to 1619 "erases the memory of many more African peoples than it memorializes," and that the "narrative arc silences the memory of the more than 500,000 African men, women, and children who had already crossed the Atlantic against their will, aided and abetted Europeans in their endeavors, provided expertise and guidance in a range of enterprises, suffered, died, and—most importantly—survived."[72] Black cultural mythology, as an intervention against the casual way scholars categorize and qualify cultural memory, avoids such pitfalls. It inaugurates a conceptual platform and variables to enable systematic critical evaluations of not only African American cultural memory (though this population is this book's national starting point) but also of broader diaspora cultural memory contexts that scholars will, hopefully, address in future works, drawing from the conceptual properties of Black cultural mythology. Black cultural mythology advances with an interest in more procedural, structural, and itemized conceptualizations of commemoration. This includes updating the historiography to reflect society's processes for acknowledging the quadricentennial as well as mining twenty-first-century commemoration practices with a lens toward how they may further reflect layers of African American commemoration philosophy. These steps help us chart what Black cultural mythology has inherited from the broad intellectual genealogy concerned with reinforcing the culture's stability and immortalization. Exploring the layers of historiography and commemoration models also helps us to decipher the levels of idea formation and theoretical directions that Black cultural mythology can offer. This offering is a contemporary organic contribution to define a more uniform methodology for analyzing the comprehensive interplay of myth, mythology, memory, heroics, and survival, including being more precise about the extent to which "commemoration" may reflect lamentation and memorialization.

Commemoration Models Post-1619

Moving toward defining a broad field of collaborative, interdisciplinary Africana cultural memory studies is an important intervention because many regions with descendants of enslaved Africans, particularly in countries or locations where their heritage is not reflected properly in the national narrative, struggle with managing heritage commemoration in the public domain. In the US model, since freedom from enslavement, white factions have contested African American culturally infused nationalism and patriotism, which has been an affront to African American *rights* to institutionalize practices of memory, agency, and autonomy based on a distinctive culture, ethos, identity, and worldview that has evolved since 1619. The year 1619 is central to these discussions from a critical race theory perspective because the chronological archive of the denial and manipulation of African rights, privileges, and identity within the precursory frameworks of English law and ensuing colonial and US law begins here. As a site of symbolic transnational encounter, the 1619 project differs from African American commemorations that scholars and activists view as cultural agency-driven remembrances and acknowledgments. The Haitian Revolution, Emancipation/Jubilee, Juneteenth, the Fourteenth Amendment, the *Brown v. Board of Education* decision, and the passing of the Voting Rights Act are some of the most prominent commemorations. Local communities celebrate the enslavement revolts of Nat Turner and Gabriel Prosser; the birthdays and prowess of leaders such as Malcolm X, Rosa Parks, Martin Luther King Jr., Fannie Lou Hamer, and more; and both annual and periodic founding and incorporation dates of institutions such as churches, fraternities, sororities, social organizations, and national organizations. Cultural commemoration takes place in vast public and private institutional domains. In these agency-driven remembrances, the more easily available archive includes African voices in primary documents. This is not so with 1619. It challenges the historians' craft, but the methodology of Black cultural mythology enables the speculative process to be liberating.

In chapter 1, I introduced the key precursors whose legacies inform this newly interpreted intellectual tradition. The ideas of exemplars, or forerunners, such as Maria W. Stewart, Shirley Graham Du Bois, Larry Neal, Maulana Karenga, Amos Wilson, and Molefi Kete Asante reveal attention to strains of idea formation that reflect processes for immortalization, sacred remembrance, and cultural mythology. But there is an additional set of commemoration practitioners who model unique layers of critical remembrance. Martin Luther King Jr.'s *Why We Can't Wait*, James Baldwin's "My Dungeon Shook: Letter to My Nephew on the Eve of the Anniversary of the Emancipation Proclamation," and perspectives from legal historian A. Leon Higginbotham, critical race theorist Derrick Bell, and poet Gil Scott-Heron reflect how African Americans have approached century-based commemoration. These commemoration sources serve as a sampling of ethical visions and convictions of what is sacred, spiritual, affirming, healing, renewing, and vital to African American remembrance. A Black cultural mythology analysis of these source suggests how these ideas have greater possibilities as philosophical premises for the field of Africana cultural memory.

Why We Can't Wait

Structurally examining King's approach to commemoration, which is actually a deconstruction, is a model for correcting US and African American deficits in advancing practices for celebrating or acknowledging milestones that, unfortunately, also still include frameworks of oppression. King published *Why We Can't Wait* in 1964, and its first chapter, "The Negro Revolution," highlights the contradictions of 1963:

> With the dawn of 1963, plans were afoot all over the land to celebrate the Emancipation Proclamation, the one-hundredth birthday of the Negro's liberation from bondage. In Washington, a federal commission had been established to mark the event. Governors of states and mayors of cities had utilized the date to enhance their political image by naming commissions, receiving committees, issuing statements, planning state pageants, sponsoring dinners, endorsing social activities. Champagne, this year, would bubble on countless tables. Appropriately attired, over thick cuts of roast beef, legions would listen as luminous phrases were spun to salute the great democratic landmark which 1963 represented.[73]

He adds, "The milestone of the centennial of emancipation gave the Negro a reason to act—a reason so simple and obvious that he almost had to step back and see it."[74] For Africana people, leisure reading should be a practice of reengaging the critical essays and histories of the past for meditation and for updating our collective historical path to the contemporary moment. As the practice of dutiful survey,[75] this is a critical methodology that determines a cyclical process of updating and inserting our contemporary struggles into the ethical problem-solving narratives and statements of the culture's corpus of exemplary critical problem solvers. King's, Baldwin's, and Bell's approaches to commemoration become models, not just critical essays, that we consider structurally for methods from which to process cultural commemoration.

In the second chapter of *Why We Can't Wait*, "The Sword That Heals," King says "in the summer of 1963 a need and a time and a circumstance and the mood of a people came together," and this was a buildup for his promotion of the tactic of nonviolent direct action.[76] His thesis is on how the commemoration moment brings together "philosophy and method" in the face of the physical, activist encounters of civil rights struggle.[77] In the twenty-first century, the commemoration moment is philosophical still, but with the privilege of theorizing from intellectual spaces that are safer than a civil rights march or the balcony of the Lorraine Motel. Black cultural mythology reiterates that we are studying the encounters and observations that Black historical actors bequeathed us, learning how to retain and utilize the legacy of four hundred years of survival in culturally specific terms. In King's era, the US Senate was not passing clarifying resolutions of cultural respect like it did in 2016 that lauded African American resilience in terms of "one of the greatest survival stories rarely told and not fully understood." In the fervor of understanding the value of the 1619–2019 quadricentennial, we can invoke the rhetorical and historical methodology that King, Higginbotham, Bell, and Scott-Heron used to deconstruct a similar commemorative event for their era—the Emancipation Proclamation centennial.

King writes, "No revolution can take place without a methodology suited to the circumstances of the period," and we, too, can question if our signification on 1619 ushers in anything revolutionary or part of radical change.[78] In his discourse, King gives a survey of methodologies from Booker T. Washington, to W. E. B. Du Bois, and finally to Garvey, and it is in the analysis of Garvey's vision for African agency that King offers discourse on the role of Africa in assessing the milestone of one hundred years since Emancipation. King emphasizes variables of heritage, achievements, roots, and progress, which are aligned with the priorities of Black cultural mythology. He credits Garvey's movement for releasing

> a powerful emotional response because it touched a truth which had long been dormant in the mind of the Negro. There was a reason to be proud of their heritage as well as of their bitterly won achievements in America. Yet his plan was doomed because

an exodus to Africa in the twentieth century by a people who had struck roots for three and a half centuries in the New World did not have the ring of progress.[79]

In 1963 King believed that a critical problem of the African American community was its inability to understand Africa as a progressive continent of future promise and as a beacon of cultural unity that is also part of the African American inheritance. American society does not routinely invoke King's civil rights era discourses on Africa in its meditations on his legacy, even those reinforced by the federal King holiday. Yet, in *Why We Can't Wait*, he offers an African American worldview and vision in terms of global African heritage, namely that what was going on in Africa in 1963 was a catalyst for US-based Black activism:

> The American Negro saw, in this land from which he had been snatched and thrown into slavery, a great pageant of political progress. He realized that just thirty years ago there were only three independent nations in the whole of Africa. He knew that by 1963 more than thirty-four African nations had risen from colonial bondage. The Negro saw black statesmen voting on vital issues in the United Nations—and knew that in many cities of his own land he was not permitted to take that significant walk to the ballot box. He saw black kings and potentates ruling from palaces—and knew he had been condemned to move from small ghettos to large ones. Witnessing the drama of Negro progress elsewhere in the world, . . . it was natural that by 1963 Negroes would rise with resolution.[80]

Structurally duplicating King's 1963 queries of quantifying the African American relationship to Africa yields a set of contemporary concerns. Hypothetically projecting his focus to Africa in the present does several things. First, it reconstitutes ongoing interest in Africa as the heritage homeland, and, by extension, insinuates a responsibility to also quantify the African American worldview in terms of the diaspora. The geographies of 1619 are Angola, Mexico, Jamaica, Bermuda, and English North America, with specific focus on the Commonwealth of Virginia and its James River basin. The year 1619 invokes questions about the life and experience of African descendants in all of these regions that could extend into numerous research questions, including contemporary science breakthroughs in heritage DNA, such as highlighting, as the blog "Trip Down Memory Lane" does, African Americans celebrities such as Isaiah Washington and Chris Tucker who have discovered their Mbundu heritage, which was revealed by DNA testing.[81] It is uncertain if these celebrities are aware of the origins of the first Angolans sold to the colony of Virginia because general histories promote their identities as Christianized, Portuguese-influenced Angolans with little reference to the details of their cultural identity. Second, it instigates a comparison between the scale of memory and commemoration throughout the diaspora. A twenty-first-century lens, cultivated by fifty years of Black studies and cultural studies' renewed framing of Black internationalism, Pan-Africanism, and comparative diaspora studies suggests that perhaps King's discourse is remiss in not framing US Emancipation in a parallel discourse with similar diaspora legal freedom moments in the Caribbean and Latin America. This has been a consistent intervention in 1619 critical discourse. Lastly, King's query suggests the practicality of using a critical survey of milestones to assess the culture's activist direction. He writes that "the disenchanted, the disadvantaged and the disinherited seem, at times of deep crisis, to summon up some sort of genius that enables them to perceive and capture the appropriate weapon to carve out their destiny."[82] His weapon is nonviolent direct action, but the contemporary tool for this is Black cultural mythology. In effect, the history of reflections on 1619 suggests the need for a formal practice of managing African American, and by extension, African diasporan cultural memory, and elevating it to a qualified theoretical place. This is the logic behind the innovative impulse to structure the framework of Black cultural mythology to deal specifically with advancing Africana conceptual and narrative agency regarding memory and heroics.

"Letter to My Nephew on the One Hundredth Anniversary of the Emancipation"

James Baldwin modeled a commemoration approach with the first essay of *The Fire Next Time*, "My Dungeon Shook: Letter to My Nephew on the One Hundredth Anniversary of the Emancipation" (1962), which originally appeared in the *Progressive* magazine out of Madison, Wisconsin. It is of interest in articulating the critical dimensions of Black cultural mythology because its theorization features literature, including its nonfiction forms, and the vision of writers, more specifically, for innovation in maintaining aesthetic memorialization. Consistently, Black writers draw on epic, legendary, and biographical historical narratives and events as source material for their creations. They signify on the culture's hero dynamics in ways that encourage cultural memory as an ongoing, and at times cyclical, discourse. Baldwin relies on the epistolary form, or letter writing, as a technique of targeted, focused, and intimate reflection. The assumed privacy and honesty of the epistolary form elevates its ideas, reflections, and confessions to the stature of unbiased truth. Furthermore, because Baldwin relies on the epistolary form not in fiction but in a collection of essays, he cements it as a legacy document with historical authenticity for readers. African American readers respond positively to his literary and philosophical acts of commemorating what is probably the most important legal action in our history. He speaks bluntly about the realities of race and racism in US and person-to-person encounters with white people and institutions. His words elevate the masculinist kinship of the uncle-nephew relationship to an African sensibility reflecting the worldview that one's brother's child is the equivalent of one's own child. He presents an Africana-centered definition of love.

Structurally, Baldwin's short letter has many features that require explication. He reveals in his first sentence that the letter is the result of five false starts. As a model of commemoration philosophy, Baldwin teaches us that historical and commemorative reflection is a critical process that requires philosophical commitment and revision in order to formulate an optimum response to the moment. Next, he affirms the identity of the recipient of the letter *physically*. Readers of this published letter learn that his nephew is of African descent. In fact, Baldwin's physical description is strategic because it relies on a narration of phenotype and strength that is universal for Black men targeted by an objectifying European worldview that views skin color, body type or physique, and gait as critical information that fuels what psychologists describe as quick, nonempathetic responses to appearance that determine racists' impulses and behaviors.[83] The Black masculinist physicality that Harlem Renaissance era poet Helene Johnson celebrates in her 1927 poem "Sonnet to a Negro in Harlem" with emphases on "your perfect body and your pompous gait,/Your dark eyes flashing solemnly with hate" and "Your shoulders towering high above the throng,/Your head thrown back in rich, barbaric song," reappears in Baldwin's description of his nephew:[84]

> I keep seeing your face, which is also the face of your father and my brother. Like him, you are tough, dark, vulnerable, and moody—with a very definite tendency to sound truculent because you want no one to think you are soft. You may be

like your grandfather in this, I don't know, but certainly both you and your father resemble him very much physically. Well, he is dead, he never saw you, and he had a terrible life; he was defeated long before he died because, at the bottom of his heart, he really believed what white people said about him.[85]

By providing a physical description of his nephew, Baldwin channels, like Johnson, the identity, power, and swagger of a Black man in Harlem as "disdainful and magnificent." These images of the Black male body are timeless, and Baldwin's reference to his nephew's physical appearance as black establishes African heritage identity immediately in the moment of commemoration. Thus, in quickly establishing genealogy—from himself, to his brother, to his nephew, to his father—he sets in motion a reflective impulse that leads the reader to link Baldwin's personal genealogy to the timeline of the 1863 Emancipation.

Readers aware of Baldwin's 1963 volume *The Fire Next Time* are often familiar with his earlier collection of essays, *Notes of a Native Son* (1955). In the title essay of *Notes*, Baldwin establishes his father's genealogy, which goes back to enslavement: "No one, including my father, seems to have known exactly how old he was, but his mother had been born during slavery. He was of the first generation of free men. He, along with thousands of other Negroes, came North after 1919 and I was part of that generation which had never seen the landscape of what Negroes call the Old Country."[86] Emancipation history as well as its commemoration is directly relevant to Baldwin's lineage, and his letter's most powerful emphasis is on fatherly Black male love that passes survivalist knowledge from one generation to the next. Baldwin's commemoration message to his nephew is to always remember that he does not have to succumb to the white world's definition of Black people.

After establishing a lineage from his family to Emancipation, Baldwin interprets time. He confesses that "as a man, you gain a strange perspective on time and human pain and effort."[87] It is constructive to isolate this reference, which introduces Baldwin's memory of his brother, because it is the path to his next commemoration point about survival, and what exactly it is that Black people must and have survived. He takes this commemorative opportunity to name America's crime: "This is the crime of which I accuse my country and my countrymen, and for which neither I nor history will ever forgive them, that they have destroyed and are destroying hundreds of thousands of lives and do not know it and do not want to know it."[88]

Baldwin's letter is about memory. He frames this commemoration blessing and its philosophy around cultural memory in terms of instructions to "never forget," "remember that," and multiple references to "survival." Per Baldwin's advice, survival depends on memory and love, and he tells his nephew that the boy was here on earth "to be loved. To be loved, baby, hard, at once, and forever, to strengthen you against the loveless world. . . . If we had not loved each other none of us would have survived."[89] Baldwin then layers survival, love, and lineage by admonishing his nephew that "now you must survive because we love you, and for the sake of your children and your children's children."[90]

The conditions of the period from 1619 to 1863 are apparent in Baldwin's historical survey of the country's desire that Blacks "perish." Baldwin narrates skin-color-based discrimination, brutality, limits on Black mobility and socialization, and white ideas of Black inferiority that have continued to be conditions of Black life in a racially hostile nation whose legal Emancipation document did not completely correct injustices. By the end of the letter, Baldwin draws on hero dynamics and ancestor acknowledgment by reminding his nephew that "in the teeth of the most terrifying odds, [his lineage] achieved an unassailable and monumental dignity."[91] The essay's title, "My Dungeon Shook," comes from an Alabama spiritual titled "Tree of Life" whose refrain is about rights to life, and Baldwin heralds this as a legacy of great poetry in reinforcing cultural memory and immortalization. Baldwin does not mention the Emancipation Proclamation by name but references the centennial measure of "one hundred years of freedom."[92] As commemoration philosophy, Baldwin's model suggests a methodology of personalizing the commemorative moment for the benefit of lineage survival.

Worldview Discourses on Emancipation and Bicentennial Commemoration

In the introduction to *In the Matter of Color: Race and the American Legal Process: The Colonial Period* (1980) A. Leon Higginbotham surveys a 1619 thesis—that it was a "godsend" for the Angolans to be transferred from Spanish enslavement to English indenture.[93] For clarification, however, this chapter's commemoration intervention directs our attention more to the 1660 Virginia Act XXII that makes reference to conditions of African race-based perpetual enslavement, even though the Act's purpose was to define penalties for English servants who ran away. Virginia's 1669 statute concerning the killing of enslaved Africans "indicated that Virginia was prepared to exploit the slave labor force to the maximum degrees possible. Virginians revealed that they were prepared to beat, mutilate, and even kill slaves in order to extract profits from their plantations."[94] Framing commemoration intervention in these terms is sobering in the assessment of defining the legacy and acknowledgment of the 1619–2019 quadricentennial.

Math is essential. Before the thirty-sixth birthday of William Tucker, the first documented Angolan/African child born in the Virginia colony and baptized on January 3, 1624, race-based enslavement had been firmly entrenched in the colony as a threat to the community of Africans, whether bond or free. Calculating and speculating on the interpersonal relationships between enslaved Angolans and other Africans imported to the colony of Virginia with the English and other European enslavers produces diverse scenarios and possibilities of bondage and oppression that white colonists practiced well in advance of the 1660 casual reference to the fact that enslavement was known to be a perpetual condition for a number of Africans—descendants of the 1619 Angolans—in the years ranging from 1619 to 1660. The 2019 commemoration moment in a Black cultural mythology theoretical framework has encouraged the whole society to stop, think, process, and speculate on this past with as much historical detail and probability for the greatest and most authentic remembrance.

David Walker wrote, "Every fourth of July celebration must embitter and inflame the minds of the slaves,"[95] and Frederick Douglass's classic speech[96] interrogating the meaning of the Fourth of July freedom holiday from a Black perspective also captures the extreme agency of the African American worldview toward questionable national holidays. Higginbotham addresses the 1776–1976 Bicentennial as a second major event in the African American cultural memory worldview: "The bicentennial roll of revolutionary heroes and events, then, symbolized one thing to white Americans but quite another to blacks. From a predominantly white perspective, as former President Nixon described it: 'the greatest achievement in the history of man. We are the beneficiaries of that achievement.' But who, until recently, did 'we' describe?"[97] In fact, the Bicentennial of US independence triggered worldview responses about commemoration's meaning for African Americans from historians as well as writers.

Poet Gil Scott-Heron captured the Bicentennial's African American point of view of European-American or white antagonistic antiheroics in the poem "Bicentennial Blues" (1990) with criticism sharp enough to jolt the public into identifying the multiple paradoxes that are connected to the discrepancies between society's view of African Americans either as agents or as objects. To Scott-Heron, "the blues," not the nation, is "celebrating a birthday."[98] The Bicentennial year of 1976 is "A year of hysterical importance / A year of historical importance: ripped-off like donated moments from the past."[99] Hysterical-historical emerges as philosophical doublespeak that licenses the reader to be free in his or her sighs of absurdity that the nation celebrates a history of freedom and independence denied to Blacks in the past, as well as in the present. His additional puns alert readers to the economics of commemoration, as he spells the celebration as "B-U-Y-centennial" and then describes society as being "bludgeoned into / Bicentennial submission / or Bicentennial suspicion."[100] The role of commemoration tourism is apparent in the Point Comfort and 1619 commemoration mission statements. Scott-Heron's philosophy of US national commemoration is one that demands a critical cultural and historical analysis of the nation's popular celebratory claims. Suspicion becomes the key concept that determines the action of approaching commemoration with a methodology of caution, distrust, and skepticism invoked by a survivalist intuition that the idea of mass celebration of a racialized, institutional past policy or condition is absurd and wrong, at least without the proper context of worldview. There is nothing left to do except shift one's methodology once Scott-Heron defines the variables of commemoration as

> partial deification of
> partial accomplishments over
> a partial period of time.
> Half-way justice.
> Half-way liberty.
> Half-way equality.
> It's a half-ass year.[101]

He summarizes that we would be "silly" to "accept anything less than the truth / about this Bicentennial year."[102]

Derrick Bell advances a related commemoration philosophy in his critique of freedom symbols and freedom documents: "American society periodically produces a symbol of redemption in the wake of unspeakable cruelties to its blacks. At the national level, the symbol is usually a document with liberating potential: the Emancipation Proclamation, the post-Civil War Amendments, the Civil Rights Acts of the 1960s and, of course, the decision in *Brown v. Board of Education*."[103] The discourse between Scott-Heron's and

Bell's ideas is connected by the debate over the extent to which the US's heroic, patriotic, and commemoration philosophy is universal enough or remediated enough away from real-time and real-era racialized meanings to make them worthy of adoption, respect, and embrace by African Americans. Bell suggests, "We are witnessing a number of black breakthroughs that resemble the first beam of sunlight of a promising new day—black mayors, the first black Miss America, the first black astronaut's ascent into space, and after many years of effort, a federal bill making Martin Luther King, Jr.'s birthday a national holiday."[104]

In a similar critique, the Scott-Heron-esque common sense of watching how racism, capitalist greed, and cultural amnesia dilute proper commemoration is the point of intervention in Alyce Elliott's school-age instructional book on *King Commemorations: A Collection of Activities* (2009). She introduces the book, admitting, "Every third Monday in January, America commemorates the birthday of Dr. Martin Luther King, Jr. He is the only African American who is honored by a National Holiday. . . . With the passing of time, many people, especially our children, are unaware of the significance of this Holiday."[105] This is an example of what Bell questions when he asks "whether the racial pattern of White symbols and black sacrifice will ever end."[106] The symbol is a national holiday on America's terms that predetermines which types of King discourses and legacy frameworks are suitable for multicultural consumption, rather than for sustaining the worldview of effective Black radical activism. Elliott's intent "is not to focus on what was, but to remember the past to prevent its recurrence. Also to imprint on the hearts of current and future generations, what one person can do when standing for the cause of justice."[107] This basic presentation of an earnest desire to acknowledge the meaning of King's legacy is suitable for school-age children, but Black cultural mythology includes a meta-analysis of enhanced variables of commemoration that incorporate a stylized language of worldview, legacy, and immortalization for stabilizing African American cultural orientations in both the academy and in the public domain.

Bell writes of freedom documents, but national commemorations are events that serve as proxies for documents. Caught up in a fervor of celebrations, citizens and institutions attempt to practice an often uninformed multiculturalism, and then they expect African Americans to be grateful for mere mention. One example of how multicultural practices related to King have gone awry appears in a study of the detriments of color-blind philosophy. Education theorists Jennifer Richardson and Richard J. Nussbaum explain that many of the teachers at one integrated school in which color-blindness was the prevailing policy were hesitant to notice students' self-segregation, actual racial differences in student suspension rates, or, even to incorporate teaching materials that represented the diversity among the student body (Schofield, 201). Furthermore, Schofield reports that race had been so de-emphasized in one classroom in this school that "one white child was surprised to learn from a member of our research team that Martin Luther King, Jr. was African American, not White" (Schofield, 2001, p. 262).[108]

The federal bill for the King holiday was approved in 1983 and went into effect on January 20, 1986, yet its commemoration is questionably inconsequential for many sectors of the US public in which citizens deny the remembrance its proper critical analysis and value-laden reflection. Black cultural mythology attributes that sustain the meaning of ancestor acknowledgment, epic intuitive conduct, hyperheroic impulses, sacrificial inheritance, and more can be primary cultural queries when considering King's legacies. Bell's commemoration philosophy structurally suggests how a national holiday such as the one for Martin Luther King Jr. is prone to be diluted by the de-racialized, color-blind approach. He predicted that

> America can be expected to offer still another freedom symbol to blacks when blacks again become insistent or when political or economic conditions indicate that such an offer will be appropriately beneficial. Blacks will again ignore the likely motivation for such a new freedom document and embrace it enthusiastically, gain from it what they can, and watch as it too . . . is retired to some other chamber.[109]

This is compatible with Scott-Heron's suspicion that African Americans need stronger, more stabilized critical tools for cultural survival to manage the culture's mythological structure, of which commemoration philosophy, in proper worldview, is a part.

These types of robust discourses on commemoration, appearing as gems of philosophy and conceptual methodology, are scattered in a diverse set of multidisciplinary sources, and the framework of Black cultural mythology is emphatic in its pressure for more comprehensive categorization, research, and subdisciplinary valuation of these ideas. Commemoration and remembrance as key concepts of formalized Black cultural mythology practices function in two ways in response to the commemoration moment of 1619. First, they compel a meditation on the intellectual portraits of Africans in 1619. This refines our understanding of this arrival as a European enslavement and Middle Passage legacy nightmare. It clarifies the commemorative moment—and not as some ingratiated story of African indentured servitude or some myth about happy, prosperous Africans in Jamestown. Second, in dutiful survey, it sends us back to the African American intellectual archive to locate sources—King, Baldwin, Bell, Scott-Heron, and certainly others—to learn how the structure of their commemoration may serve as model and methodology to inform general strategies and practices. The topic of sacrificial inheritance is also a priority in these readings, realizing that these historical actors—especially King, who lost his life because of his ideas, and Baldwin, who also experienced great emotional pain in his artistic struggles against inequality—gave up their quality of life and peace in order to serve the race.

This study compels us to view King's ideas again as contemporary, once we update them with twenty-first century cultural concerns. Problem-solving and interventionist idea formation are part of a speculative project that compels us to measure contemporary activist ethics against what was done on our behalf in the past. This is the practical effect of Black cultural mythology as a useful intellectual inquiry featuring how we take advantage of an interactive engagement with our own history and cultural mythology, as we insist on empowering African American commemoration practices. We do this through a paradigm shift away from Eurocentric and American patriotic, self-congratulatory, and culturally diluted tendencies of historical and commemorative acknowledgment and reflection. It emerges from the critical freedom to engage with interdisciplinary and transgenerational knowledge bases that yield dynamic options for advancing narrative agency reinforced by a broad intellectual genealogy and inheritance.

Enslavement Commemoration and Memorialization

There is another aspect of commemoration that goes beyond the shores of the Americas and back to the continent of Africa. In her work on the topic of African slave trade tourism, historian Ana Lucia Araujo studies how in countries such as Ghana, the Gambia, Senegal, and Benin the "heritagization"[105] of enslavement history is the center of a monument-based tourism industry. Her corpus of work features language of "slavery cultural heritage," "roots tourism," "plural memories of slavery," "commodification," and "tangible and intangible heritage" all in contexts of commemorative trends in Africa-based tourism since the 1990s.[111] The shift between Araujo's work on public memory and this study of Black cultural mythology is the latter's interest in how the public domain conceptualizes the value of African-centered agency to advance a practical methodology for demonstrating how memory functions. It functions as postenslavement mythology (beginning again and engraving identity), and it is a conceptualization that values the final product while also requiring an informed consciousness of what came before and what exists afterward.

Araujo's ideas are particularly valuable for their diaspora approaches to cultural memory. Her historical and ethnographic[112] analysis of the Atlantic enslavement trade acknowledges the institutionalization of the tourist industry. Her thesis is "the work of memory conveyed through festivals, monuments, and local museums remembering slavery and the Atlantic slave trade allows recreating, reinventing, and rethinking this painful past."[113] She relates it to concepts of "postmemory"[114] and "as transitional space where this past is relived, re-evaluated, and re-experienced."[115] Black cultural mythology manages reflections of Africana survival and the contemporary reliance on and circulation of practices that help diasporans stabilize mythological structure and cultural identity. This stabilization equips diasporans to return to the African continental sites of memorialization and heritage tourism, which Araujo features, where there is a reconciliation of enslavement history and experience. There is organic agency in starting from *home*—from the home place and regional reality of the diaspora. For Araujo, these sites are stages of reenactment. This is part of the collective cultural memory discourse, but it is a more conceptual *logic* about experience and existence. Her audience and actors are the same African Americans and African Caribbeans from whose experiences a Black cultural mythology conceptualization emerges.

Araujo practices more historical excavation to offer a narrative history of the commemoration of enslavement in Africa, and she highlights landmarks ranging from UNESCO-supported heritage sites to newer trends that demonstrate shifts away from Benin's cultural sense of enslavement history as taboo.[116] In this history, the role of festivals and conferences is strong, ranging from FESTAC 77, Ouidah 92, and the Vodun Festival that have drawn many Africana internationals to Africa for heritage tourism. But this foray into how cultural memory operates on African shores is not the same as an approach centered on what has happened on US and Caribbean shores. Araujo's survey of monuments also includes antiheroes such as the Brazilian enslavement merchant Francisco Felix de Souza, of whom she says, "a visit to a private memorial honoring a perpetrator is rather difficult to sell. African Americans, for example, hardly see in Francisco Felix de Souza and the Afro-Luso Brazilian community enough identity bonds to awaken an actual mutual interest."[117] A critique of antiheroics is also apparent in Africa's diverse monuments in shared commemorative space such as the Memorial of the Great Jubilee of 2000. This is a Catholic monument in Benin dedicated to pioneering European missionary work during the enslavement era. Araujo notes its oddity in "sending the visitors contradictory messages about the country's slave trade port" in Ouidah.[118]

Araujo notes the limited African American agency in some of the West African monuments, most strikingly in the instances when the enslaved are depicted in self-liberation rather than in victimized bondage.[119] However, her narrative documentation of heritage tourism also relates to Black cultural mythology's itemization of the ancestry, immortalization, and sacred ritual remembrance and observation. For example, her mention of Senegal's Organization for the Promotion of Traditional Medicine and its European and diaspora branches features their "Ways of Remembrance and Spiritual Connection" event for diasporan visitors. It is "a nine-day pilgrimage aiming to heal the wounds of slavery and the Atlantic slave trade. The program consists of visiting places related to the Atlantic slave trade and participation in various Vodun ceremonies" in Benin.[120] Beyond the diaspora-based maintenance of mythological structure, immortalization philosophy, and other Black cultural mythology priorities, the sacred participatory tourism that Araujo adds to Africana cultural memory discourses merges theory with travel and pilgrimage. This adds a physical, international origin encounter to mythological structures that have previously relied on ideas, narratives, orientations, and remembrance—not international heritage tourism—to celebrate survival and sustain cultural memory and mythology. Araujo specifically names African Americans and Afro-Caribbeans as the anticipated clients of African heritage tours who will appreciate "an efficient means to mourn their ancestors and to establish real or imagined connections with motherland Africa."[121]

Araujo's corpus of works has sustained the contemporary engagement with enslavement memory in historical anthropology, cultural history, and social history. Her research on the Atlantic enslavement trade in terms of history, memory, and cultural legacy is rich and usable, and is also part of the historiography on African American commemoration. She is best known for her work on the development of African diaspora tourism, but her monograph on *Shadows of the Slave Past: Memory, Heritage, and Slavery*

(2014) defines many of the key questions related to the memorial predicament of African and diasporic regions affected by the Atlantic enslavement trade. In methodology, Araujo challenges us to be centered geographically in our mapping of place and experience, ranging from specific African sites of deportation to sites in the diaspora. Her approach forces the field to be explicit in itemizing the many *sacred* sites of Africa and the diaspora where Africans lived, resisted, worked, and died, often in heroic struggle on both iconic and quotidian levels. In *Shadows of the Slave Past*, Araujo exposes inaccuracies in the Atlantic enslavement history that we have inherited in texts, in art, and in legend. She also presents a sustained comparison between enslavement memorialization in the United States and Brazil, with a persuasive narrative, suggested also by Ngugi wa Thiong'o in *Something Torn and New*, that invokes the need for African diaspora communities to mourn, which is an act of appreciation toward the ancestors and a way of honoring the descendants who survived. It is also an act of reconciliation, renewal, and healing. In terms of heroics, Araujo's comparisons between US and Brazilian experiences with society's tendency to commemorate European heroes as the most important emancipators—Abraham Lincoln and Princess Isabel, respectively—is clarifying. With precision, Araujo narrates African heritage and diaspora heroics that reflect the trajectory and outcomes of the Atlantic enslavement trade.

Black cultural mythology is an adjacent critical enterprise to Araujo's uses of the Atlantic enslavement trade as her primary referent. Mindful of, but not prioritizing, the Atlantic enslavement trade, Black cultural mythology mines survivalist philosophy and aesthetic traditions to suggest a methodology for cultural theory that retrains us to itemize the variables at work in the processes of beginning again and engraving identity on new soil. The objective is to advance liberating and practically effective cognitive and behavioral tools and directives to better sustain the Africana mythological structure.

There is room for many iterations of how cultural memory functions in diaspora communities, and while this volume addresses primarily the African American experience in the United States, it also extends the narrative quite a bit toward Afro-Caribbean perspectives, as it invites additional analysis and research. Future studies also have room to discover the unique and important memorial worldview, additionally, of Africans who were displaced from their home regions as slaves but who were left in a limbo just short of being transferred to the Americas.[122]

Joanne M. Braxton and Maria I. Diedrich's edited collection on *Monuments of the Black Atlantic: Slavery and Memory* (2004) also contributes to the discourse on ritual remembrance through travel. Their ideas are situated between Araujo's work and Black cultural mythology with critical emphasis on survival as well as on the role of writers. They speak of "our determination to survive," noting that

> informal shrines dot our sites of memory: candles, water and other offerings, like broken crockery on an ancestral tomb. And so we mark and tend our graves, for as far back as anyone's memory can reach, sometimes singing a spiritual or repeating a story that was "not meant to be told" in order to strengthen ourselves for the present journey. Like the mythical Sankofa bird, descendants of African slaves living in the wide diaspora created by the transatlantic slave trade are bearers of an "unforgettable strength" that endures and endures, manifesting itself in every aspect of culture. Black writers, artists and musicians in the New World have tested the limits of cultural memory, finding in it the inspiration to "speak the unspeakable."[123]

Survival amid new environmental and sociopolitical odds is a central inquiry that the philosophical framework of Black cultural mythology does not take for granted and seeks to explore empirically and systematically based on worldview analysis. In fact, Black cultural mythology is a primary conceptualization of a *logic* of survival, *first*. Next are concerns for what Braxton and Diedrich call "fragmented, silenced, screaming memories of slavery," as well as the matter of tourism as adjacent discourses to Black cultural mythology.[124] Nigerian Nobel Prize laureate Wole Soyinka has observed Africans' "basic curiosity about black historic reality" being "unsatisfied"[125] and their "elemental curiosity about how they survived." He articulated these sentiments in the 1970s and 1980s, prior to the 1990s surge in heritage tourism.[126] Indeed, the West African monuments and remembrance industry is a natural extension of curiosity and closure, yet from an empowered location that balances out the emotional responses to the histories and memories of the enslavement tragedy with a diasporan confidence born of survival. Like Maya Angelou in *All God's Children Need Traveling Shoes* (1986), the confidence and even ethnocentric identity of the African American expat community is based on pride in surviving, *first*, and then returning. The role of the repentance and apology memorials featured in Araujo's study, as well as in her broader study of diaspora and African modes of enslavement memory, are important to the larger collaborative enterprise of Africana cultural memory studies. Diaspora heritage travel is a powerful tool that helps the cycles of commemoration come full circle, which is an additional commemoration intervention that adds to the reconceptualization of 1619, organizational roles in planning commemorations, and the commemoration philosophies that emerged in response to the past century's heritage moments.

Chapter Three

Harriet Tubman and Aesthetic Memorialization

Chapter 1 established Harriet Tubman's role as a stable African American mythoform of great symbolic value to the intellectual tradition, setting the stage for this chapter's more sustained analysis of her centrality to Black cultural mythology. Molefi Kete Asante addresses Tubman's iconography and the primacy of history in his articulation of heroics of memory: "We are creatures of our history, and the brilliance of any liberation paradigm must be found in that history. When we know, truly know . . . that Tubman was a socialist and a revolutionary nationalist . . . we can analyze contemporary situations more accurately. . . . Our history is one of struggle and victory; this knowledge is necessary as we attempt to reconstruct and mobilize."[1] Black cultural mythology is such a philosophical reconstruction, and Asante's model of revitalizing the legacy of Harriet Tubman by defining her as more than a static textbook heroine is a vital interpretive shift.

Tubman is one of the most recognized survivors of enslavement, and society has responded to the depths of her cognitive survival, epic intuitive conduct, and hyperheroic impulses with a stable level of respect and honor that culminated in 2017 with the announcement that Tubman's image will replace Andrew Jackson's face on one side of the next iteration of the US twenty-dollar bill. The images on US currency have been a longtime reminder of power, privilege, and normalized assumptions about *who* is universally important in American history, yet the groundbreaking transition to having a woman of African descent on the currency does not sequester discourse about Tubman's centrality to Black cultural mythology. The decision to place

Tubman's image on the twenty-dollar bill, which will take effect in a matter of years, brings much satisfaction to progressives and liberals who view the replacement as an acknowledgment of the nation's diversity. However, there is much more to consider regarding Tubman's hero dynamic and the value of her cultural mythology. This chapter frames Tubman as a classical reference point in the Africana intellectual tradition, and the theoretical tool of Black cultural mythology enables a recalibrated itemization of her meaning and value. Black cultural mythology's evolution at the intersection of history and literature determines the sources that this study on Tubman follows in its quest to reveal how cultural memory practices, much of which are reconstructionist critical exercises, enliven historical figures. Tubman honorably and heroically earned the immortalization that is affirmed by Africana and American historical cultural regard. However, a revisionist itemization is required to help properly sustain the vitality of her cultural memory, much of which is presented in a form of aesthetic memorialization, which prioritizes actor, meaning, and symbolism in the mythology-memory continuum of remembrance and storytelling.

Naturally, Tubman's resistance is linked to more classical reference points such as Yaa-Asantewaa and Queen Nzingha (and even Hatshepsut)—African women who used daring and heroic tactics to fight for their people's freedom and who assumed leadership positions such as generals and pharaohs. Both ancient and traditional models have reinforced the chronology of African and diasporic epic survival. Joanne M. Braxton and Maria I. Diedrich narrate Tubman's relevance to their volume on *Monuments of the Black Atlantic: Slavery and Memory* (2004) based on Kate Clifford Larsen's contribution to the conference from which the volume emanated. They describe Tubman's value in terms of a mythology sustained by juvenile fiction that is in dire need of proper placement within historical memory. A Black cultural mythology reading of Tubman enhanced by more mature literary representations offers a biography-based mythology—elevation of the historical actor to epic storytelling—that rescues Tubman from such confinements.

As a philosophical framework that urges society to contextualize the survivalist urgency of the African American lived experiences of engraving a survivalist ethic on US soil, historiography as well as cyclical oral-written-performed-oral narrative signify on Tubman's actual epic, hyperheroic, intuitive, and cognitive-based survivalist behaviors. These are the bases of Tubman's historical and legendary *mythology*. Tubman left us with a comprehensive story of a warrior-based, genius determination to favorably increase the life chances and life experiences of the Africans who were forced to live and regenerate in an oppressive society whose restrictive barriers offered sure death to those who resisted.[2]

Black writers have been the most significant agents who have recycled historical and legendary content in their narratives with benign and innocuous creative embellishment around the root history that encourages readers and society to meditate on and to engage the culture's heroics with more creativity and depth. This conceptual corrective reorients society in its often static treatment of and conceptualization of the sacred, ritualistic, and genius accomplishments that African Americans have achieved consistently under duress. The culture's mythology is useful and effective for the formation of the culture's historical personality and is the root of the culture's memory. It links and modifies our assumptions about folk culture, cultural mythology, and memory. Folk culture addresses a group's shared past, their methods and practices of in-group socialization, worldview and consciousness-construction, and the resulting identity formation. Black cultural mythology shares much with folk culture. Tolagbe Ogunleye suggests that folk culture is "evidence of the ancient African life force and past that Africans forcibly brought to America, maintained through an expressive sense."[3] Reiterating Zora Neale Hurston's description that folk culture is "the boiled-down juice of human living," Ogunleye further paraphrases it as "the art of self-discovery as well as the first creative art of a people, shaping and rationalizing the natural laws they found around them."[4] Most useful is Ogunleye's itemized description of folk culture as representing "a line to a vast, interconnected network of meanings, values, and cognitions" that "contains seeds of wisdom, problem solving, and prophecy" including "strategies they used to resist servitude and flee their captors."[5] Its strength, she suggests, "resides in its power to communicate the social and cultural identities of the eras" because it is "a highly effective medium for teaching children about their legacy, as well as the most effective and earnest means of weaving, even thriving, through life's adversities."[6] The merit of extracting memory practices from the function of the folk tradition is apparent for Black cultural mythology's interest in cyclical and intergenerational communication.

Tubman's biography is stable, and her legacy is secure, but her culturally centered mythology is underdeveloped. To an extent it has been codified in Americanisms and become stagnated, diluted, and stifled. It is one African American legacy that has life and actuality in American youth curricula, yet her legacy experiences an unethical confinement within juvenile storytelling.[7]

The first decade of the twenty-first century witnessed an expanded historiography on Tubman through the publication of several highly credible works that honorably frame Tubman's legacy.⁸ What the contextualization of Black cultural mythology uniquely offers is a treatment of Tubman that goes beyond the descriptive, history-based approach of Catherine Clinton and Jean M. Humez, and it more innovatively and more practically theorizes her in light of myth and memory than the Milton C. Sernett volume. These volumes are exceptional scholarly products for the discipline of history, and their recurring superlative description of Tubman as an "American Hero" suggests a culturally equalizing ownership of Tubman's heroic, often as a reflection of American history's objective of offering balanced, multicultural historical storytelling. Indeed, Tubman's legacy is both American and African American, but she functions in the Africana survivalist philosophy, consciousness, mythological structure, and self-determined worldview in much more dynamic ways than those highlighted in Americanized biographies of her life and accomplishments.

In the twenty-first century, scholars have lamented that society regards Harriet Tubman as a "mythical grandmother leading fugitive slaves to freedom" (Robin Dougherty) who is stuck in the "more palatable," "elementary school version" (Mary Ethridge), that her legacy is not "up-to-date" (Eric Foner), that she is a "familiar legend" without "human dimension" (*Publishers Weekly*), plagued by "empty symbolism" without "full humanity" (Annette Gordon-Reed), "almost forgotten" (David Hubert), and in need of rescue "from the woefully inaccurate, pop-culture, Washington-chopped-down-the-cherry-tree level of scholarship found in elementary school textbooks" (Chris Patsilelis). They continue to lament that she has an unappreciated legacy (John Freeman), is too often the "heroine of children's books and biopics" that lack clarity and lack "richness of detail" (Lev Grossman), and is "more folkloric than analytical" (Catherine Clinton).⁹

Many volumes on Tubman are concerned with accomplishments, but they view her feats in a vacuum less intricately connected to an African American cultural context of sacredness, heroics, rituals of remembrance, and daily iconic value and inspiration (communion with ancestors). One critic offers an appropriate sacred, ritualistic, and ancestrally linking observation that Tubman died in 1913—the same year Rosa Parks was born. This view inadvertently features the cosmological type of spark about which Black cultural mythology is concerned in its practical, applied, and theoretical models for how we should be envisioning legacy, inheritance, and cultural memory. These linkages embody a unified ancestral system of those who are living, those who have passed on, and those who are yet to be born.¹⁰

The honest appraisals of numerous scholars and reviewers capture public sentiment and points of view about Tubman's legacy, which is too often stagnant or stuck in an unimaginative realm. In intervention, Black cultural mythology processes Tubman's biography and identity in narratives in order to reinscribe African agency in her mythological structure. In this culturally centered valuation, the primary mythical directive for Tubman comes from Molefi Kete Asante and Kariamu Welsh who frame her value to myth, noting that she is "the strongest mythical character in African American history" and is a mythoform, or heroic figure whose diligence and accomplishment for African people is central to the culture's heritage of resistance and practical ancestor acknowledgment. Asante and Welsh suggest that every time a mythoform's name is invoked it is a cultural summoning of spirit.[11] Thus, the use of mythoforms regards the sacred and ritual value of invoking the names of legendary African descended agents.

This case study on Harriet Tubman considers many of these treatments of Tubman's legacy including four major critical works since 2003, her recurring image in juvenile literature, and adult or academic literatures. Of the adult biographies, Catherine Clinton's *Harriet Tubman: The Road to Freedom* (2004), Milton C. Sernett's *Harriet Tubman: Myth, Memory, and History* (2007), Jean M. Humez's *Harriet Tubman: The Life and the Life Stories* (2003), and Beverly Lowry's *Harriet Tubman: Imagining a Life* (2007) are the most contemporarily relevant sources on Tubman. Adult audiences consume these biographies and framings of Tubman's life. Scholars and generalists with historical interest in Tubman benefit from these volumes, which provide informed and appropriately speculative narrative chronologies of Tubman's life that are important foundations from which to imaginatively consider multiple dimensions of Tubman's historic prowess, hero dynamics, humanity, and forms of cultural memory. However, the juvenile literature that has been a staple source in framing generations of impressionable core beliefs about Tubman is of particular importance.

There is a need to distinguish between society's treatment of Tubman in storytelling versus in African-centered cultural commemoration. Storytelling is based on historical chronology; on Tubman's role as an African American, American, or gendered heroic icon; and as an example of inclusionary multicultural intervention. Cultural commemoration is based on acknowledging the legacy and effect of Tubman's hero dynamics through a critical itemization of the meaning and implications of Tubman's cultural identity, worldview, and experiences. Tubman's hyperheroic behavior and epic intuitive impulses are part of an intergenerational survivalist philosophy that compels cyclical study and meditation to honor the sacred inheritance of Tubman's legacy. Maintaining Tubman's value as a cultural mythology icon is an active process.

Clinton's biography on Tubman includes an episode that merges historical storytelling and commemoration in narrative on Jubilee. The January 1, 1863 Emancipation is already an overwhelming breathtaking moment, and Emancipation is also another marker of African American "beginning again" fraught with choices identical to those anticipated on the eve of civil rights gains that W. E. B. Du Bois questioned in "Whither Now and Why?"[12] Du Bois questions what freedom will mean; however, in 1863 the answer was a purer African-centered pursuit. Africans who were formerly enslaved were still a distinctly adapting cultural group whose cultural reference points were African based on recent and recalled origins and routes to the US. Even northern and free "adapted" African strivers had carved out a US experience that was based on creative survival and achievement. The difference between the Emancipation and civil rights–era commemoration queries on what freedom should mean is that the former was not based on possibilities of integration and assimilation, including race-mixing. Du Bois describes freedom's traps in terms of the threats, if managed without cultural agency, to reduce traces of heritage and to lighten the race. From a Black cultural mythology perspective, the traces, or rather indicators, of heritage are relatively immutable, and their value and primacy in a culturally oriented life are quantifiable. Ezemenari Obasi, Lisa Flores, and Linda James-Myers help to prove this empirically with their creation of the Worldview Analysis Scale, which is a set of forty-five questions that respondents must answer on a six-point scale to measure Black and white variables of the materialistic universe, spiritual immortality, communalism, indigenous values, tangible realism, knowledge of self, and spiritualism. This tool reliably demonstrates that African Americans perceive the world in a distinct unified worldview and that European Americans do as well.[13] It is safe to suggest that the results of such a survey tool would yield even higher cultural worldview similarities if given during Tubman's era. Similarly, the variables of Black cultural mythology, such as ancestor acknowledgment, mythological structure, historical reenactment of worldview, cognitive survival, immortalization sensibility, and sacrificial inheritance, help to further advance the specificity of Africana cultural memory, which, in spite of variations in African American heritage and legacy practices, are stable, documented, and just under the surface for diaspora populations, and, if latent, they are a resuscitatable cultural identity.

Clinton's commemoration passage is among the most powerful iterations of her volume because it invites readers to celebrate Jubilee with the most important nineteenth-century pioneer of African resistance and heroics. Clinton imagines Tubman at the celebration. Her narrative recalls Frederick Douglass's and Nat Turner's anticipations of freedom, and her narrative's description of the ceremony describes abundant food, music, speakers, hymns, prayer, heroic ballads, and finally the testament and voice of Africans themselves that "few would ever forget."[14] Linking Emancipation with *remembrance* marks a central event of Africana cultural memory that benefits from an elevation to its proper place of cyclical, formal celebration and as an aspect of epic mythological storytelling. In fact, Clinton does the same in a discussion of the "leap" to freedom across Canada's border.[15]

Attentive to processes of commemoration, storytelling, heroics, immortalization, and cultural memory, the variables of Black cultural mythology are useful for measuring the effect and the cultural memory practices of storytelling about epic and legendary Africana figures. The storytelling on Tubman within juvenile literature reveals challenges that intersect with Amos Wilson's evaluations of the hero problematic among youth populations in *The Developmental Psychology of the Black Child*. An average set of juvenile literature storybooks and juvenile-aged DVD cartoons and films on Tubman aimed at first to fourth grade readers but available in school and public primary school-aged book collections and libraries reveals a host of challenges. As a group, they are reluctant to describe Tubman boldly as an African or African American hero. Instead, they forsake an Africana cultural identity for the description of an "American hero," which tends to permit children to categorize Tubman in the American patriotic realm.[16] The narratives generally begin the storytelling with a reference to "slavery," yet without a reference to Tubman's (and other enslaved Africans') African lineage. This is a cultural redirection and a missed opportunity to give agency to the African origins of modern African American identities. Juvenile literature tends to present terms such as "slave," "slavery," and "enslavement" in isolation and does not adequately historicize the phenomenon enough for children to draw culturally and racially informed conclusions that reflect Africana cultural agency, worldview, or critiques of the era's oppression. This becomes problematic especially because the juvenile narratives of books and films treat episodes in Tubman's life that require a youthful distinction between ethics and morality. Too often the outcomes of Tubman's conflicts narrated in juvenile literature are framed as a series of consequences reflecting right and wrong. Students are not equipped with a mature understanding of the enslavement system to process the ethical challenges of enslavement as a legal system that is immoral. In addition, these same challenges appear in narratives that illustrate Africana resistance and bold choices to follow a path of freedom and personhood.

The category of juvenile narratives also presents Tubman's heroics in isolation from other Africana heroics of the era. Even when a Tubman book is part of a historical or biographical series, there is limited emphasis on a collective consciousness to frame African American heroics. This suggests a lack of cultural development and worldview that artist and children's author Faith Ringgold is able to correct and redirect in her children's book *Dinner at Aunt Connie's House* (1993), which includes Tubman among the pantheon of important African American women. This book is a children's narrative adapted from Ringgold's story quilt painting titled "The Dinner Quilt," which depicts a family gathering for a special dinner for which Aunt Connie has embroidered the names of twelve historically important Black women on the placemats.[17]

The key feature that represents a Black cultural mythology innovation is Ringgold's objective to induce a "magical" engagement between children, family, and the ancestors. She explains that the book "is an expression of my belief that art can be more than a picture on the wall—it can envision our history and illustrate proud events in people's lives. And what's more, it can be magical!"[18] From a Black cultural mythology reading, Ringgold's objective that the ancestor acknowledgment, immortalization sensibility, ritual remembrance, aesthetic memorialization, cyclical storytelling, and historical reenactment of worldview embodied by *Dinner at Aunt Connie's House* should be *magical* transitions into a methodology—an important cultural process and outcome of children's literature. The children first encounter the paintings in the attic, but their encounter is based on the fact that the women in the paintings call out and summon the children, who are receptive to learning about culture. Following the sound of a strange noise in the attic, Melody hears a voice say, "Come in, Melody. . . . We would like to talk to you." It is Rosa Parks who is the spokesperson for the group, and she tells the children, "Your aunt Connie created us to tell you the history of our struggle." Their presentation at dinner was to be a secret, and Aunt Connie had hidden them up there with plans to reveal the paintings at dinner.

At dinner, Melody ponders, "only Lonnie and I knew that today's dinner was extra special. It was magical." After hanging the paintings around the dining room wall for the dinner event, something transcendent happens. "Aunt Connie's paintings were no longer hanging on the dining room walls but sitting in the chairs around the table as our dinner guests. Aunt Connie's voice [initially narrating the women's heroics and experiences] faded into the background, and our family disappeared" as each woman shared her experience in her own testimonial voice.[19] In the final conversation between Lonnie and Melody, the protagonists of the book, Melody anticipates future dinners with her own husband and children, saying, "We will have delicious family dinners, and they will be magical just like Aunt Connie's, and our children, Lonnie, will be just like us."[20]

Ringgold's contribution to Black cultural mythology is requisite to finding ways to enable cultural heroic storytelling to be *magical*. The features of a magical engagement are using images, managing communion with the ancestors in an intergenerational arrangement that includes adults and children, presenting the event with intrigue at routine gatherings such as family dinners, and creating a cultural environment of respect and heritage interest that is powerful enough to enable the narratives of the culture's hero dynamics to come to life with creativity and imagination. Though a fictive tale, Ringgold's innocuous embellishments are a culturally reinforcing creativity that sustains cultural mythology and memory. Ringgold is in company with other artists such as Romare Bearden, Jacob Lawrence, and Joseph Holston who depict Tubman and the Underground Railroad. Ringgold's storytelling style is emancipatory, and parents need not fear sharing a book of juvenile literature with their elementary school-aged children that, like African American children's author Glennette Tilley Turner's *An Apple for Harriet Tubman* (2016), has an image by illustrator Susan Keeter showing a bloody, beaten, and tattered-clothes image of Tubman as a child.

The juvenile literature sometimes complies with a child's developmental worldview, but this often means encouraging children to focus on "the moral of the story" that relates less to African American history. This creates confusion about the precise antiheroic force in Tubman's saga, which is the US system of enslavement and its racism. Black cultural mythology variables help to initiate a needed critical shift to address legacy and to deconstruct narratives of African American heroics that are not adequately framed within proper Afrocentric cultural agency. The tendency to describe Tubman as an American hero is pervasive. The juvenile texts do not seek to deconstruct Americanism, but that does not preclude an additional recognition of Tubman as an Africana hero or a contextualization of Tubman within a pantheon of Black cultural mythological figures. She is indeed part of a pantheon of survivors and heroes whose stories and feats require grounding in both individual and collective sacred, ritualistic, ceremonial remembrance.

Clinton offers an interesting passage that exposes the Africanness of the enslaved populations in the South. When Tubman arrives to help organize self-liberated Africans in the Sea Islands and Gullah regions, she realizes how urban she is and her cultural distance from the more African-infused language and mores. She bridges the initial distinction between herself and the more culturally identifiable Africans with humble and communal behavior. Clinton describes the Gullah enslaved as having African parents. Layered with the statistic that there were four million Africans in the South and half a million Africans in the North at Emancipation, this distinctiveness that Tubman notices reiterates that freedom was an achievement of *Africans* in America.

Juvenile literature's tendency to feature symbols, motifs, tropes, and language familiar to children often emerges as a distraction to the cultural integrity and sacred nature of what Tubman accomplished. Turner's book *An Apple for Harriet Tubman* focuses on Tubman's love and desire for shiny red apples. While "working" in the slave master's orchard she sneaks a bite and is caught. The overseer angrily whips her, tears her clothing, and gives her lifetime scars. When she is older and after escape, she plants apple trees in her own yard and shares the fruit with her community. The moral of the story is that in time, a person can grow her own apples instead of stealing from the slave master and getting punished for doing something wrong. The narrative uses words such as "unkind" (moralizes that the slave mistress was not nice); "not fair" (that enslaved Africans did all the work); "favorite job" (as if Tubman's task to pick apples was something fun and enjoyable); "whipped" (as if Tubman is to blame for breaking a rule that ends in corporal punishment); "ran away" (what children do when they do not get their way); and "angry" (as in the slaveholder was angry when Tubman ran away, which suggests she did something wrong). These tales do not adequately present the enslavement system as the antihero (or villain) to firmly draw the lines of justice for children to understand. Doing so would interfere with the American patriotic ideology of good citizenship that is infused in the primary school curriculum. Can we imagine a storybook on "The Sad History of What Citizens of the United States Did to Africans during Enslavement" that is a primer that children encounter before they read a Tubman storybook? In fact, a real patriotic discourse could be framed around the fact that Tubman relocated her family and other Africans to Canada, where, by 1850, half of the Afro-Canadians were American-born yet denied rights as citizens.[21]

The DVD format of *An Apple for Harriet Tubman* shows Tubman, at all ages, smiling a lot and uses background music that is sweet and cheery and not nuanced enough to suggest the danger and doom of what Tubman combatted. Other juvenile texts routinely compare a description of Tubman's home (a shack) with the plantation owner's home (a mansion), permitting children to capture a vision of Tubman's deprivation of what society favors as the ideal "house" or "home." The works use words such as "play," "living with family," "work," "whipped," "punished," "hid," "friendly," "runaway," "homeless," "hated," "wild," "sang songs," "threatened men with guns," "poor," "worked as a cook," and other storytelling phrasings that can get easily convoluted in a child's youthful consciousness, leaving Tubman's story with more holes and uncertainties than with a coherent culturally infused and balanced historic, heroic tale.

From an adult literary commemoration perspective there are several examples that speak differently to Tubman's aesthetic memorialization. May Miller's play "Harriet" from *Negro History in Thirteen Plays* (1935), Laini Mataka's poem on Tubman entitled "freedom's divas should always be luv'd" (1994), and Carolyn Gage's short play, *Harriet Tubman Visits a Therapist* (2011), reflect traditional and innovative options for (re-)presenting Tubman's hero dynamic. This sample tests the critical capacity of Black cultural mythology tools to effectively manage Tubman's hero dynamic. Furthermore, the discourses from the deliberations to put Tubman on the next twenty-dollar bill are also informative in considering the interventions on commemorations of Tubman.

May Miller's 1935 play on Harriet Tubman survives as the standard traditional play on the heroine. Errol Hill gave it new life in his collection *Black Heroes: 7 Plays* (1989). He credits Miller's depiction for its balanced revelation of "some of the personal and emotional issues at stake in becoming a runaway, thus stressing the humanity of the slaves—a factor important to recognize both in the context of the history of those times and for dramatic characters to achieve credibility on the stage."[22] The one-act play dramatizes two plantations' anticipation of Tubman's return and rescue of more enslaved Africans, and Miller uses dramatic circumstance rather than hagiographic praise dialogue to permit characters, even those who oppose Harriet, to bear witness to her hero dynamics, resistance-based cognitive survival, hyperheroic impulses, and epic intuitive conduct. The African community is confident about her prowess. Tubman's brother Henry says, "Ain't no trouble Harriet can't beat," and his girlfriend Catherine calls her "an angel" and "a good woman."[23] When Tubman makes her first appearance on stage, "The men and women fall on their knees and kiss her dress," indicating how they honor and revere her in the real time of the era.[24]

Miller weaves into Tubman's characterization traces of psychological and physiological intuitive heroics when Tubman says, "Ah always knows when thar is danger near me. 'Pears lak mah heart go flutter, flutter, an' they may say, "Peace! Peace! As much as they lak; Ah know its gwine to be war."[25] The text uses biblical references to indicate antiheroics when the matriarch Sabena donates rope to tie up a fellow enslaved man, Sandy, who is trying to capture Tubman. Sabena describes him as one of the "limbs o' Satan," while others call him "Judas o' yo' own people" and "two-faced devil."[26] Miller even constructs the play with a sense of womanist solidarity between Tubman and Catherine, who is heroic in her activism to preempt Sandy's plan to corner Tubman. Tubman says, "An' you ain't thinkin' Ah'd be a-leavin' no smart gal lak you behin'," which suggests Tubman's investment in the next generation of women freedom fighters.[27] This early dramatic vision of Tubman serves as a traditional model, and Black cultural mythology is also attentive to the speculative nature of contemporary works on Tubman.

Octavia Butler's novel *Kindred* (1979), though set in the US Bicentennial year of 1976, summons a high respect for Tubman's survival and instincts. The core fantasy element of *Kindred* is that Butler relies on time travel back to the antebellum era to compel readers to engage in a more holistic meditation on the nation's self-congratulatory commemoration. In Butler's artistic vision, neither a culturally grounded Black woman nor her liberal white husband—armed with the contemporary privileges of being educated, of having professions as creative writers, of being historically aware, and of successfully managing an interracial marriage—have the power and efficacy to expertly navigate the perils of the enslavement era. The novel is a thick description of survivalist philosophy as Dana and Kevin Franklin try to pack a "survival kit" (clothes, books, maps, medicine, knives) to protect themselves when they are drawn into the antebellum world and into the novel's chronicle of lessons and mores that enslaved Africans on the plantation share about their tactical approach to biding their time until freedom. Several passages honor Tubman and humble readers whose contemporary egos compel us to think too highly of our hypothetical ability to survive such a treacherous era of the past. On one of the trips, when Dana's white male enslaving ancestor, Rufus Weylin, summons her back to the past, she packs a book. Dana's literacy and the book's documentation of the abolitionist movement offend Rufus, and she ponders:

> And there was other history that he must not read. Too much of it hadn't happened yet. . . . And there were two important slave children right here in Maryland. The older one, living here in Talbot County, would be called Frederick Douglass after a name change or two. The second, growing up a few miles south of Dorchester County was Harriet Ross, eventually to be Harriet Tubman. Someday, she was going to cost Eastern Shore plantation owners a huge amount of money by guiding three hundred of their runaway slaves to freedom. And farther down in Southampton, Virginia, a man named Nat Turner was biding his time. There were more. I had said I couldn't do anything to change history. Yet, if history could be changed, this book in the hands of a white man—even a sympathetic white man—might be the thing to change it."[28]

Dana's historical reflection in the Bicentennial moment tests her awareness of the past and the freedom at stake if she is too trusting of whites in a way that would betray the heroics of Douglass, Tubman, Turner, and others. In another passage, the legacy of Tubman's heroics emerges to humble Dana's assumptions of intellectual and survivalist superiority enabled by her late twentieth-century privileged existence. After her failed escape attempt, which empowered the plantation owner, Tom Weylin, to revel that "educated nigger don't mean smart nigger, do it?," Dana concedes that "nothing in my education or knowledge of the future had helped me to escape. Yet in a few years an illiterate runaway named Harriet Tubman would make nineteen trips into this country and lead three hundred fugitives to freedom. What had I done wrong?"[29] Butler is an admirer of Tubman's heroism, and this appears in at least one other novel, Butler's *Parable of the Sower* (1993). In this novel, even borrowing Tubman's aesthetic of sometimes disguising herself to look like a man, a Black teenage girl—Lauren Olamina—leads a group of social apocalypse survivors to freedom from southern to northern California.

In the collection *Restoring the Queen* (1993) Laini Mataka presents the poem "freedom's divas should always be luv'd," which she dedicates to Harriet Tubman and the Black psychiatrist Frances Cress Welsing. While the poem is a memorial speculation on Tubman's prowess that restores life and ignites Tubman's feminine aesthetic beyond the often gruff and static images society receives of Tubman, the dedication serves as a link that connects the revolutionary prowess of the past (Tubman) with the present (Welsing). The dedication is praise and encouragement of the continuum of Black women's activism and agency. Welsing is an outstanding social critic of racism and white supremacy based on her expertise in using the tools of psychiatry to study racism as a pathology. Tubman, of course, challenged this pathology through the physical act of self-manumission as well as ensuring the freedom of others.

The free-verse, free-form poem is seven stanzas long, most of which use the repeated refrain, "i like to think" to speculate on, in a Black cultural mythology style of meditation on cultural heroics, what the poet believes Tubman deserved. The poem is about love, and the poet, likely knowing that Tubman's first husband did not run away with her, replaces him with "a big, sudanese-looking war-lord" who is unknown because "history just never got his name."[30] As an intervention on memorialization and on the celebration of Tubman's hyperheroism, Mataka uses poetry to give Tubman a loving companion who laid a "quilted cloud" on the ground for her to collapse upon after her journey. In the poet's imaginings, Tubman's man always prepared a meal and a warm fire to welcome her home. He washed her hair, carried her to bed, and even cried if she returned later than expected.

Mataka captures Tubman's heroics in descriptions such as "bodacious flights" amid "unbelievable weariness" in acknowledgment of the sacrificial inheritance African Americans received from Tubman's freedom efforts. She features the physical toll Tubman's heroic flights took on her body as "aches" and "wounds."[31] The poem gives Tubman a sense of femininity that enlightens a gender-based cultural memory beyond the "general"-like cemented neutral expression that is the trademark look of Tubman. Of course women are generals and warriors, but society's narratives on Tubman rarely assess her womanhood in terms of gender complementarity toward a man or lover. In this revision that depicts Tubman's femininity, the process implies that Mataka meditated on Tubman's identity as a woman, which the poem captures in descriptions of Tubman as "a fragile creature / of living ebony" who "fell into his arms laughing."[32] In fact, in terms of method, there is a line in the poem in which the poet admits, "becuz i love harriet, / i had to speculate this pome."[33] She adds:

> i adore harriet and when it comes
> to being loved by a Blackman
> i like to think she had it like that
> and if she didn't
> *she shouldve!*[34]

The poem's central features are love and speculation, and Mataka offers these as a methodology for managing hero dynamics and cultural memory. The poem reflects historical accomplishment, the physical scars of freedom activity, and spirituality, as Tubman's companion did "spiritual / somersaults / to gain God's attention" on Tubman's behalf.[35] Mataka's reflection on Tubman is that she deserved love and protection from a male companion, in spite of the ways she proved capable of taking care of herself. The poem reenvisions Tubman's image for contemporary audiences in ways that counter the sterility of the trademark images of Tubman. The genre of poetry relies on figurative language and sustaining imagery, and in this sample Mataka reincarnates the memory of Tubman in unique womanist memorialization and speculation that reflect love and gender complementarity. The poem is an ideal companion to the early twenty-first-century biographies on Tubman that reveal more human details such as Tubman's love of laughter, jokes, fun, and dancing and documentation of a committed and enduring second marriage to a younger man.

Mataka's poem, as well as Carolyn Gage's short play *Harriet Tubman Visits a Therapist: A Play in One Act* (1996), are relevant samples of cultural mythology works on Tubman because they both engage in contemporary speculation on Tubman's persona. Like many of the biographers and juvenile literature authors, Gage is not African American. However, she specializes in "non-traditional roles for women" and is attentive to women who have been "erased from history."[36] The play targets preteen and teen audiences and has two African American women characters—Tubman and a therapist in her midtwenties. Writers depict Tubman in cultural memory as a feisty, push-the-envelope character, yet Gage's first presentation of Tubman at the therapist's office describes her body language in defeatist and submissive terms—"She stands waiting for orders, head bowed"—yet the reader learns that Tubman was pretending to be submissive.[37] This is a complicated play to digest because the characterizations do not make sense from an Africana culturally centered perspective, sustained even briefly here by Miller's traditional and Mataka's contemporary depictions that reflect Tubman's positive effect on the culture's collective consciousness. Gage's choice to give the therapist the identity of a "light-skinned African American woman who wears the clothing of a contemporary middle-class therapist" is odd, and it suggests a breach in gender solidarity for freedom. Miller also writes another character (but not a woman) as obstructionist. Sandy is also a "light-skinned" enslaved man who opposes Tubman, but Miller does not give him a sense of agency through character development as Gage does with the therapist. This is also in contrast to Mataka's theme in the poem "freedom's divas," wherein a contemporary Black woman acts in love and in tribute to both Tubman and Welsing to construct a cyclical meditation on a Black hero's well-being.

The Americanization of Tubman that exists in the juvenile literature is exacerbated in Gage's play for teen audiences; from a Black cultural mythology critical perspective, the play does more harm than good. The play has positive narrative elements such as showing Tubman's awareness of other self-emancipation leaders. Gage elevates Tubman's hyperheroics particularly by dramatizing Tubman's reverence for Nat Turner and his revolt. It reveals Tubman's resistance-based cognitive survival by giving Tubman a single-minded voice on freedom and survival in spite of the threat of death. However, positioning another Black woman as an apologist for the evils of enslavement is an antiheroic characterization that is not true historically and is a deconstructive rather than a productive cultural memory characterization in the contemporary era. Discerning Black parents would object to their children reading or experiencing a performance of this play because its black-on-black conflict fails to offer a culturally logical stance that could sustain mythological structure. Given Gage's commitment to empowering women through staged narratives, she inevitably sacrifices a light-skinned African American woman character in favor of empowering Tubman, which is an incomplete and misguided class-based heroic. The effect of *Harriet Tubman Visits a Therapist* as a contemporary speculation on African American hero dynamics is bittersweet because of its convoluted sacrifice of the traumatized African American therapist who behaves, irreconcilably, as an agent of oppression for women like Tubman. Additionally, there is an irreconciled imbalance in costuming. The modern executive suit of the therapist is juxtaposed against Tubman's enslavement era costume and functions as an unresolved difference. While writers have the authority to weave dynamic narratives that can advance or deconstruct historical and invented personas, texts such as Gage's speculation on Tubman envisions an irregular conflict for a hero who is held in such sacred regard in Black cultural mythology and broader Africana cultural memory traditions.

An awareness of Black cultural mythology's critical variables as tools to manage and assess the culture's maintenance of memory practices and hero dynamics illuminates a crisis in perspective and agency, particularly in the case of Tubman. With the impending release of new currency bearing Tubman's image, one can expect that the public will continue to engage with her legacy; Sernett indicates that she is among the most known American and African American achievers. On a different scale of intervention, Tubman is a prime historical candidate for programming and curricula that transmit critical Black cultural mythology conceptual tools to school-age children to enhance their ability to itemize the dimensions of mythology, heroics, survival, and immortalization. They are likely familiar with Tubman's existing heroic persona, but there is much to be gained in the critical shift of engaging with her legacy in a more conceptually enhanced aesthetic memorialization.

Chapter Four

Haiti as Diaspora-Wide Mythology

The philosophy of Black cultural mythology emerges on behalf of Africana freedom in the Western Hemisphere to acknowledge a debt of conceptual gratitude to the iconic Republic of Haiti. Its theorization proceeds with a foundational recentering of the superlative of the Haitian Revolution as the first diaspora-wide mythology. Domestically and internationally, contemporary citizens seem to forget that Haiti was part of a triptych of black internationalism and literary movement activism that linked (1) the US New Negro/Harlem Renaissance movement, (2) Haiti's Indigenisme/Indigenist movement, and (3) the French African and Caribbean Négritude movement. Black cultural mythology is attentive to the commemorative, memorial, symbolic, narrative, social justice, and survivalist relevance of historically documented episodes. These episodes reflect usable models of hyperheroism, epic intuitive conduct, and resistance-based cognitive survival. Collectively, this set of enhanced language of hero dynamics serves as a conceptual lens that prompts the critical reflexivity needed to re/situate the cultural memory of Haiti. Haiti's monumental feats and its ensuing narrative mythological rendering possess cyclical vitality as living history and functional memory. From an internal diaspora-gazing African American cultural lens, Haiti is eternally relevant. Black cultural mythology introduces revitalized contexts for a contemporary assessment of Haiti's value to Africana cultural memory.

This chapter is a study of the effect of the Haitian Revolution and its heroes on Black cultural mythology and the phenomenon's role in Africana cultural memory. By rebuilding the narrative of Haiti's unique commemoration value, predicated on its success as a freedom agency and on its revolutionary ethos, this study draws conclusions that are distinct from the theses of several contemporary works on Haiti's meaning in the realms of political memory and culture as well as in the literary imagination. The distinction reflects an interest in asking Black cultural mythology questions of the memorial and speculative representations found in African American and diaspora literatures on Haiti's history and personas. These questions are based largely on Black cultural mythology variables such as immortalization sensibility, ancestor acknowledgment, sacred observation, ritual remembrance, mythological structure, historical reenactment of worldview, and aesthetic memorialization. The chapter offers a discourse simultaneously about the critical philosophy on Haiti's priority relevance in the timelines and episodes in Africana worldview and epistemology. This chapter also features diaspora literatures and literary criticism on the topic of Haitian heroics, and suggests an extension of Toussaint Louverture's transnational ancestor status in the Afroeuropean diaspora.

Haiti's revolutionary origin is a most unusual historical episode of shared African world heroics. It is a significant source of diaspora freedom mythology, and the early nation's allure pervades Black writing. This chapter's approach to Haiti specifically considers not only the nonfiction narratives of Black cultural mythology but also its application as a literary methodology. In the literary domain, Haiti is the source of a creative, imaginative, yet historically engaged repertoire of writing that, honed over the years, has captured the Haitian Revolution's history, intrigue, symbolism, ethics, and heroics. African American and Caribbean writers have most often utilized the Haitian Revolution as a sociohistorically reflective literary source that often helps to comparatively measure Africana agency, and this compels a Black cultural mythology reading.

The Haitian Revolution is, therefore, a dynamic transregional episode of beginning again and engraving a new revolutionary identity in the Americas. As both a legacy of war and embattlement and as a historical period of majestic personalities forging a national identity as a manifestation of new hemispheric Africanity, the Haitian Revolution demanded hyperheroic and resistance-based cognitive behavior for the sake of cultural, national, and hemispheric survival. A Black cultural mythology reading of Haiti's revolutionary legacy is a narrative not of chance but of intuitive epic conduct that, when narrated through the Black literary imagination, emerges as mythology. Applying the framework of Black cultural mythology to the study of the Haitian Revolution in the literary imagination introduces a rich discourse on the cross-fertilization of diaspora heroics over time, over genre, and even over gender formations.

A Black cultural mythology reading of diasporan literature on the Haitian Revolution is not satisfied with celebrating the bibliography of works on Haiti and its heroes from the revolutionary period. The bibliography is vast, so for the limited and inaugural effort of defining and contextualizing Black cultural mythology, this chapter takes a selective approach to the inclusion of representative texts whose analyses are suitable for introducing several premises of Haiti's value within Black cultural mythology's contemporary structure. The analysis features Haitian-themed works from canonical authors of the African American literary tradition, and contextualizes it among Caribbean works such as Edouard Glissant's *Monsieur Toussaint* (1961) and Derek Walcott's *Haitian Trilogy* (2002), both important because of their inherent commemoration objectives.

The histories, the nonfiction essays, and the fiction genre texts that scholars usually cite as part of the bibliography on the Haitian Revolution and its heroes are diverse. The vision that each author pursues to reflect his or her interest in the Haitian Revolution as a phenomenon varies and reflects the complexity of a thirteen-year war with multiple battles and fronts and contests on an island defined by the enslavement system. The Revolution revealed the competing interests of field hands, house hands, biracial actors of various social status, and at least three European powers, as well as the anxieties and dreams of races/cultures of people in the diaspora who either feared or eagerly anticipated the effect that this island's power struggle would have on their mainland. Literary readers may not have the attention span for the meandering details of the numerous versions of the actual historical event. It takes *mythology*, which is simplified storytelling that narratively utilizes the core factual variables of an event or phenomenon and assumes license to enhance the story's dimensions with benign or innocuous embellishment. This process is about storytelling and transmitting cultural memory, and the narrative benefits from being structured in ways that home in on the philosophical and humanistic complexities presented narratively and symbolically in literature.

In the case of the Haitian Revolution, its actors of African descent are not homogeneous. They switch sides. There is a leadership dimension whose clarity is further exacerbated by notions of hierarchy, ascension, inheritance, not to mention competing philosophies, African-centeredness, strategic militarism, discretion, the challenges of having access to power, and the maintenance of conflicting public-vs.-private personas. There are spiritual and ancestral elements that invigorate the freedom behaviors.

The Haitian Revolution is not only the subject of numerous narratives with symbolic weavings of intrigue and good storytelling, but it is also the first diaspora-wide freedom epic—the first diaspora-wide mythology. There is double (at least) mythological import in the phenomenon that Black writers have recycled the Haitian experience in their texts. Frederick Douglass described Haiti as "the original pioneer emancipator of the nineteenth century."[1] C. L. R. James links the Haitian Revolution to the continuum of Pan-Africanism that led to African independence.[2] Jacob Carruthers describes it as proof that Blacks could "wage modern warfare" and "perfected the art of guerrilla warfare," which immerses the saga of freedom within the narrative trope of military conquest and the patriotism reinforced by the commitment to battle.[3]

These characterizations of Haiti in African diasporic cultural memory are both literary and socio-literary, making them suitable for discourses subsumed under the revisionist interest of Black cultural mythology. The literary focus on applied functionality necessitates that beyond the humanities pursuit of exhausting philosophical questions of the conflict and resolution (or not) addressed in literary engagements of the Haitian Revolution, we fulfill a discourse whose trajectory is compatible with social-science-oriented pursuits. From a Black cultural mythology critical point of view, after we exhaust textual analysis, an additional set of inquiries emerge based on a study of the philosophical basis of writers' intentions when they recycle aspects of the Haitian Revolution in their texts. This perspective is also concerned with the location of society's consciousness about the continuum of the Haitian experience from the era of its inaugural mythology to the present. In media representations, Haiti is merely a land of natural disaster, poverty, and political unrest. Yet Haiti's revolution and subsequent independence are part of a continuous heroic of epic proportions.

Literature has the potential to inspire a reproduction of the models, power, and conviction of freedom behaviors that can be useful in contemporary and future cultural pursuits. The writer's craft affects society's consciousness of the relationship between cultural survival and cosmological factors (worldview, spiritual worldview, cycles of human empowerment, and connectivity) that may be regenerated by recycled heroic-themed literature. Thus methodologically, the literary assumptions regarding the engagement of Black texts on or about aspects of the Haitian Revolution are transcendent, as they engage with and then move beyond the traditional academic pursuit of criticism and move toward the civic and applied responsibilities of reader-response. Through its critical variables, Black cultural mythology encourages society to consider sophisticated cultural and intersectional inquiries after and beyond the act of textual analysis. The corpus of texts on Haitian Revolution themes invokes unique diaspora-wide sensibilities.

Toussaint Louverture is a hero of the Americas whose identity embodies Africa and whose legacy still demands attention and revision from the survey of traditional, recent, and reprinted sources, including "lively" biographies[4] such as Victor Schoelcher's *Vie de Toussaint Louverture* (1982), historical studies such as C. L. R. James's *The Black Jacobins* (1936) and Aimé Césaire's *Toussaint Louverture* ([1961] 2000), and historical dramas such as James's *Toussaint Louverture: A Play in Three Acts* ([1934] 2012) and Edouard Glissant's *Monsieur Toussaint* ([1961] 2005). The latter work of creative fiction supports a philosophy of Black cultural mythology as Glissant's various prefaces from multiple editions offer a vocabulary of heroics that helps characterize the depths and sacredness of legacy objectives in the Black experience in the Americas. Glissant describes his play as a "prophetic vision of the past"[5] and grounds this description in the context of "revolutionary destiny"[6] and the "presentation of a historical datum."[7] He introduces the Haitian revolutionary leaders as founders, initiators, and prophets.[8] Black cultural mythology borrows liberally from the rationale that inspires his treatment of Louverture's legacy. He explains:

> For those whose history has been reduced by others to darkness and despair, the recovery of the near or distant past is imperative. To renew acquaintance with one's history, obscured or obliterated by others, is to relish fully the present, for the experience of the present, stripped of its roots in time, yields only hollow delights. This is a poetic endeavor.
> Struggling with, and in, history is our common lot. Thus, often from opposing sides, the literary work strives to diminish the same basic insecurity of being.[9]

Glissant's treatment of Louverture, introduced with clear philosophical statements addressing the relationship between historical legacy and creative literature, is a model of the depths of cultural consciousness channeled in the legacy work managed by writers with a cultural vision. Glissant's attention to the role of ancestors, whether it is an interpretation of Louverture's "relations with his deceased companions" or the hero's "casual communication with the dead" powerfully suggests a spirit of witnessing and dimensions of firsthand testimony that are foundations of the intergenerational transmission of Black cultural mythology.[10]

The Black cultural mythological tendencies of the literary corpus of texts on the Haitian Revolution are important to explore. They reveal a concern not only for the leadership acumen of Louverture and other leaders but also a concern for cosmology. For example, in *Monsieur Toussaint*, Glissant relies on cosmological and ancestral evaluations of how to judge Louverture's soul. The drama follows Louverture's conscience as he proceeds to his death in an allegorical process of guiding the reader to consider whose point of view is the most culturally legitimate when we seek an authoritative recommendation for how to value the greatest strategist and martyr of the Haitian Revolution. Glissant's text compels readers to view Louverture's ancestor status and his spiritual value along a continuum of African activists and heroes since enslavement—François Mackandal, Dutty Boukman, and Hyacinthe Moyse, the nephew whose execution Toussaint authorized in response to treason.

The literary texts invert the stereotypical and romantic historical motifs of associating and comparing Louverture to Napoleon, in particular, and with wartime hero stories, as a generalist trope. This analysis also calls into question the icons of gender relationships and complementarity that writers derive from the record of the Haitian Revolution. The presidential palace's imitation of French court life is one part of the context, but a review of the role that spousal equality or that love plays in the maintenance of heroics is a consistent topic in the literature. Widows carry on the legacy of their fallen husband-leaders. Daughters also bear the burden, and writers have found ways to imaginatively feature the daughters, the widows, and even the love stories. The framework of Black cultural mythology also reserves an analytical space for antihero dynamics, and manipulative mistresses seem to fall into this category. Glissant presents Toussaint's wife as an alienated, bitter, sorrowful widow. The secondary love story in Langston Hughes's *Emperor of Haiti* (1936) dramatizes relationships between Jean-Jacques Dessalines's generals and his wife as well as the biracial damsel who betrays Dessalines in an example of intraracial hatred. In the play *Genefride* (1935), Helen Webb Harris imagines that Toussaint's daughter (a daughter he never had, in reality) was in love with his executed general, which caused her to betray her father's wishes by planning an ethical, albeit late, intervention to preserve her lover's life (ahistorical, but a healthy speculation that enhances Louverture's hero dynamic all the same). Then there is the imaginary friend and innocent childhood love-story of Ntozake Shange's excerpt from *for colored girls who have considered suicide / when the rainbow is enuf* (1977) when, for the lady in brown, Louverture immortalizes from the shelves of the adult reading section and embodies (or possesses) the young boy who bears his name and his bravado. In *Christophe's Daughters* (1935), May Miller's love story between Henri Christophe's daughter and her traitorous lover is part of narrative antiheroics.

In a Black cultural mythology theorization, the writer functions as an interesting and visionary voice in the way he or she recycles the mythology of the Haitian Revolution. The Haitian Revolution and the strategic narratives on its key leaders, Toussaint Louverture, Jean-Jacques Dessalines, and Henri Christophe, represent the first *diaspora-wide freedom epic* and the first *diaspora-wide mythology* that, consistent with the time-transcending meanings of "epic" and "mythology," survive as part of the continuum of the global Africana historical narrative. In 1857 Rev. James Theo Holly wrote, "This Revolution is one of the noblest, grandest, and most justifiable outbursts against tyrannical oppression that is recorded on the pages of the world's history."[11] David Walker, in his 1829 appeal, wrote, "Hayti (is) the glory of the blacks and the terror of the whites."[12] Carruthers also clarifies that "Haiti was not the first independent Black nation in the western hemisphere (that honor belongs to Palmares established circa 1595 in northern Brazil and destroyed in 1694) but it was the most successful Black revolt against the European colonial system."[13] Michael Dash writes, "Haiti emerges as an inexhaustible symbol designed to satisfy material as well as psychological needs" including "images of mystery, decadence, romance, and adventure" that offered "enduring fascination."[14] He adds, "If the Haitian revolution was America's nightmare, it fulfilled the most passionate dream of Black Americans."[15]

Africana writers value the topic of the Haitian Revolution for many reasons. The Haitian Revolution scared white people/Europeans who were accustomed to dominance and treating African people as objects, not subjects. It was masterfully heroic, and it provided an African-centered romantic impulse for the imagination: a Black republic, a Black kingdom, presidents, courts, romantic ethical conflicts, and what Dash describes as "refinement" and "pageantry."[16] It offers an African-centered aesthetic and cultural hero dynamics, among other things. In the African American literary tradition on Haiti, both Dessalines and Louverture have powerful legacies. Carruthers's volume *The Irritated Genie* is a celebration not of Louverture, but of his successor Dessalines, who removed the stigma of being Black. Carruthers evaluates the African vs. Western interpretation of Dessalines' heroic vs. antiheroic status, respectively, and draws our attention to the literary genre of the speech tradition in order to support his thesis. In Carruthers's vision,

Dessalines reclaimed and immortalized the value of Black skin. The Revolution itself disproved so many stereotypes of black inferiority that it opened up a space for literary visions beyond racial vindication and the traditional bipolar model of race. It gave us heroic icons that made Africans in the Americas part of the larger African world—the diaspora. Carruthers cites the intrigue with the vision of Black leaders in Haiti waging war against Europeans. Without knowing their exact links to Africa, diasporans were in fraternity with Haitians.

The Haitian Revolution gave Africana cultures the first Black superheroes, international heroics with a feat so significant that writing about some aspect of the Haitian Revolution was almost like a rite of passage for early Black writers. William Easton observed in 1893 that

> the Negro alone fails to immortalize his distinguished dead, and leaves to the prejudiced pen of another race, the office, which by a proper conception of duty to posterity, very properly becomes his destiny. What religious pen of the race has written of Benedict the Moor; of the sainted Africans, Monica and Augustine; or sang in stately verse the deeds of the heroic Hatiens; or sought to turn the light of truth on the historic greatness of ancient Ethiope?[17]

Quoted in Carruthers's introduction to *The Irritated Genie*, this late nineteenth-century observation is an additional voice to add to that of Maria W. Stewart, who campaigned for the race's immortalization and also acknowledged the Haitian model. In the contemporary era, Black writers have fulfilled this duty to posterity, and teachers and professors of this literature have a duty, as well, to itemize this mythology as an important conceptual category in knowledge transmitted on cultures of African descent. The Haitian hero dynamic is central to a diasporic conceptualization of tactical freedom, and Haiti as a point of reference is alive and well for Haitians, Caribbean populations, scholars, and those with a high cultural and historical consciousness. Contemporary critical thought and scholarship on the interplay between radical and conservative approaches to structural African independence offers a host of perspectives that would prompt fruitful debate. Awareness of the role of Haiti is significant to training in history, Black psychology, and research methodology. Thus, literature revitalizes the centrality of Haitian cultural memory and mythology as a reference point for Africa as well as for the diaspora.

Black Cultural Mythology in Literary Visions of the Haitian Revolution

Genefride by May Miller and *Christophe's Daughters* by Helen Web Harris appear in *Negro History in Thirteen Plays* (1935), compiled by Willis Richardson and May Miller, and Carter G. Woodson historicized the literary effort with his introduction to the volume that, like Carruthers, extends the meaning of Haiti for at least a generalized Africa. Woodson is ardent in his cultural demand for historically meditative dramas: "There are such few worthwhile plays on the stage that we do not miss much in not keeping abreast with the theatre of today"[18] In contrast, he celebrates that

> the playwrights herein represented have the vision of the Negro in the new day. They have undertaken to dramatize every phase of his life and history. Their conception of this task, we are delighted to note, shows no restriction to any particular period or place. The Negro is presented as a maker of civilization in Africa, a contributor to progress in Europe, and a factor in the development of Greater America.[19]

He considers the book to be "another step of the Negro toward the emancipation of his mind from the slavery of the inferiority complex. The Negro has discovered that he has something to dramatize."[20] It is logical to view Black cultural mythology as an intervention related to Woodson's call for new vision and for cultural-literary work that represents the diaspora or "Greater America." In the preface, May Miller predicts and affirms the license to build narrative mythology, or embellished cyclical storytelling, from history: "The writers have not attempted to reproduce definitive history, but have sought to create the atmosphere of a time past or the portrait of a memorable figure."[21] These are early Black cultural mythology goals that are more fervently manifested in a canon of works whose themes reflect Haitian heroics and cultural iconography.

Haiti appears in the African American literary tradition liberally, though works on Haiti are not routinely a part of the African American literary canon, which could be open to debate or to remedy. *The Norton Anthology of African American Literature* (2004) does not index any references to Haiti or Louverture. There is an entry on Louverture in *The Oxford Companion to African American Literature* (1997). The Schomburg Center's *The Essential Black Literature Guide* references Louverture only in the entry for Ntozake

Shange's *for colored girls*. Fortunately, and as an accolade to one of the most visionary African American literary companions, Gene Andrew Jarrett's *A Companion to African American Literature* (2013) includes not only a dedicated chapter on "The Constitution of Toussaint: Another Origin of African American Literature," by Michael J. Drexler and Ed White, but also nearly a dozen additional broad references to Haiti.

Many canonized authors have made contributions to the diasporan literary tradition on Haiti.[22] This study features representative well-known literatures selected from among the many. The larger category includes Arna Bontemps's novel *Drums at Dusk* (1939); Langston Hughes's play *Emperor of Haiti* (1963); Ralph Ellison's short story "Mister Toussan" (1941); Lorraine Hansberry's unfinished play, "Toussaint," collected in *To Be Young, Gifted, and Black* (1969); Ntozake Shange's choreopoem from *for colored girls who have considered suicide / when the rainbow is enuf* (1975); Edwidge Danticat's short story "A Wall of Fire Rising," from *Krik? Krak!* (1991); and Charles Johnson's epistolary sketch on the Haitian Revolution from the collection *Soulcatcher and Other Stories: Twelve Powerful Tales about Slavery* (2001). For an exhaustive study of the bibliography of literatures on the Haitian Revolution, Philip Kaisary's *The Haitian Revolution in the Literary Imagination: Radical Horizons, Conservative Constraints* (2014) and Marlene Daut's *Tropics of Haiti: Race and the Literary History of the Haitian Revolution in the Atlantic World, 1789 to 1865* (2015) are encyclopedic. However, for this selective reading and analysis of Africana mythological structure in diaspora Haiti literatures, the scale is suitable for a comparative textual analysis based on Black cultural mythology variables, one that is also informed philosophically and historically by sources such as Albert Hunt's *Haiti's Influence on Antebellum America* (1988).

The repertoire of key texts reflecting Haiti's broad impact as Black cultural mythology is worth exploring in this chapter because each author's creative literary vision imparts a practical philosophy on cultural memory. Dramatist, critic, and anthologist Errol Hill compiled *Black Heroes: 7 Plays* (1989) because of a yearning to contribute to a recognition of a Black heroic that Black cultural mythology, as a contemporary framework, embodies:

> In past times social conditions were inimical to the recognition of black heroes whose lives have been largely unheralded and unrecorded. But if such conditions no longer exist, if in fact the leaders of American history and culture are ready to accept Afro-American men and women of renown in the pantheon

of American heroes, then efforts . . . should be made to "right the wrongs of history" by identifying black heroes and ensuring that they are appropriately memorialized for present and future generations. The publishing of this play collection is a step in that direction.[23]

Hill suggests that the gains of the civil rights era "appear to be in abatement."[24] He insists that "the nation as a whole needs to recognize that blacks as well as whites have produced their share of heroes who deserve to be honored for their contribution to the nation and to humanity."[25] Hill is emphatic in the introduction to qualify the imbalance of memorialization of Black performers and exemplars in key social categories (e.g., sport, science, activism, and so forth). In fact, Hill's introduction engages with a noticeable set of cultural memory terminologies such as memorial, honor, inspiration, race pride, recognition, progress, and heroic criteria. Hill's introduction emerges as a treatise on heroics. Yet he frankly acknowledges the antiheroic, that "of course, heroes to one group are villains to another. Heroes are not universally admired because they tend to embody the values and needs of the community that honors them."[26] Hill anthologizes Langston Hughes's play *Emperor of Haiti* as the collection's first chronological entry representing the year 1791. He characterizes Hughes's protagonist, the Haitian leader Jean-Jacques Dessalines, as Caribbean and frames the dilemma in terms of the historical fact that "the United States refused to recognize the first free and independent nation in the Western World—the black republic of Haiti—because it maintained a slave society itself."[27] Hill introduces the play by exposing the United States in a context of antiheroics. Hill's treatise is also remarkable because he theorizes the author's role in participating in the transmission of history:

> While these heroes have their place in history, it should be noted that the playwrights who have chosen to write about them are not historians. They do not feel bound to reproduce historical events as they occurred. Rather it is their aim to organize episodes based on the life of their hero so as to create the social atmosphere in which he lived and against which his actions may be judged. The playwright seeks to portray the essence of his hero's character in terms of a dramatic conflict that, when staged, will capture and hold the interest of an audience. Some license for invention is allowed the writer, provided he does not distort what is known

and felt about the character's virtues and failings. What most playwrights strive to present is the hero's confrontation with himself in light of his goal so that he may become knowledgeable about the effect of his actions, thus enlightening an audience as to their necessity or inevitability. Because the writer wishes his hero to be a sympathetic figure, this act of self-confrontation is apt to be ennobling to the character.[28]

Hill's philosophical description of heroics and its processes balanced between author and historical heroic persona is a profound introduction to the compilation's first play on Haitian Jean-Jacques Dessalines. Even Hill's inclusion of a biographical sketch of the *hero* of the play is a unique Black cultural mythology contribution. His logic suggests that if audiences are aware of the protagonist's public career then the audience may better experience "the sweep of the hero's triumph and agony" or it may help to "bring into sharp focus the distinctive character of the hero in responding to these periods of crisis."[29] What Hill has constructed in this introduction is a guide for methodologically approaching the heroic subject. His instructions reinforce what Black cultural mythology features as "meditation"—that writers construct heroic characters with noninterruptive literary embellishment with a goal of encouraging society to study and reflect on the dilemmas, problem-solving prowess, and conscientiousness of the hero during either victory or defeat. The final outcome of such meditation is to either reinforce the cultural memory and sacred inheritance gained from the hero's epic intuitive impulses and hyperheroic conduct or to become empowered and resourceful from engaging with a cultural crisis and resolution whose model may serve as a tool for cognitive survival for realistic and symbolic cultural needs.

Langston Hughes wrote *Emperor of Haiti* in 1936. After Hughes had made multiple revisions, Hill published his final 1963 version. In 1989, Hill excavated the play, and his method of merging history and dramatic literature in a compilation is one of the best methodologies for transmitting Black cultural mythology in drama. The four-page history on Dessalines and the Haitian Revolution is necessary background for an audience experiencing the historical hero's drama on stage. Hill suggests that Hughes's play is the third African American play on Haiti, after William Edgar Easton's *Dessalines* (1893) and Lesley Pinckney Hill's *Toussaint L'Ouverture: A Dynamic History* (1928). Hill's historical narrative precursor to the play captures the emotional stress of a national leader. First he credits Hughes's play for revealing Dessalines's challenge to rule a Haiti "deeply rent with psychological, racial, and social scars," and then he describes Dessalines's fervor to succeed in his leadership effort to pay homage "as a sacred trust to the hundreds of thousands of lives sacrificed in the fight for liberty."[30] This description corroborates the cosmological and ontological value of Black cultural mythology sensibilities, which is a testament to underscoring the sacredness of African survival in the diaspora.

A prominent and well-known African American work on Haiti is Ralph Ellison's short story "Mister Toussan," originally published in 1941 in the *New Masses*[31] and anthologized in *Flying Home and Other Stories*.[32] Ellison gives Buster and Riley, the child protagonists of "Mister Toussan," robust and self-assured confidence and authority, as they critically measure Africana heroics against the wasteland that whiteness has prepared for them. This could be borne out of what Ellison scholar John F. Calhoun describes as Ellison's early desire "to subvert the world and make reality over" in images that merge the grit and savviness of local, working-class Black men with what the world deemed classical.[33] Calhoun also observes a general Ellisonian interest in "the impact of geography on personality" that suggests at least a measure of the "shapes and guises of black experience from about 1920 to 1945."[34] Calhoun's no-fault description of the story slightly mutes the Black cultural mythology effect of Haiti and Louverture, but his broader description of Ellison's skill in imbuing his short story characters with "conscientious consciousness" is suggestive.[35] Calhoun describes the plot of "Mister Toussan" as two boys "improvis[ing] a tall-tale version of Toussaint Louverture's historical exploits in the manner of call-and-response until the symbolic action of their language emboldens them to plot sneaking after some cherries that white man Rogan has declared off-limits."[36] This is one narrative of the story, but in a Black cultural mythology reading, the structural elements of backstory, cause and effect, rising action, in-text revelation of the source of the story's theme, and historical role-play corroborate an intact and functional mythological structure on which readers pause and then engage in a process of cultural memory, memorialization, and cyclical meditation for intergenerational benefit. This is a story that we tell and retell (or read and reread) because the boyish mirth of adventure and rural rites-of-passage bravado to partake in the neighbor's forbidden fruit are recognizable and nostalgic contexts for the more dominant textual effect of maintaining the culture's heritage hero dynamics through a literary act of cultural memory. Conveying the meaning of Haiti and its leadership through the structure of the short story has been particularly effective for the legacy and acclaim of "Mister Toussan." It has benefited from the short story's brevity, permitting readers to absorb in one sitting the genre's succinct action and language, its masterful command of the senses, and its innocent presentation of how the power of the hero dynamic in the child's imagination tempers the pitfalls of cultural pathos to stabilize the effect of the story's modeling of victorious consciousness.

"Mister Toussan" invokes Black cultural mythology satisfaction because the boys respond to a Black teacher's faithful execution of her duties to impart Black history and achievement to school-age children. This is the intergenerational seed that enables the narrative to become a performance celebrating resistance-based cognitive survival and historical markers of African hyperheroic prowess and epic conduct. The boys perform a historical reenactment of Africana worldview, and their action-filled storytelling is an example of aesthetic memorialization that is more about rites of passage than summoning the bravado to sneak fruit from a neighbor's garden.

Many scholars and writers have a testimony of when they first encountered the epic mythology of the Haitian Revolution and its heroes such as Louverture and Dessalines. In "Mister Toussan," the premise of the story is racial socialization. It begins with the boys acknowledging that a neighbor has surplus produce, but because of racism he will not share with them. The boys have a mature racial consciousness, and they conclude that "white folks ain't got no sense."[37] The background music of Riley's mother singing "I Got Wings" influences the boys to have a conversation about where they would fly if they indeed had wings. They generally decide that a good place to fly is where "colored is free," and Buster decides that his destination will be Africa. The boys debate the myths and stereotypes about Africa. Mythological structure prevails, as they recall that both a Black parent and a Black teacher had conveyed knowledge and empowerment about African resources and kingdoms and about "one of them African guys named Toussan" who had "come from a place named Hayti" and who had "whipped Napoleon!"[38]

As an episode of reenactment of Africana hero dynamics and worldview, the boys' action-packed performance play is a memorable rite of passage for which Ellison even poses a wordplay worldview binary in which he corrects, "not Taar-zan, dummy, Toou-zan!"[39] This signifies on the value of African-derived heroics as a self-defense from European racial and colonial assaults on African world heroic sensibility.

The boys settle on nicknaming Louverture "Sweet Papa Toussan," which localizes his heroic identity on the scale of familiar folk culture. In this embracing the hero into familiarity and cultural intimacy, the boys add

Louverture to the African American pantheon of storytelling best imparted by "old folks like grandma," who, in the boys' judgment, is one of the adults that *can* actually tell a story the right way.⁴⁰ In innocuous embellishment, the boys imagine Sweet Papa Toussan's prowess, not completely knowing how the story ends. Then, they discuss:

> "It sho is a good story," said Riley.
> "Hecks, man, all the stories my teacher tells us is good. She's a good ole teacher—but you know one thing?
> "Naw; what?"
> "Ain't none of them stories in the books! Wonder why?"⁴¹

The boys continue to meditate on how Sweet Papa Toussan fought domination by whites, and they resolve to ask the teacher to tell them more about him. Black teachers, especially since the era of segregated or Black neighborhood schools, have always known that Haitian history has significant meaning for African Americans, the diaspora, and the world. Carruthers's version of this encounter is that

> as long as I can recollect, my first acquaintance with the Haitian Revolution came from my 8th grade Music teacher in Dallas, Texas. I remember her only as Mrs. Bailey. She amazed a class of Black children with what sounded like a fairy story of how black descendants of Africans, Toussaint, Christophe and Dessalines, had destroyed the best armies of Europe and won their independence way back in olden days. I have ever since been inspired to seek out the whole story of this event.⁴²

Another youthful episode, comparable to Ellison's heroic "Mister Toussan," appears in Ntozake Shange's *for colored girls who have considered suicide / when the rainbow is enuf*, in the remembrances of lady in brown, the choreopoem's protagonist. The reflection is a womanist rites of passage memory set in St. Louis in which a girl revolts against the lack of available Black cultural texts that are advanced enough for the natural genius of African American children in her public library's section of youth literature. She has a choice between George Washington Carver and Louverture, and she selects Louverture, fondly befriending this historical character on a first name basis. At eight years old, she takes him as her imaginary friend and her boyfriend. Toussaint, in his full autobiographical dynamics, emerges as her Black male protector against the social elementary school cruelties and the larger 1955 assaults (e.g., integration after *Brown v. Board of Education*, Emmett Till, Rosa Parks' arrest) of whiteness, racial violence, and racism.

Shange's literary vision of Louverture reveals many elements of Black cultural mythology. In her childhood, the lady in brown needed the hero dynamic of Louverture for mental and emotional empowerment, like Buster and Riley, to survive as a Black child in a racist world. The lady in brown benefits from ancestor acknowledgment and the heroic persona's resistance-based cognitive survival, which results in a plan to protect her from the antiheroics of the library's discrimination through its summer reading program. The library baits Black children with a summer reading contest but disqualifies them for reading advanced historical narratives (from the adult reading room) such as the historical account the lady in brown discovered on Louverture. In her reenactment of worldview, she follows the instructions of Louverture who has now emerged as an imaginary friend, when he says, "lets' go to Haiti."[43]

The genre of children's literature has several popular books that manage the childhood impulse to run away, and Shange, too, uses the memory of the lady in brown to frame this seminal childhood memory of escape within African American sociohistorical reality. Yet, by invoking the legacy of the Haitian Revolution and the hero Louverture, Shange practices immortalization sensibility in a womanist way, demonstrating that a male hero also functions to inspire Black women. Through her library book on Louverture, the lady in brown communed with him and summoned his heroic spirit into her space, meditatively.

The lady in brown's memory of running away reveals the Black cultural mythology property of reconciliation and renewal, which in this case is based on ancestral naming. When she runs away, she encounters a boy whose name is, ironically, Toussaint Jones. This important transference of hyperheroics and epic memory through naming implies cultural destiny. The exchange is transformative:

> I am on my way to see
> TOUSSAINT L'OUVERTURE in HAITI
> are ya any kin to him
> he dont take no stuff from no white folks
> & they got a country all they own
> & there aint no slaves'
> That silly ol boy squinted his face all up

> 'looka heah girl
> i am TOUSSAINT JONES
> & i'm right heah lookin at ya
> & i don't take no stuff from white folks
> ya don't see none round heah do ya?
> & he sorta pushed out his chest.⁴⁴

Shange's textual resurrection of Louverture suggests ways ancestors embody and influence the present as aid, inspiration, kinship, and healing. This literary act also models a relationship between young readers and historical texts, reinforcing the importance of allowing children to benefit from the literary canon, reflecting legacy empowerment at the earliest age possible, within the maintenance of mythological structure. Ellison framed his aesthetic memorialization of Louverture in a balanced gender context that showed the cultural influence of a singing mother, a historically aware father, a dedicated and mothering teacher, and an autonomous freedom setting for Black boys to play, role-play, and engage in dialogue that helps to reaffirm the agency of finding their empowered place in the world. Shange's womanist vision demonstrates girlhood intellectual prowess and historical awareness that helped the lady in brown sift through selecting a mate based on the normative assumption that heritage names have cultural and survivalist power. In fact, Ralph Ellison, in his short story "Mister Toussan," never uses the word "Caribbean" or "Haitian" to describe Louverture. He was an African in a place called Haiti. It allowed Black readers to give the heroic personality an iconic potential to embody the average, everyday Black person such as Ntozake Shange's Toussaint Jones from "lady in brown" (St. Louis 1955), who could be Toussaint *Brown*, Toussaint *Smith*, Toussaint *Williams*, Toussaint *Johnson*, or Toussaint *Armstrong*. The name Toussaint is a spiritual invocation of anticipating that any Black child bearing this name will have ancestral guidance of greatness.

Like Ellison's and Shange's literary creations that immortalize aspects of the Haitian Revolution, Haitian American writer Edwidge Danticat also uses a child's persona to illuminate sacred remembrance of the Haitian Revolution. In her collection of short stories, *Krik? Krak!* (1991), Danticat conveys a uniquely Caribbean worldview, and through "A Wall of Fire Rising," Danticat focuses not on Louverture or Dessalines, but on Boukman, the spiritual leader of the fervent first ritual moments of the Haitian Revolution. Danticat empowers the tale with African agency in descriptions of Boukman as not merely an enslaved African but as a "slave revolutionary," which is an important distinction in the art of mythological storytelling.⁴⁵

Wilson C. Chen's analysis of *Krik? Krak!* highlights aspects shared by a Black cultural mythology interest in the Boukman story when he observes, "Danticat's stories construct imaginative discourses of community by invoking, hybridizing, and reworking folklore and legends of the black Atlantic as well as twentieth-century literary retellings of these narratives."[46] Chen cues readers to be aware of the story's "historical complexity and intertextual dimensions [that] call for more elaborate treatment."[47] However, when Chen explores Danticat's "highly significant vernacular literary antecedents, both oral and written," he does so regarding Danticat's interest in gender and the trope of flight.[48] Similar to Black cultural mythology's priorities, he does briefly frame the story's meaning within Haiti's revolutionary mythology. He writes, "At the same time the story engages with Haitian revolutionary folklore, including the types of representation found in Alejo Carpentier's retelling of the Haitian Revolution in his novel, *El reino de este mundo* (1949), translated into English as *The Kingdom of this World*."[49]

The story's setting is a family shack in Haiti. Danticat plants liberal cues of the routines of subsistence existence, ranging from the gourds used for dining, the meager preparations, and spatial descriptions that emphasize smallness, such as Little Guy's "sleep corner" and serving the meal on the floor. However, the family's evening attention on celebrating Little Guy's role playing Boukman in the school play infuses the narrative with a sense of glory and pride that, at least in the beginning of the story, overshadows poverty and the meagerness of the family's existence. Semia Harbawi observes, "Edwidge Danticat's aesthetic endeavors seem to converge towards the performance of a 'rite of memorialisation' that mainly consists in the revisualization of trauma as the pledge of regeneration. Memorialisation acts as a periapt to ward off the devastating effects of literal/psychic death: invisibility and oblivion."[50]

Danticat compels the reader to understand, mostly through invoking the family's sense of confidence, pride, and sacred inheritance, that Boukman is a powerful figure of their cultural memory. Little Guy's mother, Lili, the most essential figure in the story, manages the household's mythological structure—its coherent narrative of the culture's heritage value that powerfully transmits legacy and confidence to the next generation. Lili narrates Little Guy's accolade of being selected to play Boukman, and she fulfills her cultural mythological role as mother in the call and response structure of training Little Guy to understand the grand legacy of Boukman. She encourages Little Guy, saying, "My love, Boukman is the hero of the play," and then she cheers and coaxes his national pride.[51] She says, "Remember who you are . . . a great rebel leader. Remember, it is the revolution."[52] Her coaching of his historical reenactment of a revolutionary worldview, which, culturally and even spiritually, she knows well, layers the mythological reenactments in the story.

Lili is aware of the function of "destiny," as she implores her husband not to place their son's name on a years-long wait list for employment at the sugar mill. Not only will her son perform Boukman but he will also embody Boukman in the highest form of ancestor acknowledgment, immortalization sensibility, sacred observance, and ritual remembrance. She encourages him as if she is a part of the 1791 crowd of enslaved but revolutionary Africans summoning collective consciousness and the resolve to be free. She announces, "He is Boukman."[53] Then she rhetorically challenges her son, asking, "What is the only thing on your mind now, Boukman?"[54] The role-play that produces the answer demonstrates, very much like it did for Ellison's Buster and Riley, a powerful African-centered performance of memory of the culture's epic intuitive and hyperheroic dynamics:

> "Freedom!" Shouted the boy, as he quickly slipped into his role.
> "Louder!" Urged Lili.
> "Freedom is on my mind!" Yelled the boy.[55]

Lili holds her breath in reverence and anticipation as Little Guy, "like the last burst of lighting out of a clearing sky," performs the speech for his father, and the narrative conveys the majesty of this humble reenactment:[56]

> It was obvious that this was a speech written by a European man, who gave to the slave revolutionary Boukman the kind of European phrasing that might have sent the real Boukman turning in his grave. However, the speech made Lili and Guy stand on the tips of their toes from great pride. As their applause thundered in the small space of their shack that night, they felt as though for a moment they had been given the rare pleasure of hearing the voice of one of the forefathers of Haitian independence in the forced baritone of their only child. The experience left them both with a strange feeling that they could not explain. It left the hair on the back of their necks standing on end. It left them feeling much more love than they ever knew they could add to their feeling for this son.[57]

Remembrance is spiritual, physical, intergenerational, ancestral, and renewing. In Danticat's Haitian vision, love of family is infused with love of heritage and heroics, and this prose moment of Black cultural mythology is one of the most consistent examples that fulfills Amos N. Wilson's description of and emphasis on the function of cultural mythology within the realm of the Black family. After the performance and reflection, as meditation on heroics is a central feature of Black cultural mythology, Lili says, "Long live Boukman and long live my boy."[58]

However, Danticat's "A Wall of Fire Rising" employs Black cultural mythology in a more tragic signification than the other well-known examples of Ellison and Shange. Danticat seems to borrow or at least share with Ellison's "Mister Toussan" an interest in the trope of flight and the protagonists' desire and bravado to partake in metaphorically forbidden fruit. For Buster and Riley, the forbidden fruit is their white neighbors' surplus apples and cherries, which he refuses to share. The boys' reflections on flight represent a desire to reach a place where Black people are free. In "A Wall of Fire Rising," the father, Guy, has a sustained obsession with flight, symbolized by the locked up hot air balloon possessed by the Arab Haitians who own the community's sugar mill, which does not provide full employment to Guy and many other heads of household seeking work. Danticat's bold and emotionally effective comparison between the memory of the oppression, or *antiheroics*, against which the Haitians revolted, and Guy's contemporary oppression as an unemployed provider, overwhelms the reader with tragedy, as Little Guy spontaneously and ritualistically performs his Boukman speech as a eulogy for his father, who, like Boukman, seemed also to proclaim, *"we shall all let out one piercing cry that we may either live freely or we should die."*[59] Legacy kinship and filial piety converge in the story's conclusion, and Chen's reading of Danticat's prose for the brilliantly sustained implications of flight offers a transcendent note of hope as he highlights "African diasporic cosmology" to suggest that Guy's death was actually a flight home to be among the ancestors.[60]

Charles Johnson's contribution to the African American literary tradition's valuation of the Haitian Revolution appears in *Soulcatcher and Other Stories: Twelve Powerful Tales about Slavery* (1998), which has a sardonic epistolary tale called "A Report from St. Domingue." Johnson takes a unique approach to signifying on the meaning of the Haitian Revolution by permitting the reader to infer meaning from gazing upon a confidential government correspondence from Theobald Wedgwood, a fictionalized consul, who writes in reportage to his boss, President Thomas Jefferson, to share his impressions of an 1804 post-Revolution diplomatic visit to Haiti to meet with Toussaint Louverture. Johnson is well known for his satire, and this epistolary tale requires multiple readings to discern the meaning and implications of the white supremacist Jedi-style racial trickery that saturates the narrative and challenges the reader's comparative sociohistorical filter. Johnson's literary choice to expose the private and confessional observations, which a diplomatic subordinate reveals to his superior, mimics government and pundit voices of contemporary politics who cannot help but reveal their prejudices.

The official document and its backstage prejudicial nuances both reveal tactical racism and the dysfunctional illogic of using one's power to discriminate against *equals*. This is indeed Johnson's thesis on Haiti, its revolution, its leadership, and US and European prejudicial diplomacy—that Haiti's revolution was legitimate, and in diplomacy, Haiti was an equal nation, whose equality Thomas Jefferson and others rejected and then attempted to subjugate. However, in "A Report from St. Domingue" even a subordinate consul is literally *unable* to narrate Haiti's and its leadership's inferiority.

The genre of the epistolary form, or letter writing, is so imbued with the expectation of honesty, in spite of bias or sway, that the letter's report becomes a primary archival document that cannot deny Haiti's accolade, Louverture's brilliance, and Dessalines's patriotic tactical effectiveness (even in his choice of Voodoo methods, which, though a religion, the letter derides). In addition, on every page Wedgwood admits that the US strategized to undermine Haiti's sovereignty, primarily because of racism. As one of the more recent African American literary significations on cultural mythology related to Haiti, Johnson implores a double marionette socio-literary device. This is seen when a puppet character (Jefferson as an agent of US racism) controls another puppet character (Wedgwood); because neither is an honest puppeteer, the performance easily reveals its flaws. In this case, the flaws are the diplomatic and racial biases stacked against Haiti. From a Black cultural mythology critical lens, Johnson uses the antihero (Wedgwood as an agent of Jefferson and the United States) to articulate Louverture's and Haiti's hero dynamics through the epistolary narrative and historical reenactment of worldview. Wedgwood could not control the natural impulses of human instinct and observation and force a narrative of inferiority on Haiti and its leaders. In fact, the "Report" becomes a counterarchival literary document that challenges Jefferson's *Notes on the State of Virginia* when Wedgwood writes:

Clearly, as you state, the white race is blessed with greater beauty and in America is destined—as if by divine decree—to be the black man's master, to guide him as the parent does the child, and surely this is for the Negro's own good, lest he, in a state of freedom, fall deeper into savagery. No, none of these matters do I question as I revisit your *Notes*. But I have begun to wonder since our arrival at Le Cap, and after such close contact with Negros such as Jacques Dessalines (during their Revolution he cried to the other slaves, "Those who wish to die free, rally round me now," which is hardly different than our own Patrick Henry's "Give me Liberty or give me death"), if perhaps the lower standards and performance you so precisely observed in the Virginia slaves are not innate, after all.[61]

Johnson's collection *Soulcatcher* was the literary companion to the PBS film series and historical volume *Africans in America*, and Johnson shares anecdotes that align his early revisionist poring over the historical archive with a similar survey of US history in preparation for the creativity that became *Soulcatcher*. He proceeds philosophically, and creates his compelling stories as clever, African-centered, agency-driven narratives that explore the often muted and incomplete worldview of African American experience in transmitted histories. For Johnson, this survey "unveiled the fascinating and often ambiguous anecdotes, ironies, back-stories, and paradoxes that inevitably arise when human beings for centuries live within an execrable social arrangement they know is unjust and fragile and ultimately doomed."[62] To prepare for this literary exploration of the role of Haiti in African American history, Johnson paid close attention to "marvelous grist for the mill of fiction" in the form of "the racist alarm Thomas Jefferson felt over Toussaint L'Ouverture's victory in Haiti."[63] Johnson's literary gift is his vision and craft in managing cultural heroics.

Explicating these well-known examples of Haitian heroics in the African American literary tradition demonstrates how the language and terminologies of Black cultural mythology are useful tools for itemizing the value and function of cultural hero dynamics. In a more elaborate study, there would be room to explicate other models such as Arna Bontemps's *Drums at Dusk* (1939) and diasporan works such as the Cuban Alejo Carpentier's *The Kingdom of This World* (1949, first translated into English in 1957), C. L. R. James's *Black Jacobins* (1938), and Derek Walcott's *The Haitian Trilogy: Plays* (2002).

Walcott's collection offers a multilayered narrative method through the presentation of a three-play epic telling of "the story of his native West Indies as a four-hundred-year cycle of war, conquest, and rebellion."[64] The second play in the trilogy, *Drums and Colours*, addresses the "the slave revolt against French rule in Saint Domingue" and was "commissioned for the first and only West Indian Federation, with emblematic images from Caribbean History."[65] Like Glissant's *Monsieur Toussaint*, created with commemoration in mind, Walcott's *Trilogy* reflects his understanding of the Haitian Revolution as an "upheaval, a necessary rejection of the debasement endured under a civilized empire, that achieved independence. The revolution is as central to the play as it is to the history of the island," and the framework of Black cultural mythology extends its centrality to the worldview of African American experience, as well.[66]

Expanding the Ancestor Status of Transnational Louverture

Louverture is a revered ancestor, and his effect in this frame of memory is a regional phenomenon for the Western Hemisphere whose historical experiences intersect with enslavement. A methodology that applies the framework of Black cultural mythology, layered with models of literary memorialization and social memorial practice, supports a hypothesis that Toussaint Louverture has the capacity to be an icon of shared heroics for European-born, immigrant, and transnational African and Caribbean populations, as well as for African and diaspora visitors to Europe (France), based on the fact that Louverture's grave is in France and is a site of pilgrimage. The image is clear in Glissant's play *Monsieur Toussaint*, which places a reflective and dying Louverture in a cell at Chateau de Joux in the Jura Mountains in France from where he communes with and debates his legacy with ghosts of his past. History confirms that Napoleon's army kidnapped and forced Louverture into exile from Haiti; that his remains lay in an unmarked location at Fort de Joux; and that contemporary Haitians make pilgrimages to the Fort's obscure location in order to pay their respects.

In 2004, for the bicentennial celebration of Haitian independence, actors performed Glissant's play on location at Fort de Joux. This performance—affirmed through a type of ancestral communicative practice—reiterates how Louverture's memorialization has sacred site value for the Haitian nation and on European soil, literally through his grave site. Such contexts of history, literary vision, ritual, memory, sacred sites, and ancestor acknowledgment are features of the critical philosophy of Black cultural mythology, and they present a discursive opportunity to consider the sacredness of Louverture's legacy on European land. The concept of diaspora concedes that sites where people of African descent have created culturally significant communities expand the map of the African world, and this is no less true for monumental sacred sites such as the grave of Louverture. It is vital to African global legacy awareness to reiterate Louverture's iconic status and meaning to the broad diaspora. Louverture's revolutionary activism was on behalf of African people displaced to the Caribbean and to the Americas. His leadership role and the Haitian Revolution, itself, inspired a conceptual and reciprocal fraternity with Africans on multiple coasts where their continuity and worldview were affected by European enslavement, colonialism, and imperialism. This extends Louverture's value to legacy-minded Afroeuropean populations who learn about him and honor him based on the historical memory and cultural memory of his capture and exile to France. This adds a dimension of shared legacy and continuum to a global sense of collective heroics. Neither artificial nor imagined, Louverture's activity, exile, death, and memory constitute a legitimate Pan-African, cross-cultural, and transatlantic hero dynamic.

Carruthers globalizes Louverture's activism, noting, "Let's be clear, Toussaint espoused the ideology of world revolution in his day," and he is part of a multinational group of revolutionaries who "were waging war against an international power structure that oppressed mankind in general."[67] History records the leadership differences between Toussaint and Dessalines in a familiar, debatable binary similar to those between Booker T. Washington and W. E. B. Du Bois and Malcolm X and Martin Luther King Jr., and other ideological differences about freedom. Critics anticipate that the Revolution presents valuable lessons in sociopolitical realities as well. In *The Irritated Genie* (1985), Carruthers linked the Haitian Revolution to his observations on apartheid South Africa, noting that "leaders in the more recently successful and still continuing armed struggles of Southern Africa apparently have ignored the Haitian Revolution."[68] He further globalizes the potential of Haiti's historical model, suggesting that Ghanaian independence in 1957 "tended to obscure the Haitian Revolution."[69] These observations are interesting and pose the challenge for us to further explore Carruthers's data and to update the contemporary and ongoing way Haitian history serves as a revolutionary primer. Carruthers provides an extended explanation:

The leaders of the more recently successful and still continuing armed struggles in Southern Africa apparently have ignored the Haitian Revolution. These revolutionary Blacks seem to be more inspired by the Russian, Chinese, Vietnamese and Cuban revolutions than the one truly successful Black revolution in modern history. They apparently never quoted Dessalines, although they have found much inspiration in the words of Marx, Lenin, Mao Tse Tung, Ho Chi Min[h] and Fidel Castro. They do not preach "death to the whites," rather they speak of expelling the imperialists. They do not vow "Conquer or Die," rather they fight to force the colonial power to negotiate. The do not execute the white assassins of the Black race, rather they ask many whites to stay and help rebuild their country. . . . The European settlers who were the exploiter and assassins in Kenya, Zambia, and even Zimbabwe, have not been executed or even indicted. To the contrary, many are living in those same African territories as respectable and affluent citizens or honored guests.[70]

Carruthers's fiery, though generalized, comparison instigates for us to naturally mine the Haitian Revolution for its tactics that can be inspiring and replicated in subsequent contests of African and diaspora combat and confrontation. The heroes Jean-Jacques Dessalines and Toussaint Louverture had opposing tactical preferences, which also appears in the literary treatments. Carruthers's thesis is that Dessalines's tactics of European exclusion from postrevolutionary structures were more logical for Haiti's long-term freedom than Louverture's diplomatic tactics of negotiation, forgiveness, and European collaborative restoration of the country, particularly the diplomatic trickery that is responsible for Louverture's capture, imprisonment at Fort de Joux, and his death.

In considering Carruthers's contention, there are multidirectional conversations. In journalist Marjorie Valbrun's article, "Mandela and the Black Diaspora" (2013), she synthesizes the heroics and cultural memory of Nelson Mandela and the Haitian Revolution:

Mandela personified the bravery of my Haitian ancestors. Like them, he clung unapologetically to the notion that self-determination was a birthright, not a right bestowed or denied by self-appointed ruler-occupiers. Mandela made tangible the native history I was taught to be proud of, but to which I couldn't always relate. He was the living embodiment of the long dead heroes of the Haitian Revolution. He also kept Martin and Malcolm alive for me, despite their assassinations a few years before I arrived to my adopted country as a little girl.[71]

The Revolution influenced media content and reportage on at least three continents whose enslavement societies or economic interests, or both, necessitated blow-by-blow news accounts of this thirteen-year war, waged from August 21, 1791 to January 1, 1804. Colonial and European newspapers transmitted full accounts of the Revolution's progress and implications for France, Spain, and Britain's economic and political interests. Literate economic classes of not only Europe but also of the Americas consumed the news and information. In addition, the news became part of the folk narrative and orally and clandestinely recounted current events transmitted by free, enslaved, illegally educated or noneducated, and nonliterate masses in the Caribbean, the United States, and South, Central, and Latin America. The record of the Haitian Revolution is part of the foreign policy archive of many European and American governments. It is evident why writers (including filmmakers) and artists from diverse cultural backgrounds have acknowledged the epic mythology potential of the Haitian Revolution as source material for their creativity.

There are barriers to cultural memory involving the Haitian Revolution. Some scholars observe a level of contemporary obscurity of information and literature about the Haitian Revolution and its freedom mythology—and this is the silence and anonymity to which the critical framework of Black cultural mythology responds by highlighting Black writers' tendencies to recycle cultural heroics. Carruthers cites a "general historical conspiracy to relegate the event to the dim shadows of insignificance."[72] He adds that "the leaders and masses of revolutionary Africa know little or nothing about that overwhelming victory of a group of African people over the most advanced armies of Europe in the late 18th and early 19th century."[73] Dash describes this as whites using Toussaint's courage and martyrdom in narratives that used a "rhetorical strategy designed to keep Haiti at a distance," similar to sanitizing Black heroics to fit white objectives.[74] Dash characterizes the Haiti-America relationship over the years as affected by the "logic of American expansionism and the attendant demonizing of Haiti."[75] Carruthers also suggests that the revolution caused whites to modify their approach to Black elites. In favoring Dessalines over Louverture, he writes, "Outstanding Blacks like Toussaint were held up like models. Whites well knew the difference between a Toussaint and a Dessalines. The European tried to defame and expunge the Great Liberator Dessalines from history."[76]

Fort de Joux is a sacred African space and a monument (though the French did not intend it to be) of shared ancestral value. This site is a key example of international Africana heroics. It is a historical legacy and memorial continuum that enriches Africana diaspora history and heritage in a geography that, though European, many people of African descent now call home. This exploration of Haitian hero dynamics merely scratches the surface, but seeks to challenge us to consider whose point of view is the most culturally legitimate when we seek an authoritative recommendation for how to value an Africana strategist and martyr in the mythological structure of the Haitian Revolution and its legacy.

At Fort de Joux, on August 29, 1954, the French government placed a stone cross memorial at the foot of the fort (this was initiated by the Haitian ambassador to France, Léon Thébaud). In Paris, on the wall of the Panthéon, there is a memorial inscription placed in 1998 that reads "Combattant de la liberté; artisan d l'abolition de l'esclavage, héros hatien mort déporté au Fort-de-Joux 1803" (Fighter for liberty, strategist of the abolition of enslavement, Haitian hero died in exile [or deportation] at Fort-de-Joux 1803). These two memorials suggest an apology for the persecution of Louverture, and they are sites of Afroeuropean *sacred space*. No one can contest Europe as a site of home and heritage to the generations of its citizens of African descent from many different nations, islands, territories, and départements; when there is a *sacred* space of African culture, this enhances one's affirmation of "home" in the diaspora. This is not as a vindication, but reflects what happens when a culture matures in its new environment as it remembers its ancestors (however it is that the ancestor came to "reside" eternally in this new space).[77]

Guy Antoine is the creator of the Haitian website "windowsonhaiti.com," and in his statement of purpose, he describes Haitians as having "an identity deeply rooted in spirituality and in collective remembrances." He is Haitian American, naturalized, and he made the pilgrimage to Fort de Joux, alongside the Haitians who live in Europe, and this models a confraternity that represents not only Haitian sensibilities but also Haitian Afroeuropean sensibilities (linked as well to Caribbean Afroeuropean sensibilities, and inevitably shared Afroeuropean sensibilities). Thus, the implications of cultural memory, commemoration, sacred remembrance, immortalization sensibility, and mythological structure bloom in the multitudinous contexts of Haitian cultural mythology. Haiti as the first diaspora-wide mythological epic evolves in continuous globalized heroics and memory, which reinforces Haiti's central epic value in the African diaspora worldview from which Black cultural mythology emanates and brokers an expanding intellectual tradition.

In conclusion, Black cultural mythology aims to expand our effectiveness in balancing tradition and innovation in intellectual, genealogical, historical, and creative phenomena. Black cultural mythology pauses on Haiti's value as the first diaspora-wide epic mythology, but there are numerous intriguing paradigm shifts signified by Haiti's superlative processes.

Chapter Five

Richard Wright's Navigation of the Antihero

The fiction and nonfiction of African American writers, including Richard Wright, reveal latent idea formation on what we now describe as Black cultural mythology. As a heretofore barely categorized contribution to African American diasporic worldviews concerned with *beginning again* and engraving identity on new soil, the corpus of mythological thought should be reexamined for mining its tradition beyond the mere folkloric and updating this new awareness as a contribution to the African American literary canon. Black cultural mythology is attentive to the formation and maintenance of elements of an Africana heroic and survivalist mythology that relates to intergenerational heritage practices and icon transmission. African American writers' art and analyses inform a narrative of legacy that draws from both history and the creative imagination to define and interpret heroic and *antiheroic* characters and events. Examining Richard Wright's novel *Native Son*, and related criticism aligned with the priorities of the framework of Black cultural mythology, reveals extended dimensions of Wright's contribution to the African American literary canon in areas of heroics, antiheroics, folk culture, and myth.

What Black cultural mythology offers as the antihero dynamic is equivalent to the strategy of vilification that Molefi Kete Asante identifies in his early work as a pioneering theorist on African American myth, *Rhetoric of Black Revolution* (1969). Vilification

> is the agitator's use of language to degrade an opponent's person, actions, or ideas. When the agitator speaks of former

vice-president Humphrey as a "political chameleon," or former president Johnson as a "buffoon," he is engaging in vilification [which is] always concerned with using caustic or bitter language against one person. The person vilified is usually well-known to the audience; indeed, it is the dynamic of the strategy that the audience can identify the person vilified as a leader of the opposition. Thus, vilification is almost always directed toward a conspicuous leader of the opposition rather than toward an unknown personality.[1]

By calling out the name of the antihero, the agitator presents the audience with an opportunity for catharsis. Asante used the term "anti-hero" within a general discussion of Black mythology and mythmaking as early as 1969. In later work, he defines this with more precision, framing it as a matter of Black leadership on the matter of cultural autonomy that permits African Americans "to imagine a culture of resistance as well as a reconstructive culture."[2]

The emphasis in African American memory practices on valuing the culture and legacy of resistance emerges as a key determinant for which Black achievers and leaders are given mythological status. African American writers do not routinely use their art forms to support the mythology of Black achievers (e.g., Clarence Thomas or Condoleezza Rice) whose legacy of leadership serves the American-centered and Eurocentric status quo rather than a platform for pro-Black cultural resistance. So, the discourse of antiheroics reflects the culture's collective judgment and interrogation of any persons or institutions (Black, white, or other) whose behaviors are perceived to be in opposition to Black self-determination and prosperity. In the models from the exemplars, Asante addresses antiheroics in his reversal of Christopher Columbus's mythology, and Maria W. Stewart decries internal and external behaviors that reduce the culture's capacity to immortalize itself through achievement. David Walker, whose *Appeal* (1829) emerges in chapter 7's Black cultural mythology literary history as a seminal work on the mythological worldview in the literary tradition, directs the community to divest itself from the antiheroics of Africans whose loyalty to whites or unwillingness to educate themselves is betrayal, and to reject white trickery aimed at keeping Africans in bondage through religion and emigration schemes. Wright's contribution to the discourse of antiheroics is part of this broad tradition, with a philosophical fluidity about realism, inevitability, and regenerative cultural goals that are enhanced by a critical Black cultural mythology reading.

A Black cultural mythology reading of *Native Son* models an updated critical approach to the novel that draws on the best of literary scholarship related to the novel's heroics, myth, mythology, folklore, and psychology. Wright describes Bigger Thomas as "dispossessed," "disinherited," and as having a "cultural hunger," but a Black cultural mythology reading measures Bigger against a positive standard of African American *inheritance* and *possession* whose depths are deciphered through the framework.[3] Of course, this is revisionist and is a polemic to Wright's vision that "the civilization that gave birth to Bigger contained no spiritual sustenance, had created no culture which could hold his allegiance and faith, had sensitized him and had left him stranded, a free agent to roam the streets of our cities, a hot and whirling vortex of undisciplined and unchannelized impulses."[4] In fact, regarding Bigger Thomas, whether literally or symbolically, his version of *antiheroics* responds to this description of the depths of his void, in comparison to how African Americans as agents and as literary characters tend to labor toward an objective to create a heroic self.

The concepts of the hero, folk, folk culture, folklore, and myth as they appear in *Native Son* are informed by Wright's personal critique of *Native Son*, the philosophy of folklore that appears throughout his nonfiction writings, and a handful of critical texts on a variety of his complete works that address the folk tradition and myth. Folk narratives are valuable to younger generations because of the intergenerational transmission of the culture's strengths, wit, mores, accolades, and protection. Readers wonder about Bigger's models of legacy, and relying on an answer derived from a historical-biographical approach to literary analysis, Wright's confession about his childhood is informative: "I lived the first seventeen years of my life in the South without so much as hearing of or seeing one act of rebellion from *any* Negro, save the Bigger Thomases."[5] This implies that the Biggers of Wright's experience are types of folk heroes as well as folk casualties, and the question pivots on whether or not they have violent endings for the greater good. Bigger No. 1 challenged others and "took his way, right or wrong."[6] Bigger No. 2 duped exploiting whites for the food, shelter, and clothing he needed to survive. Bigger No. 3 defied whites by taking free services, such as seats at the movies without paying. Bigger No. 4 defied southern customs and taboos, but the cost was his sanity. Finally, Bigger No. 5 confrontationally sat in white sections of the streetcar without paying. Wright based his character on Bigger "types" that he encountered through his early life. And Bigger is uniquely complex in a Black cultural mythology reading because he is a heroic antihero, this time in the sense that his prowess is remarkable and effective for his goals but is in opposition to ethical norms. In the theorization of Black cultural mythology there is room for a period of antiheroics—as the figure resists oppression and finds his or her way through dislocation or dysfunction—on the path to eventually attaining a final heroic destiny. The five Biggers are fearless in the face of life and death, while the character Bigger is fearless in death rather than in life.

Wright provides exclusive commentary on his interpretation of the African American folk tradition, including myth, in "Blueprint for Negro Writing," and his analysis also indicates directions for what has emerged as Black cultural mythology. Wright suggests that "in the absence of fixed and nourishing forms of culture, the Negro has a folklore which embodies the memories and hopes of his struggle for freedom."[7] But he asks, "How many John Henrys have lived and died on the lips of these black people? How many mythical heroes in embryo have been allowed to perish for lack of husbanding by alert intelligence?"[8] Wright's interpretation of folklore also shows a similar conceptualization of the African American need to engrave identity and begin again on American soil, when he observes that in folklore "are those vital beginnings of a recognition that mark the emergence of a new culture [African American] in the shell of the old [African]."[9] He also compares African American existence to "a tree which must live or perish in whatever soil it finds itself."[10]

Wright's "Blueprint" offers guidance for writers, in particular, and theorists, in general. His remarks powerfully relate to the folk tradition and Black cultural mythology. For him, writers and theorists "must have in their consciousness the foreshortened picture of the *whole*, nourishing culture from which they were torn in Africa, and of the long, complex (and for the most part, unconscious) struggle to regain in some form and under alien conditions of life a *whole* culture again"[11] (emphasis in original). Even in his photographic history *Twelve Million Black Voices*, Wright organizes photographs and a narrative of Black experience that is mythological in its rough images of endurance and survival:

> We black folk, our history and our present being, are a mirror of the manifold experiences of America. What we want, what we represent, what we endure is what America *is*. If we black folk perish, America will perish. If America has forgotten her past, then let her look into the mirror of our consciousness and she will see the *living* past living in the present, for our memories go back, through our black folk of today, through the recollections

of our black parents, and through the tales of slavery told by
our black grandparents, to the time when none of us, black or
white, lived in this fertile land.[12]

Wright's concern with memory, the living past, recollection, tales, and a
homeland beyond America's shores relates to "a need to resist annihilation"[13]
and is aligned with the features of Black cultural mythology. Yoshinobu
Hakutani and Robert L. Tener in the afterword to Wright's posthumous
collection, *HAIKU: This Other World* (1998), observe, "Wright's exploration
of the Ashanti convinced him that the defense of African culture meant
renewal of Africans' faith in themselves. He realized for the first time that
African culture was buttressed by universal human values—such as awe of
nature, family kinship and love, faith in religion, and a sense of honor."[14]

Wright is consistent in featuring the African American's African roots
in his analyses, despite occasional sarcasm about his personal regard for
roots. Ironically, and even with a bit of complexity, in *White Man Listen!*
(1964) Wright introduces his work with a disclaimer that he is a "rootless
man" who does not "hanker after . . . as many emotional attachments,
sustaining roots, or idealistic allegiances as most people," even though his
cultural analyses document these within the population.[15] Nonetheless, in
his writings on the blues, he does emphasize the role of heritage and folk
consciousness in leaving a record of Black achievement on American soil.
First in speculation, then in confirmation, Wright humorously handles
this task in the foreword to Paul Oliver's *The Meaning of the Blues* (1963).
Imagining a 1623 planter's logic as he rationalizes the oppression of Africans,
Wright muses about the planter's expectation that history and posterity will
not record his oppressive deeds. The planter says to himself, "I'm free to
buy them [Africans] and work them on my tobacco plantation without
incurring the wrath of God. Moreover, these odd black creatures will die
early in our harsh climate and will leave no record behind of any possible
sufferings that they might undergo."[16] Wright then writes of how the record
of the blues inevitably "deluded" the planter:

> They left a vivid record of their sufferings and longing in those
> astounding religious songs known as the spirituals, and their
> descendants, freed and cast upon their own in an alien culture,
> created the blues, a form of exuberantly melancholy folk songs
> that has circled the globe. . . . How was that possible? I stated

above that the possibility of those shackled, transplanted blacks ever leaving behind a record of their feelings about their experiences in the New World ran smack against historical odds.[17]

Wright's intention in addressing heritage, heroics, myth, and the folk tradition is to interrogate the meaning of African American life in the United States. In the literary criticism of Wright's work, however, scholars have a wide array of approaches to these topics of folk traditions, hero dynamics, heritage practices, legacy tools, and ancestor acknowledgment and how they compare to the conceptualization of Black cultural mythology.

Robert Butler's introductory essay to *Native Son: The Emergence of a New Black Hero* (1991) directly addresses the theme of heroics, particularly the waves of reception and reinterpretation of *Native Son*. Regarding treatments of folkloric elements, he gives honorable mention to Blyden Jackson's 1969 biographical essay that credits the novel for capturing southern cultural elements despite Wright's migration from the South. In addition, Butler's analysis of Houston Baker's *Long Black Song: Essays in Black American Literature and Culture* (1972) is highly relevant to the idea of Black cultural mythology. He observes, "Baker draws revealing parallels between Bigger Thomas and trickster heroes like Brer Rabbit, bad-man heroes like Stackolee, and revolutionary figures like Nat Turner."[18]

Michel Fabre's treatment of Wright's use of myth is based on the short story, "The Man Who Lived Underground," from *Eight Men* (1938). He does not offer an extended orientation to myth, but his observations on the hero are poignant:

> Without stretching the structure of the narrative, we can easily construe the underground adventure of Wright's hero as an existential parable, but also as a quasi-mythological quest that uses certain techniques such as are found in myths or folk narratives. We find obstacles to overcome, a "sesame" or magical instrument, a guarded treasure, infractions and punishments, adverse destiny and protective divinity, going beyond the human condition and the fall that occurs after such hubris. . . . Whether the story is studied as a detective story, myth, fantasy, or history of the creation of human values . . . [it] presents us with the same humanist message that says that man acquires his identity from other men.[19]

Fabre's interest in mythology is based on the story's structural and plot proximities to the tale of Robinson Crusoe.

C. James Trotman's edited collection on *Richard Wright: Myths and Realities* (1988) features a discussion of myth primarily in his introduction that confirms that the study is not about myths, per se, but about "fresh responses" to Wright's work.[20] In particular, Trotman writes, "The title for this volume of symposium essays directs attention to the aesthetic complexity inherent in Wright's narratives. The *myths* and *realities* are conceptual instruments for speaking both generally and specifically about Wright's narrative constructs and human passions."[21]

Eugene Miller in *Voice of a Native Son* (1990) examines myth with a bit more depth, relating it first to Wright's "own personal share of the Afro-American artist's concern with naming his own terrain."[22] Miller suggests that Wright participated in a tradition inherited from nineteenth-century writers for whom "in writing of the American experience in a new environment, he had to use in his surface narrative the images of a thing considered diminished, ugly, by those not of that environment or experience" and that he had to find ways "to forge a link between that level and myth."[23] Miller's early attention in the text is to Wright's "folkloric transformulations" in several short stories, in *Pagan Spain*, in *Twelve Million Black Voices*, and in *Native Son*. With respect to *Pagan Spain*, Miller examines Wright's engagement of white folkloric folk motifs. Referencing *Twelve Million Voices*, Miller emphasizes the "folk religious behavior and psychology" that seem to characterize the emotional escalations between Bigger and Mary.[24] His analysis of the mythic elements in Wright's fiction climaxes with an association between mythology and Voodoo. He writes, "The mythology that blooms in this section of *Native Son* is that of voodoo, and it is virtually present in the religious form that Wright knew . . . the phenomenon of possession."[25] Miller analyzes symbolism and the function of the loas of Haitian Voodoo that are possibly at work in Bigger's "trancelike possession" that enables him to silence Mary and destroy the evidence of his crime.[26] Miller's New Criticism analysis of *Native Son* extends the novel's intuitive cosmology, suggesting that "Wright was undoubtedly no more aware of the mythic voodoo dimension he was giving this section of *Native Son* than he was of the source in his own experiences of the emotion-laden images of the black male in the white woman's bedroom and the disapproving white mother."[27] Miller invokes a psychoanalytical interpretation of the novel's compatibility with African-Caribbean religious mythology.

This overview of the extent to which the topics of folk traditions, heroics, and myth have been applied to studies of *Native Son* reiterates the unique possibilities of analysis within the framework of Black cultural mythology and poses larger possibilities for the collective, cross-disciplinary approaches to the subfield of African cultural memory studies. Yet Wright's literature is appealing as a model of and critique of revolutionary violence as it relates to revolutionary or revolt-based heroics as well as to antiheroics. Wright's personal, youthful watchfulness for "rebellion" also informs a Black cultural mythology reading of *Native Son* that charts the evolution of the character Bigger Thomas from its Black male folkloric archetypes[28] and considers Bigger's antiheroic revolutionary violence against historical models of praised Black male revolt that also used a revolutionary violence. This comparison permits an engaging philosophical contribution to Black cultural mythology because the literature inspires a discussion of the heroic productivity of violence measured against the traditions of Black nationalist revolt, from the enslavement era to the present.

The memory of heroics enacted through necessary struggle (which can have an inherent element of violence even as self-defense) is a tricky matter in cultural memory studies, as seen in the 2018 national crisis about Confederate monuments juxtaposed against public memorials to enslavement revolt leaders such as Nat Turner and Gabriel Prosser. Black cultural mythology's attributes of hyperheroic impulses, epic intuitive conduct, hero dynamics, and sacrificial inheritance are rarely combined in a discussion of the antihero. However, when we itemize survival, people of African descent, ranging from Prosser and Turner to the fictionalized Bigger Thomas, are responding to identical types of oppression. Responding to oppression is honorable, yet the choice of response (group revolt vs. homicide) compels society to make a judgment concerning the nature of heroics/antiheroics. The fictive symbolism inherent in the predicaments and choices of Wright's protagonist is what links factual and hyperbolic responses to oppression. Critics sustain a discourse about this, even though it is not linked directly to Black cultural mythology's itemization of antiheroics. For example, John Reilly suggests that "violence is a personal necessity for the oppressed. When life in society consists of humiliation, one's only rescue is through rebellion,"[29] which aligns Bigger's motivation with the revolt heroes of the Black American past (Gabriel Prosser in Virginia in 1800, Denmark Vesey in South Carolina in 1822, and Nat Turner in Virginia in 1831).

Houston Baker's analyses of Wright's use of the African American folkloric and heroic traditions are foundational observations that help illuminate *Native Son*'s suitability for a contemporary Black cultural mythology reading:

Black folklore includes countless examples of strong black men giving "a faint, wry, bitter smile" or the final, destructive thrust to the revered symbols of white America, and Bigger Thomas's act is simply a continuation of this heritage. . . . Since black Americans were kept illiterate by the laws of the land during much of their history, they could not challenge the general American view of the black man in poetry or prose. And when black writers did take pen in hand, polemical demands (the need to castigate slavery and caste in America) and the bare formal requirements of their craft exerted pressures that relegated the true folk heritage to a somewhat minor role. This does not mean that the folk heritage was forgotten; . . . But Richard Wright's *Native Son* was the first black novel that captured its full scope and dimension.[30]

Baker reflects on the inheritance of resistance, linking nineteenth-century African American nationalists and revolt leaders to Bigger Thomas. He specifies that "the voices of David Walker, Nat Turner, Frederick Douglass, Martin Delaney, and a disheveled group of black forced laborers . . . resound in Bigger's words."[31] Baker addresses the hero in Wright's novel: "Wright's theme and his hero were drawn from the folk history to which he was the heir," and "Wright successfully translated the values of an oral tradition into written form."[32] Baker's discussion of "heirs" adds much to the discourse now categorized as Black cultural mythology, as it reiterates aspects of ancestor acknowledgment and the historical reenactment of worldview. While Baker confirms Wright's contributions to the legacy of named and unnamed heroic activity of Black folk, he also identifies the complexities of Wright's interpretation of his artistic creation: "The author did not miss the mark in his attempt to create an appropriate representative of black folk culture, but his interpretation of his own paradigmatic creation is simply too narrow."[33] This observation lends additional support to the legitimacy of applying a Black cultural mythology analysis to *Native Son*, including asserting that Bigger is a complex antihero, whose choices, though symbolic, must be deciphered by the culture in its willingness to transmit best practices of survival.

Similar to the nationalist positions of nineteenth-century revolt leaders, the defense offered by Bigger's white attorney, Boris Max, of Bigger suggests that African Americans are at war with the US's systems of oppression, which condones self-defensive violence. However, Bigger's violence continues to be abstractly motivated, misunderstood, and often difficult to assess as a historically modeled example of Black revolt. It is a revolt that is self-destructive, rather than wholly inspiring. Max's defense gives credibility to a level of Bigger's spirit of revolt that, at first, sounds similar to the heroes of the past. He says, "Every sunrise and sunset make him guilty of subversive actions. Every movement of his body is an unconscious protest. Every desire, every dream, no matter how intimate or personal, is a plot or a conspiracy. Every hope is a plan for insurrection."[34] This description equates Bigger's spirit of revolt with his forefathers, yet he fulfills his revolt in a mode of antithetical prowess.

In one interpretation, Bigger's death is not a productive, meaningful, heroic death, but a useless death that brings little hope to those who remain.[35] Thus, Bigger's death is even more antiheroic because his memory does not inspire, and he is not catapulted by death into ancestor status. This synthesis of literary analysis and African cultural worldview beliefs supports the updated canonical treatment of *Native Son* within the framework of Black cultural mythology.[36] The trend has been to decry the victimization apparent in *Native Son*, but a Black cultural mythology reading of *Native Son* offers, instead, a lamentation that historical models failed to function as inspiration and ancestral protection for the character.

Fiction can inspire practical discourse about a culture's legacy of resistance, and Wright's commentary about Bigger being a Black nationalist is informative here. To Wright, "He was an American because he was a native son; but he was a Negro nationalist in a vague sense because he was not allowed to live as an American. . . . his nationalist complex was for me a concept through which I could grasp more of the total meaning of his life than I could in any other way. . . . Yet, Bigger was not nationalist enough to feel the need of religion or the folk culture of his own people."[37] With this view of his literary creation, Wright links Bigger to a version of antiheroics similar to the distinction that David Walker draws in his *Appeal* between African people who express a unified consciousness of achievement and those whose selfishness or indiscretions stand in the way. These are comparative articulations of antiheroics. When Wright speaks of this tradition of Black nationalism, of which activists and philosophers such as David Walker and exemplar Maria W. Stewart are a part, he gives license for critics to measure Bigger's life variables against a historical continuum that can reveal African American culture's close proximity to and departure from the cultural maintenance of religion and rebellion.[38] Bigger rejects religion, while most of the models of revolt use religion to advance their passion for freedom. Bigger's predicament and behaviors reflect a *loss*. Enslaved and free, and also striving, Africans in America had the tools in earlier periods—the drive, the self-determination, forms of spirituality, and even "articulate verbal expressions"—to productively fight oppression, yet in the next century the Biggers of the United States were arguably less able to find a productive orientation to these tools.[39]

The criteria for Black nationalism reflects a variation of self-determination, having an African-centered image of God or spiritual base, economic determination, separation from whites, an economic development program, harsher critiques of the race's nonliberating behaviors, and a willingness to die for the freedom of the future. Identifying Bigger as an antihero can be based on him as a *Black nationalist antihero* or as a *Black antinationalist hero* because his life reflects a manipulation of most of the variables of Black nationalism. He is antireligion and devoid of spirituality. Wright places him in a "No Man's Land."[40] He is dissociated from the folk and from his family, and Wright shares that he had to "show what oppression has done to Bigger's relationships with his own people, how it had split him off from them."[41] Economically, he throws money away with Bessie's dead body and is not interested in working the fairly decent job as a chauffeur (many of the Black nationalists or freedom fighters, including Toussaint Louverture and Gabriel Prosser, were coachmen, which gave them mobility and status that enabled their liberation agenda). He is hard on the race—willing to kill a kinsman (Bessie) for not following through with his plan for escape—yet this particular act of violence is non-heroic, compared to more conventional survivalist heroics such as Harriet Tubman who was known to threaten potential deserters who could jeopardize the group's safety by putting a gun to their heads.

Bigger is willing to die for the feeling of aliveness that the act of murder produces, yet it is a bad death—individualistic and needlessly self-sacrificing. The death does not benefit the future liberation of the community. Additionally, Bigger does not possess verbal skills of self-defense and persuasion. He "did not offer in his life any articulate verbal explanations," which handicapped his ability to summon the sustaining myths of the culture and participation in the oratory and utterances that Asante describes as an essential communion with the culture's mythologies.[42] Mythological structure ensures that African Americans encounter their legacy, often through storytelling, speeches, and historical literatures, during their early life cycle.[43] Wright suggests that Bigger revolted because "he had become estranged from the religion and the folk culture of his race," but historical figures of Black cultural mythology revolted because of the opposite spiritual location—they were enmeshed with the experiences of spirituality and of commitment to their race.[44] These perspectives reinforce the complexities of interpreting Bigger as *antiheroic*.

Bigger's nonfunctional death (or bad death if interpreted on the assumption that antiheroic is also antiancestral) also directs our attention to the legacy consciousness of the many versions of Bigger Thomas that Wright discerns in his view of the folk. The act of meditating on diaspora histories to learn tools of cultural survival presumes that we engage in temporal comparisons between oppressive conditions of the past, subsequent eras, and the present. The contemporary era has the greatest benefit and flexibility to access versions of freedom, literacy, mobility, technology, resources, capital, and media that are tools of resourcefulness, yet Wright notes a "lack of inner organization" that suggests dysfunction in both the psychology and historical grounding of the character.[45]

The creative characterization of Bigger Thomas as irredeemably depraved is antiheroic on these terms, alone, and is a prompt for readers to consider that for a Bigger Thomas to exist, there may be a deficit in the ways immortalization, hyperheroics, and epic intuitive conduct were maintained in Bigger's development, which is symbolic for actual Black populations who share Bigger's predicament. We do not neglect *Native Son* because of its overwhelming sense of victimization. Instead, there is an embrace of Wright's plot innovation and of the model characterized by a Bigger Thomas because, conceptually, it encourages readers to assess the antihero's distance from the ideal, cognitively resistant worldview that can locate and utilize legacy tools that inspire and model Black cultural mythology attributes such as reconciliation and renewal. This implies a deliberateness in the norms of cultural transmissions of myth, mythology, and memory, especially in the transmission of culturally relevant models of challenge that end in triumph. The feat of prevailing through types of cultural rites of passage is a process for ensuring that future generations locate from within a confidence in their abilities to achieve survival on the scale of the ancestors. This was the problematic that faced Dana in Octavia Butler's *Kindred*. She believed that her 1976 modernity reflected individual survival skills, yet she had fewer skills than the enslaved Africans in the early nineteenth century who were companions in bondage. The goal is to acquire a guiding sense of knowledge of *what* the ancestors have endured and survived and *how* contemporary generations can duplicate the past's successful responses or temperaments.

There are a series of textual episodes in which Bigger's thoughts and behaviors indicate Black cultural mythology concerns, framed in terms of inheritance, a desire for the cultural logic and support of the home place, and a desire for greater self-esteem. These are variables associated with Amos Wilson's description of mythological structure as well as the priorities of the exemplars who modeled a range of possibilities for immortalization and for having an active relationship with stabilizing cultural mythology. Shortly after killing Bessie, Bigger reflects, "If only someone had gone before and lived or suffered or died—made it so that it could be understood."[46] Bigger desires to "walk and be at home, in which it would be easy to tell what to do and what not to do."[47] He expressed a similar wish for "a new pride" or a "vast configuration of images and symbols whose magic and power could lift him up and make him live so intensely that the dread of being black and unequal would be forgotten."[48] In the novel's legal scenes, in Max's defense of Bigger, he describes Bigger's crime as "one of the darkest crimes in our memory."[49] This passage relates memory and *infamy*, which is an even more complex aspect of antiheroic mythological memory, suggesting that the mythology (in this case maintained in imaginative fiction) has the capacity to not only commemorate but also to *warn* against what not to do.

Bigger's antiheroics reflect pride and hubris regarding his most notorious crime, as he lamented how the act of murder "had created a new world for himself." He was anxious about his ability to maintain his infamy and evasive prowess, and "he did not want it said that he had done all the things he had done and then had got caught for stealing a 3-cent newspaper."[50] During the hunt for Bigger, "Several hundred Negroes resembling Bigger Thomas were rounded up . . . for investigation."[51] The power of "resemblance" in Black cultural mythology is usually favorable (e.g., to resemble a proud ancestor, to look like Malcolm, Martin, or another hero is usually a good thing). Related to infamy, reputation is also central to positive mythology. While no legendary figure is perfect, the acts and deeds of one's life, usually linked to liberation and self-determination, are the cores of heroism, even though some heroic figures reach their heights after prevailing through a period of transformation from a period of folly to one of honor. Bigger began as "mean and bad, but sane" and "sullen and contrary," but through a Black cultural mythology lens, we can predict that orientations to cultural mythology and memory have a strong enough force to renew a healthier sense of survival beyond moments of the antiheroic.[52]

Bigger's antiheroism is a liability to members of his community. In his blind quest for survival, he is willing to kill other Black community members such as Ellen and her husband, who resided in the apartment building with the "For Rent" sign. He says, "I would've had to kill 'em both if she saw me." Bigger expresses a unique antiancestral wish, which is too radical to be described in existential terms as a mere wish to have never been born. In an African cosmological sense, the ancestry is made up of the living, the deceased, and the unborn. Heroes acknowledge the hand of fate as a vision of guidance or blessing. Ironically, in the opening pages of the novel's third book, "Fate," Bigger "looked wistfully upon the dark face of ancient waters upon which some spirit had breathed and created him . . . feeling that he wanted to sink back into those waters and rest eternally."[53] He desires to return to the unborn cycle of the ancestry, which is a peculiar request. He does not desire to cease to exist, but he seeks peace in that abstract, former state of rest. This is a sort of cowardice or refusal to live well toward leaving a legacy of good deeds. However, in another sense, it could be Bigger's acknowledgment that his life force is not strong enough to survive among the living.[54]

In Black cultural mythology, sacred observation, ritual remembrance, and respect for sacrificial inheritance are priorities in how the culture regards death and memorial. The life cycles that we remember are retained and recycled in oral and written traditions because the death transitions represent the culmination of sacrifice on behalf of others. At life's end, one's deeds should be honorable and worthy of remembrance. In *Native Son*, white society seeks to define the meaning of Bigger's death. This lack of agency to control the symbolic meaning of one's death is another characteristic of antiheroics, this time associated with the White community. In corroboration of this, "They were determined to make his death mean more than a mere punishment. . . . they were going to use his death as a bloody symbol of fear to wave before the eyes of the black world . . . a helpless spectacle of sport for others."[55]

Inevitably, Wright's attempt to show the horrors of American racism was successful, but each generation's distance from *Native Son*'s literary heyday and from America's social and legal landscape of Jim Crowism demands an innovative reading that verifies the timelessness of Wright's novel. The answer to *why* Bigger fell to such depths is as easy to understand as are the cycles of inequality and oppression in the United States that sadden and prompt us to activism when we face contemporary conditions of oppression that foster the deaths of Trayvon Martin, Michael Brown, or Sandra Bland. Approaching an analysis through the lens of Black cultural mythology permits us to use a literary character to stress a point about the need for historical role models, culturally based education, and active intellectual engagement of the legacy of men and women who *engraved identity* and *began again* amid the challenging fronts of US racism.

This analysis also functions to address issues of the African American literary canon with respect to teaching texts like *Native Son* in ways that account for its period relevance as well as alternative meanings of the novel in *contemporary* contexts of race, society, and culture. Native Son maintains credibility in contemporary anthologies despite some opinions that Bigger Thomas's Jim Crow era overt victimization is outdated. In response, then, to the demands of a contemporary readership that has had unique modern racial experiences, a Black cultural mythology reading of *Native Son* is an effective critical intervention. It is a liberating approach to the novel through which viewing Bigger as a formal, mythological *antihero* permits an expanded contextualization of Wright's work. In fact, Wright himself wrote, "Tradition is no longer a guide. The world has grown huge and cold. Surely this is the moment to ask questions, to theorize, to speculate, to wonder" through fresh readings of earlier eras that seem overwhelmed by the contexts of its period's victimization.[56]

Chapter Six

Mythical Malcolm in an Age of Marable

As a theoretical corrective that reinforces regard for Black survivalist achievement and legacy by staking claims to a documented mythology that defies reductionist interpretations, Black cultural mythology is a useful philosophical framework from which to engage Manning Marable's *Malcolm X: A Life of Reinvention* (2011), particularly in the context of living history, biography, and the challenge of heroic memory. As one of the most debated contemporary revisionist biographies on an acclaimed African American persona, Marable's volume and its criticism are of particular interest to Black cultural mythology.[1] Specifically, this chapter is a consideration of the extent to which critical biographical perspectives, the framework of living Black history, and the implications of heroic memory relate to Malcolm X's legacy and *mythological* status. Malcolm's mythological status is the heroic cultural memory that emerges from the set of autobiography, biographies, narratives, stories, or beliefs transmitted about his real life and those which evolve from modestly embellished or speculative accounts, including creative literature. Malcolm's mythological status is most functional for members of his culture, and it elevates him to the status of *phenomenon*, wherein his identity, persona, feats, and accolades have influence and effect. For a period of Malcolm's life in memoriam, the public cautiously managed his heroic within a space of commemorating only the portion of his legacy whose pro-Black nationalism was not offensive to conservative American expectations.

Mythology serves Black psychosocial well-being. The effectiveness of theorizing mythological status as a practical application of Black cultural mythology and cultural memory practices increases when we view it for its

Black psychological value. Borrowing from *The Developmental Psychology of the Black Child* (1987), we find that Amos N. Wilson's approaches to framing *mythological structure* and *mythological methodology* ground this analysis of debates about Malcolm X's legacy because Wilson itemizes a set of cognitive and developmental variables that are at stake when the culture's mythology is *not* intact. If Marable's *Malcolm X: A Life of Reinvention* (hereafter referred to as *Reinvention*) will inevitably deconstruct Malcolm X's legacy as a mythoform, valued with cultural precision in chapter 1's discussions of Maulana Karenga's formative 1960s vision of mythology, spirituality, and remembrance, then the revisionist biography instigates a cultural loss. Viewing mythology as an indispensable intergenerational element for transmitting a proper worldview for the sake of cultural well-being from childhood to adulthood is a practical framework from which to interpret the effect and the meaning of the debates on Marable's *Reinvention*, as well as the value of other significant works in the canon on Malcolm X. The effectiveness of this framework is well-characterized by Wilson's suggestion that mythology should "permit new points of view . . . lead to new discoveries, provoke new questions, create new problems that must be solved in new ways, [and] jolt the imagination."[2] From the psychologist's point of view, there is no contradiction if a figure's legacy is represented by both literal and speculative accounts of agency and if these differing approaches are merged. The critical reviews on *Reinvention* determine the impact that *Reinvention* will have, over time, on Malcolm X's mythological structure.

Malcolm's legacy is well aligned with the topic of myth. In historical and cultural criticism, several sources feature the topic of myth as both a productive and nonproductive approach, as a key concept for learning how to interpret Malcolm's value. In "Myths about Malcolm X" (1969) Reverend Albert Cleage is prophetic and clarifying about the uses of Malcolm's myth. Relevant to the immediate frenzy in 2011 over the meaning and impact of Marable's biographical approach to Malcolm in *Reinvention,* Cleage's words surface as a healing salve, "Don't be afraid, brothers, don't be afraid—I am not hurting the image of Malcolm. I am just trying to save it because you are about to lose it, you are about to forget what Malcolm said."[3] Cleage continues, "Malcolm the man is in danger of being lost in a vast tissue of distortions which now constitute the Malcolm myth."[4] Cleage intervenes to correct two views: that post-Mecca Malcolm was an integrationist and that Malcolm's interest in internationalizing the African American struggle put faith in the United Nations to solve the problem. Cleage then imagines the optimum effect of a more credible Malcolm myth/mythology when he writes that "until you get power, Malcolm X is just a memory. When we get power, we will put his statue in every city, because the cities will belong to us. Then we can do him reverence. But until we get power, let's not play with images and myths."[5] Cleage's vision for a functional mythology is related to the power of African Americans to memorialize and to commemorate legacy using state-sanctioned space in the form of monuments.

Cleage's measure of the culture's ability to advance its mythology (the power to erect monuments) is echoed in Molefi Kete Asante's title essay from *Malcolm X as Cultural Hero and Other Afrocentric Essays* (1993) when Asante explores Malcolm's value as cultural hero, links this to a description of Malcolm as a "cultured individual," and ultimately defines culture based on Maulana Karenga's seven constituents of culture, including the culture's mythology.[6] Later in the volume, Asante also provides an extensive analysis of the role of architecture and buildings in sustaining mythology. Some sources engage with myth and mythology with subtlety, but Cleage's contextualization applied to *Reinvention*'s effect is a bold assertion of how myth functions in the cultural nationalism embodied in memory practices and formations associated with icons such as Malcolm.

In *Making Malcolm: The Myth and Meaning of Malcolm X* (1995), Michael Eric Dyson balances Malcolm's use as an icon and hero with a survey of the conservative perspective that "ensures an attention to detail that guards against romantic fictions and unrestrained myths."[7] He reminds us that mythology has degrees of being restrained, embellished, or romanticized. He observes, "All of us who have a stake in the meaning and myth of Malcolm's life will continue to do battle, will continue to disagree about how and why Malcolm's memory is used one way or another, even as we make wildly different uses of his career."[8] However, his final contribution to framing Malcolm's collective memory value is in the suggestion that Malcolm's legacy can help to protect Black males from "the staggering array of difficulties that hound and hurry them from the cradle to the grave" particularly in the Reagan-Bush-Clinton administrations that reinforced the stereotypes of Black males as problems and instigated entrapment for Black male children with their "juvenilization of crime."[9] Dyson's use of Malcolm's mythological legacy as an intervention for young Black males is significant in framing Malcolm's mythology, and it is directly related to Wilson's interpretation of mythology as a necessity for and an indicator of well-being in youth populations.

Scholars, critics, biographers, family members, dissenters, clergy, and bibliographers have published volumes on Malcolm's legacy since his death and autobiography, but those that significantly advance Malcolm's mythological value are of the greatest interest for an analysis of biography, living history, and the challenges of heroic memory. When critics assess Malcolm's heroics, mythology is implied, and the ways scholars knowingly and unwittingly concede to this as a measure of Malcolm's identity is of interest even though the subjects of myth and mythology are rarely indexed in the canon on Malcolm X. *The Cambridge Companion to Malcolm X* (2010), edited by Robert E. Terrill, does not feature myth as an itemized category.[10] *The Malcolm X Encyclopedia* (2002) edited by Robert L. Jenkins also does not address myth. Its entry on the 1999 "Commemorative Postage Stamp" is important because commemoration is a feature of cultural mythological practices.[11] In comparison, *Malcolm X: A Historical Reader* (2008) and its essays edited by James L. Conyers Jr. and Andrew P. Smallwood significantly chronicle analyses of Malcolm's mythological value.[12] Conyers offers a diverse historiography of myth-based critiques of Malcolm's legacy, drawing from works by Dyson, Gerald Horne, and Hank Flick.[13] Several other contributors frame their surveys of myth in contexts based on Horne's seminal historical review, "'Myth' and the Making of 'Malcolm X'" (1992).[14] Other essays reveal the intersections of history and literature that permit creative speculation on the historical narrative for the sake of literary and oral storytelling, and delineate the paradigm shift from which critics assess Malcolm's racist myth.[15]

Black cultural mythology, Black psychological valuation of mythology, and the ways in which debates on the topic of myth appear in critiques of Malcolm's legacy are priorities in the analysis of how Marable's *Reinvention* functions in the applied historiography of Malcolm X. With attention to theoretical considerations from Black cultural mythology as well as to Marable's early introduction to the Malcolm X project in his *Living Black History: How Reimagining the African-American Past Can Remake America's Racial Future* (2006), much is revealed in conducting a content analysis of the first wave of book reviews on Marable's *Reinvention*. The central inquiries are the following: (1) Is *Reinvention* consistent with the framework of "living Black history" that Marable used to introduce his objective for pursuing a magnum opus biography on Malcolm? (2) What is the relationship between Marable's methodology of "reimagining" and processes of mythology? (3) What effect does *Reinvention* have on Malcolm's mythological structure? (4) How do the criticism and reviews on *Reinvention* negotiate the challenges of heroic biography in the context of its relationship to African American mythology?

The answers to these questions have implications for both methodology and mythology. Marable's chapter "Malcolm X's Life-After-Death: The Dispossession of a Legacy" from *Living Black History* is a precursor to *Reinvention* in which he discloses his interest in a corrective biographical project on Malcolm X. This chapter is Marable's condensed survey of Malcolm's broad legacy and includes assessments of mythmaking, which Marable approaches as "the fabric of myth and legend."[16] A reminder of the distinction between myth and mythology is appropriate here. Myth, particularly in Marable's approach, often refers to generalizations, falsehoods, romanticizing, stereotyping, and historical inaccuracy. In contrast, mythology emphasizes heroic storytelling and the intergenerational transmission of legacy, wherein modest, restrained, and *not* overly romantic embellishment and exaggeration are creative techniques that elevate the legacy transmission process to the level of aesthetic memorialization, as it gains life, visibility, and momentum as a topic of creative literature. In such an engagement, which can be an oral or written one, aesthetic engagement sustains the process of remembrance and engagement with a legacy figure, including the use of conceptual hyperbole, symbolism, metaphors, gestures, inflection, imagined dialogues, and reconstructed historical dramatization.

Marable's methodology of "living Black history" frames civic capacity as one's ability to reject the trends of historical amnesia as a means of transformation:

> Let us approach the construction of a new black history from the vantage point of the evolution of black consciousness over time. . . . As racialized populations reflect upon the accumulated concrete experiences of their own lives, the lives of others who share their situation, and even those who have died long ago, a process of discovery unfolds that begins to restructure how they understand the world and their place within it. That journey of discovery can produce a desire to join with others to build initiatives that create space, permitting the renewal or survival of a group, or a celebration of its continued existence despite the forces arrayed against it.[17]

"Living Black history" includes possibilities for creative speculation on African American history through imagining "alternative pasts" and considering "counterfactual history," commemoration, reconstructing memory, distinguishing how culture affects public memory and the language of memory, reconstructing Black narratives using archival data, understanding the problem of "the suppression of black counternarratives," how "iconic personalities . . . have practical and powerful consequences in shaping civic behavior and social consciousness," and how "access to power . . . can alter how a group will remember its most dynamic figures."[18] Marable uses vivid terminologies that itemize the variables of memory and mythology. He frames "living Black history" as an "intervention" that will "honor the sacrifices of those African Americans who died to achieve freedom by interpreting accurately what they actually said and did, and then making the information available."[19] As "an honest interaction with the raw materials of the past" Marable's methodology of "living Black history" is a tool for invigorating African American mythological structure. The question, then, is how consistent is this "living Black history" treatment of Malcolm with Marable's approach to the life and legacy of Malcolm X in *Reinvention*.

The challenge to heroic memory inherent in Marable's approach to Malcolm's legacy in *Living Black History* is to respect that the weight of Malcolm's mythological structure is just as relevant before Marable's "corrective" biography as it is afterward. Wilson's work on mythology establishes that mythology is a process that evolves with new discoveries, new questions, and new problems, and that it can be "self-generating."[20] It is appropriate, then, to view Marable's attempt to "repossess" Malcolm from "dispossession" in *Living Black History* as a new contribution to an ever-evolving mythology. Marable asserts that "the real voice and vision of Malcolm X has been, and is presently being dispossessed from the intellectual and cultural memory of black America," and his emphasis on cultural memory in *Living Black History* further links his work to the processes of mythology.[21]

To what extent do the critics and reviewers of Marable's *Reinvention* acknowledge the mythological processes at work with the presentation of a revised narrative on Malcolm X's legacy? A content analysis of the reviews provides significant data, but it is first necessary to show the continuity of Marable's critical legacy process from *Living Black History* to *Reinvention*.

Biography is a form of mythology. Three sections of *Reinvention*—the prologue, chapter 16 (briefly), and the epilogue—reveal the legacy objective of the volume, and this objective is synonymous with the mythological process. Biographies contribute to a historical figure's mythology as refinement, reiteration, reinforcement, and even sometimes as antiheroics. Marable's prologue to *Reinvention*, titled "Life beyond the Legend," is a very structured introduction that he uses to state the purpose of his volume; to summarize

Malcolm's legacy, his personas, key sources and texts on Malcolm; and to explain how the volume diverges from previous renaissances of Malcolm's legacy. More subconsciously related to aspects of mythological structure, the prologue highlights a lexicon for and conceptual orientation to African American mythology.

The objective of *Reinvention* is "to go beyond the legend to recount what actually happened in Malcolm's life," and much of the prologue through which Marable frames the domain of this objective is a summary of the Malcolm chapter in *Living Black History*.[22] Marable equates legend with myth, as described above. Structurally, the prologue begins with a management of legacy based on commemoration of a site (the Audubon Ballroom), a narrative of death at the site, and the date of death. Marable recounts the history and present state of the Audubon Ballroom in order to reinforce its value as an African American monument. He offers a concise narrative of Malcolm's last hours and of his assassination. He then commemorates February 21, 1965 as a memorial date in African American cultural memory. These are significant junctures of Malcolm's mythological structure. If we compare the more sacred and ritualistic response that Maulana Karenga and the US organization had to Malcolm's death, documented in Keith A. Mayes's *Kwanzaa: Black Power and the Making of the African-American Holiday Tradition* (2009), Marable's efforts are rather static. This is a reminder of the varying levels of enthusiasm for and investment in the behavioral aesthetics of mythology.

Marable then shifts to introduce the challenges of Malcolm's legacy and renaissance. He does this by characterizing *The Autobiography of Malcolm X* as a project of multicultural icon-making. He contests the *Autobiography*'s genre-status as an autobiography based on his critique of an imbalanced collaboration between Malcolm X and Alex Haley—an author with an agenda of his own—on an autobiography that was completed after Malcolm's death. His view of Malcolm's renaissance is that it was limited by hip-hop's figurative portraiture summoned in the lyrics of the genre as well as by Malcolm's assimilation by conservative politicians. This is an assessment of antiheroics, wherein Marable identifies hip-hop and politics as forces that are interruptions to a stable and traditionally meaningful iconography.

Marable uses the prologue to delineate his view of what constitutes authenticity in structuring one's life story. Marable can be accused of negating an individual's rights and privileges to discretion and privacy in the name of what he contends is a commitment to historical, "factual truth," and he can be accused also of questioning Malcolm's right to *reinvent* himself.[23] Marable is intent on presenting the inconsistencies, the partial fiction, the masks, the method acting, the distortions, and the embellishments of Malcolm's personality and personas and of the ways society remembers him. This execution of *Reinvention* challenges heroic memory by its potential to deny a multilayered interpretation of a remarkable man who not only meant many different things to many different people, but who also journeyed through the mid-twentieth-century relying on his skill and capacity to negotiate a flexible identity as a key source of his cultural survival and agency. In a Black cultural mythology reading, Marable's objectives tamper with ancestor acknowledgment, quantifications of what the culture has inherited from Malcolm, and the logic of immortalization, as they blur the line between heroics and antiheroics. In the prologue Marable presents the process of reinvention as a problematic that requires deconstruction, rather than as a highly cultivated survival skill.

In the end, Marable contributes to the mythological process by using the legacy of Malcolm X as a model for discerning the line between truth and fiction or history and myth, while at the same time demonstrating the cognitive processes for evaluating an individual's mythological structure. His featured interpretation of the meaning of hero, cultural memory, folk culture, self-invention, legend, image, martyr, iconic figure, historical figure, and resurrection is a context of the mythological process that should not be overlooked, even as society remains a bit disgruntled that Marable sought to humanize an iconic figure whose flaws and potential inconsistencies have not troubled his admiring public.

While readers would expect chapter 16, on life-after-death, to significantly address Malcolm's value as a memorialized icon, instead it chronicles blame for his death, the Nation of Islam (NOI) leadership succession, and the Little/Shabazz family infighting about the narrative authority over Malcolm's memory and related matters. The chapter has two indicators of potential discursive turning points for Malcolm's "posthumous image" advanced by jazz musicians and his "posthumous rehabilitation" under Wallace Muhammed's period of leadership of the NOI, but only the former is developed. Marable is also attentive to the "new memory" of the NOI under Wallace Muhammad, which was enabled by the destruction of earlier NOI archives.

It is in the epilogue where Marable revisits the assessment of Malcolm's mythological value, albeit without ever using the word "mythology." Mythological language, terminologies, and contexts abound in this section—iconic status, inclusion in the pantheon of multicultural heroes, leader, folk hero, masking in terms of the roles Malcolm has played, muse, and memory as a radical humanist. In contrast to the prologue's presentation of Malcolm's reinvention as a problematic skill of transformation, in the epilogue Marable commends Malcolm's reinvention. He writes, "Malcolm's strength was his ability to reinvent himself, in order to function and even thrive in a wide variety of environments."[24] Elaborating on the implications of reinvention, Marable extends his interpretation of this process to include Malcolm among icons of Black resistance, or "black outlaws," such as the nationalistic Gabriel Prosser and Nat Turner, the folkloric Stagger Lee, and Tupac Shakur.[25] He credits Malcolm with literally encouraging commemoration through cultural celebration in his public addresses to Black crowds. He reiterates the Black Aesthetic Movement's regard for Malcolm as muse, and he insinuates that Malcolm had the capacity to be a counselor or psychologist for the masses due to his perception of the "group psychology" of African Americans.[26] A unique, prophetic contribution is Marable's indication that Malcolm's future legacy is as an icon of Muslim "jihadist reinvention."[27] Such characterizations and affirmations of Malcolm's currency as symbol and icon are directly related to the mythological process.

In the epilogue, Marable reminds us of the merits and tasks of the biographer: "The biographer charts the evolution of a subject over time, and the various challenges and tests that the individual endures provide insights into the person's character."[28] The data, new perspectives, and new archival details that collectively advance an expanded account of Malcolm's lifelong worldviews and effect have the potential to invigorate the mythological structure of Malcolm's legacy by permitting the culture to *perform* more informed stories of Malcolm's legacy. In Black cultural mythology, this is an aspect of the historical reenactment of worldview. In the epilogue, Marable's description of Malcolm as "consciously a performer, who presented himself as the vessel for conveying the anger and impatience the black masses felt" is conversant with the characteristic that mythology can be performance that animates the subject in order to make his legacy more memorable.[29] Recalling Wilson's characteristics of mythological structure and mythological methodology, it is essential to link Malcolm's life and trajectory as one of the "organic historical-experiential events" or "symbols" that carry "psychosomatic, personal and interpersonal, subjective and objective, conceptual and emotional, [and] conscious and subconscious meanings."[30] This capacity of myth to impact the culture is a reminder of the freedom of Black cultural mythology to use heroics and legacy as a means of "reality testing, broad environmental mastery, ego strengthening, integrating the self with social reality, [and] the facilitation of intellectual and thought development."[31] The legacy analysis of Malcolm X is a model that can be applied to a host of figures.

Mythology and the Challenge of Heroic Memory

A final question about the effect *Reinvention* has had or will have on the mythology of Malcolm X concerns the ongoing challenge of heroic memory, and this is measured by whether or not the general readership views or interprets this biographical project as a contribution to mythology. There are numerous reviews on *Reinvention* published in the press and in scholarly journals, and this next exploration considers the extent to which reviewers, as authoritative and historically informed voices in the public domain, organically or deliberately use and interpret variables of mythology.

The critical reception of *Reinvention*, based on the large body of general and academic critique in primarily book review form, is diverse and includes a significant number of essays that are so thorough the reviewers even critique other reviews. Nonetheless, the reviews uniquely advance matters of mythology. The conversations and observations are rich, discursive, historical, and dialogic. They serve as indicators of the challenges to heroic memory because, collectively and innately, they participate in a debate about Malcolm's mythological status, couched in corroborations of and, conversely, objections to Marable's narrative effect on what was, heretofore, a stable and functional mythology on Malcolm X. A few of the reviews use the term and gauge the value of "myth," and fewer use and engage the term "mythology." The words "myth" and "mythology" appear in interesting contexts that reveal how critics value these terms as well as disregard them for their implications. Maulana Karenga mocks Marable's objective to save Malcolm from "the alleged mythological conceptions of him hosted and harbored by those too appreciative of Malcolm to see his flaws."[32] Darryl Lorenzo Wellington observes, "Haley's *Autobiography* captured Malcolm X's mythic dimensions, but his myth is dated—and Marable does not quite succeed in updating it."[33]

The reviews produce an inherently de facto survey of mythology, primarily through their use of language—terms, phrasings, and key concepts—that delineates critical facets of mythological structure; through clarifications of the function of the genres of biography and autobiography; and through evaluations of whether or not *Reinvention* has the capacity to add to, subtract from, or reframe the memory and meaning of Malcolm primarily for Africana audiences. A basic challenge to managing heroic memory is lexical. The content of our words, conversations, stated beliefs, and interpretations insistently reflect a concern for mythological structure, but we have hardly enumerated its value since two of the Black Arts Movement's spokesmen, Karenga and Neal, itemized cultural mythology as a central component of Black culture.

A study of the reviews reveals a rich *mythological vocabulary* that measures memorial value and potential based on Malcolm's life experience: exalted, iconic figure, iconic stature, iconic resonance, legend, emulated, leader/leadership, hero, image, virtual saint, clipped from the sky, subject to a public craze, popular standing, cultural afterlife, cultural symbol of black self-worth, publicly commemorated, cultural icon, enduring, significant, influential, admired, inspiring, empowering, "David-versus-Goliath dimension,"[34] comparable to the status Christopher Columbus holds for Italian Americans,[35] "a saint of defiance, an enemy of indifference,"[36] "could have been Olympian,"[37] forefather, elegant emblem, reputable, cultivated, metaphorical, revered national figure, "rendered in granite,"[38] father-hero, apotheosized, idolization, subject to the "hagiographic formula,"[39] influential, ennobling, empowering, martyred, resurrected, affirming, "uncompromising Black heroism,"[40] icon of "heteronormative masculinity,"[41] mythic legend, Malcolmology, symbol of Black manhood, part of the political imagination, "durability as a model,"[42] mythological conception, famous, beloved, resuscitated, of quality and status, and worthy of portraiture. Surely this list resonates with direct variables of mythological structure, with the attributes and properties of Black cultural mythology, and with the total Africana cultural memory enterprise.

A handful of reviewer insights are poignant and demand critical exploration due to the contexts they provide on the status quo of myth and mythology. These exceptionally valuable reviews offer unique and illuminating critical depth and additional variables. Amiri Baraka views *Reinvention* as an attempt to " 'reduce' Malcolm's known qualities and status" by removing him "from the context and character of an Afro American revolutionary" and by "challenging" and "dismantling that portrait by redrawing him."[43] He rejects the implication of *Reinvention* as well as the Black elite back-cover blurbs that suggest, as he sarcastically states, that "we were following flawed leaders with flawed ideas." Karenga affirms Malcolm's mythology and describes his "durability as a model of African and human excellence and achievement of his people."[44] A review in the journal *Culture* reiterates Karenga's and Baraka's uncompromising commitment to preserving Malcolm's mythological structure, albeit through a culturally belittling review that takes issue with the scholar-activists' investment in "protecting (or exaggerating) Malcolm's influence" and on Karenga's "focus on how history's ennobling aspects can enrich the lives of those who study the past."[45] The essay underscores *Reinvention*'s deconstructionist threat with the inquiry and answer, "Why tarnish one of black America's most powerful icons in a tabloid, tell-all book? But the book is not that. Marable simply seeks to demystify Malcolm; that seems irreverent to those who demand hagiography."[46] This is not the only review that introduces hagiography, the study of saints or the creation of biographical saints. Also, it is not the only review to suggest that Malcolm is mystified and enigmatic, two descriptions that are irrelevant to Malcolm's affirmed mythological status in life and afterlife. Those terms suggest that Malcolm had a puzzling, confusing, obscure, and mysterious personality and persona, for which a small case can be made. However, Malcolm's more prominent and documented mythological status is impervious, as these conditions have not reduced the power of his legacy.

In the same vein, the idea of resuscitation also appears in the reviews. Abdul Alkalimat challenges this, writing, "Perhaps the most cold-blooded negation is his [Marable's] statement that Malcolm has to be resurrected for Black people, where most certainly he should have said most white people. Black people have never forgotten Malcolm X, and certainly the state and white intellectuals have not either. He was more of an icon in the Black radical tradition than even Martin Luther King, Jr."[47] Wellington suggests that what Malcolm left us is a "story arc" based on his journey and that this answers the question, "'Why Malcolm today?' better than any of the biographical trivia or assassination intrigue" promoted in *Reinvention*.[48] Alkalimat summarizes, "Marable advances an argument that separates Malcolm from his legacy, a legacy that was in fact us, the Black liberation movement."[49]

The critique of genre appears in several reviews. Clarence Lang considers, "Autobiography often melds truth and fiction. But biography is also an ethically open-ended process that hands the writer power to represent people unable to represent themselves. . . . In impact, if not by intent, the book sets a stage for ongoing conversation about the importance of historical biography to social movement theory."[50] Touré credits the 1965 *Autobiography* as the source that has kept Malcolm current, but he writes, "all autobiographies are, in part lies. They rely on memory, which is notoriously fallible, and are shaped by self-image. They don't really tell us who you are but whom you want the world to see you as. . . . He has some failings, but Malcolm is still the empowering figure his autobiography showed us he was."⁵¹ Empowerment is indicated in many of the attributes of Black cultural mythology, but here Touré links them in understood cosmological and ontological terms that imply mnemonic influences. Memory, remembrance, and commemoration are the types of broad variables at stake in critics' warnings about how Marable's *Reinvention* is culturally oppositional. However, Black cultural mythology's attributes extend the language needed to continue to preserve the heroic and survivalist value of legendary ancestors such as Malcolm X. Malcolm's capacity as epic, sacrificial, renewing, immortalized, hyperheroic, and cognitively resistant is better itemized by the contribution of Black cultural mythology theorizations and terminologies.

Some reviews provide commentary on Black intellectual common sense about the limitations and contradictions inherent in narrative forms. Yohuru Williams gives credit to the critical thinkers who knew that the 1965 autobiography's "neat presentation of Malcolm's life as a quintessentially American morality tale has, for instance, always been at odds with the complex man many knew Malcolm to be."⁵² He continues, "Most lofty historical figures have been clipped from the sky by revelations that cast their actions in a different light. . . . What Marable confirms, both for the historian and the biographer, is that lives are messy and untidy, and that reconstructing them requires the utmost care."⁵³ Alkalimat adds a clarifying perspective on the value of an icon's metamorphoses through his or her life's journey when he writes, "My argument is that Malcolm's life is not a self-invention process intended through Malcolm's agency, but a global process that summed up the journey so many were to make from the oppressed, through the street, to Black self-determination, to revolutionary. . . . and on that basis people held and hold Malcolm in the highest regard and lived and are living the life he epitomized."⁵⁴ These types of commentaries confirm how *Reinvention* challenges the line between heroics and antiheroics, which, in terms of Malcolm's life, is transitional and developmental rather than moral. Alkalimat's observation about how a personal journey toward the heroic is not always perfect is an unanticipated truth that has reappeared in numerous discourses on heroics, myth, and mythology.

Several reviews call for greater analytical depth and enhanced tools for the analysis of legacy, and the philosophy of Black cultural mythology responds to this request. Lang writes, "We still know less, however, about the complex framing processes involved in forging and maintaining activist identities and self-narrative."⁵⁵ He also asserts that it was Malcolm's iconic stature that is responsible for turning scholars toward immersive cultural study. If *Reinvention* is guilty of deconstructing Malcolm's mythology, it could, in applying Lang's measure, do damage by weakening an influence that has had the stability to inspire generations to theorize phenomena that remain unaddressed in academic arenas that marginalize the study of people of African descent. Finally, Lang calls for new conceptual productivity in the form of "renewed political imagination."[56] Black cultural mythology responds to this as well because maintaining the variables associated with the hero dynamic requires imagination, as creative writers have aptly demonstrated in their sociopolitical uses of iconic personas and episodes in their storytelling. Wellington is impressed with Marable's research but writes, "Something is missing. The book provides a great deal, but what is needed today is more than the particulars. . . . Rather, the reader needs an interpretation of the historical significance of Malcolm X."[57] Again, as seen in the itemization of Black cultural mythology's vast intellectual tradition, over and again critics have desired and called for an enhanced lens from which to engage memorial phenomena; this is when and where Black cultural mythology enters.

When Aziz Rana observes, "as Malcolm's iconic stature has grown, the memory of his political beliefs and commitments has faded,"[58] he affirms Malcolm's existing mythological status, but credits *Reinvention* with linking mythology with politics. He describes this activity as "recovering the political actor beneath the cultural icon,"[59] which is a more tempered observation than those that pretend that Malcolm's legacy needed to be resuscitated. Alkalimat's criticism is among the most compelling that recall the contemporary and future value of Malcolm's mythological status: "In short, Marable fabricates a Malcolm X who would not take militant and revolutionary action against the global war on poverty, and degradations of today. That's why we have to speak up: to respect our legacy and affirm our future."[60] This observation not only describes the function of mythology but it also rejects Marable's careless tendency in *Reinvention* to permit the sordid details of Malcolm's life to mimic the antihero. Similarly, an equally careless and hostile review claims, "He presents reams of evidence that should demote Malcolm X from the exalted standing he enjoys among many progressives of various stripes. Yet Marable was simply unwilling to go where his own narrative should have taken him."[61] The negative connotation of this review, ironically, concedes the resilience of Black cultural mythology, and the author does not understand that mythology is indeed a central variable of Black culture. He laments, "The most serious deficiency in Marable's study is his failure to extricate himself from the pull of the Malcolm X legend."[62] Imagine that. Malcolm's mythology cannot and should not be dismantled by what Karenga calls "scavenger history."[63] As the common sense of Alice Walker reminds us, no culture throws away its genius.

Several review essays conclude that the minimal effect of *Reinvention* is that it is a catalyst for renewed dialogue on Malcolm. Alkalimat assuages the potentially negative impact of the biography by introducing his review with the expectation that the biography "will help us to get a deeper understanding of Malcolm X and the times we're living in now. This will not be a direct result of what Marable has done, but of what needs to be done because of what he has done."[64] *Reinvention* indeed instigates the need to consider the idea formation and effect of Black cultural mythology, with reminders of its sociopsychological relevance advanced in Wilson's research. Black cultural mythology challenges us to regard the continuity of struggle within the framework of conceptual resistance and survival. *Reinvention* not only challenges us to achieve greater clarity about the attributes at stake in biography and memorial narrative but it also implies a tool of comparative methodology to advance Africana cultural memory studies.

The interplay between *Reinvention* and the critical reviews emerges as a remarkable phenomenon in which a record of legacy must battle with a revisionist artifact. Black cultural mythology strengthens the tools that will ensure the resilience of African American epic lives that have the right to be valued on culturally relevant terms. Mythological structure and mythological methodology are latent and implied dynamics of the ways we negotiate the record and motives of legendary actors with waves of new generations' (re-) assessments of legacy. Marable's challenge to Malcolm X's mythology is but one example among a pantheon of iconic and legendary African American figures whose mythology may one day be contested. It is productive to have a healthy respect for the value of Black cultural mythology, which includes advancing clear definitions and domains for distinguishing myth from mythology and being aware of when the subtleties and usages intersect. Its epistemological agency is a culturally specific approach to preserving and promoting legacies and hero dynamics that have sustained the culture through its processes of survival, despite moments of bleakness and mourning.

It is easier to measure the variables of nonfiction literature that illuminate the lived experience of legendary figures like Malcolm X. When the genre shifts from nonfiction (such as biography and autobiography) to more imaginative, symbolic, and abstract fiction genres, society wavers and second-guesses its right to respond to the text just as Baraka, Karenga, Alkalimat, and others used editorials and book reviews to defend Malcolm

X's empowering legacy. Imaginative texts demand synthesized methodologies drawing from both literary criticism and Black cultural mythology theorizations. The autobiographical-biographical challenge between Malcolm's and Marable's narratives initiates a discourse on Black cultural mythology's function in terms of African American literary history and criticism.

Chapter Seven

Imaginative Rights

The [Africans] had to build their own Pantheon of famous men, didn't they? The Mandingo marabout was proud of his ancestors and he was right. . . . What wonderful things the white man has accomplished! . . . What about us? . . . What about us? They let us stand back and admire. Isn't that enough?[1]

—Maryse Condé, *Heremakhonon*

Ancestral imperatives, indeed. . . . But . . . WHICH ancestors among which?[2]

—Albert Murray, *Seven League Boots*

As a tool for literary criticism, Black cultural mythology affects how we respond to fiction and nonfiction literary narrative traditions of heroic remembrance. The innovation of offering a set of new critical attributes matures and stabilizes diasporic cultural memory practices. The framework challenges society to perfect the art of cultural commemoration in the most specific and refined ways possible. Black cultural mythology intervenes theoretically to support a more profound analysis of historical and creative artifacts to protect the culture against having its record of ingenuity, resilience, and survival descend into obscurity. Black cultural mythology is thought-provoking as society considers the exceptionalism as well as the challenges of the African American predicament of being a "nation within a nation."

Komozi Woodard's contemporary critique of cultural nationalism suggests that it is still an impactful description.[3] In the framework of

Black cultural mythology, cultural nationalism has implications for power, citizenship, public displays of symbolic cultural unity, and commemoration. It reinvigorates the transnational value of the Republic of Haiti in order that whenever media or society mention Haiti, the world never forgets its revolutionary superlative. It deciphers and resists how Harriet Tubman's grit is sterilized in feel-good juvenile narratives that constrain the epic and hyperheroic dimensions of her activism. It gives us new ways to read Richard Wright's Bigger Thomas, so that his fate is not so easily digested as villainous but is seen more alongside the competing ideological nobility of *Black Panther's* Erik Killmonger. It chronicles prototype activism in the vocal ways pro-Africana intellectuals rang the alarm when Marable's biography emerged as a cultural nonnegotiable, as he dared to deconstruct Malcolm's largely intact legacy.

Black cultural mythology helps to restore healthy centered worldviews, encouraging the citizenry, intellectuals, and Black families to gain proficiency with lexical tools and perspectives that equip them to speculate on the past with better clarity about the epic feat of survival in the narrative of beginning again and engraving identity on new soil in the diaspora. This renews respect and admiration for the microbehaviors and microsurvivals of ancestors whose freedom dreams are fulfilled in the lives of present and future forebears. The tools of Black cultural mythology give us confident dexterity to analyze critically the paths and tributaries between encounter, resistance, enslavement, freedom, and self-determination and how this journey deserves to be experienced as sacred remembrance. Merging the sacred with meditation, which is modeled exceptionally well by creative writers, literature emerges as a constant artifact that recycles the plots and pinnacles of the African American cultural record and demands that society take notice and engage. Linking this function of literature with Black cultural mythology's robust discursive cues enables us to itemize diaspora history and its retelling in a spirit of commemoration and affirmation that we control and manage through the confidence of the mythological structure.

Black cultural mythology also functions as literary criticism to help society understand the artistry, vision, and cultural commitment of Africana writers whose cyclical, historical storytelling enlivens the commemorative and memory-based processes of writing's function as a conduit to capture and advance the oral-written-oral cycle of cultural communication in remembrance and letters. In 1937 Richard Wright observed that "a new role is devolving upon the Negro writer. He is being called upon to do no less than to create values by which his race is to struggle, live, and die." He added, "he can create the myths and symbols that inspire a faith in life."[4] He further suggests the role of the imagination when he says that Black writers "have begun to feel the meaning of the history of their race as though they in one life time had lived it themselves throughout all the long centuries."[5] He refers to the consciousness that the writer must have that supports his or her cultural envisioning. He insists that "the imaginative conception of a historical period will not be a carbon copy of reality. Image and emotion possess a logic of their own."[6]

These theoretical considerations about the intersection of Black creative writing and mythology are important to the explication of literature such as Robert O'Hara's play *Insurrection: Holding History* (1996), which is a prototype of the way Black cultural mythology functions as a critical theorization. *Insurrection* has that "magical" quality that artist and author Faith Ringgold itemizes as an outcome of proper legendary mythological storytelling. The way writers use the past and frame the shifts in Africana worldview from Africa to the diaspora is reflected when Wright observed:

> Negro writers will rise from understanding the meaning of their being transplanted . . . in all of its social, political, economic, and emotional implications. It means that Negro writers must have in their consciousness the foreshortened picture of the *whole*, nourishing culture from which they were torn in Africa, and of the long, complex (and for the most part, unconscious) struggle to regain in some form and under alien conditions of life a *whole* culture again.[7]

The framework of Black cultural mythology and its critical and conceptual priorities are a manifestation of Wright's anticipation.

Frantz Fanon's view of national culture relates to the writers' activity when he notes, "the oral tradition—stories, epics and songs of the people, which formerly were filed away as set pieces—is now beginning to change. The storytellers who used to relate inert episodes now bring them alive and introduce into them modifications which are increasingly fundamental. There is a tendency to bring conflicts up to date and to modernize the kind of struggle which the stories evoke together with the names of heroes and the types of weapons."[8] The philosophical framework of Black cultural mythology is indeed this modernization. Fanon suggests that the imaginative process is an "invocation" and is "remodeled."[9] He explains that "the emergence of the imagination and of the creative urge in the songs and epic stories of a colonized country is worth following. The storyteller replies to the expectant people by successive approximations, and makes his way, apparently alone but in fact helped on by his public, towards the seeking out of new patterns, that is to say national patterns."[10] This is no less true in the colonization process in the United States and the broader diaspora.

Naturally, Black cultural mythology is also pedagogy. James Baldwin gave an unfavorable review of Shirley Graham's *There Once Was a Slave: The Heroic Story of Frederick Douglass* because the volume was too celebratory. Baldwin reasoned, "There is a tradition among emancipated whites and progressive Negroes to the effect that no unpleasant truth concerning Negroes is ever to be told," and he considered Graham's alleged participation in this tradition to be "crippling." Baldwin adds, "Douglass was first of all a man—honest within the limitations of his character and time, quite frequently misguided, sometimes pompous, gifted but not always a hero, and no saint at all. Miss Graham . . . has reduced a significant, passionate human being to the obscene level of a Hollywood caricature."[11] Such strong words reflect Baldwin's interest in the urgency of mending "interracial understanding," but libraries classify Graham's book as juvenile fiction, which has a more basic, presentational, educational agenda. Nonetheless, Baldwin's evaluation reflects three possible theories. First, perhaps Baldwin believed that young learners are capable of understanding the passion, politics, and negotiations of adult society and should therefore be offered more mature and complex presentations of the meaning of the past. Second, Baldwin's sense of hero dynamics was as realistic and as complex as is human nature, so human flaws do not subvert an individual's potential to be heroic. Third, perhaps Graham's accomplishment, as Baldwin notes, of making "Douglass a quite unbelievable hero," was a deliberate act of embellished storytelling to support Douglass's transformation from the realms of history into mythology. It is a rich speculation to imagine how Baldwin would have responded to Marable's *Reinvention*.

The bibliography and sources from which a discussion of imaginative rights emerges is vast. While autobiography, biography, and even historical fiction are important genres for transmitting a general historical and nonfiction frame story from which creative writers draw, the interest in imaginative rights is the creation, function, and effect of writers' innocuous embellishment of nonfiction legacies. In the African American context, the New Negro movement emerges in literary history as the era that initiated robust cyclical storytelling drawing on the hard-won and sifted out pantheon of African world heroics that Maria W. Stewart and Black press editors demanded to stabilize the culture's immortalization philosophy and practice. The genre of drama was the conduit for this, coupled with the genre of poetry, with key nineteenth-century models of odes and elegies from writers such as Paul Laurence Dunbar and canonized others.

Fiction cannot be ignored, as Arna Bontemps, in the post–New Negro thirties penned classics on the heroics of the Haitian Revolution and African American enslavement revolt in *Drums at Dusk* (1939) and *Black Thunder* (1936), respectively. The incubation of heroics and its aesthetic literary possibilities ripened during the first half of the twentieth century as literary and cultural media such as the *Crisis* and *Negro World*, the black press, children's serials such as *The Brownies' Book*, and narratives of African American historical chronology saturated Black intellectual and cultural life. This was further stabilized by the activity of the early Negro studies movement and the academic and cultural institutionalization of Black history through the efforts of George Washington Williams, Carter G. Woodson, and Lorenzo Johnston Greene. Viewing this intellectual genealogy of broad Africana historical and cultural interest in its own agency is an orientation to exploring the *continuum* of African diaspora life, experience, specificity, cultural creation, and memory. From this vantage point, a twenty-first-century interest in the imprints of legacy and heritage behaviors is nothing more than a natural culmination of a cultural view of itself that has been ripening for over a century and that has been reflecting on its long view of survival for even longer. This view of African American identity and letters underscores the logic of an early twenty-first-century theoretical and itemized framing of Africana cultural memory practices offered as Black cultural mythology.

Chapter 3 introduced aesthetic memorialization, cyclical storytelling, and narrative embellishment on Harriet Tubman's historical and still-emergent identity, while chapter 4's coverage of Haiti relied on literary history and cultural criticism to better explore the nation of Haiti's prominent place in diaspora worldviews and memory. The thesis of both chapters required a pairing between historical and literary evidence, yet this chapter's goal is to explore the broad literary bibliography implications of Black cultural mythology as well as more in-depth literary criticism on dynamic examples of authors taking full advantage of imaginative rights to create new orientations to African American cultural heroics. The key texts for a Black cultural mythology literary criticism are Charles Johnson's *Dreamer: A Novel* (1997), Colson Whitehead's *John Henry Days: A Novel* (2001), and Robert O'Hara's play on Nat Turner, *Insurrection: Holding History* (1998). However, first, as a partly bibliographic essay, this chapter introduces a brief literary history covering the diverse and relevant texts that stabilize Black cultural mythology as a literary genre.

My critical anthology, *Literary Spaces: Introduction to Comparative Black Literature* (2007), was the first source to itemize Black cultural mythology as a prominent categorization of global Black literatures. The anthology's chapter on Black cultural mythology included speeches, poetry, and historical essays from writers representing Grenada, the United States, South Africa, Brazil, and Jamaica. Aside from the section in the anthology *Literary Spaces*, there are only a couple of published works on the topic, including literary and cultural criticism on poetry memorializing Malcolm X, a cultural theory study that mines Black studies theorizations on the topic of myth as a precursory discourse on Black cultural mythology, and a study on Paul Robeson that explores the cross-genre relationship between the adaptation of his memoir into a documentary.[12]

Black Cultural Mythology in the Literary Tradition

Defining Black cultural mythology not only as a conceptual framework of African American identity and worldview but also as a literary tradition with a documented origin and development challenges us to frame a narrative of its derivation, which stabilizes it within the literary canon. This inquiry is a backward-gazing revisionist exercise that acknowledges the genius of the Black Arts Movement's vision of, yet *limited development and theorization* of, a Black aesthetic mythology as a defining criterion for Black art and culture.

Neal's theorization informs the quest to define Black cultural mythology's origin and legacy as a *literary tradition* (Karenga's approach is not literary) by providing criteria that give direction to identifying early examples of Africana cultural creative production that advances or theorizes mythological structure. One comprehensive work emerges from the African American tradition of rhetoric and persuasion—David Walker's *Appeal to the Coloured Citizens of the World, but in particular, and very expressly, to those of THE UNITED STATES OF AMERICA* (1829). This persuasionist abolitionist document reflects the balance between diaspora and African American views and is a reference point and prototype for the earliest prominent sources of Black cultural mythology. Its formal publication and circulation in 1829, its ongoing availability, and its idea formation are superlative. Its central value as a cultural conceptualization that helps define the tradition of Black cultural mythology is its vision for Africana mythological structure in the predicament of beginning again.

In company with Walker, it is no wonder that Maria W. Stewart's speeches share the fervor to immortalize the race in the Black nationalist vision of its formation beyond enslavement. St. Lucian/Trinidadian Nobel laureate in literature Derek Walcott also contributes to the selection of Walker's *Appeal* as a reference point and prototype for one of the earliest prominent sources of Black cultural mythology. As a remarkable literary visionary, Walcott canvassed US history as source material for heroic plays, and published *Walker and Ghost Dance: Plays* (2002) representing the revolutionary heroics of David Walker in *Walker* and of Sitting Bull in *Ghost Dance*. Also in 2002, Walcott released *The Haitian Trilogy: Henri Christophe, Drums and Colours, The Haitian Earth*, and these two volumes represent Walcott's elevation of diaspora heroics to the level of diasporic mythological consciousness. In *Appeal*, Walker references Haiti with enthusiasm and honor. Additionally, Walker and immortalization philosophy foremother Stewart were compatriots in the abolitionist struggle. Thus, Walcott's literary vision helps to merge diasporan Black nationalist consciousnesses that contributes to the Black cultural mythology literary tradition.

In terms of the literary tradition, Black cultural mythology is also part of folk culture, which editors frame in *The Norton Anthology of African American Literature* (2004) as the first segment of the literary tradition—"The Vernacular Tradition."[13] Excerpts from David Walker's *Appeal* are in *Norton*'s second section, "The Literature of Slavery and Freedom." Both Walker and Stewart appear as compelling foundational thinkers in the *Norton* anthology, and a conceptual rereading of their value to creative production and literary conceptualization is a contemporary intervention in literary history.

The central requisite of this intervention is prioritizing the study of *worldview* and *continuum* within literary discourses.[14] Worldview is compatible with "ethos," or the character and disposition of people of African descent that cultural historian Sterling Stuckey suggests African Americans fashioned as a distinct cultural point of view during the enslavement experience.[15] Worldview is a set of philosophical assumptions and designs for living that reflect culturally specific categories, queries, and logic formation drawn from a continuum of in-group historical experiences and developments.[16] Thus, placing Black cultural mythology within the narrative of the African American literary tradition is an exercise of both merging and expansion. The category is an asset to the discussion of oral, vernacular, folk, survival, and abolitionist traditions. A detailed and refined understanding of abolitionist traditions—those aimed at ending enslavement—is a clarification that this activism is infused with visions for Black nationalism and for normalized Black lives empowered by self-determination and cultural choice in the design of nation and community. This includes a place for mythological structure.

Black cultural mythology should appear at multiple intervals in the collective narratives of the African American literary tradition, from folk culture, to abolition, to the New Negro movement institutionalization of heroic storytelling obsessed with featuring Haiti and then featuring domestic heroics. Black cultural mythology is vital to frameworks for understanding Black Arts and Black Aesthetics, and it resurfaces cyclically in contemporary African American literary practice, which can be subsumed under the larger category of Africana cultural memory.

This conceptual addition to framing the Africana worldview in creative production refines and reorders canonical timeliness so they more accurately capture the continuum of mythological idea formation and cross-fertilization that is stable and cyclical. Charting Black cultural mythology in the literary tradition helps to transmit critical tools to aid society in identifying the golden threads of hero dynamics, ancestor acknowledgment, immortalization philosophy, epic intuitive conduct, hyperheroic sensibility, sacrificial inheritance, cognitive survival, and historical and cultural reenactments of worldview in literature whether folk culture, essays, poetry, drama, biography, autobiography, prose, fiction, or film.

Many works emerge as priority reading in the literary bibliography of Black cultural mythology. The conceptual categories help to arrange and qualify the different approaches, even though era, genre, movement, and theme are also useful categorizations. The era approach considers heroic and mythological creative production commensurate with existing categories of the African American canon and its key anthologies. A genre approach has a bit more diversity. For example, the study of genres of biography, autobiography, memoir, and personal narrative that represent ancestral acknowledgment, hyperheroics, epic intuitive sensibility, cognitive survival, ritual remembrance, and inheritance can be read alone or comparatively using the conceptual categories. But studying the texts also benefits from *pairings* with documentary and film, which visually elevate the presentation of heroics with the added dimension of eyewitness testimony and collective communal assessment of cultural memory.[17]

Black cultural mythology genre studies for poetry, short prose, fiction, and drama are easily managed categorically or in comparative literary analysis. There is a host of commemorative poetry in honor of or dedicated to Frederick Douglass, Harriet Tubman, Martin Luther King Jr., and Malcolm X, as well as a hearty collection of dramatic works on Black heroes. The critical contextualization of Black cultural mythology has dynamic possibilities for the genre of speculative fiction not only for the genre's visionary and utopic manipulations of time, place, space, and geography but also for its transcendent approach to the existential possibilities of heroic ancestors who, in the writers' hands, have the capacity to embody different human, physical, and temporal realities.

Documentary film is another featured genre for hero dynamics and pedagogy because school audiences and community programs benefit from audiovisual media exposure to African American, African, or diaspora biography, heroics, or legendary activity. The difference in relying on a Black cultural mythology intervention is that there is now a unified set of attributes or critical variables to reinforce the value and itemized analysis of Africana heritage. The critical categories stabilize our understanding of the sacred, survivalist, and commemorative value of legacies of beginning again and of engraving identity on new soil. Media options include documentaries and films on Ralph Bunche, Ida B. Wells-Barnett, Patrice Lumumba, Paul Robeson, Malcolm X, Madame C. J. Walker, Amiri Baraka, A. Philip Randolph, Marcus Garvey, Ralph Ellison, Emmett Till, and Nat Turner.

A movement approach would feature models of mythology and memory from the perspective of literary generations. For the New Negro movement, it would be on broadly ancestor-based heroics such as Toussaint Louverture and Gabriel Prosser who appear in the works of Langston Hughes, May Miller, and Arna Bontemps and on sociopolitical character satire such as George Samuel Schuyler's *Black No More*, which covers such caricatures as W. E. B. Du Bois, Marcus Garvey, and Madame C. J. Walker. Even Hughes's collection of Jesse B. Semple stories captures popular and communal discourses on cultural heroics. From the indignant generation,[18] which includes Richard Wright, Alice Childress, Ralph Ellison, James Baldwin, and Lorraine Hansberry, Black cultural mythology categorizations of cognitive survival, antiheroics, reconciliation and renewal, and commemoration philosophy indicate ways this generation fused hero dynamics with more cultural memory-inspired sociopolitical commentary and criticism. Louverture continues to be a literary priority, represented by Ellison's short story "Mister Toussan," which transmits the intellectual yearnings and potential of children influenced simultaneously by the history and perspectives they encounter from media, the curriculum, good teachers, and their parents. Childress,

Baldwin, and Hansberry all have works on and carefully placed references to Louverture as well as cultural commentary that refines culturally centered perspectives on commemoration. Childress even extends her dramatic work to consider a broad pantheon of African and diasporic heroics in the serialized incidental, end of workday monologues eventually anthologized in *Like One of the Family* (1956).

The conjoined Black Arts and Black Aesthetic Movements represent a bold stance of cultural agency in literary production, and their theorizations of the meaning of mythology and memory influenced the remainder of the twentieth century and are apparent in pre- and postmillennia mythology visions of Black writers. This began with socio-literary responses to the civil rights and global Pan-African anticolonial era losses of Malcolm X, Martin Luther King Jr., Medgar Evers, and Patrice Lumumba. A discourse emerges between intergenerational heroics (beyond Louverture and the Haitian Revolution), as poets, dramatists, and fiction writers cyclically engage with the past through memories of Frederick Douglass and Harriet Tubman, and through respect for the hyperheroic activism of freedom fighters such as Fannie Lou Hamer.

The late twentieth-century literary models of heritage reflection began to evolve toward both mythological considerations as well as memory configurations. The Black women's literary movement has produced and instigated stable discourses on philosophies of remembering, and this also appears as a priority for contemporary men's writing. To provide optimal examples of Black cultural mythology as literary criticism and categorization, this chapter highlights several literary works that compel a Black cultural mythology reading based on the content and creativity with which authors deliberately recycle the historical record to urge readers into an active, participatory, and visionary encounter with the culture's hero dynamics and mythological structures.

There are several works that are conceptual triumphs for their presentation of the possibilities of Black cultural mythology in contemporary African American literature. Charles S. Johnson's *Dreamer: A Novel* (1998) uses the tropes of physical recognition and naming to compare and contrast the passions and vulnerabilities of Martin Luther King Jr. in his final days with a con man look-alike whom King's inner circle recruits to help manage King's busy schedule of appearances.[19] Colson Whitehead's *John Henry Days* (2001) captures the nation's diverse points of view about legend and heroics in the wake of a West Virginia ceremony to introduce the John Henry postage stamp. This novel is the final source excerpted in the *Norton* (2004) anthology, and its description is a propos for Black cultural mythology reconceptualization. The editors explain that "the novel poses serious questions about the possibility of heroism in the postmodern age and about the relation of young privileged African Americans to their history," which is an invitation to introduce Black cultural mythology as a new critical framework to respond to the need for more advanced tools with which to manage the continuum of African American experience and memory. Finally, Robert O'Hara's *Insurrection: Holding History* envisions a psychodramatic and psychosocial living Black history of Nat Turner. An explication of these three works reveals the nuances and applicability of theorizations of cultural heroics in literary criticism.

Readers will notice the lack of Black women's heroic and mythological literature in this section on literary criticism. However, Black women's texts from writers such as Maria W. Stewart, Shirley Graham Du Bois, May Miller, Laina Mataka, Faith Ringgold, Edwidge Danticat, Ntozake Shange, Toni Morrison, Gayl Jones, and more already appear liberally in earlier chapters featuring key critical discussions. These women writers' texts tend to bloom in either poetry, in one-act dramas, in short prose, or in stylized nonfiction. Or, in their longer works—novels—the writers situate setting, era, nuance, and subtle textual signifiers to reveal recognizable but transformative storytelling that digresses from core, documented histories. As Evelyn Jaffe Schreiber describes the memory phenomenon in the works of Toni Morrison, she notices how Morrison trades the historical for the personal: "Her characters, drawn from historical events or everyday communities, search for a meaningful place in the world, succeeding or failing through personal and cultural memory."[20]

In expanding its function to literary criticism, Black cultural mythology inspires the ongoing mining and classification of all relevant texts that imaginatively embellish and revitalize legendary personas and events in recognizable ways to chronicle the mythological power of narrating diaspora survival. Regarding the gender balance, there is space in the emergent tradition of Black cultural mythology literary criticism for all perspectives that reflect aspects of the cultural memory attributes, such as narratives of epic intuitive conduct (perhaps *Free Enterprise: A Novel of Mary Ellen Pleasant* by Michelle Cliff), immortalization (possibly *Venus* by Suzan-Lori Parks), resistance-based cognitive survival (conceivably *Wild Seed* and *Kindred* by Octavia Butler), historical reenactment of worldview (maybe Shay Youngblood's *Black Girl in Paris* or Nalo Hopkinson's *Midnight Robber*), and antiheroics (satirically, *The America Play* by Suzan-Lori Parks). The current study prioritizes an analysis of texts that feature *sustained* reflections on *well-known* heroic personas. However, for future studies the critical framework is also promising for excavating the meaning and function of texts that feature little-known, unknown, or common folks' radical episodes of survival, fraternity with the ancestors, more localized heroics, and perhaps martyrdom, the latter of which a historical figure's victimization, unintentional sacrifice, or resistance is inspiring (e.g., Emmett Till's gruesome 1955 murder). Infamous and notorious personas and episodes may also enter the critical realm of Black cultural mythology, which, in its affinity to folk culture, acknowledges the value of radical and unlawful Black prowess, particularly episodes that are responses to oppression (e.g., Richard Wright's character Bigger Thomas or Margaret Garner's 1856 act of infanticide on which Toni Morrison bases her 1987 novel *Beloved*).

In this inaugural model of Black cultural mythology as literary criticism, I limit the criticism to texts that are *immersion* works about publicly celebrated heroics, rather than lesser known ones. The included speculative works about the legacies of King, John Henry, and Nat Turner respond to heroic scale, as the texts document nineteenth- and twentieth-century legends whose feats captured the attention of the nation, the colonial hemisphere, and the world. Tales of these men's feats and accolades emerged and evolved during eras that elevated the histories of famous men in a society in which men had certain social advantages that supported a male leadership model, even in oppression. And, sadly, each man's personal heroic tale is embedded in types of violence, physical contest, and death (enslavement, revolt, life on the chain gang, death by exhaustion, and assassination) that caused these men to emerge from their respective eras as martyrs. The corpus of such biographical or semibiographical fiction by Black women or on well-known womanist heroics is smaller, yet such literary criticism will be naturally forthcoming as additional scholars and theorists help to grow the archive and help to identify more women's literary texts that would benefit from the critical tools of Black cultural mythology.

Charles Johnson's *Dreamer*: Humanizing the Mythology

Charles Johnson experiments creatively with the Black cultural mythology binary between hero dynamics and antiheroics in *Dreamer: A Novel* (1998), which juxtaposes Martin Luther King Jr. with a doppelganger who serves as his casual double. The antihero in this case is a flawed hero who either has the capacity to gain understanding or nobility or a character that lacks heroic qualities and who is not necessarily redeemable. The differential between King and his double, Chaym, poses a sustained dilemma for the reader whom Johnson teases and tempts to grapple with the ethics of valuing one identical human over another. Johnson gives Chaym Smith a moniker reminiscent of words such as "shame" or even "chasm," meaning a marked division, a separation, discontinuity, and difference, and the name Chaym is also in proximity to the word "chiasma," which is a crossing or intersection of two tracts. Also, in Hebrew, L'Chaim or L'Chayim is a toast meaning "to life," which signifies on either King's impending assassination or on the life-or-death possibilities of King's destiny. The duality posed by the comparison and intersection of two versions of a famous and immortalized leader compels readers to proceed thoughtfully and philosophically, and it is compatible with comparative achievement narratives such as Wes Moore's memoir, *The Other Wes Moore: One Name, Two Fates* (2010).

Johnson relies on biblical mythology to frame King sometimes as a Messiah and sometimes as one whom "violence followed . . . like a biblical curse."[21] Within a Christian heroic he was "God's athlete."[22] In a philosophical, humanistic heroic, he was "celebrated as the heir of Thoreau."[23] As a leader waging battle, he was "*leading his generals in the siege.*"[24] Johnson summarizes his superlative as "more tired, acclaimed, hated, gaoled, and hunted than any other Negro in History, but living this close to death was . . . inevitable.[25] The novel's prologue frames King's rather complicated mythology. He was in tune with the culture's plight as

> the memories came washing over him in waves—the poor living like chattel, children dynamited in a church, Watts burning for six days, the death threats spewing through the telephone at his wife—on those nights he wept for the blood spilled by his enemies, for his own life's lost options, for the outrageous fragility of what he hoped to achieve in a world smothering in materialism.[26]

The prologue compels a Black cultural mythology reading with its poetic and sad litany of King's trials as well as his achievements. *Dreamer*'s speculation on King provides a detailed impression of the processes and stages of a hero's epic intuitive conduct, hyperheroic sensibility, and resistance-based commitment to cognitive survival. Johnson's historical-biographical method of creating literature based on acute historical research is apparent in the novel's *meditation* on King, and it is a marvel that Johnson duplicates this immersion also for King's foil, Chaym. This process supports the novel's characterizations, which for King means that the reader gains access to both his insecurities and the public antiheroics of the era that fuel them. The opposition attempted to threaten King's dynamism:

> Never a day passed when he did not read that his stature was diminished, his day of leadership done, and he could not ignore his critics if he was, as he so often claimed, committed to the truth. Twelve times he'd been imprisoned in Alabama and Georgia jails, stabbed once, spat upon, and targeted for death so many times he could say, like the Apostle Paul, "I bear in my body the marks of the Lord."[27]

Johnson also notes King's "twelve years of sacrifice" that some youth ignored in favor of characterizing him as an Uncle Tom. This compels an even more reflective consideration of the Black cultural mythology attribute of sacrificial inheritance that might not be recognized as a contribution by future generations.[28]

Familiarizing readers with King's soul and both mortal and immortal versions of personhood, the prologue credits King's collective superpower as "the severe discipline that black manhood calls for in the twentieth century."[29] It ends by planting the seed for the novel's *binary of* reconciling opposites, as well as its *duality*—that one man can be both heroic and normal. The novel emerges as a speculative fantasy from a tired and beleaguered King who "longed to escape 'the strain of being known . . . I've been faced with the responsibility of trying to do as one man what five or six people ought to be doing.' "[30] Another binary is the tension between versions of King in public memory. Joseph Darda critiques societal complacency about King's legacy. With the unfortunate state of memorial affairs, King's "name and image can be found everywhere and yet rarely with any context or complexity."[31] This echoes the commemoration observations related to King in chapter 2, where an interventionist approach helps renarrate King's transnationalism and his grounded cultural radicalism concerning interpretations of African American historical progress. Darda categorizes the novel with language such as reimagining and remembering that places it firmly within the purview of Black cultural mythology. Darda's other effective phrasing related to Black cultural mythology is the notion of *rematerializing* that counters the *dismembering* of King as a liberal rather than as a radical. Darda's interest in memory is how "Johnson's fiction encourages us to rethink black freedom struggles not as frozen in history but as ongoing and under threat."[32] This point of view parallels Black cultural mythology's philosophical assertion that the function of past-to-present meditations on history and survivalist cultural memorial processes is to stabilize ongoing African American orientations to freedom.

Johnson uses the young, twenty-four-year-old volunteer Matthew Bishop to narrate much of the novel, and his observations as "a man of no consequence at all" help to situate the novel's thesis about the relationship between heroes and average people. Matthew has a memorial awareness that centers the processes of memory tested by his reminiscences about his late mother:

> Since her death it was as if she'd never lived, and now only existed in memory, in me during those times when I thought of her, which were less and less each year, and when I ceased to be, it seemed to me, all vestiges of her would vanish as well. (Often I tried to reconstruct her face, and found I could not remember, say, her ears. How could I forget my own mother's ears?) In her mind, the minister was a saint.[33]

This association between his mother's regard for King and his own struggles with processes of memory and forgetting reinforces Johnson's authorial commitment to exploring aspects of what is now Black cultural mythology. In fact, Johnson includes nostalgia and celebration for many ordinary people referenced in the narrative such as memories of the "egoless" and "self-forgetful" Mama Pearl who was known among the young Southern Christian Leadership Conference as "everybody's grandmother."[34]

Matthew introduces King to Chaym, and Johnson structures the moment of encounter between King and Chaym, his "double," with existential possibilities. As Matthew describes the scene, "Far beyond interested, he looked spellbound. Then shaken. He might have been peering into a mirror, one in which history was turned upside down, beginning not in his father's commodious, two-story Queen Anne-style home in Atlanta but instead across the street in one of the wretched shotgun shacks crammed with the black poor."[35] The resemblance as well as the binary were clear as "his eyes squinted, the faint smile on his [Chaym's] lips one part self-protective irony, two parts sarcasm, as if he carried unsayable secrets (or sins) that, if spoken, would send others running from the room."[36] Despite his resemblance to

King, Chaym was "the kind of Negro the Movement had for years kept away from the world's cameras: sullen, ill-kempt, the very embodiment of the blues."[37] Chaym described them as twins and in a surprising colorful metaphor suggested a sort of divine history to explain the two of them, "I figured God f____ up and missed with me, but He had you for backup."[38] Chaym's background of juvenile homes, poverty, Korean War injury, and hard times contrasts with King's life and choices, and Matthew has a sense that Chaym's appearance and objectives are based on hustle and conspiracy enabled by his photographic memory and slick talk.

The text reiterates the irony and sarcasm that pervade Chaym's character, yet it also introduces the word "synchronization" to suggest the magnetism that links the two men after their encounter.[38] Cleary Chaym is the antihero, King's opposite, who has "an inverted Midas touch so that everything he brushed against transmogrified into crap."[40] For Chaym, bouts of memory loss, perhaps from a Korean War trauma, caused his life to be "a nightmare, a ghastly joke on everything he'd once dreamed of becoming."[41] He is an uneven, even frightful personality who seems bent on capitalizing on his likeness to King. Matthew notices how "he was staring at us—like a fugitive peering at a comfortable bourgeois family through their window as they eat dinner, oblivious to his presence, and on his face was that unsettling smile as he critically scrutinized King."[42] These introductory passages on Chaym invoke a level of mysterious, horror-film fear because Chaym lurks and behaves like a threatening impersonator. He tells Matthew, "I don't just want a job . . . I want a li'l of what the good doctor in there has got in such great abundance. . . . *Immortality.*"[43] This is certainly not what Maria W. Stewart had in mind when she poured out her soul to reiterate the value of immortalizing the race.

Introducing Chaym as not merely a twin, a doppelganger, or double but as a possibly threatening *impersonator* who desires King's *immortality* is a frightening prospect that is also an ingenious twist of fictional storytelling. Johnson's narrative merges hero dynamics and antiheroics not so much in the context of commemorating or memorializing, but in a plot twist of envy. It was as if "he took a delicious pleasure in publicity that diminished the man he so resembled and clearly revered."[44] In the end, Chaym's antics are not threatening, but he is cerebral, calculating, brilliant in his own way that is completely different from that of King, and almost *villainous* in his imaginings of the benefits of resemblance. This dichotomy between the heroic King, as the martyr that society memorializes, and Chaym, as the hustler who is either "damned" or "fallen," challenges King by "shak[ing] his certainty that all were equal in the eyes of the Lord."[45]

King's team considered Chaym's possibility as a decoy, a duplication and deflection that introduces new critical possibilities beyond the expectations of Black cultural mythology, yet Johnson's narrative challenges the practical application of King's values by using Chaym's appearance to challenge King's philosophy on equality. King thinks, "in no other way than the somatic were they equal. In fact, they were like negatives of each other."[46] In this passage, the text introduces the possibilities of envy and jealousy that others in King's circles have for him. It also introduces the term "chasm," related to "the danger of his becoming a pariah among the Negroes if he didn't somehow soften the separateness, the chasm his talent created between himself and others."[47] To soften the harsh conclusion he was drawing about the value of his talent ("natural gifts") and destiny versus that of the Chayms of the world, King lists the accolades of talented others such as Harry Belafonte, Paul Robeson, Joe Louis, Claude McKay, Ollie Harrington, and Jacob Lawrence. A Black cultural mythology theoretical reading will never ignore such a pantheon expounded upon in a literary text.

In fact, in another passage, Amy, Matthew's love interest within the Southern Christian Leadership Conference, recounts the mythological structure of her southern relatives who urged her to duplicate the entrepreneurial prowess of Jean Jacques Pointe de Sable (Chicago founder and merchant), Madame C. J. Walker (queen of a beauty empire), and Robert Bogle (famous Philadelphia caterer). The novel's emphasis in this section is on cultural survival as Amy recounts the communal philosophy of her great-grandfather. Matthew "hungered for the sense of history she had, the confidence and connectedness that came from a clear lineage stretching back a century."[48] Johnson's focus in this novel is not only on hero dynamics but also on myriad variables of Black cultural mythology related to ancestry and heritage practices. They do not go uncontested, however. Chaym is annoyed by Amy's narrative of her family's hero dynamics, and he attempts to shatter the story by announcing, "Memory is mostly imagination."[49] This proclamation is one of many examples in the text where Johnson plants a philosophical or discursive query on memory that prompts the reader to pause for further reflection. Chaym's observation is not wholly untrue; instead, it is the magic of remembrance that storytellers may innocuously embellish a narrative to give it life and to construct the way it serves a family's or a culture's mythological structure. This is an act of well-being and survival.

Chaym studies to be like King, with a confidence to be more like King than King himself. This preparation makes him suitable to fulfill minor appearances, such as accepting an award. The dichotomy between Chaym and King is most apparent when, immediately before the award appearance, Matthew spies Chaym sneaking away to shoot heroin while in his role as King. Chaym has a meltdown before he can fulfill his role as a decoy, and from the church kitchen he listens to King perform. In this passage, Johnson suggests an even deeper heroic *dysfunction*, that after twelve years of obsessively studying his look-alike, Chaym cannot deliver and is upset. He says, "That was *my* stuff. Not things I've ever said, but stuff I've felt. Like my spirit is trapped in his . . . like he gives my soul a voice."[50] This passage suggests Chaym's transcendent, transformative obsession with King and with embodying King's identity. In literature, this impulse is suggestive of a prefantasy conceptual device that would take interesting flight in the genre of science fiction or speculative fiction. It could also be a function of dysfunctional *twinning*, wherein identical twins are born with unequal abilities that haunt their lifelong relationship to one another.

Chaym gets shot during a moment of impersonating King on the ride home, as an elderly Black man feigns awe to gain proximity to attempt assassination. During his convalescence, he looks less and less like King. He grows his hair out in an Afro hairstyle, wears dark sunglasses, and chews gum to the extent that, while waiting for the train, a college student asks, "Excuse me, sir, are you LeRoi Jones?"[51] Johnson cleverly redirects the narrative away from Chaym and begins to use it to document the histories and legacies of the civil rights era as well as more localized histories such as that of southern churches. Chaym reappears antiheroically submitting to the FBI's blackmail that persuades him to work as an impersonator to discredit King, possibly as a womanizer, and more, while King eventually succumbs to the harshest assault of antiheroics—the assassin's bullet.

Johnson's novel *Dreamer* adds a new dimension to Black cultural mythology because he exposes the intersections between hero and antihero, or even hero and villain. This juxtaposition is a universal trope in storytelling, including in the text's references to Cain and Abel, Romulus and Remus, and Jacob and Esau, which signify on the possibility that heroics are based on point of view. There is a universal truth differentiated between competing groups or entities, that one group's hero is the opposing group's antihero. In African American history, there have been pairings of opponents such as W. E. B. Du Bois versus Booker T. Washington and Martin Luther King Jr. versus Malcolm X, but Johnson writes of twinship or brotherhood born of more existential parallels. In heroic and commemorative discourses Johnson's artistry draws attention to the hero's effect and influence on possibilities with a double, decoy, impersonator, stand-in, imposter, doppelganger, replacement, reinvention, look-alike, mistaken identity, alter ego, counterfeit, twin, split personality, déjà vu, a mimic, role-playing, and an opposite. Addressing these predicaments within the realm of ancestor acknowledgment or through relational proximity represented by resemblance, cultural reincarnation, genealogy, or inheritance is an exciting direction that Johnson's text poses for Black cultural mythology.

John Henry Days and Intercultural Mythology

A Black cultural mythology study of the legendary figure John Henry is in some ways closely related to chapter 2's topic of commemoration and chapter 3's exploration of Harriet Tubman's aesthetic memorialization because it adds a "Reconstruction to Nadir" period narrative on cultural icons to the discussion of contemporary cultural memory practices. Éva Tettenborn nicely introduces the heroic philosophy on which Colson Whitehead's *John Henry Days* stands by linking the mythological discourse to Patrice Rankine's discussion in *Ulysses in Black* (2006). Rankine considers "the cultural context in which the hero acts," and Tettenborn summons Rankine to remind readers of *John Henry Days* of the challenges of fostering an African American cultural heroics.⁵² The struggle is to reject the ways America manifests its intent to reduce African American men's "heroic possibilities."⁵³ Much of the novel features masculinity (Pamela Street being the exception).

The academic character in Colson Whitehead's *John Henry Days*, the ethnographer Guy Johnson, corroborates the value of legend, which extends to its symbolic literary meaning as well, in the confirmation that "for Guy, the question of whether the John Henry legend rests on a factual basis is, after all, not of much significance. No matter which way it is answered the fact is that the legend itself is a reality, a living functioning thing in the folk life of the Negro."⁵⁴ And the blues singer-songwriter Moses reveals the process of meditating on the ancestor to thoughtfully memorialize his struggle:

> Most John Henry songs he's heard from people, they tend to talk about the race and the man's death. He sang a version like that a few times but it never sounded right to him. The words "nothing but a man" set him thinking on it: Moses felt the

natural thing would be to sing about what the man felt waking up in his bed on the day of the race. Knowing what he had to do and knowing that it was his last sunrise. Last breakfast, last everything.[55]

Through numerous characters and similar confessional episodes in *John Henry Days*, Colson Whitehead pens an epic, comprehensive literary vision of an African American heroic figure. Whitehead uses the African American protagonist, J. Sutter, who applies the processes of investigative journalism and reportage merged with adjacent human curiosity about cultural group behavior, to suggest a more complicated cultural mythology about an African American man and legend. John Henry's life is perfect for Whitehead's imaginative effort because his life spanned the southern industrial revolution, and his memory is stable and multisymbolic to a multicultural set of characters and communities. This differs from Sylvie Bauer's contention that what Whitehead offers is a smorgasbord of commemoration sensibilities that fall short of cultural "stability and fixity" concerning John Henry's mythology.[56] But perhaps the novel only signifies on the legendary figure in order to prompt a mythological self-assessment in its readers, particularly African American cultural readers.

In Whitehead's literary vision, John Henry's legacy and value are simultaneously relevant for Black dimensions of cultural memory, white dimensions of regional legacy and heritage, labor industry iconic empowerment, regional tourism, family nostalgia, sacred space, and personal identity, from which emerge many individual and collective conflicts that require resolution or intervention. The novel features a corps of journalists, and much of the banter prefigures media ideology concerning what is newsworthy and the power of the media to memorialize its subject. The novel's discourses on cultural mythology and memory are so layered that *John Henry Days* emerges as a central contemporary novel in the creative literary genre of Black cultural mythology. Readers experience layers of point of view, including chapters imagined from the life of John Henry as he performed with superhuman resolve on the railroad and diverse cultural examples that suggest the diversity of ways that people—regardless of race, culture, and region—worship, revere, and commemorate. John Henry is both a legendary African American persona and a universal one, which stretches the theoretical possibilities of Black cultural mythology's variables as both culturally distinct and possibly usable for shared, cross-racial, heroics. Antiheroics also play a part, in which interpreters with different worldviews prioritize different parts of the John

Henry narrative. For some, the man is the hero; for others, the machine is the hero.

This critical deconstruction of the legendary is what Scott Nelson's John Henry historiography *Steel Drivin' Man* (2006) explores as a legend that is actually based on the collective hyperheroics of numerous steel-driving men named "John."[57] It also pairs nicely with the structurally comparable analysis of collective contemporary points of view on Malcolm X's lasting mythological structure, maintained in spite of and even revitalized *because of* Manning Marable's potentially mythology-damaging biography, *Malcolm X: A Life of Reinvention*.

The title *John Henry Days* literally refers to the novel's culmination of an annual commemorative event, John Henry Days, a weeklong celebration in the small towns of Hinton and Talcott in West Virginia. The novel introduces layers of cross-cultural heroic queries that cue a philosophical explication in terms of Black cultural mythology. It compels a study of the meaning of immortalization, the role of the ballad or song, and the interplay between history, memory, and authorial license to embellish in the process of mythology-sustaining storytelling. It also addresses the difference between a festival and commemoration, the parallels between contemporary and past struggles that have shared racial and cultural premises, the role of postage stamps in commemoration, and how heroes parallel everyday folk. It features the historical archive, festivals and commemoration practices, fairs and reenactments, the politics of museums and antiquing, song tributes, the difference between the folk hero and the agency of the legendary hero, and the function of cultural memory. It also addresses antiheroics and the economic commodification of memorial activity.

The prologue is a masterful introduction to the conceptual possibilities of where the novel's plot may go. It admits that there is no single version of truth to sustain society's beliefs about the man or memory because, through a series of written accounts and messages that function as ethnographic responses to a researcher's call for information on John Henry, it confesses that variations of truth and recollection make memory fluid and contested. Michael K. Walonen suggests this view with an emphasis on how "contemporary African American historical fictional discourse is not so much a means of recapturing past realities or straightforward or unambiguous vectors, as it is a mythical textual exploration of the past."[58]

Whitehead emboldens the myth and legend interests of the novel by introducing both brief and sustained mention of numerous legendary, historical, folk culture, and regional examples of memory, legacy, heritage, inheritance, monument, and memorialization. These range from John Henry, Pecos Bill, Paul Bunyan, and Mighty Casey, to Harpers Ferry, the Beatles, comic book heroes, and rap icons.

Whitehead introduces the term "mythology" in his discussion of the cult of the railroad that sustains regional labor pride, an intergenerational work ethic, and working-class identity. The celebration towns have a regional legacy, notably, "They are railroad towns, Hinton and Talcott, and everybody who lives here has railroad in their bloodline."[59] Benny, the thoughtful young proprietor of the humble Talcott Motor Lodge where the journalists stay, relocated there as a teen and "feels out of place when confronted with the railroad nostalgia of the two towns, that is to say nearly every waking moment."[60] However, "he is learning to understand the mythology of his adopted home. He is learning how to wait for the train."[61]

The novel introduces many branches of heroics and mythology, which are paralleled by the sensational embellishments and infamy of stereotype, celebrity, exaggeration, superlative, gossip, ghosts, antiques, media attention, and icons of pop culture. The group of journalists has fraternal familiarity with each other, and their conversations debate things such as their "legendary gluttony," good times, and the greatest bands and other superlatives related mostly to American music, pop culture, and movement icons in mythological ways that border on nostalgia and cult following.[62]

The white citizenry's generic Americanist legacy of the novel's folk stamp commemoration event proceeds with its own sense of legacy and heroics. The postmaster general's speech introduces one lens of commemoration. He speaks proudly about the region's history and the sacrifices of men.[63] He does acknowledge John Henry's status as formerly enslaved, and goes on to note that "his great competition with the steam drill is a testament to the strength of the human spirit."[64] He adds that the Post Office is "proud to honor such an American."[65] The novel also has a sustained discourse on the possibility of John Henry as a diversity matter. He is one of four folk heroes in the stamp series, and a postal employee says, "You know. They got three white ones, you gotta mix it up these days."[66] One journalist shares his diversity story: "'We used to read the story of John Henry in kindergarten,' Tiny says. 'The school board told the teachers they couldn't teach Little Black Sambo anymore, so they switched over to this picture book of John Henry's competition. Positive imagery.'"[67] White citizens have a sense of competing heroics and mythology within the social interplay of race. In J. Sutter's reflections after his near-death experience with choking, Whitehead plants a profound critical analysis of the ways juvenile literature and cartoons manipulate the implications of the hero's enslavement background, similar to chapter 3's discussion of the same tendency with Harriet Tubman.

Sutter is critical of the myths about John Henry because the hero's birth and death are linked inextricably with his *destiny* in most tales and representations. Critic Peter Collins questions if "J's problem is that he is not traumatized enough by history," which reflects the character's journalistic economic depravity.[68] Like the protagonist Ron in Robert O'Hara's Black cultural mythology play, *Insurrection: Holding History*, J. Sutter also wonders if the heroic feat that ends in death is really a victory: "John Henry was dead. He died with a hammer in his hand, just as he said he would on the day he was born. He beat the machine and died doing it."[69] As a child, he asked his teacher, "Mrs. Goodwin, if he beat the steam engine, why did he have to die? Did he win or lose?"[70] With the haphazard credential of philosopher, curator, and historian on John Henry due to her father's immersion of their lives within the legend's archive, Pamela also questions whether the John Henry work songs were resistance, condemnation, or lamentation. The men who sang of John Henry might have had a different objective, conveying, "His fight was foolish because the cost was too high."[71]

The chapters meander in documentation of folk cultural practices, including one about a John Henry balladeer in omniscient narrative that captures the creative processes in which personal, folk, heroic, and mythological sensibilities converge. J. Sutter is even repelled by any level of treatment of Black exceptionalism, accusing white smiles of being "some kind of overcompensation for slavery."[72]

Defensively, J. Sutter views the whites of Talcott as antiheroic descendants of the railroaders who watched John Henry die. Sutter points out the commemorative silence on John Henry's race and culture in the towns' celebration, as he realizes that he and Pamela are the only Black people at the festival. He ponders, "Honoring a black hero and them the only folks in the room. John Henry the American."[73] J. Sutter's positionality is as an a-cultural journalist, one who is not moved by African American cultural nuances. He finds himself in positions in which commemoration and heroics taunt him. Always aware of the Black face-count in the room during John Henry Days, he has an ironic brush with death that places him conceptually between John Henry and Marvel Comic Black heroes. Ignoring the teenage African American soloist who performs a Robeson-esque version of "The Ballad of John Henry," Sutter sneaks away to binge on free prime rib. He chokes, and while succumbing to a slow death (before a last-minute rescue), he sees only visions of the Avengers and the Black superhero Luke Cage. He is further sarcastic toward the teenage boy singing more than twelve stanzas of the ballad. He is distraught at his own shallowness and with the lack of noble heroics in his seemingly final moments. Collins interprets much of the novel's haunting as "not just a cultural haunting but an economic haunting. That is to say, the novel's ghosts serve as a way of reinjecting the past into a market that relentlessly transforms history into a commodity."[74]

As an exploration into Africana cultural memory, several characters and predicaments from *John Henry Days* emerge to offer historical and philosophical depth to the processes of memory and memorialization. Related to chapter 3's discussion of commemoration, Whitehead's fictional John Henry Days event is challenged to offer a sincerer racial and cultural remembrance beyond the John Henry activities and "John Henry barbecues."[75] William Wiggins's *O Freedom!* reminds us of how distinctly communal Black barbecues are, even in ancestral remembrance.

J. Sutter is the African American junketeering freelance journalist who reluctantly accepts the job to cover the West Virginia commemoration. He has "been very conscientious about staying away from the forge of his race's history," and he accepts the gig in order to maintain a record of daily free meals on the media circuit.[76] His path toward taking commemoration and hero dynamics seriously is circuitous, as he gets distracted by myriad possibilities such as how the "white cannibals" in West Virginia will cause the story of his "martyrdom to live on in black fable."[77]

Pamela Street is one of the most compelling Black cultural mythology characters because she has the task of managing both personal and cultural legacy, in a double jeopardy of cultural mythology. She rejects the mythology and eternal life of John Henry in "sibling rivalry," as she shared her childhood with a three-foot replica of the man and witnessed the evolution of her father's obsession.[78] However, at six years old, when her family encountered the figure of John Henry in the antique store, she too was in awe, acknowledging, "The hammer's impending but stalled convergence with the spike had a spooky presence to it and Pamela felt a chill; it was a fragment of something larger fallen from above, eternal forces glimpsed for a second."[79]

She considers her father's John Henry home museum collection, which suffocated the family home, to be "his remains." An oversaturation of hero dynamics that bordered on hoarding give her an initial skeptical and mechanical relationship to cultural memory, though the text reveals this as a stage of mourning her father's death. She attends the festival to liquidate her inheritance—her father's coveted collection of John Henry memorabilia—by donating it to a local museum. Whitehead introduces her character not as an asset to cultural mythology but as a victim of it. In an original approach to antiheroics, Pamela is too jaded to support artifact or aesthetic memorialization because her life has been smothered by the crowded claustrophobia of "repositories for things of no immediate purpose but infinite quantifiable value."[80] Even Howard University and Tuskegee University rejected the collection as a potential donation. The text groups museums and storage units as tombs and mausoleums that help to quantify the death, rather than the life, of memory. She hated John Henry and "the bills from the storage facility . . . distilled her hatred for John Henry into a convenient monthly statement."[81]

Pamela's narrative plants the first seeds for us to know her father, Mr. Street, and John Henry metaphorically joins the family almost as an adoptee, secured in the backseat with six-year-old Pamela and "swaddled in her favorite red blanket, her blanket."[82] This adoptee, endowed with "eternal forces," advances from being a well-earned hobby for a successful and hard-working hardware store owner to an "addiction" and "fixation" whose obsession represented Mr. Street's transferred and misplaced devotion away from his family and in favor of weekend "pilgrimages to antique shows and fairs."[83] Mr. Street even spent her school clothes money on John Henry artifacts. His devotion to celebrating, preserving, and *assembling*[84] John Henry seemed to be commemoration and sacred remembrance gone awry in a modern rite of obsessive reincarnation or resurrection reminiscent of an Africana mythological twist on Frankenstein. In Pamela's description, Mr. Street did not participate in healthy cultural heroics that celebrated the postenslavement capacity of the Black male body as a machine forging its own agency against an industrial revolution that attempted, still, to commodify it. Instead, Pamela's narrative shifts to admit the tomb-like evolution of her family's home: "The Street household smelled of her father's rotting mania and the sour reek of Pamela's and her mother's snuffed lives."[85] Reinforcing the mausoleum nature of her home, there was a poster in their dining room of "John Henry sprawled dead on his back, surrounded by the witnesses of his feat, arms spread wide like Christ's and his hammer in his hand, he died with his hammer in his hand."[86] Whitehead permits this poster to replace the stereotyped image of Jesus in traditional, twentieth-century Black homes, as a type of religious mythology and symbolism.

Black cultural mythology appears in its extreme in Whitehead's characterization of Mr. Street, as he assembles artifacts in a dysfunctional ritual remembrance that is antithetical to the maintenance of mythological structure that benefits the Black family and adds to its wholeness. It is a dysfunctional heroic nostalgia that has a double effect as Pamela grieves her father's death and is challenged to liquidate his trove of earthly possessions—her inheritance. This is one of the novel's dilemmas, pivoting on the processes of the personal layered with the legendary that inform Pamela's choice to either forsake her personal inheritance or relinquish it as a sterile donation of artifacts for a museum.

By design, Whitehead's *John Henry Days* documents the broad social and cultural histories related to John Henry, and he frames his epic narrative to represent a comprehensive demographic sampling of worldviews, commensurate with the novel's ethnographic prologue. The tools of Black cultural mythology help distinguish between mythology in an Americana worldview and mythology in an Africana worldview with particular relevance for African Americans. The character transformations of the African American cynic, J. Sutter, and the commemoration-traumatized daughter, Pamela Street, are traditional. They successfully reinforce the novel's effect in the African American literary canon of prioritizing an exceptional and distinct African American worldview in processes of cultural memory. At the festival, Sutter and Pamela pair off toward what becomes a ritualistic pilgrimage to the smaller, secluded, and possibly original "John Henry tunnel of old wives' tales."[87] It is in this sacred space where each character comes to terms with the actual and symbolic healing and renewal effect of John Henry on their lives. For Pamela, "Standing here now, I thought I would never be here because I hated it all. Listening to the same old stories out of his mouth every day. John Henry, John Henry. But being here now."[88] For Pamela, the festival held an additional meaning. She prepared by smuggling her father's ashes onto the airplane that would deliver her (and him) to this historical town of his obsession. Following her father's old map, she and Sutter trek up a mountain in search of John Henry's grave. There, they bury her father's urn:

> She asked him if he had to die to bring this weekend into being. All his life he wanted something like this weekend, a celebration of John Henry. His collection would have been a star attraction, he could have made speeches. . . . The crowds finally would have come to his museum. She asked him, would this have still happened, the fair, the museum, if he was still alive. Or did he have to give up on himself for this to happen. The price of progress. The way John Henry had to give himself up to bring something new into the world.[89]

After this interment, Whitehead includes a brilliantly speculative chapter on Mr. Street that chronicles the days on end that he prepared for and waited for visitors to stop in to see his John Henry museum. He planned to "elaborate on the theme of the march of technology and the march of progress and the prices paid. In the end what was important was not the machine but the man."[90] Mr. Street honored John Henry and wanted to share knowledge of his heroic breadth with the community for the legend's example of "possibility."[91] Yet, "the speech slept in his mouth," perhaps uttered in requiem by Pamela as she found thoughtful words to offer over his grave.[92]

For J. Sutter, the ritual releases him from the consuming stagnation of his impersonal journalistic career as he asks, "What if this were your work? To best the mountain. Come to work every day, two, three, years of work, into this death and murk, each day your progress measured by the extent to which you extend the darkness. How deep you dig your grave. . . . This place defeats the frequencies that are the currency of his life. Email and pagers, cell phones . . ."[93] This is meditation in the best tradition of Black cultural mythology literature. The final effect on J. Sutter is a reflection on "decades of healing and forgetting. How long does it take to forget a hole in yourself?"[94] Jaya Shrivastava refers to this as how "J. Sutter's metarepresentational ability not only allows him to recall past occurrences but also enables him to revise the information recollected."[95] In her view, "by evaluating information he gathers on John Henry's legend and by keeping track of his own evolving perception, he gradually changes his opinion and ascribes meaning to the folkloric architecture of the John Henry story."[96] J. Sutter's transformation is stimulated by Mr. Street's legendary commitment to John Henry and Pamela's museum donation. These emerge as centerpieces for the real human-interest story J. Sutter must report from John Henry Days.

In addition to the well-developed characters who experience the John Henry Days event only to discover that it sparked within them a philosophical understanding of Black cultural mythology and dimensions of Africana cultural memory, Whitehead seems aware that an epic text on traditional African American hero dynamics must have requisite mention of Toussaint Louverture. The revolutionary is duly acknowledged, and is included in Whitehead's critical excavation of the ways singer, actor, and activist Paul Robeson performed John Henry in 1940 in the musical of the same name along the path of developing his own cultural heroics, although noticed and countered antiheroically by the FBI and the US government.

Inevitably, Whitehead's *John Henry Days* is another key work in the genre of Black cultural mythology. Its value is its power to measure, comprehensively, the impact of a *folkloric* African American hero dynamic that retains vitality in spite of society's competing and uncertain narrative of John Henry's life and mortality. Whitehead's work is a departure from Johnson's philosophical measure of men in his contrast of heroic versus average human worth highlighted by differences between the honorable Martin Luther King Jr. and his con artist doppelganger. The final example of imaginative rights addresses a third dimension—*speculation*—of literary models of Black cultural mythology that sustain African cultural memory studies.

Robert O'Hara's *Insurrection: Holding History*

Nate Parker's visual biography on Nat Turner, *Birth of a Nation* (2016), was a nicely timed media challenge for society to practice public domain diversity wherein a distinctly African American heroic empowered the African American resistance narrative from the big screen. The nation had just witnessed eight years of a Black president, and the film emerged during the election cycle that would inevitably force dichotomous racial ideas and racialized national memories to the surface. Indeed, this biopic film is a biographical contribution to Black cultural mythology. However, this chapter prioritizes Robert O'Hara's dramatic literary contribution to Black cultural mythology to represent Nat Turner in a play—*Insurrection: Holding History* (1998). *Insurrection* is more compelling because O'Hara, who admits his "imagination lives in Overdrive," presents a complex play that challenges members of society to define the domains and memorial sequences of their personal and cultural mythologies.[97] The play's meditative, imaginative, and temporal crossings simulate heretofore unexpressed possibilities of cultural memory, and Black cultural mythology is a critical tool that gazes deeply into the play's function and effect. This is commensurate with O'Hara's dramatic philosophy:

> I think of myself as participating in what I like to call The Theater of Choke. I do not want my work to go down easily. . . . I want you to Gasp. To have to work what you see and read down into your Gut. . . . I had to *work* to create it, and you should have to *work* to experience it. I want you to see and read my work and Choke. It should not dissolve in your mouth, instead

it should be one of those Hard Candies. . . . Maybe one of those "Fireballs" . . . that you have to suck on it as it stings your gums and then finally you get to the point where you can crunch it up in your mouth and then you can swallow it but only after much hard work.[98]

This colorful statement of objective is an appropriate companion to the hard-won agency of Black cultural mythology, whose aim is to frame an African American survivalist worldview in terms of immersion and cultural agency. The survivalist demands of the historical heroic record were unscripted, yet they were transmitted in ways that generations of Africans in the diaspora could retain and utilize for cultural survival. Similarly, the final product of cultural memory and cultural mythology requires grounded conceptual tools, such as the itemizations of the philosophy of Black cultural mythology, that have the ability to give meaning to the vast expanse of memorialization, ancestry, inheritance, and cyclical sacred observance, whose representation, as O'Hara demonstrates, has no limits, though it remains culturally recognizable.

O'Hara's philosophy centers the imaginative rights of a long tradition of writers who recycle Africana or diasporic hero dynamics in their narratives in a procreative act of cultural stabilization. Studies on O'Hara's play focus overwhelmingly on the queer identities in the play, and a cultural mythology analysis is a critical redirection. Rebecca Balon's study explores matters of enslavement sexuality, but she does credit the play for how its themes and effect "reinhabit the world of American chattel slavery in order to supplement the historian's record with an imaginative exploration of the experience of the enslaved."[99] Faedra Chatard Carpenter notes the "inherent capaciousness of our historical narratives" and reacts to O'Hara's shifting of history. She writes, "O'Hara extends these concepts of non-linearity and multiplicity by revealing the performativity of history itself. History (like performance) may be documented or re-enacted."[100] Black cultural mythology's conceptual tools support a structured analysis in this new direction that expands the corpus of existing criticism on *Insurrection*, and the broad frameworks of Balon's and Carpenter's studies reveal an interest in further considering the intersection of history, consciousness, and recollection.[101]

Insurrection: Holding History is an atemporal speculative drama about the symbolic, yet practical and functional, relationship between personal and collective cultural hero dynamics and cognitive survival. The drama centers the historical narrative, action, and worldview of the African American enslavement revolt leader, Nat Turner, who in 1831 led a revolt in Southampton County, Virginia. Turner's memorial legacy is as a prophet who was inspired by a spiritual force and visions to strike for Black freedom with Old Testament biblical wrath and with New Testament sacrificial leadership. O'Hara's creative vision to merge the family lineage of protagonist Ron Porter (a twenty-five-year-old academic, stressfully meeting his dissertation deadline for a degree in slavery studies) with the enslavement experience and heroics is a striking example of Black cultural mythology's interest in the relationship between ancestor acknowledgment, immortalization sensibility, sacrificial inheritance, and mythological structure practiced within family memory and generally linked to broad communal hero dynamics. The play itself is an aesthetic memorialization and a reenactment of cultural worldview, as O'Hara structures seven acts of magical realism through a methodology of writing drama as "a Bullet through Time."[102]

The play's title features the act of insurrection, which is a reference to the memory of Nat Turner's freedom event. The subtitle, *Holding History* is O'Hara's cultural memory intervention that suggests the need for action and engagement of history for optimum cultural survival. O'Hara artistically signifies on a personal event—the passing of his grandfather and the patriarch's appearance in a dream—to use the genre of drama to recommend a new form of mythological structure. Mythological structure reflects how family and community reinforce cultural self-esteem in group members by exhibiting, transmitting, and cultivating a functional relationship with their own historical worldview. This serves as inspiration and as a model for enhanced intergenerational future cultural existence. O'Hara's innovation to mythological structure is the play's revelation of what "holding history" actually means for lineage survival.

The central commemorative event of *Insurrection* is the annual birthday party for Ron's formerly enslaved, 189-year-old great-great-grandfather, T.J., who aside from a few symbolic working parts, is catatonic. His working eye and one good toe are symbols of heritage traumas from enslavement that he physically carries to transmit the family's history to future generations. It is similar to the long list of scars that Dana and her husband Kevin receive from their sporadic time travel from 1976 California to early nineteenth-century, antebellum Maryland. In *Insurrection*, Ron does not party because he is busy studying Thomas Ruffin Gray's 1831 pamphlet *Confessions of Nat Turner*, searching for a new meaningful conceptual breakthrough to better illuminate Nat Turner's meaning in history. He gives an extended confession about his new obsession:

RON (*Lit. quick*): yeah, iii don't know where it came from but I can't git it outta my head and I have nothing new to say about him or slavery there's nothing new about the fact that he lost his mind and started slashin' folks and okay we survived OKAY ALREADY i mean so what throughout history millions of people have survived horrible events and american slavery is MINUTE when you think about it in terms of what happened during the Crusades and even the uh i don't know I mean turner's revolt was NUTHIN compared to how those brothas and sistas were kickin' up in Haiti okay nat turner/slavery BIG DEAL move on but it won't let me Go!!¹⁰³

At a later point in the play, Ron shows Nat Turner the book *Confessions of Nat Turner*, and the two deconstruct its credibility, with Turner questioning, "i'm supposed to have tol' this white lawyer i never even heard of all my thoughts all my ideas all my life stories?" to which Ron replies, "we know all of it can't be absolutely true but."[104] This is the same conversation that African Americans wish they could have with Antony and Isabell—from the 1619 Angolan group—to ascertain how they came to name their Angolan-Virginian son William Tucker. Nonetheless, such revisionist markers are central features of *Insurrection* that cement its Black cultural mythology value. O'Hara even joins the corps of writers who signify on Haiti within a Black cultural mythology sensibility. Also, the dramatist's itemization of the variable of "survival" further corroborates a Black cultural mythology reading of *Insurrection*.

After this year's birthday party, Ron begins to have visions, and the silent, noncommunicative patriarch, whose presence is more like an aboveground ancestor or the near-dead maintained in stasis, is able to telepathically communicate with his great-great-grandson to share his final request—a desire to travel home with him. Ron obliges, yet the drive detours to present-day Southampton, Virginia, where the insurrectionist past and the present merge into an ordered temporal chaos that is inevitably transformative. T.J. reveals, "i waited 75 years sayin' nuthin ta nobody barely movin' even I waited 75 years fo' you ta understand the favor I need to ask ya. . . . Drive me. Carry me. Push me. Take me. Home."[105]

As a play within the speculative genre, *Insurrection*'s time travel facilitates an enactment of one of the genre's central inquiries of "What if?" Carpenter describes this as a "use of the fantastical to emancipate African American history and identity."[106] O'Hara writes all characters, past and present, with the same linguistic dialect and with the same idioms such as "don't know nuthin 'bout nuthin," which is a timeless tool of feigning ignorance for the sake of survival.[107] This device is a bridging of past and present that O'Hara uses to suggest the timelessness of historical meaning and instructional cultural memory, including racial predicaments as well as the identification of racial personas (e.g., the interchangeability of the white motel Clerk Wife of the present and Mistress Mo' Tel of the plantation era past). The central question that Ron faces as history holds him and compels him to better interpret the meaning of Turner's experience and revolt appears in a series of speculative "what if?" moments.

Like Butler's character Dana from *Kindred*, Ron's contemporary expectation of freedom and justice disqualifies him from surviving in the past. T.J. must rescue him twice—once from interfering in an overseer's whipping that results in Ron's whipping and another from an impromptu decision to remain in the enslavement past. O'Hara's presentation of a functional philosophy of historical respect and honor through the wise and ancestral cross-generational gazing of the great-great-grandfather—T.J.—is the play's most profound contribution to Black cultural mythology ideations of sacred observation, ritual remembrance, sacrificial inheritance, and reconciliation and renewal. Even as a historically educated twenty-five year old, Ron had not yet achieved reflexive cultural understanding. T.J. interprets Ron's naivete and lack of plantation era understanding in several key instances. He rebukes, "what the hell did you think you was gonna see som' picture-book technicolor dream fantasy you on a plantation boy plantations gats slaves white folks treat slaves lak shit and the ones claim they treat they slaves good treat they slaves lak *good shit* so nah you brace up and learn ta shut up o' I'm gon' take yo' ass back home ratt nah you gat it?"[108] The mythological journey functions to educate Ron, the emergent historian, about the deeper meaning of the revolt experience from Nat Turner's enslavement era. T.J. must intervene with extended explanations of the differences between the past and present and of Ron's unpreparedness to survive in the past. He instructs, "Ronnie you gotta learn yo' place there are times when you say what you gotta say and there are times when you keep all that stuff ta ya'self."[109] Ron's character develops from these exposures, and when he is overflowing with questions, T.J. confirms, "it ain't lak what you read in 'em books, is it?"[110]

Ron's exposure to the Nat Turner era is transformative in unexpected ways that suggest a methodological need to layer the facts of historical narrative with Africana survivalist logic, which is a purer form of agency than hindsight. T.J. refused to die for 189 years until he is able to teach this lesson to his great-great-grandson. Ron attempts to interfere with the revolt plans because he views it as thwarted and as a loss resulting in meaningless deaths. T.J.'s counterpoint as someone who can say "i LIVED it!!" provides an eyewitness testament of the event's intergenerational narrative value.[111] In the most compelling dialogue of the play, T.J. calms Ron's emphatic plea to change history by giving the most precise explanation of the processes of what Black cultural mythology operationalizes as sacrificial inheritance:

> T.J.: i brought you heah ta learn. ta listen. not change nuthin we change in oura OWN time. not. in. othas.
>
> you wake up ev'ry mornin' breathin' the AIR that NAT TURNER fought fo' you ta breathe and you sleep ev'ry night wit no FEAR cuz that crazy. nigga. SHOUTED Out at the Moon askin' his Gawd fo' a way thru dis trouble and you think you can show up back heah and BLOCK that!!! ronnie you are who you are because them people that's gon' git shot up hung up cut up is what will 'llow you ta enter them doors of that fancy college ya go ta read them wordy books and write them thesis papers SEE these niggas heah cain't understand that ALL they know is that they wanna be FREE and that's what they plannin' ta Do
>
>> So they gon' WIN
>> they might DIE
>> but they gon' WIN
>> You. da Proof.
>> *(the SLAVE and the FREE MAN*
>> *Clock each other.)*
>> slavery.
>> ends.[112]

Another transformation is Ron's growing appreciation for the supernatural spirit forces of life, which the play poses as both an indication of God as well as of the peace and assurance that come from the embrace of the past—literally "holding" history:

> T.J.: . . . you know them times in the quiet when ya feel ya'self lift a little? n'ya know there's somethin' there liftin' the weight?

at those times when ya know there's somethin' that's holdin' ya steady pushin ya through carryin' ya over? ya ever feel that way sometimes ronnie? light on ya feet even in times of trouble?

RON: yes, sir. sometimes.

T.J.: then that's somethin ta believe in.
    call it what you want.[113]

O'Hara explores the more communal aspects of heritage celebrity, even though he draws heavily from the historical archive to reproduce the epic ideas of the hero, in this case Nat Turner. O'Hara additionally creates a vision to explore the value of the hero's contemporaries (in this case T.J.) whose participation, camaraderie, shared vision of physical, cognitive, and intergenerational survival, and eyewitness memorial account are part of the processes of sustaining the culture's hero dynamics. This conceptualization of a *community* of heroics includes the memorialized leader as well as unnamed and un- or underacknowledged actors who were also heroic. This view of collective heroics challenges us to name another heroic figure in Nat Turner's revolt (or in Gabriel Prosser's, or Denmark Vesey's). The criticism that juvenile narratives of Harriet Tubman—except Ringgold's *Dinner at Aunt Connie's*—rarely give heroes a community of contemporaries is reinforced here. O'Hara reiterates the value of nonhagiographic heroics and of recalling the community of heroism, which merges icons of collective narrative history as well as icons of personal lineages. Both are ancestrally active and have a claim to the power to protect and preserve their progeny. Even Ron's aunt Gertha and cousin Octavia experience an involuntary embodiment of enslavement memory.[114] The character, or *presence*, Mutha Wit, as the omnipresent and temporally omniscient mother of the emergent ancestor, T.J., demonstrates this when she rescues Ron from an escalating rural episode of policing. The white Southampton officer begins the routine of overpolicing that often ends in Black male trauma or death. However, upon hearing (or sensing) Mutha Wit's presence warn, "GET YO HANDS OFFA MY GREAT-GREAT-GRANDSON," the officer retreats and disappears.[115] O'Hara's drama reminds readers and viewers of the potential power of famous and lineage ancestors, and he even makes a subtle case for the ideal relationship between elders and youth. Perhaps, they should be "buddies," which implies greater communion and fellowship between generations.[116] This is apparent especially when Ron and T.J. travel back to the Turner insurrection period and T.J. reverts to his real appearance in that era, as "a handsome fit young man."[117] Though the following is an example from contemporary popular culture, in Jill Scott's song "Wake Up Baby" (2011) the persona recounts a life lesson when her grandmother told her, "But once upon a time, I was young and fine, too," as the matriarch's warning for a young lady to proceed with better self-preservation.[118] O'Hara suggests that such relationships within the ancestral cycle are inevitable.[119]

The analysis of O'Hara's complex historical play blooms by using Black cultural mythology concepts. The irony of the author's characterizations is that the only narrative the family had of the patriarch T.J. was that he lived during enslavement, yet he was part of the insurrection community that survived. T.J. held the history in his memory and refused to die until his shared memory transmitted tools for cultural survival to the next generation. Ron described freedom as being:

> lost
> i feel lost
> sometimes
> without a connection
> without a linkage
> without a
> past
> . . . story . . .
> but now—[120]

The play ends with Ron floating back to the present, with Ron holding T.J., the embodiment of his personal and collective cultural history. The body and "corporeal" experience, as Carpenter observes, relate to memory: "The material body–and the cultural memories it contains–can represent a uniquely powerful form of historic documentation."[121] Ron has learned the lesson of Black cultural mythology, and he says, "I am holding history in my arms."[122] Instead of the text indicating "The End," O'Hara writes, "the Beginning," which parallels Black cultural mythology's conceptual interest in the culture's beginning again and engraving identity on new soil.

This chapter's coverage of the canon, literary history, and the literary possibilities of Black cultural mythology serves as a map and a guide to initiate further articulation of the ways cultural heroics continue to manifest creatively in Africana literary and artistic cultural production. Black cultural mythology leads society in a frequent and natural critical understanding of the intersections of history and literature, including demarcating fact from storytelling and embellishment, with an appreciation for the balance that maintains legacy in the hands of the socially responsible writer. The framework also reinvigorates an acute critical understanding of the culture's heroic models, including those developed from the leadership and activism of leaders of past revolts, whose motives and cultural convictions are not so far removed from those of contemporary leaders of political, social, and cultural movements. Society's engagement with the attributes of Black cultural mythology will have an impact on equipping society to emerge toward more effective practices of honoring legacies. It also has implications for defining a more concisely articulated African American patriotism based on the idea formation of both male and female models of immortalization discourse and commemoration philosophy, including the future of Black holidays, monuments, and museums whose effect and vitality can be enhanced by practices of refining our sense of their mythological meaning.

In essence, the philosophical intervention of Black cultural mythology metaphorically gives Black History Month a facelift, a brain transplant, or a terminal degree, as the vibrant itemization of variables of legacy, heritage, and heroics infuses both the month of February and the daily lives of those who respect and admire diasporic epic intuitive conduct, hyperheroic impulses, cognitive survival, and inheritance maintained by narrative and visual memorialization.

A stable corpus of Black cultural mythology is maintained in the traditions of Africana art such as the visual representations of history and heroics maintained by painters such Jacob Lawrence and Joseph Holston, by photographers such as Gordon Parks and Charles "Teenie" Harris, sculptors, collagists, muralists, commemorative postage stamp artists, and even musicians who rely on rhythm, sound, instrumentation, and the voice to create with an impulse toward performing songs commemorating the culture's collective survival. This specificity meanders away from cultural memory studies' interest in collectivity—collective *identity* and collective *memory*. Collective *survival* is indeed something different, and its markers of remembrance reflect the ongoing national affront to Africana personhood that has defined the nature of African existence since 1619 as a hyperheroic and resistance-based response to oppression.

The sources of Black cultural mythology are infinite, and many are suitable for the critical inquiry of younger students or laypersons. The objective is to develop communal patterns and practices of philosophically meditating on the past in search of best cultural orientations to survival.

Laini Mataka expertly models this process in poems such as "freedom's divas should always be luv'd" because she takes the license to ponder, reflect, and imagine moments in the life of a cultural hero—Harriet Tubman.[123] Like Graham Du Bois's imaginings on Douglass, Black cultural mythology gives license and authority to breathe life into cultural heroes. Thus, the embellishments of storytelling or the imaginings of what life was like for the ancestors—and even the deeds and feats of the living great—are part of a procreative exercise that does not interfere with an adjacent commitment to ensuring the sanctity of the formal *historical* record. Instead, the process enhances the community's awareness of its heritage by encouraging those in the present to commune with the legacies of the past for the benefit of the future.

Black cultural mythology's variables encourage society to transpose sources for use by diverse audiences. In an essay on traditional African education, Felix Boateng confirms that for traditional, non-Westernized societies, methods of "intergenerational communication" and "cultural transmission" are the equivalent of "Western formal education."[124] Briefly, such a traditional education relies on the effective use of shared linguistic practices such as the performance and exchange of fables, myths, stories, legends, proverbs, and folktales, as well as other more organized communal rituals.[125] This reference is significant as a reminder that oral cultural practices—the structure of what families say, repeat, perform, and riddle in their home lives—are types of communicative training. Black cultural mythology reinscribes the value of these practices. For youth and generalist, nonacademic behaviors toward storytelling and other literary approaches to historical commemoration, the act of reading or viewing cultural sources, in part or even in digestible excerpts (poems, prose, articles, historical summaries, timelines, documentaries) are casual, routine, and lifestyle practices the keep us engaged with episodes of the culture's mythological structure. The digital-age availability of imaginative sources, including film, fosters mythological practices as a cultural institution. School curricula, which are constrained by policies that overvalue student performance on standardized tests at the expense of more flexible learning, limit the ability of a teacher (like the teacher in Ralph Ellison's "Mister Toussan") to integrate casual cultural instruction into lessons. However, instruction and exposure in the home, afterschool programs, church activities, PTAs, community centers, and one-on-one tutoring and mentoring are routes for the inclusion of strategies of Black cultural mythology that will sustain diasporan culture for future generations. The imaginative pool of epic literary creativity on the culture's intuitive and cognitive hyperheroic narrative of survival is the culture's aesthetic wealth. This wealth translates into a trove of communicative and affirming artifacts relevant in academics and in leisure. Writers have managed imaginative rights in literature to ensure the culture's entertainment, enrichment, historical personhood, philosophical elevation, and *survival.*

Conclusion

Introducing Africana Cultural Memory Studies

When a culture elevates the narrative of its survival—not merely the memory of its heritage—to a conceptual mythological status, the philosophical refinement permanently revives the intellectual cycles of wonder and analysis. A philosophical intervention has been this book's first concern, particularly in modeling how the conceptual framework of Black cultural mythology is one of many approaches that can now be categorized as Africana cultural memory studies. Imaginative rights are its closing concern, which reflects the vitality of cultural mythology and cultural memory within literary texts, movements, and criticism that confer a broader sense of how Black writers creatively reimagine the past to serve a specific cultural function: transmitting possibilities for assessing and duplicating survival. Their efforts sustain cyclical storytelling of the culture's mythology. The storytelling—with its innocuous and benign imaginative and stylistic embellishment of core historical activities and feats, or *mythology*—sustains processes of cultural memory by reviving the stages of the oral-written-oral tradition in which the behaviors of recollection, writing, and retelling are cyclical and self-sustained processes in the culture's intergenerational self-awareness.

Though it was important to exhibit how Black cultural mythology relates to existing cultural memory scholarship, for several reasons I refrained from *immersing* this study within contemporary paradigms of the field of cultural memory studies, which assumes and reflects core Americana and European orientations—mostly concerning the Jewish Holocaust, the nation-state, migration, trauma, war, personal narrative, lore, and slavery. The first reason for maintaining a strict Africana cultural exceptionalism is that the conceptualization of an Africana framework for translating cultural memory into an even more concise configuration of cultural mythology emerges from within a distinct organic experience of excavating from within an immersion in diaspora consciousness and worldviews. This domain allowed Africana cultural priorities and norms to diffuse, ferment, and emerge with the authenticity of an original, yet tradition-based, manner of critical specificity nurtured from within an organic cultural incubation.

The second reason is that the current field of cultural memory studies has yet to demonstrate a sustained or convincing interest in Africana worldviews beyond "slavery" and "museums." Diasporan Africans have been remarkably motivated survivors, and the analytical depth and critical theorizations of these survivors' relationships with the past is dynamic, far beyond the traumas of the oppressive institution of slavery or its artifact representation in museums. An oversaturation of enslavement memory overdetermines the power of the institution of slavery at the expense of exploring the multidimensionality of Africana consciousness and agency of cultural survivors in the Americas. Black cultural mythology accepts the challenge to construct better tools for critically exploring this multidimensionality.

The process of deciphering when and where mainstream American and European cultural memory discourses are attentive to the Africana experience began with a survey of the field's priorities and key subject areas from the program and debates of the inaugural Transcultural Memory conference for the Centre for the Study of Cultural Memory in 2010. It was an initiative of the Institute of Germanic and Romance Studies of the University of London School of Advanced Study, and it coincided with the release of Astrid Erll and Ansgar Nünning's *A Companion to Cultural Memory Studies*. The survey was not promising. Even though the conference gathered cultural memory specialists from around the world, the inclusion of Africana perspectives and participants was negligible. Cultural memory ideas reflecting Africana worldviews and experiences were largely absent, invisible, unaddressed, objectified, and in the margins of discourse. A few presentations approached topics of enslavement, empire, and the postcolonial museums that help societies (Britain, France, Brazil, Benin) reconcile the enslavement past.

The closing plenary session on "The Politics of Memory" by Michael Rothberg, author of *Multidirectional Memory: Remembering the Holocaust in the Age of Decolonization* (2009), was troubling.[1] An intellectual conflict arose when Rothberg used perspectives from W. E. B. Du Bois to advance an aspect of Holocaust memory studies. It was a complex thesis—that critical analyses of the historical and modern performances of genocide and violence against Africans and Jews are more intersectional that we realize. As a professionally trained Africana Studies expert in the audience, I yearned for cultural agency in the discourse. African-centered perspectives had been largely absent during the conference, yet the sustained examination of Du Bois's ideas served only Holocaust memory studies. It was a positive engagement to be reminded that Du Bois is a universal scholar whose intellectual legacy benefits more than the Africana enterprise. However, the moment assured me of the urgency of my own project, developing the theorization of Black cultural mythology and categorizing the scope of a broader, collaborative, and cross-disciplinary Africana cultural memory studies.

Although a few Africana/diaspora-oriented texts provided a general sense of some aspect of African American memory, the deficit of not having a comprehensive, culturally organic Africana conceptual framework for memory studies was glaring and problematic. As a remedy, *Black Cultural Mythology* is the first comprehensive, Africana-immersed text on myth, memory, mythology, and heroics. It introduces Africana cultural memory studies as an *intellectual tradition* with sustained cultural genealogies that allow us to historicize its development and track the germination, circulation, and application of its key concepts.

In such a study, which classifies a new tributary of the Black intellectual tradition on mythology and cultural memory, I locate the theoretical vision in a liberated distance *away* from the usual and customary Western approaches to myth and mythology.[2] For this inaugural book, it is essential to retain the culturally explicit African diasporic orientations to legacy, memory, and survival to sustain the integrity of its epistemologies. Itemizing the historiography of Africana mythology draws attention to variants of mythology, including myth and mythoform as well as metavariables such as *revivification* or *mythification/mythication*.

Inevitably, the philosophical theorization of Black cultural mythology is foundational to reorganizing how people value the processes of survival from an Africana worldview. From this orientation, contemporary generations are increasingly more intellectually equipped for multidimensional, cross-subject area, and revisionist interpretations of history, autobiography, legend, formal and informal narrative practices, and remembrance processes that prompt the creation of new knowledge forms. Introducing Black cultural mythology conceptually has been a challenging project, and the topic mandates the creation of additional volumes and complementary studies to address adjacent topics and contexts not yet or not fully explored. For example, the visual arts and music are two categories that, unfortunately, require an additional study. The category of visual arts would include an analysis of how the works of artists such as Jacob Lawrence, Romare Bearden, Joseph Holston, and others participate in contemporary intellectual traditions related to Black cultural mythology. A study of Black cultural mythology in music or ethnomusicology would generate dynamic idea formation on traditional, African, diasporic, folkloric, calypso, blues, gospel, jazz, soul, Afro-Pop, R&B, rap, hip-hop, and spiritual examples of heroics and legacy instituted by the artistic vision of a host of musicians who sing or perform ancestral, praise-song, and heroic tributes in their diverse cultural artistries.

Caribbean, African, and transatlantic experiences with related heroic and mythological phenomena are not much addressed in this volume, though by design. Cilas Kemadjiv imagines the possibilities of postcolonial mythologies linked to Africana cultural memory studies through his envisioning of charismatic memory (per politico-literary uses of the legacy of Haitian leader Jean Jacques Dessalines) applied to works by Caribbean writers such as Jean Metellus, Aimé Césaire, Maryse Condé, and Boubacar Boris Diop.[3] This indeed is compatible with aspects of Black cultural mythology and may help with the incorporation of additional translocal and transatlantic possibilities of cultural mythology as sacred inheritance. Such literary meditations are part of what Christina Sharpe refers to as "wake work," noting that, "Wakes are processes; through them we think about our dead and our relations to them. They are rituals through which to enact grief and memory. Wakes allow those among the living to mourn the passing of the dead through ritual."[4] Sharpe also prioritizes "observance," understood as the traces and symbols that are remnants of the past processes of living that cry out to be understood and theorized.[5] Her philosophical and cultural perspectives on aspects of memorialization mark her work as part of an emergent collaborative, interdisciplinary cadre of scholars whose ideas can sustain Africana cultural memory studies.

The growing trail of scholarly works on cultural memory that participate in broad definitions of Africana and Diaspora studies is evidence that something important is emerging. Lisa Woolfork's *Embodying American Slavery in Contemporary Culture* (2008) is easily overlooked because its title does not alert readers to the book's central viewpoints related to arranged bodily re-enactments of enslavement experiences, enslavement-themed tourism, rememory, and the ritual participation of African American cultural celebrants, with evidence drawn from literature, social and community-based cultural activism, and even the repertoire of comedian Dave Chappelle. Ana Araujo's work on enslavement memory, memorialization, and tourism is a powerful contribution from the discipline of history and includes volumes such as *Shadows of the Slave Past: Memory, Heritage, and Slavery* (2014), *Crossing Memories: Slavery and African Diaspora* (2011; coedited with Mariana P. Candido and Paul E. Lovejoy), *Public Memory of Slavery: Victims and Perpetrators in the South Atlantic* (2010), *African Heritage and Memories of Slavery in Brazil and the South Atlantic World* (2015), *Politics of Memory: Making Slavery Visible in Public Space* (2012), and *Living History: Encountering the Memory and History of the Heirs of Slavery* (2009). Celeste-Marie Bernier's work on enslaved heroism is a closely related project that emerges from the field of American studies. In fact, Bernier's *Characters of Blood: Black Heroism in the Transatlantic* (2012) is a study of six iconic, transatlantic Africana personas, including Harriet Tubman, Toussaint Louverture, and Nat Turner, who also appear as topics of interest in this inaugural treatment of the framework of Black cultural mythology.[6] With a sustained reflection on *art*, Bernier initiates, in a different yet equally detangling intervention, conversations on aesthetics, the arts, commemoration, and heroics.

The field of literary criticism also has a compelling and growing number of works that help to advance a broader, collaborative, and multidisciplinary field of Africana cultural memory studies. I address some of these outstanding works in the introduction, but here I reiterate their greater value for readying the field for a more theoretical consideration of mythology and memory that has a greater permanence for the intellectual tradition. Nancy Peterson's *Against Amnesia: Contemporary Women Writers and the Crises of Historical Memory* (2001), Ron Eyerman's *Cultural Trauma: Slavery and the Formation of African American Identity* (2001), Timothy Spaulding's *Re-Forming the Past: History, the Fantastic, and the Postmodern Slave Narrative* (2005), and Marni Gauthier's *Amnesia and Redress in Contemporary American Fiction: Counterhistory* (2011) stress the intersections of history and literature, somewhat in conversation with this volume's anchor chapter on imaginative rights. Sources such as Saidiya Hartman's *Scenes of Subjection: Terror, Slavery, and Self-Making in Nineteenth-Century America* (1997) and *Lose Your Mother: A Journey along the Atlantic Slave Route* (2007), Salamishah Tillet's *Sites of Slavery: Citizenship and Racial Democracy in the Post–Civil Rights Imagination* (2012), and *Mapping Generations of Traumatic Memory in American Narratives* (2014), edited by Dana Mihailescu, Roxana Oltean, and Mihaela Precup, are also striking studies that, when categorized as part of the emergent field of Africana cultural memory studies, reveal the diversity of perspectives in conversation, and possibly debate, with Black cultural mythology.

The consciousness and subconsciousness of survival among generations of Africans in the diaspora since enslavement is the basis of a profound recollection. National patterns of ignoring, denying, and concealing the histories of African diaspora legacy compete with a worldview that Black life and ancestry are sacred. Institutionalized and systemic racism deconstruct the value of Black cultural mythology as schools, streets, and neighborhoods named in honor of Black legacy figures represent structures and infrastructures infused not with heroics, but with memories of neglect, ghettoization, hard times, racial oppression, and segregation that make the "heroic naming of place" backfire in urban and rural landscapes. Legacy mismanaged denies, deconstructs, and alters the agency of Africana heroics.

To combat this and to be a catalyst for renewed synergy for how we engage with heritage, this book's chapters have explored aspects of Black cultural mythology through processes of historical excavation and reinterpretation. The study has explored historical, conceptual, applied, and analytical models of Black cultural mythology that are philosophically grounded in some of the most dynamic, yet understudied, efforts to move the culture's thinking toward the memorial, mythological, and the sacred. The careful excavation of exemplars—Stewart, Graham Du Bois, Neal, Karenga, Wilson, and Asante—indicates that this orientation to African American mythology is, actually, a delayed enterprise. The genealogy of ideas about inheritance, ancestor acknowledgment, immortalization, heroic impulses, the sacredness of survival, and epic hyperheroism has been here all along. Linking it to the vast repository of scattered idea formations about myth and memory as well as to commemoration historiography is a luxury of interdisciplinarity that extends the power of discourse. Furthermore, rereadings of commemoration philosophy and revising or updating topics, such as Tubman's hypervisibility and retheorization, Haiti's presence as an active mythology, Wright's bold vision of antiheroics, and the resilience of Malcolm's epic status, challenge us to engage in a more meditative process of cyclically studying even the superlatives for new ways of extending their meaning and effect.

This book is the result of over ten years of research and idea formation, including teaching four unique upper-level seminars that linked the topic to the field of African American folk culture. The record of teaching cultural mythology and cultural memory courses reflects back on Maulana Karenga's decision-making process about which subject areas to include in *Introduction to Black Studies* (1982), which is still a central textbook in the field. Based on this criterion that subject areas will "coincide with course titles," we are at a juncture of innovation for Africana cultural memory studies.[7] In recent years, over a dozen institutions have offered a related course in fields such as African American studies, history, American studies, public policy, and conflict studies. (See table 8.1.)

Table 8.1. List of University Courses on Africana Cultural Memory

Pittsburgh	Africana Cultural Memory
Tufts	African American Memory & History
Gettysburg	Memory & Meaning in African American Culture
Lehigh	Sites of Memory: Cultural Monuments & Urban Spaces
Leiden	Slavery & Memory in the Black Atlantic (Netherlands)
Buffalo	Issues of Identity and Memory in Contemporary Africana Art
Goucher	Bad Spirits: Trans-Atlantic Slave Trade in History & Memory
Stanford	Sites of Memory [study abroad in South Africa]
Pennsylvania	Black Feminist Approaches to History & Memory
Dickinson	Memory & Memorialization [Charleston, SC, local history tour]
St. Paul (CA)	Special Topics in Conflict Studies: Conflict and Memory
Duke	Monuments and Memorials: Publ. Policy & Remembrance of Racial History
Sewanee	Place, Memory, & Identity [American studies]
Columbia	Slave Memory in Brazil
Northwestern	Memory Studies [graduate]
Northwestern	Performing Memory in the Black World
Howard	Seminar in Comparative History: Memory and Heritage of Slavery

Beyond its curricular potential, the conceptual framework of Black cultural mythology has numerous intellectual and practical implications. The attributes are original in their categorization as a *set* of properties and tools excavated and stylized from ideas and nuances circulating within the intellectual tradition. The study of Black cultural mythology documents *cultural logic* and behavior wherein positive cultural identity is directly proportionate to a healthy sense of cultural memory and awareness. It also celebrates aesthetic prowess as it alerts us to approach speech, storytelling, literature, and art as imaginative significations that redirect us to nearly archaeological, search-and-rescue missions to excavate even more threads of sustained ideas about the heroics of survival. Such diverse philosophical and historical variables require an organizational conceptual work that captures the tradition of African American memorial consciousness and behavior and is reliable for academic and practical application.

As a tool for expanding our sense of the culture's survival, Black cultural mythology is allied with significant educational imperatives based on its association with early child development categories of identity, personhood, and self-esteem. In fact, the critical conceptualization of Black cultural mythology will help to reform the static approaches to annual Black History Month celebrations wherein practitioners, historians, teachers, and laypersons will be motivated by new language and applications to devote less energy to mere fact-recitation and more time and intellectual energy to exploring the cultural logic and sacred reasoning that inform a community's commemoration enterprise. In addition, this project is allied with initiatives to reconsider philosophies and assumptions related to the maintenance of monuments, culturally relevant architecture, public domain saturation of heroic images and iconography, and practices of heroic/antiheroic naming.

In the critical anthology *Literary Spaces: Introduction to Comparative Black Literature* (2007) I first introduced the concept of "Black Cultural Mythology" as one of several core categories of analysis for African diasporic literatures. It emerged from research on African American memorialization responses to Malcolm X's death, namely the collective behaviors' similarities to West African funeral dirge practices. I am indebted to Dudley Randall and Margaret G. Burroughs's edited collection *For Malcolm X: Poems on the Life and Death of Malcolm X* (1969) for planting seeds of wonder about Africana sacred memorial consciousness that inspired what has emerged as Black cultural mythology. As my research segued away from the dirge toward theorizations of heroics in the US and the Caribbean since the enslavement encounter, I appreciated scholar and activist Sam Yette's suggestion that I use the phrasing of "hero dynamics" instead. The project has benefited from years of research, of conference workshopping, of exploring the dimensions of the topic in waves of teaching, and of excavating the historical and cultural archives of African American, Caribbean, African, and even Afroeuropean experience to finally inform this comprehensive volume introducing the critical framework of Black cultural mythology.

This topic owes a genealogical debt to Larry Neal and Maulana Karenga for introducing the category of "mythology" into the culture's conceptual vocabulary with their treatises and discussion on criteria for Black culture and myriad philosophical debates and clarifications during the Black Arts Movement and beyond. It was a great fortune to locate Amos Wilson's research on psychology and mythological structure, nestled in the brief final chapter of *The Developmental Psychology of the Black Child*. Discovering Molefi Kete Asante's overlooked, earliest career scholarship on African American myth is another important intellectual tradition unearthed over the course of my research. Collectively, these and other dynamic past intellectual contributions stabilize this book's introduction to a multidimensional philosophy of Black cultural mythology as a broad critical framework with distinct assumptions, attributes, and priorities.

Africans in the diaspora have lived with a daily obsession with mastering feats of freedom and justice, impelled by cognitive and physiological responses to the threats of bodily and emotional harm. This study could almost rely on the science of adrenaline and neurological impulses of fight or flight to explain how African diasporic life is a remarkable and victorious narrative of survival. This philosophical shift to theorizing these impulses implores readers to understand the pragmatic and authentically lived meaning associated with the term "mythology."

The stereotypes of stagnation that constrain February as Black History Month in the United States become a central, practical order of symbolic business related to invigorating heritage practices. Viewing Black cultural mythology as an inheritor and contemporary manifestation of Carter G. Woodson's lifelong work on reinforcing historical respect and maximizing African American historical consciousness is an intervention for Africana social, cultural, political, and community institutions. As a tool for public impact, it pushes for a revitalized awareness of the philosophical and phenomenological stability of Africana cognitive survival that calls out from between the lines of the historical narrative of beginning again and engraving identity on American soil.

It is an honor to present this theoretical work to clarify the relationships between cultural ideas of immortalization, forced geographical relocation, the agency of survival, memory as resistance, centered iconography, heroic marginalization, mythological silence and competition, and the role of legacy in communal and individual identity. Sacred memory is a self-actualizing and resistance behavior. Inevitably, advancing Black cultural mythology as a curricular innovation to Africana studies and clarifying diverse cross-disciplinary research on aspects of Africana negotiations with the past announces the potential of a unified Africana cultural memory enterprise. This book invites robust comparative discourse among the collaborating disciplines, fields, and communities that advance a vision for best practices in capturing the vitality of diasporic specificities of myth, memory, and mythology. The progressive exchange among scholars and in spaces of the public domain promises to be a dynamic expansion.

Notes

Preface

1. U.S. Government Publishing Office, "400 Years of African American History Commission Act," Senate Report 114–341, September 6, 2016. https://www.govinfo.gov/content/pkg/CRPT-114srpt341/html/CRPT-114srpt341.htm.

2. Joe Hagan, "Michael B. Jordan's Technicolor Dreams," *Vanity Fair*, November 2018. https://www.vanityfair.com/hollywood/2018/10/michael-b-jordan-cover-story.

Introduction

1. Salamisha Tillet, *Sites of Slavery: Citizenship and Racial Democracy in the Post–Civil Rights Imagination* (Durham, NC: Duke University Press, 2012), 103.

2. Molefi K. Asante, *Afrocentricity* (Trenton, NJ: Africa World Press, 1988), 24. As an alternative to the West's universal timelines of AD or BC, the cultural reference point for Njia offers ABA to designate After the Beginning Again (after 1619), while BBA references history Before the Beginning Again (before 1619).

3. Maurice Halbwachs, *The Collective Memory* (New York: Harper and Row, [1968] 1980), 156.

4. Carol P. Marsh-Lockett and Elizabeth West, *Literary Expressions of African Spirituality* (New York: Lexington Books, 2013), 1.

5. Saidiya V. Hartman, *Scenes of Subjection: Terror, Slavery, and Self-Making in Nineteenth-Century America* (New York: Oxford University Press, 1997), 4.

6. Saidiya Hartman, *Lose Your Mother: A Journey along the Atlantic Slave Route* (Farrar, Straus and Giroux, 2007), 7.

7. Saidiya Hartman, *Scenes of Subjection*, 3.

8. Hartman, *Scenes of Subjection*, 176.

9. Ron Eyerman, *Cultural Trauma: Slavery and the Foundation of African American Identity* (New York: Cambridge University Press, 2001), 1.

10. Eyerman, 2.

11. Nancy Peterson, *Against Amnesia: Contemporary Women Writers and the Crises of Historical Memory* (Philadelphia: University of Pennsylvania Press, 2001), 15.

12. Peterson, 14.

13. Peterson, 55.

14. Peterson, 1.

15. Mack Freeman, "Peterson, Nancy G. *Against Amnesia: Contemporary Women Writers and the Crises of Historical Memory*," *Biography: An Interdisciplinary Quarterly* 25, no. 4 (2002): 701.

16. A. Timothy Spaulding, *Re-Forming the Past: History, the Fantastic, and the Postmodern Slave Narrative* (Columbus: Ohio State University Press, 2005), 124.

17. Spaulding, 127.

18. Jan Assman, "Communicative and Cultural Memory," in *A Companion to Cultural Memory Studies*, ed. Astrid Erll and Ansgar Nünning (New York: Walter de Gruyter, 2010), 110.

19. Assman, 110–11.

20. Assman, 117.

21. Assman, 113.

22. Jeffrey K. Olick, "From Collective Memory to the Sociology of Mnemonic Practices and Protocols," in *A Companion to Cultural Memory Studies*, ed. Astrid Erll and Ansgar Nünning (New York: Walter de Gruyter, 2010), 156.

23. Olick.

24. Olick, 156.

25. Renate Lachmann, "Mnemonic and Intertextual Aspects of Literature," in *A Companion to Cultural Memory Studies*, ed. Astrid Erll and Ansgar Nünning (New York: Walter de Gruyter, 2010), 307.

26. Colson Whitehead and Donna Seaman, "The Carnegie Interview: Colson Whitehead," June 21, 2017. American Library Association Book Club Central, http://www.bookclubcentral.org/2017/06/21/the-carnegie-interview-colson-whitehead/.

27. Herman Beavers, "Bondage as Discipline: Pedagogy as Discomfort in *The Sorcerer's Apprentice*," in *Charles Johnson: The Novelist as Philosopher*, ed. William R. Nash and Marc C. Conner (Jackson: University Press of Mississippi, 2007), 55.

28. Charles Johnson, *I Call Myself an Artist: Writings by and about Charles Johnson* (Bloomington: Indiana University Press, 1999), 81.

29. Trudier Harris, *Martin Luther King Jr., Heroism, and African American Literature* (Tuscaloosa: University of Alabama Press, 2014), 26.

30. Harris, *Martin Luther King Jr.*, 2.

31. Harris, *Martin Luther King Jr.*, 3–4.

32. Harris, *Martin Luther King Jr.*, 11–12.

33. Harris, *Martin Luther King Jr.*, 24, 25.

34. Harris, *Martin Luther King Jr.*, 137.

35. Harris, *Martin Luther King Jr.*, 137.

36. Milton C. Sernett, *Harriet Tubman: Myth, Memory, and History* (Durham, NC: Duke University Press, 2007), 7.

37. Sernett, 7.

38. Quoted in Sernett, 7–8. The original source is David W. Blight, *Beyond the Battlefield: Race, Memory, and the American Civil War* (Amherst: University of Massachusetts Press, 2002), 2.

39. Sernett, 8.

40. Sernett, 8.

41. Sernett, 8. This list of terms comes directly from Sernett's discussion.

42. Pierre Nora, "Between Memory and History: *Les Lieux de Mémoire*," in *History and Memory in African-American Culture*, ed. Geneviève Fabre and Robert O'Meally (New York: Oxford University Press, 1994).

43. Pero Dagbovie, *The Early Black History Movement, Carter G. Woodson, and Lorenzo Johnston Greene* (Urbana: University of Illinois Press, 2007), xi.

44. Dagbovie, xi.

45. Dagbovie, xi, xiii, 6.

46. Dagbovie, 2, 5, 7.

47. See the preface to Carter G. Woodson, *African Heroes and Heroines* (Washington, DC: Associated Publishers, 1944).

48. Woodson, *African Heroes and Heroines*.

49. Woodson, *African Heroes and Heroines*, 7.

50. Burnis R. Morris, *History, the Black Press, and Public Relations* (Jackson: University Press of Mississippi, 2017), 14.

51. Morris, 14.

52. Dagbovie, *Early Black History Movement*, 44.

53. Houston A. Baker Jr., "Theoretical Returns," in *African American Literary Criticism: A Reader* (New York: New York University Press, 2000), 421.

54. Baker, "Theoretical Returns," 421.

55. Baker, "Theoretical Returns," 422.

56. Baker, "Theoretical Returns," 422.

57. Alison Moore, "Historicizing Historical Theory's History of Cultural Historiography," *Cosmos and History: The Journal of Natural and Social Philosophy* 12, no. 1 (2016): 258.

58. Moore, "Historicizing," 261.

59. Cilas Kemadjiv (trans. R. H. Mitsch), "Postcolonial Mythologies: Jean Metellus and the Writing of Charismatic Memory," *Research in African Literatures* 35, no. 2 (2004): 92.

60. Ngugi wa Thiong'o, *Something Torn and New: An African Renaissance* (New York: Basic/Civitas Books, 2009), vii, x. These descriptions are from Ngugi's chapter titles and general discourse throughout the book's collection of speeches originally delivered between 2002 and 2007.

61. Ngugi, 63–64. Ngugi quotes Zora Neale Hurston from Carla Kaplan, ed., *A Life in Letters* (New York: Anchor Books, 2005), 518–20.

62. Ngugi, 64.

63. See Walter Hawthorne, "Review of *Crossing Memories: Slavery and African Diaspora* edited by Ana Lucia Araujo, Mariana P. Candido, and Paul E. Lovejoy," *New West India Guide* 88, nos. 1–2 (2014): 110–12.

64. Hawthorne, 110–12.

Chapter 1

1. Larry Neal, "The Black Arts Movement," in *Visions of a Liberated Future: Black Arts Movement Writings by Larry Neal*, ed. Michael Schwartz (New York: Thunder's Mouth Press, 1989), 62–80. The essay first appeared in *Drama Review* 12 (1968): 29–39.

2. Even the biography project that Shirley Graham Du Bois undertakes in the mid-twentieth century is included in this tradition. Because Graham Du Bois wrote nearly a dozen biographies, her vision and work are unique, different from the occasional production of biographies such as John Hope Franklin's volume on George Washington Williams and Nell Painter's volume on *Sojourner Truth: A Life, a Symbol*. Milton Sernett's volume on Harriet Tubman is the closest volume available that layers biography, symbolism, and memory, even though it does not theorize the broad cultural memory or mythology project.

3. Contemporary publishers generally omit the subtitle of Douglass's *The Heroic Slave* which is *A Thrilling Narrative of the Adventures of Madison Washington, in Pursuit of Liberty*.

4. Marilyn Richardson, *Maria W. Stewart, America's First Black Woman Political Writer: Essays and Speeches* (Bloomington: Indiana University Press, 1987).

5. Richardson, xiii.

6. Richardson, xiv.

7. Richardson, xv.

8. Richardson, xv.

9. Richardson, xv.

10. Richardson, xvi.

11. Ebony A. Utley, "A Woman Made of Words: The Rhetorical Invention of Maria W. Stewart," in *Black Women's Intellectual Traditions: Speaking Their Minds*, ed. Kristin Waters and Carol B. Conaway (Burlington: University of Vermont Press, 2007), 55.

12. Jami L. Carlacio, "In Their Own Words: The Rhetorical Practices of Maria Stewart and Sarah Grimke," PhD diss., University of Wisconsin, Milwaukee, 2001, 5.

13. Carlacio, 9, 10, 11.

14. Jennifer Rycenga, "A Greater Awakening: Women's Intellect as a Factor in Early Abolitionist Development, 1824–1834," *Journal of Feminist Studies in Religion* 21 (2005): 31–59.

15. Rycenga, 32.

16. Rycenga, 33, 36.

17. Rycenga, 37.

18. Rycenga, 48.

19. Marcia Riggs, *Can I Get a Witness? Prophetic Religious Voices of African American Women* (Maryknoll, NY: Orbis Books, 1997). Riggs focuses on Stewart's call to preach and her heavenly visitations.

20. Judylyn S. Ryan, *Spirituality as Ideology in Black Women's Film and Literature* (Charlottesville: University of Virginia Press, 2005), 42.

21. Kathy L. Glass, introduction to *Courting Communities: Black Female Nationalism and "Syncre-Nationalism" in the Nineteenth-Century North* (New York: Routledge, 2006), 1.

22. Glass, 1, 37.

23. Glass, 39.

24. Ida Young, "Keeping Truth on My Side: Maria Stewart," in *Black Lives: Essays on African American Biography*, ed. James Conyers (Armonk, NY: M. E. Sharpe, 1999), 120, 119.

25. Molefi K. Asante and Kariamu Welsh, "Myth: The Communication Dimension to the African American Mind," *Journal of Black Studies* 11 (1981): 387–95.

26. Asante and Welsh, 391.

27. Glass, *Courting Communities*, 45.

28. Maria W. Stewart, "An Address Delivered before the Afric-American Female Intelligence Society of America," in *Maria W. Stewart, America's First Black Woman Political Writer: Essays and Speeches*, ed. Marilyn Richardson (Bloomington: Indiana University Press, 1987), 55.

29. Maria W. Stewart, "Religion and the Pure Principles of Morality, the Sure Foundation on Which We Must Build," in *Maria W. Stewart, America's First Black Woman Political Writer: Essays and Speeches*, ed. Marilyn Richardson (Bloomington: Indiana University Press, 1987), 31.

30. Stewart, "Religion and the Pure Principles of Morality, 34.

31. Shirley Wilson Logan, *"We Are Coming": The Persuasive Discourse of Nineteenth-Century Black Women* (Carbondale: Southern Illinois University Press, 1999), 23–43.

32. Asante and Welsh, "Myth," 393.

33. Asante and Welsh, 41. Logan gives significant evaluations of Stewart's traditional nationalism and Ethiopianism and concludes that Stewart "invoked an African past for strength and inspiration" rather than for its possibility as a "literal national homeland" (41).

34. Maria W. Stewart, "Farewell Address to Her Friends in the City of Boston," in *Maria W. Stewart, America's First Black Woman Political Writer, Essays and Speeches*, ed. Marilyn Richardson (Bloomington: Indiana University Press, 1987), 70.

35. Rycenga, "Greater Awakening," 55. Also, for a discourse on liberation theology, see Stacey M. Floyd-Thomas and Anthony B. Pinn, eds., *Liberation Theologies in the United States* (Cambridge: Cambridge University Press, 2004).

36. Stewart, "An Address Delivered at the African Masonic Hall," 57.

37. Stewart, "Masonic Hall," 49, 59.

38. St. Lucian/Trinidadian writer and Nobel laureate Derek Walcott, whose literary creativity spans Africa and the diaspora, uses the legacy of David Walker in the play *Walker* (2002) and the legacy of the Haitian Revolution in *The Haitian Trilogy: Three Plays* (2002) to survey African American and diasporan cultural mythology. Thus, Stewart's investment in print culture merges with the contemporary publication of print culture sources in what can be interpreted as a continuum of Black cultural mythology.

39. Stewart, "Masonic Hall," 57.

40. Stewart, "Afric-American Female Intelligence Society," 54.

41. Stewart, "Masonic Hall," 56.

42. Stewart, "Masonic Hall," 57.

43. Richardson, *Maria W. Stewart*, xiv.

44. Rycenga, "Greater Awakening," 56.

45. Rycenga, 50.

46. Jean Fagan Yellin, *Women and Sisters: The Antislavery Feminists in American Culture* (New Haven: Yale University Press), 48.

47. Rycenga, "A Greater Awakening," 47. Rycenga refers to John Adams's *Sketches of the History, Genius, Disposition, Accomplishments, Employments, Customs, Virtues, and Vices of the Fair Sex, in All Parts of the World* (Boston: Bumstead, 1807).

48. The funeral program should be considered a document of history, particularly in the practices of elders such as John Henrik Clarke, who fused the meaning of eldership, passing, and immortalization by writing his own eulogy to be printed in the program for his funeral in July 1998. Clarke's funeral program has been used as a teaching tool to illuminate a practical Black cultural mythology, as Clarke wrote of seeing Kwame Nkrumah and others welcoming him into the afterlife.

49. Frances Ellen Watkins Harper, *A Brighter Coming Day: A Frances Ellen Watkins Harper Reader*, ed. Frances Smith Foster (New York: Feminist Press, 1990), 270.

50. Harper, *Brighter Coming Day*, 46, 49–50.

51. Frances Ellen Watkins Harper, *Iola Leroy: Or, Shadows Uplifted* (Mineola, NY: Dover, [1893] 2010), 194.

52. Anna Julia Cooper, *The Voice of Anna Julia Cooper*, ed. Charles Lemert and Esme Bhan (New York: Rowman and Littlefield, 1998), 164.

53. Cooper, 176.

54. Cooper, 182.
55. Cooper, 182.
56. Cooper, 182.
57. Cooper, 186.
58. Gerald Horne, *Race Woman: The Lives of Shirley Graham Du Bois* (New York: New York University Press, 2000), 1, 12, 149. The final description is from Alesia McFadden's "The Artistry and Activism of Shirley Graham Du Bois: A Twentieth Century African American Torchbearer," PhD diss., University of Massachusetts, Amherst, 2009.
59. Quoted in Horne, *Race Woman* 21.
60. Quoted in Horne, *Race Woman*, 263. Letter was from April 5, 1977. Dixler wrote her dissertation on women in the Communist Party.
61. Jodi Van Der Horn-Gibson, "Dismantling Americana: Sambo, Shirley Graham, and African Nationalism," *Americana: The Journal of American Popular Culture, 1900 to Present* 7, no. 1 (2008): 4.
62. Robert Dee Thompson Jr., "A Socio-biography of Shirley Graham Du Bois: A Life in the Struggle," PhD diss., University of California, Santa Cruz, 1997.
63. Julia Mickenberg, "Civil Rights, History, and the Left: Inventing the Juvenile Black Biography," *MELUS: The Journal of the Society for the Study of Multi-Ethnic Literatures* 27, no. 2 (2002): 65–93.
64. McFadden, "Artistry and Activism."
65. Horne, *Race Woman*, 101.
66. Horne, *Race Woman*, 104.
67. Horne, *Race Woman*, 102.
68. Horne, *Race Woman*, 102, quoted in Horne, *Race Woman*, 101.
69. Horne, *Race Woman*, 104, 105.
70. Horne, *Race Woman*, 107.
71. Discussed in McFadden, "Artistry and Activism."
72. Quoted in Horne, *Race Woman*, 106.
73. Quoted in Horne, *Race Woman*, 43.
74. Quoted in Horne, *Race Woman*, 215.
75. Horne, *Race Woman*, 15.
76. McFadden, "Artistry and Activism," 323, 326.
77. Elizabeth Ross Haynes, *Unsung Heroes* (New York: DuBois and Hill, 1921).
78. Quoted in McFadden, *Artistry and Activism*.
79. James Baldwin, "Smaller Than Life," review of *There Once Was A Slave* by Shirley Graham, in *Baldwin: Collected Essays* (New York: Library of America, 1998), 577–78. The original essay appeared in the *Nation*, July 19, 1947.
80. Baldwin. "Smaller Than Life," 577.
81. Baldwin. "Smaller Than Life," 577.
82. Baldwin. "Smaller Than Life," 578.

83. Horne, *Race Woman*, 103–4.
84. Quoted in Horne, *Race Woman*, 215.
85. Horne, *Race Woman*, 242.
86. Horne, *Race Woman*, 104.
87. See McFadden, "Artistry and Activism," 27n.
88. Alex Haley, *Roots: The Saga of an American Family* (Boston: Da Capo Press, [1976] 2016).
89. See McFadden, "Artistry and Activism," 316.
90. Horne, *Race Woman*, 150.
91. Horne, *Race Woman*, 151.
92. Horne, *Race Woman*, 151.
93. McFadden, "Artistry and Activism," 274, 287.
94. Henry Louis Gates and Nellie Y. McKay, eds., *The Norton Anthology of African American Literature, 2nd Edition* (New York: W. W. Norton, 2004), 1848.
95. Neal, "Black Arts Movement," 62.
96. Neal, "Black Arts Movement," 73.
97. Neal, "Black Arts Movement," 73.
98. Neal, "Black Arts Movement," 78.
99. Neal, "Black Arts Movement," 64.
100. Larry Neal, "And Shine Swam On," afterword to *Black Fire: An Anthology of Afro-American Writing*, ed. LeRoi Jones and Larry Neal (New York: William Morrow, 1968), 639.
101. Neal, "And Shine Swam On," 647.
102. Neal, "And Shine Swam On," 647.
103. Neal, "And Shine Swam On," 646.
104. Neal, "And Shine Swam On," 653.
105. Neal, "And Shine Swam On," 654.
106. Neal, "And Shine Swam On," 655–56.
107. Neal, "And Shine Swam On," 638, 639, 131.
108. Neal, "And Shine Swam On," 128.
109. Neal, "And Shine Swam On," 129.
110. Neal, "And Shine Swam On," 130.
111. Neal, "And Shine Swam On," 210–11.
112. Neal, "And Shine Swam On," 130.
113. Amiri Baraka, introduction to *Black Fire: An Anthology of Afro-American Writing*, ed. LeRoi Jones and Larry Neal (New York: William Morrow, 1968), x.
114. Baraka, introduction to *Black Fire*, xi.
115. Baraka, introduction to *Black Fire*, xiv, xv.
116. Baraka, introduction to *Black Fire*, xvii.
117. Larry Neal, *Visions of a Liberated Future: Black Arts Movement Writings by Larry Neal*, ed. Michael Schwartz (New York: Thunder's Mouth Press, 1989), 148.
118. Neal, *Visions of a Liberated Future*, 148.

119. Charles H. Fuller Jr., "Black Art Is Socio-Creative Art," in *Modern American Poetry: Documents from the Black Arts Movement*, http://www.english.illinois.edu/maps/blackarts/documents.htm (accessed January 1, 2019). See also the original source, *Liberator* (April 1967): 8–10.

120. Fuller.

121. Fuller.

122. See Larry Neal, "Some Reflections on the Black Aesthetic," in *The Black Aesthetic*, ed. Addison Gayle (New York: Doubleday, 1971), 12.

123. Neal, "Some Reflections," 12.

124. Neal, "Some Reflections," 13.

125. Neal, "Some Reflections," 14–15.

126. Neal, "Some Reflections," 15.

127. Molefi Kete Asante, "Location Theory and African Aesthetics," in *African Aesthetics: Keeper of the Tradition*, ed. Kariamu Welsh-Asante (New York: Praeger, 1994), 55.

128. Molefi Asante, *Malcolm X as Cultural Hero and Other Afrocentric Essays* (Trenton, NJ: Africa World Press, 1994), 31.

129. Asante, *Malcolm X*.

130. Ron Karenga, "On Black Art," *Black Theatre* 3 (1968): 9–10.

131. Henry Louis Gates Jr. and Nellie Y. McKay, eds., "Maulana Karenga," in *The Norton Anthology of African American Literature, 2nd Edition* (New York: W. W. Norton, 2004), 2086.

132. I am grateful for an extended email correspondence with Maulana Karenga between January 28 and February 13, 2019 in which he answered my questions about the origin of "mythology" as one of the seven criteria and provided a useful list of sources that contributes to understanding the historiography of Black Arts mythology ideas. Karenga shared that the idea of mythology dates back to 1965.

133. Maulana Karenga, *Kawaida Theory: An Introductory Outline* (Inglewood, CA: Kawaida Publications, 1980), 23.

134. Karenga, *Kawaida Theory*, 23–28. Here Karenga gives a detailed explication of "The Negatives" as well as "The Positives" of religion, according to Kawaida philosophy. The ideas are so culturally centered and profound that it would be difficult for lay readers to presume to know the critical depth and clarity of Karenga's deciphering of the role of function of religion in African American culture.

135. Maulana Karenga, "Overturning Ourselves: From Mystification to Meaningful Struggle," in *Essays on Struggle: Position and Analysis* (Los Angeles: University of Sankore Press, 2016), 25–26. This essay originally appeared in the *Black Scholar* (October 1972): 6–14.

136. August Wilson and Sandra Shannon (interviewer), "August Wilson Explains His Dramatic Vision: An Interview," in *Conversations with August Wilson*, ed. Jackson R. Bryer and Mary C. Hartig (Jackson: University Press of Mississippi, 1991), 128.

137. Maulana Karenga, *Introduction to Black Studies* (Los Angeles: Kawaida Publications, 1982), 36.

138. Maulana Karenga, *Introduction to Black Studies* (Los Angeles: University of Sankore Press, 1993), 26.

139. Molefi Kete Asante, *Maulana Karenga: An Intellectual Portrait* (Cambridge, UK: Polity, 2009), 96–97.

140. Asante, *Maulana Karenga*, 96–97.

141. Asante, *Maulana Karenga*, 148.

142. Quoted in Asante, *Maulana Karenga*, 96. This discussion appears in an unpublished conference paper, "Kawaida and the Kemetic Concept of *Seankh* (Revivification): Insights into Renewing Ourselves in the World," presented at the Cheikh Anta Diop International Conference, October 13, 2007.

143. In the private email correspondence from February 13, 2019, Maulana Karenga described this trajectory: "Finally, mythology, which is treated as religion (spirituality and ethics) here, is for Kawaida one element of culture. Thus, as a philosophy of life and struggle, Kawaida deals with this essential ground in African culture, placing it in the context of the culture as a whole. And I have developed new and expanded concepts and positions in this area with my seminal studies and works, *Maat, The Moral Ideal in Ancient Egypt: A Study in Classical African Ethics* (2006) and *Odu Ifa: The Ethical Teachings* (1999) as well as numerous articles and papers within these subject areas and fields."

144. Keith A. Mayes, *Kwanzaa: Black Power and the Making of the African-American Holiday Tradition* (New York: Routledge, 2009), 68–69.

145. Mayes, 69.

146. Asante, *Maulana Karenga*, 94–95.

147. Asante, *Maulana Karenga*, 95.

148. Maulana Karenga, *Kawaida and Questions of Life and Struggle: African American, Pan-African, and Global Issues* (Los Angeles: University of Sankore Press, 2008), 1.

149. Karenga, *Kawaida and Questions*, 1.

150. Karenga, *Kawaida and Questions*, 21.

151. Karenga, *Kawaida and Questions*, 21.

152. Karenga, *Kawaida and Questions*, 21.

153. Quoted in Mayes, *Kwanzaa*, 70. This citation is from the interview, "Observance Set for Malcolm X," *Los Angeles Sentinel*, February 3, 1966, 4.

154. Amos N. Wilson, *The Developmental Psychology of the Black Child* (New York: Africana Research Publications, 1978), 215.

155. Wilson, 215.

156. Wilson, 207.

157. Wilson, 214.

158. Wilson, 215.

159. Wilson, 215.

160. Wilson, 190.

161. Wilson, 190.
162. Wilson, 196.
163. Wilson, 196.
164. Wilson, 200.
165. Wilson, 200.
166. Wilson, 107.
167. Wilson, 196.
168. Wilson, 207.
169. Wilson, 207.
170. Molefi Kete Asante [Arthur L. Smith], *Rhetoric of Black Revolution* (Boston: Allyn and Bacon, Inc.), vi.
171. Molefi Kete Asante and Steven Robb, *The Voice of Black Rhetoric: Selections* (Boston: Allyn and Bacon, 1971).
172. Asante, *Rhetoric of Black Revolution*, 13.
173. Asante, *Rhetoric*, 16.
174. Asante, *Rhetoric*, 16.
175. Asante, *Rhetoric*, 18–19.
176. Asante, *Rhetoric*, 34.
177. Asante, *Rhetoric*, 36.
178. Asante, *Rhetoric*, 36–37.
179. Molefi Kete Asante [Arthur L. Smith], *Language, Communication, and Rhetoric in Black America* (New York: Harper and Row, 1972).
180. Asante, *Language, Communication*, 296.
181. Asante, *Language, Communication*, 298.
182. Asante, *Language, Communication*, 299.
183. Molefi Kete Asante and Peter A. Anderson, "Transracial Communication and the Changing Image of Black Americans," *Journal of Black Studies* 4, no. 1 (1973): 69.
184. Asante and Anderson, 72.
185. Asante and Anderson, 73.
186. Asante, *Afrocentricity*, 1.
187. Asante, *Afrocentricity*, 1.
188. Asante, *Afrocentricity*, 4.
189. Asante, *Afrocentricity*, 6.
190. Asante, *Afrocentricity*, 6.
191. Asante, *Afrocentricity*, 7.
192. Asante, *Afrocentricity*, 14.
193. Asante, *Afrocentricity*, 14.
194. Asante, *Afrocentricity*, 20.
195. Asante, *Afrocentricity*, 65.
196. Asante, *Afrocentricity*, 65–69.
197. See Molefi Kete Asante and Abdulai S. Vandi, *Contemporary Black Thought: Alternative Analyses in Social and Behavioral Science* (Beverly Hills, CA: Sage,

1980), which includes several essays by Asante, including his chapter 3 essay entitled "International/Intercultural Relations" where he briefly addresses mythology (51–52).

198. Molefi Kete Asante, "Television's Impact on Black Children's Language," in *Contemporary Black Thought: Alternative Analyses in Social and Behavioral Science*, ed. Molefi Kete Asante and Abdulai S. Vandi (Beverly Hills, CA: Sage, 1980), 184–85.

199. Asante and Welsh, "Myth," 391.

200. Asante and Welsh, "Myth," 394.

201. Asante and Welsh, "Myth," 395.

202. Molefi Kete Asante, "The Ideological Significance of Afrocentricity in Intercultural Communication," *Journal of Black Studies* 14, no. 1 (1983): 6.

203. Asante, "Ideological Significance," 9.

204. Asante, "Ideological Significance," 10.

205. Asante, "Ideological Significance," 13.

206. Asante, *Afrocentricity*, 24.

207. Asante, "Ideological Significance," 15–16.

208. Asante, "Ideological Significance," 16.

209. Asante, "Ideological Significance," 16.

210. Molefi Kete Asante, *The Afrocentric Idea* (Philadelphia: Temple University Press, 1987), 96.

211. Asante, *Afrocentric Idea*, 96.

212. Asante, *Afrocentric Idea*, 98.

213. Asante, *Afrocentric Idea*, 99.

214. Asante, *Afrocentric Idea*, 98, 99.

215. Asante, *Afrocentric Idea*, 100.

216. Asante, "Ideological Significance," 12.

217. Molefi K. Asante, *Kemet, Afrocentricity, and Knowledge* (Trenton, NJ: Africa World Press, 1990), 8.

218. Asante, *Kemet, Afrocentricity, and Knowledge*, 9.

219. Asante, *Kemet, Afrocentricity, and Knowledge*, 10.

220. Asante, *Kemet, Afrocentricity, and Knowledge*, 10.

221. See Du Bois's essay "Whither Now and Why" from the collected speeches in *The Education of Black People* (Amherst: University of Massachusetts Press, 1973).

222. Asante, *Kemet, Afrocentricity, and Knowledge*, 12.

223. Asante, *Kemet, Afrocentricity, and Knowledge*, 19.

224. Molefi Kete Asante, *Malcolm X as Cultural Hero and Other Afrocentric Essays* (Trenton, NJ: Africa World Press, 1993), 18.

225. Asante, *Malcolm X*, 82.

226. Asante, *Malcolm X*, 82–83.

227. Asante, *Malcolm X*, 82.

228. Asante, *Malcolm X*, 82.

229. Molefi Kete Asante, *Kemet, Afrocentricity, and Knowledge* (Trenton, NJ: Africa World Press, 1992), 61.

230. See Asante's essay in *Malcolm X* on "Image Dragons after Our Hearts."

231. Asante, *Kemet*, 168.

232. John Oliver Killens, "A Symposium: Black Power: Its Meaning and Measure: John O. Killens," *Negro Digest* 16, no. 1 (1966): 33.

233. Toni Morrison, "The Site of Memory," in *Inventing the Truth: The Art and Craft of Memoir*, ed. William Zinsser (New York: Houghton Mifflin, 1995), 98.

234. Morrison, "Site of Memory," 91–92.

235. Toni Morrison, "Rootedness: The Ancestor as Foundation," in *The Norton Anthology of African American Literature, 2nd Edition*, ed. Henry Louis Gates Jr. and Nellie Y. McKay (New York: W. W. Norton, 2007), 2287.

236. Morrison, "Rootedness," 2289.

237. Morrison, "Rootedness," 2289.

238. This collection does not approach memory as a broad cultural concept. Instead, it is about different scholars' memories of their experiences and encounters with Toni Morrison.

239. Although the novel *Kindred* does not fit the criteria for this book's final chapter on literary criticism, it poses a compelling intellectual challenge for future studies that may critically analyze *Kindred* from a Black cultural mythology lens. Octavia Butler alerts readers of the 1976 Bicentennial setting by merely referencing July 1976 as the setting. The novel's creative reliance on themes of ancestors and its fantasy use of time travel would stretch Black cultural mythology's definitions of immortalization, epic-intuitive conduct, resistance-based cognitive survival, and even antiheroics. The criticism of *Kindred* uniformly mentions the Bicentennial setting as a commemorative whose axiology Butler questions but not as a sustained discourse related to cultural memory.

240. Audre Lorde, *Zami: A New Spelling of My Name* (Berkeley, CA: Crossing Press, 1982).

241. Heather Russell, *Legba's Crossing: Narratology in the African Atlantic* (Athens: University of Georgia Press, 2009), 58.

242. Russell, 60.

243. Russell, 61. In the blocked quote, Russell quotes Henry and offers pagination as 84–85.

244. Suzan-Lori Parks, *The America Play and Other Works* (New York: Theatre Communications Group, 1995), 4–5.

245. Richard Wright, "Blueprint for Negro Writing," in *The Richard Wright Reader*, ed. Ellen Wright and Michele Fabre (New York: Harper and Rowe, 1978), 98.

246. Wright, "Blueprint," 100.

247. Wright, "Blueprint," 106.

248. Wright, "Blueprint," 104–5.

249. Paul Robeson, *Here I Stand* (Boston: Beacon Press, [1958] 1988), 100.

250. Fanny Lou Hamer, *To Praise Our Bridges: An Autobiography*, taped and edited by Julius Lester and Mary Varela (Jackson, MS: KIPCO, 1967).

251. Hilary Teague, "Liberia: Its Struggles and Its Promises," delivered in 1846, in *Masterpieces of Negro Eloquence, 1818–1913*, ed. Alice Dunbar Nelson (Mineola, NY: Dover, [1914] 2000).

252. Wilson J. Moses. *Afrotopia: The Roots of African American Popular History* (New York: Cambridge University Press, 1998), 3.

253. Quoted in Sandra G. Shannon, "Audience and Africanisms in August Wilson's Dramaturgy: A Case Study," in *African American Performance and Theater History: A Critical Reader*, ed. Harry J. Elam and David Krisner (New York: Oxford University Press, 2001), 155.

254. Cornel West, "Philosophy and the Afro-American Experience," in *African-American Philosophy*, ed. Tommy Lott and John Pittman (New York: Wiley-Blackwell, 2006), 16.

255. George Yancy, *What White Looks Like: African American Philosophers on the Whiteness Question* (New York: Routledge, 2004), 70.

256. Addison Gayle, "Blueprint for Black Criticism," *First World* 1, no. 1 (1977): 41–45.

257. Sherley Anne Williams, *Dessa Rose* (New York: William Morrow, 1986), 6.

258. Quoted in Karanja Keita Carroll, "A Genealogical Review of the Worldview Concept and Framework in Africana Studies-Related Theory and Research," in *African American Consciousness Past and Present, Africana Studies, Volume 4*, ed. James L. Conyers Jr. (New Brunswick, NJ: Transaction Publishers, 2011). See also Dona Richards, "European Mythology: The Ideology of 'Progress,'" in *Contemporary Black Thought: Alternative Analyses in Social and Behavioral Science*, ed. Molefi Kete Asante and Abdulai S. Vandi (Beverly Hills, CA: Sage Publications, 1980), 59–79.

259. See the discussion of impermanent mortality, based on Maria W. Stewart's model, in Christel N. Temple, "The Cosmology of Afrocentric Womanism," *Western Journal of Black Studies* 36, no. 1 (2012): 23–32.

Chapter 2

1. See "Do African Americans Feel Lucky Their Ancestors Were Slaves?," *Yahoo! Answers*, August 1, 2014. https://answers.yahoo.com/question/index?qid=20140801202215AANF7o1.

2. Hillary Crosley, "Crazy Talk: Slavery Was a Blessing in Disguise," *The Root*, October 6, 2012, http://www.theroot.com/crazy-talk-slavery-was-blessing-in-disguise-1790893592.

3. Crosley. See also Jon Michael Hubbard, *Letters to the Editor: Confessions of a Frustrated Conservative* (Bloomington: iUniverse, 2009). http://www.theroot.

com/articles/culture/2012/10/crazy_talk_slavery_was_blessing_in_disguise_says_jon_hubbard.html.

4. See "The White Side of the Black Story," *Quora*, https://www.quora.com/The-White-Side-of-the-Black-Story-BUCHANAN-TO-OBAMA-By-Patrick-J-Buchanan-What-is-your-opinion-of-Mr-Buchanans-take-on-this-issue-I-am-not-saying-I-agree-with-him-nor-have-I-verified-his-statistics-I-want-to-know-your-opinion-of-what-he-wrote (accessed July 17, 2018).

5. See Christel N. Temple, "Communicating Race and Culture in the 21st Century: Discourse and the Post-Racial/Post-Cultural Challenge," *Journal of Multicultural Discourses* 5, no. 1 (2010): 45–63, quote at 45.

6. Nathan Huggins, "Integrating Afro-American History into American History," in *The State of Afro-American History: Past, Present, Future*, ed. Darlene Clark Hine (Baton Rouge: Louisiana State University Press, 1989), 157–68.

7. William H. Wiggins, Jr. *O Freedom! Afro-American Emancipation Celebrations* (Knoxville: University of Tennessee Press, 1987), xi.

8. Wiggins, xi.

9. Wiggins, xi.

10. Wiggins, 108.

11. Wiggins, 82.

12. Mitch Kachun, *Festivals of Freedom: Memory and Meaning in African American Emancipation Celebrations, 1808–1915* (Amherst: University of Massachusetts Press, 2003), 9.

13. Kachun, 9.

14. Kachun, 9. In particular, see Kachun's introduction, which suggests many of these topics.

15. Quoted in Kachun, 152.

16. Kachun, 152.

17. Quoted in Kachun, 152.

18. Kachun, 161. These are the names of heroes who appear in this section of Kachun's chapter.

19. Kathleen Ann Clark, *Defining Moments: African American Commemoration and Political Culture in the South, 1863–1913* (Chapel Hill: University of North Carolina University Press, 2005), 2.

20. Clark, 5.

21. Clark, 6.

22. Clark, 9.

23. Clark, 9.

24. Clark, 11.

25. Clark, 91.

26. Clark, 91.

27. Clark, 62–63.

28. Clark, 63.

29. Kachun, *Festivals of Freedom*, 250–51.

30. Ishakamusa Barashango, preface to *Afrikan People and European Holidays: A Mental Genocide, Book One and Book Two* (Baltimore: Afrikan World Books, 2001). The author adds, "Generally, holidays have a special political and cultural significance, in short they are institutions of the mind and as such can be and most often are used as control mechanisms. . . . Participating in European politico-cultural holidays is destructive to the true nature of Afrikan Genius, the genius that laid the foundations of the world."

31. Mayes, *Kwanzaa*, xxi.

32. Quoted in Mayes, xxi.

33. Mayes, xxi.

34. Mayes, xxi.

35. Mayes, xxii.

36. Mayes, xxiii.

37. Mayes, xxi.

38. Mayes, xxi, xxiv.

39. Mayes, xxii.

40. "Project 1619: Arrival of the First Africans in Colonial America." http://www.project1619.org/10.html (accessed September 26, 2017).

41. "Project 1619: Arrival."

42. Wiggins, *O Freedom!*, 121–22. In a personal interview with Mr. Mingo Scott, October 18, 1972, Wiggins learned of the value of annual "ritualized readings" of the Emancipation Proclamation, which also helped to politicize celebrants.

43. See http://project1619.org/10.html (accessed October 21, 2015).

44. See "Pilgrimage to Point Comfort August 20, 2016." http://www.project1619.org/index.html (accessed September 27, 2017).

45. See http://project1619.org/8.html (accessed October 21, 2015).

46. See "Actual Date First Africans Arrived in English North America Revealed." http://www.project1619.org/index.html (accessed September 27, 2017).

47. "Actual Date Africans Arrived."

48. See "Mission," Hampton Virginia 2019 Commemorative Commission, http://hamptonva2019.com/about/mission/ (accessed October 29, 2017).

49. "Mission."

50. Since 2016, the event has been updated from "African Arrival Day" to "African Landing Day," but the event includes identical types of activities. See the schedule of events for "African Landing Day," http://box5485.temp.domains/~rojecwf4/events/african-landing-day/ (accessed August 15, 2019).

51. Associated Press, "Rededicating Historical Marker for Arrival of First Africans," August 20, 2015, http://www.newsplex.com/home/headlines/Rededicating-Historical-Marker-for-Arrival-of-First-Africans-322430332.html.

52. See "American Evolution: Virginia to America, 1619–2019," https://catalog.hathitrust.org/Record/100105441 (accessed October 29, 2017).

53. "American Evolution."

54. "American Evolution."

55. "American Evolution."

56. Ana Lucia Araujo, *Shadows of the Slave Past: Memory, Heritage, and Slavery* (New York: Routledge, 2014), 41.

57. Kadiatu Kanneh, *African Identities: Race, Nation, and Culture in African Ethnography, Pan-Africanism, and Black Literature* (New York: Routledge, 1998), 123.

58. See "The First Africans," *Jamestown Rediscovery*. http://historicjamestowne.org/history/the-first-africans/ (accessed October 16, 2107\).

59. See "Virginia's First Africans," http://www.encyclopediavirginia.org/virginia_s_first_africans#start_entry (accessed October 16, 2017).

60. Ashley Barnett, "*1619: The Making of America*," *Early American Literature* 49.2 (2014): 607–11.

61. Barnett, 608. Here, Barnett emphasizes historian Ben Vinson's examination of the "Afro–Latin American View" of 1619.

62. Barnett, 607.

63. Barnett, 608.

64. Barnett, 608. In this conference review, Barnett describes Calvin Pearson's ideas as opening presenter.

65. Barnett, 609.

66. Barnett, 608.

67. Barnett, 608.

68. Barnett, 609.

69. Michael Guasco, "The Fallacy of 1619: Rethinking the History of Africans in Early America," in *Black Perspectives*, African American Intellectual History Society blog, September 4, 2017, http://www.aaihs.org/the-fallacy-of-1619-rethinking-the-history-of-africans-in-early-america/.

70. Guasco.

71. Guasco.

72. Guasco.

73. Martin Luther King Jr., *Why We Can't Wait* (New York: Penguin, 1964), 22–23.

74. King, 25.

75. See *Transcendence and the Africana Literary Enterprise* (New York: Lexington Books, 2017) in which Christel N. Temple introduces features of literary Africology as a transcendent, Africana disciplinary-based methodology, including Africana reader-response, bibliographic shift, pairing, isolation, canon summary, idea formation modeling, disciplinary competency, applied functionality, limited narrative product or artifact, Africana phenomenology, multidimensionality, and dutiful survey.

76. Temple, *Transcendence*, 27.
77. Temple, *Transcendence*, 27.
78. Temple, *Transcendence*, 34.
79. Temple, *Transcendence*, 33.
80. Temple, *Transcendence*, 22.
81. See "Trip Down Memory Lane" (blog), https://kwekudee–tripdownmemorylane.blogspot.com/2013/06/mbundu-ambundu-people-angolas.html (accessed October 24, 2017).
82. King, *Why We Can't Wait*, 36.
83. See Jennifer Richardson and Richard J. Nussbaum, "The Impact of Multiculturalism versus Colorblindness on Racial Bias," *Experimental Psychology* 40, no. 3 (2004): 417–23, and Alesso Avenanti, Angela Sirigu, and Salvatore M. Aglioti, "Racial Bias Reduces Empathic Sensorimotor Resonance with Other-Race Pain," *Current Biology* 20, no. 11 (2010): 1018–22.
84. Helene Johnson, "Sonnet to a Negro in Harlem," in *Norton Anthology of African American Literature*, ed. Henry Louis Gates Jr. and Nellie Y. McKay (New York: W. W. Norton, 2004), 1353.
85. James Baldwin, *The Fire Next Time* (New York: Vintage International, [1963] 1992), 3–4.
86. James Baldwin, *Notes of a Native Son*, in *James Baldwin: Collected Essays* (New York: Library of America, [1949] 1998), 63–64.
87. Baldwin, *Fire Next Time*, 4.
88. Baldwin, *Fire Next Time*, 5.
89. Baldwin, *Fire Next Time*, 7.
90. Baldwin, *Fire Next Time*, 7.
91. Baldwin, *Fire Next Time*, 10.
92. Baldwin, *Fire Next Time*, 10.
93. A. Leon Higginbotham, *In the Matter of Color: Race and the American Legal Process: The Colonial Period* (New York: Oxford University Press, 1980), 20.
94. Higginbotham, *In the Matter of Color*, 36.
95. Quoted in Higginbotham, *In the Matter of Color*, 386. Here Higginbotham quotes Truman Nelson, *Documents of Upheaval* (New York: Hill and Wang, 1969), 6. Also, it is in Walker's *Appeal*, 27, 76.
96. Douglass's well-known speech is "What to the Slave Is the Fourth of July," which he delivered on July 5, 1852, at Rochester, New York's Corinthian Hall, to the Rochester Ladies' Anti-Slavery Society.
97. Higginbotham, *In the Matter of Color*, 5.
98. Gil Scott-Heron, *So Far, So, Good* (Chicago: Third World Press, 1990), 64.
99. Heron, *So Far*, 64.
100. Heron, 65.
101. Heron, 65.

102. Heron, 65.
103. Derrick Bell, "An American Fairy Tale: The Income-Related Neutralization of Race Law Precedent," in *The Derrick Bell Reader*, ed. Richard Delgado and Jean Stefancic (New York: New York University Press, 2005), 118.
104. Bell, "American Fairy Tale," 121.
105. Alyce Elliot, preface, *King Commemorations: A Book of Activities* (N.p.: Create Space Independent Platform Publishing, 2009), 5.
106. Bell, "American Fairy Tale," 122.
107. Elliott, *King Commemorations*, 5.
108. Richardson and Nussbaum, "Impact of Multiculturalism," 418.
109. Bell, "American Fairy Tale," 122.
110. Ana Lucia Araujo, "Welcome the Diaspora: Slave Trade Heritage Tourism and the Public Memory of Slavery," *Ethnologies* 32, no. 2 (2010): 145–91.
111. Araujo, "Welcome."
112. Araujo, "Welcome," 145.
113. Araujo, "Welcome," 145.
114. Araujo, "Welcome," 145. She references Marianne Hirsch's *Family Frames, Photography Narrative, and Postmemory* (Cambridge: Harvard University Press, 1997).
115. Araujo, "Welcome," 145. She references Régine Robin's *La mémoire saturée* (Paris: Stock, 2002).
116. Araujo, "Welcome," 155, 156.
117. Araujo, "Welcome," 164.
118. Araujo, "Welcome," 169.
119. Araujo, "Welcome," 165, 167.
120. Araujo, "Welcome," 170.
121. Araujo, "Welcome," 173.
122. Araujo, "Welcome," 173.
123. Joanne M. Braxton and Maria I. Diedrich, eds., *Monuments of the Black Atlantic: Slavery and Memory* (New Brunswick, NJ: Transaction Publishers, 2004), 1. This collection is from efforts of the College of William and Mary's Middle Passage Project and the Collegium for African American Research, based at the Westfälische Wilhelms-Universität in Münster, Germany, which held the conference "Monuments of the Black Atlantic: History, Memory, and Politics" on May 24–28, 2000 in Williamsburg and Hampton, Virginia.
124. Braxton and Diedrich, 7.
125. Wole Soyinka, *Myth, Literature, and the African World* (New York: Cambridge University Press, 1976), 6.
126. Wole Soyinka, "The African World and the Ethno-Cultural Debate," in *African Culture: Rhythms of Unity*, ed. Molefi Kete Asante and Kariamu Welsh Asante (Trenton, NJ: Africa World Press, 1990).

Chapter 3

1. Asante, "Ideological Significance," 15.
2. See Robert O'Hara's *Insurrection: Holding History* on Nat Turner, in which the play removes the death sting from the assassination of Black revolters and conceptualizes such heroic activity as behavior intended to positively affect posterity—just as Maria W. Stewart's calls for immortalization did the same.
3. Tolagbe Ogunleye, "African American Folklore: Its Role in Reconstructing African American History," *Journal of Black Studies* 27, no. 4 (1997): 435.
4. Ogunleye, 436–37.
5. Ogunleye, 436.
6. Ogunleye, 436.
7. Shirley Graham Du Bois's biography project is remarkable because of its audience; even James Baldwin did a book review of one of her volumes as an adult reader.
8. See Catherine Clinton's *Harriet Tubman: The Road to Freedom* (New York: Little, Brown, 2003); Jean M. Humez's *Harriet Tubman: The Life and the Life Stories* (Madison: University of Wisconsin Press, 2003); Milton C. Sernett's *Harriet Tubman: Myth, Memory, and History* (Durham, NC: Duke University Press, 2007); and Beverly Lowry's *Harriet Tubman: Imagining a Life* (New York: Doubleday, 2007).
9. Clinton, *Road to Freedom*, xi.
10. See John Freeman's 2004 jacket cover review.
11. Asante and Welsh, "Myth."
12. W. E. B. Du Bois, "Whither Now and Why," in *The Education of Black People: Ten Critiques, 1906–1960* (New York: New York University Press, 2001).
13. Ezemenari Obasi, Lisa Flores, and Linda James-Myers, "Construction and Initial Validation of the Worldview Analysis Scale," *Journal of Black Studies* 39, no. 6 (2009): 937–61.
14. Clinton, *Harriet Tubman*, 161.
15. Clinton, 101.
16. In *Harriet Tubman: Hero of the Underground Railroad* by Lori Mortenson (North Mankato, MN: Picture Window Books, 2007), Tubman is "the bravest American hero."
17. In *Dinner at Aunt Connie's House* (1993), Faith Ringgold features the same twelve women from her painting, *The Dinner Quilt*: Harriet Tubman, Maria W. Stewart, Bessie Smith, Mary McLeod Bethune, Augusta Savage, Billie Holiday, Zora Neale Hurston, Dorothy Dandridge, Marian Anderson, Fannie Lou Hamer, Sojourner Truth, and Madame C. J. Walker.
18. Faith Ringgold, *Dinner at Aunt Connie's House*, afterword (New York: Hyperion Books for Children, 1993); pages not numbered.

19. Ringgold, afterword.
20. Ringgold, afterword.
21. See Clinton, *Road to Freedom*, 104.
22. Errol Hill, *Black Heroes: 7 Plays* (New York: Applause Theatre Book Publishers, 1989), 103.
23. May Miller, *Harriet Tubman*, in *Black Heroes: 7 Plays*, ed. Errol Hill (New York: Applause Theatre Book Publishers, 1989), 105, 107.
24. Miller, *Harriet Tubman*, 111.
25. Miller, *Harriet Tubman*, 112.
26. Miller, *Harriet Tubman*, 115, 116.
27. Miller, *Harriet Tubman*, 116.
28. Octavia Butler, *Kindred* (New York: Beacon, [1979] 2003), 140–41.
29. Butler, *Kindred*, 175, 177.
30. Laini Mataka, *Restoring the Queen* (Baltimore: Black Classic Press, 1994) 59.
31. Mataka, 59, 60.
32. Mataka, 59.
33. Mataka, 60.
34. Mataka, 61.
35. Mataka, 61.
36. "Carolyn Gage," https://carolyngage.weebly.com/bio-and-vitae.html (accessed August 15, 2019).
37. Carolyn Gage, *Harriet Tubman Visits a Therapist*, in *Under Thirty: Plays for a New Generation*, ed. Eric Lane and Nina Shengold (New York: Vintage Books, 2004), 444.

Chapter 4

1. Quoted in Jacob Carruthers, *The Irritated Genie: An Essay on the Haitian Revolution* (Chicago: Kemetic Institute, 1985), 113.
2. Carruthers, 113. Also see C. L. R. James, *A History of Pan-African Revolt* (Chicago: C. H. Kerr, [1969] 1995), 1–20.
3. Carruthers, 112, 12.
4. Edouard Glissant, *Monsieur Toussaint: A Play*, trans. J. Michael Dash and Edouard Glissant (Boulder: Lynne Rienner, [1961] 2005), 15.
5. Glissant, 15.
6. Glissant, 15.
7. Glissant, 13.
8. Glissant, 11.
9. Glissant, 15–16.
10. Glissant, 6.

11. Carruthers, *Irritated Genie*, 2.
12. Carruthers, 1.
13. Carruthers, xviii.
14. Carruthers, 1, 11.
15. Carruthers, 11.
16. Michael J. Dash, *Haiti and the U.S.: National Stereotypes and the Literary Imagination* (New York: St. Martin's Press, 1997), 12.
17. Carruthers, *Genie*, xx.
18. Carter G. Woodson, introduction to *Negro History in Thirteen Plays*, ed. Willis Richardson and May Miller (Washington, DC: Associated Publishers, 1935), iii.
19. Woodson, "Introduction," v.
20. Woodson, "Introduction," v.
21. May Miller, preface to *Negro History in Thirteen Plays*, ed. Willis Richardson and May Miller (Washington, DC: Associated Publishers, 1935), vi.
22. I appreciate Gary Ashwill's essay on "Toussaint L'Ouverture" in the *Oxford Companion to African American Literature* because he offers a useful bibliographic survey of key models of how writers and historians have captured the meaning of Louverture's heroics. He cites Michael Dash's *Haiti and the United States: National Stereotypes and the Literary Imagination* (1988) and Alfred N. Hunt's *Haiti's Influence on Antebellum America: Slumbering Volcano in the Caribbean* (Baton Rouge: Louisiana State University Press, 1988). I add several other signifying works to this: Edouard Glissant's *Monsieur Toussaint* (1961), Ntozake Shange's *for colored girls . . .* , Arna Bontemps's *Drums at Dusk*, Derek Walcott's *Haitian Trilogy* (*The Haitian Earth*, *Henri Christophe*, . . .), Langston Hughes's *The Emperor of Haiti*, "Genefride" by May Miller, "Christophe's Daughters" by Helen Webb Harris, Lorraine Hansberry's unfinished play "Toussaint," Margaret Walker's poem "The Ballad of the Free," Ralph Ellison's short story "Mister Toussan," *The Tragedy of King Christophe* by Aimé Césaire, C. L. R. James's (now published play) *Toussaint L'Ouverture*, C. L. R. James's (revision of the play into historical fiction) *Black Jacobins*, Aimé Césaire's *Toussaint Louverture* (1960), Leslie Pinckney Hill's *Toussaint L'Ouverture: A Dramatic History* (1928), Shirley Graham Du Bois and Selden Rodman's coauthored plays *Deep Rivers* and *The Revolutionists*, William Easton's play *Dessalines*, and Langston Hughes's play *Troubled Island*.
23. Hill, introduction to *Black Heroes*, vii.
24. Hill, vii.
25. Hill, vii.
26. Hill, ix.
27. Hill, x.
28. Hill, xi.
29. Hill, xi.
30. Hill, 5.
31. Ralph Ellison, "Mister Toussan," *New Masses* (November 4, 1941), 19–20.

32. Ralph Ellison, *Flying Home and Other Stories*, ed. John F. Calhoun (New York: Random House, 1996).

33. John F. Calhoun, introduction to *Flying Home and Other Stories*, by Ralph Ellison, ed. John F. Calhoun (New York: Random House, 1969), xix.

34. Calhoun, xxv.

35. Calhoun, xxviii.

36. Calhoun, xxix–xxx.

37. Ellison, "Mister Toussan," 19. This is reprinted in *The Unz Review: An Alternative Media Selection,* https://www.unz.com/print/NewMasses-1941nov04-00019/ (accessed March 10, 2019).

38. Ellison, "Mister Toussan, 19.

39. Ellison, "Mister Toussan," 20.

40. Ellison, "Mister Toussan," 20.

41. Ellison, "Mister Toussan," 20.

42. Ellison, "Mister Toussan," xix.

43. Ntozake Shange, *for colored girls who have considered suicide / when the rainbow is enuf* (New York: Scribner Poetry, 1977), 27.

44. Shange, 30.

45. Reviewers such as the *San Francisco Chronicle* acknowledged the collection as a source on some of the myths "that sustained generations of Haitians" (inside front book cover), which reflects an awareness of Haitian nationalism based on the history of its successful revolution.

46. Wilson C. Chen, "Figures of Flight and Entrapment in Edwidge Danticat's *Krik? Krak!*," *Rocky Mountain Review* 65, no. 1 (2011): 36.

47. Chen, 36.

48. Chen, 37.

49. Chen, 37.

50. Semia Harbawi, "Writing Memory: Edwidge Danticat's Limbo Inscriptions," *Journal of West Indian Literature* 16, no. 1 (2007): 37.

51. Edwidge Danticat, *Krik?! Krak!* (New York: Vintage Contemporaries, [1991] 1995), 54.

52. Danticat, 55.

53. Danticat, 55.

54. Danticat, 55.

55. Danticat, 55–56.

56. Danticat, 56.

57. Danticat, 57.

58. Danticat, 57.

59. Danticat, 80.

60. Chen, "Figures of Flight," 44.

61. Charles Johnson, *Soulcatcher and Other Stories: Twelve Powerful Tales about Slavery* (New York: Harcourt, 1998), 62–63.

62. Johnson, *Soulcatcher*, xii. See Charles Johnson's preface to *Soulcatcher*, which was added to the collection in 2001, xii.

63. Johnson, *Soulcatcher*, xiii, xii.

64. See the back cover description's thematic precision in marketing the value of Walcott's collection that "carved a place in the modern theatre for the history of the West Indies." This is less focused on African American mythological points of view of the meaning of revolutionary activity in the Caribbean, but the discourses are complementary.

65. Derek Walcott, preface to *The Haitian Trilogy: Henri Christophe, Drums and Colours, and The Haitian Earth: Plays* (New York: Farrar, Straus and Giroux, 2002), vii.

66. Walcott, "Preface," viii.

67. Walcott, *Haitian Trilogy*, 114.

68. Carruthers, *Irritated Genie*, 113.

69. Carruthers, 113.

70. Carruthers, 113–14, 15.

71. Marjorie Valdun, "Mandela and the Black Diaspora," *Colorlines*, December 8, 2013, https://www.colorlines.com/articles/mandela-and-black-diaspora.

72. Carruthers, xvii.

73. Carruthers, xvii.

74. Dash, *Haiti and the U.S.*, 10.

75. Dash, ix.

76. Carruthers, 11.

77. See Guy S. Antoine, "Toussaint's Body: Antoine Comments and Speaks of His Visit to Fort de Joux," http://faculty.webster.edu/corbetre/haiti-archive-new/msg10107.html (accessed August 15, 2019) and Antoine's "Statement of Purpose" for the blog "Windows on Haiti," http://windowsonhaiti.com/windowsonhaiti/note-ed.shtml (accessed August, 15, 2019).

Chapter 5

1. Asante, *Rhetoric of Black Revolution*, 26–27.

2. Asante, *Malcolm X*, 29.

3. Richard Wright, "How Bigger Was Born," in *Native Son* (New York: Harper and Row, [1940] 1989), xx. This appeared originally in the *Saturday Review of Literature*, June 1, 1940.

4. Wright, "How Bigger Was Born," xix.

5. Wright, "How Bigger Was Born," xiii.

6. Wright, "How Bigger Was Born," ix.

7. Richard Wright, "Blueprint for Negro Writing," in *The Richard Wright Reader*, ed. Ellen Wright and Michele Fabre (New York: Harper and Row, 1978), 41.

8. Wright, "Blueprint," 41.
9. Wright, "Blueprint," 41.
10. Wright, "Blueprint," 41.
11. Wright, "Blueprint," 47.
12. Richard Wright, *Twelve Million Black Voices* (New York: Thunder's Mouth Press, [1941] 2002), 146.
13. Molefi Kete Asante, *An Afrocentric Manifesto: Toward an African Renaissance* (Malden, MA: Polity Press, 2008).
14. Yoshinobu Hakutani and Robert L. Tener, afterword to *HAIKU: This Other World* by Richard Wright (New York: Arcade Publishing, 1998), 295.
15. Richard Wright, *White Man Listen!* (Garden City, NJ: Doubleday, 1964), xvi.
16. Richard Wright, foreword to *Blues Fell this Morning: Meaning of the Blues* by Paul Oliver (New York: Cambridge University Press, [1963] 1990), 7.
17. Wright, "Foreword," 8.
18. Robert Butler, *Native Son: The Emergence of a New Black Hero* (Boston: Twayne, 1991), 19.
19. Michel Fabre, *The World of Richard Wright* (Jackson: University Press of Mississippi, 1985), 102, 105.
20. C. James Trotman, ed., *Richard Wright: Myths and Realities* (New York: Garland, 1988), xi.
21. Trotman, xiv.
22. Eugene Miller, *Voice of a Native Son: The Poetics of Richard Wright* (Jackson: University Press of Mississippi, 1990), 57.
23. Miller, *Voice of a Native Son*, 57, 58.
24. Miller, *Voice of a Native Son*, 45.
25. Miller, *Voice of a Native Son*, 46.
26. Miller cites the symbolism of the "flaming furnace, knife, and ax" and their association with loas representing "fire and war, with blacksmithing and iron, their icons decorated with sabers and machetes" (51). He notes Bigger's killing occurs on a Saturday, similar to the "favored day of voodoo rituals" (51) and associates Mary with the "seductive and sensual behavior" of the "mythic figure of Erzulie," the "sea goddess" (53).
27. Miller, *Voice of a Native Son*, 57.
28. Maria K. Mootry examines this theme in "Wright's Male Heroes and Female Characters Are Archetypes" in *Readings on Native Son*, ed. Hayley R. Mitchell (San Diego: Greenhaven, 2000). Though it is a straightforward, linear analysis of the classic archetype, it is remarkable for being a part of the small group of criticism that uses the language of heroics in considering *Native Son*.
29. John Reilly, afterword to *Native Son* (New York: Harper and Row, 1989), 395.
30. Houston Baker, *Long Black Song: Essays in Black American Literature and Culture* (Charlottesville: University of Virginia Press, [1972] 1990), 134, 135.

31. Baker, *Long Black Song*, 135.
32. Baker, *Long Black Song*, 136.
33. Baker, *Long Black Song*, 138.
34. Richard Wright, *Native Son* (New York: Harper and Row, [1940] 1989), 367.
35. See Ode S. Igede's "Context, Form, and the Poetic Expression in Igede Funeral Dirges," *Africa* 65, no. 1: 80, in which he describes the meaning of a "good death" that is worthy to be publicly celebrated and its application to Malcolm X's murder and legacy in Christel N. Temple, "Literary Malcolm X: The Making of an African American Ancestor," in *Malcolm X: A Historical Reader*, ed. James L. Conyers Jr. and Andrew P. Smallwood (Durham, NC: Carolina Academic Press, 2008), 172.
36. In this sense, Black cultural mythology's methodology is very much aligned with aspects of the Afrocentric paradigm concerning "orientation of [a] text" to emphasize "a *defense of African cultural elements* as historically valid in the context of . . . literature" as well as "an intense interest in *psychological location* as determined by symbols, motifs, rituals, and signs," including their absence in the experience of culturally displaced characters such as Bigger Thomas. See Molefi Kete Asante's "African Betrayals and Recovery for a New Future," in *Africa in the 21st Century: Toward a New Future*, ed. Ama Mazama (New York: Routledge, 2007), 76.
37. Wright, "How Bigger Was Born," xxiv.
38. Wright, "How Bigger Was Born," xxv.
39. Wright, "How Bigger Was Born," xxv.
40. Wright, "How Bigger Was Born," xxiv. Also, Max's defense (369–70), which suggests "prison" would be a more fulfilling home for Bigger than being in society, also counters the Black nationalist interpretation of nation/land.
41. Wright, "How Bigger Was Born," xxvi.
42. Wright, "How Bigger Was Born," xxvi.
43. Wright, "How Bigger Was Born," xxv. Also, see Molefi K. Asante and Kariamu Welsh's "Myth: The Communication of the African American Mind," in which the authors suggest that Black orators and speakers intuitively draw on the culture's heroics in their persuasive speech.
44. Wright, "How Bigger Was Born," xiii.
45. Wright, "How Bigger Was Born," xxi.
46. Wright, *Native Son*, 226.
47. Wright, *Native Son*, 226.
48. Wright, *Native Son*, 256.
49. Wright, *Native Son*, 354.
50. Wright, *Native Son*, 226, 227.
51. Wright, *Native Son*, 229.
52. Wright, *Native Son*, 351.

53. Wright, *Native Son*, 255.
54. In Nigerian Ibo cultures, when a child is born, dies, and is born again in a repetitive cycle, it is called an *ábíkú*. Bigger's desire could be interpreted as a variation of this death cycle worldview, which is also held responsible for miscarriages, wherein the child remains in the spirit world.
55. Wright, *Native Son*, 256.
56. Wright, "Blueprint," 49.

Chapter 6

1. See Herb Boyd and Ron Daniels, eds., *By Any Means Necessary: Malcolm X: Real, Not Reinvented: Critical Conversations on Manning Marable's Biography of Malcom X* (Chicago: Third World Press, 2012), which includes over thirty responses from immediately mobilized scholars and public intellectuals to Marable's alarming new biography on Malcolm X. See also Jared Ball's and Todd Steven Burroughs's *A Lie of Reinvention: Correcting Manning Marable's Malcolm X* (Baltimore: Black Classic Press, 2015). These collections are important to the legacy discourses on Malcolm, but this chapter is a review of the first wave of book reviews published in the first six months after Marable's release of *Reinvention*. Capturing the quick, intuitive response of the general public in news magazines as well as journals reflects an immediate, gut-level reaction to *Reinvention*.
2. Wilson, *Psychological Development of the Black Child*, 196.
3. Albert Cleage, "Myths about Malcolm," in *Malcolm X: The Man and His Times*, ed. John Henrik Clarke (Trenton, NJ: Africa World Press, 1990), 16.
4. Cleage, 14.
5. Cleage, 26.
6. Asante, *Malcolm X as Cultural Hero*, 25, 31.
7. Michael Eric Dyson, *Making Malcolm: The Myth and Meaning of Malcolm X* (New York: Oxford University Press, 1995), 151.
8. Dyson, xxv.
9. Dyson, 167, 168.
10. Robert E. Terrill, ed., *The Cambridge Companion to Malcolm X* (Cambridge: Cambridge University Press, 2010).
11. Robert L. Jenkins, ed., *The Malcolm X Encyclopedia* (Westport, CT: Greenwood Press, 2002), 69.
12. James L. Conyers Jr. and Andrew P. Smallwood, eds., *Malcolm X: A Historical Reader* (Durham, NC: Carolina Academic Press, 2008).
13. Conyers and Smallwood, 21–22.
14. Gerald Horne, "'Myth' and the Making of 'Malcolm X,'" *American Historical Review* 98, no. 2 (1992): 440–50.

15. Conyers and Smallwood, *Malcolm X*, 168, 169, 182, 330.

16. Manning Marable, *Living Black History: How Reimagining the African-American Past Can Remake America's Racial Future* (New York: Basic Books, 2006), 174.

17. Marable, *Living Black History*, 36.

18. Marable, *Living Black History*, 34, 30, 29, 24–25, 22, 20, 19, 16.

19. Marable, *Living Black History*, xix.

20. Wilson, *Developmental Psychology*, 196.

21. Marable, *Living Black History*, 175.

22. Manning Marable, *Malcolm X: A Life of Reinvention* (New York: Penguin Books, 2011), 12.

23. Marable, *Malcolm X*, 10.

24. Marable, *Malcolm X*, 479.

25. Marable, *Malcolm X*, 480–81.

26. Marable, *Malcolm X*, 482.

27. Marable, *Malcolm X*, 486.

28. Marable, *Malcolm X*, 479.

29. Marable, *Malcolm X*, 480.

30. Wilson, *Developmental Psychology*, 190.

31. Wilson, *Developmental Psychology*, 107.

32. Maulana Karenga, "Reinventing Malcolm with Marable: Pursuing Pathology by Another Name," review of *Malcolm X: A Life of Reinvention* by Manning Marable, *Los Angeles Sentinel* (April 21, 2011), A7.

33. Darryl Lorenzo Wellington, "A Man for Many Seasons," review of *Malcolm X: A Life of Reinvention* by Manning Marable, *Dissent* (September 9, 2011): 103.

34. Touré, "Criminal, Minister, Humanist, Martyr," review of *Malcolm X: A Life of Reinvention* by Manning Marble, *New York Times Book Review* (June 19, 2011), BR18.

35. Aziz Rana, "The World House," review of *Malcolm X: A Life of Reinvention* by Manning Marable, *Nation* (October 11, 2011), 35.

36. Rana, 35.

37. Wellington, "Man for Many Seasons," 100.

38. William Jelani Cobb, "Malcolm X: The Man, The Myth, the Mystery," review of *Malcolm X: A Life of Reinvention* by Manning Marable, *Crisis Forum* (Summer 2011): 25.

39. Adeyinka Makinde, "Manning Marable's Malcolm X—a Life of Reinvention," review of *Malcolm X: A Life of Reinvention* by Manning Marable, *Daily Independent* (Lagos) (June 25, 2011).

40. Clarence Lang, "Manning Marable and Malcolm X: The Power of Biography," review of *Malcolm X: A Life of Reinvention* by Manning Marable, *Solidarity*, http://www.solidarity-us.org/node/3358 (accessed February 25, 2012).

41. Lang.

42. Karenga, "Reinventing Malcolm with Marable," A7.
43. Amiri Baraka, "Amiri Baraka Reviews Manning Marable's Malcolm X," May 10, 2011, http://www.theblacklistpub.ning.com/profiles/blogs/amiri-baraka-reviews-manning.
44. Karenga, "Reinventing Malcolm with Marable," A7.
45. Salim Muwakkil, "Malcolm's X-Factor," review of *Malcolm X: A Life of Reinvention* by Manning Marable, *Culture* 25, no. 7 (2011): 28.
46. Muwakkil.
47. Abdul Alkalimat, "Rethinking Malcolm Means First Learning How to Think: What Was Marable Thinking? And How?," review of *Malcolm X: A Life of Reinvention* by Manning Marable, June 2011, http://brothermalcolm.net/marable/pdf/alkalimat.pdf.
48. Wellington, "Man for Many Seasons," 103.
49. Alkalimat, "Rethinking Malcolm."
50. Lang, "Power of Biography."
51. Touré, "Criminal, Minister, Humanist, Martyr," 18.
52. Yohuru Williams, "Malcolm X: A Life of Reinvention," review of *Malcolm X: A Life of Reinvention* by Manning Marable, *Race & Class* 53, no. 2 (2011): 94.
53. Williams, "Malcolm X," 96.
54. Alkalimat, "Rethinking Malcolm."
55. Lang, "Power of Biography."
56. Lang, "Power of Biography."
57. Wellington, "Man for Many Seasons," 102.
58. Rana, "World House," 35.
59. Rana.
60. Alkalimat, "Rethinking Malcolm."
61. Randall Kennedy, "Imagining Malcolm X," review of *Malcolm X: A Life of Reinvention* by Manning Marable, *American Prospect* 22, no. 6 (2011): 56.
62. Kennedy.
63. Karenga, "Reinventing Malcolm with Marable," A7.
64. Alkalimat, "Rethinking Malcolm."

Chapter 7

1. Maryse Condé, *Heremakhonon* (Washington, DC: Three Continents Press, 1982), 5, 9.
2. Albert Murray, *Seven League Boots* (New York: Vintage International, 1997), 138. This is also paraphrased in Bernard Bell, *The Contemporary African American Novel: Its Folk Roots and Modern Literary Branches* (Amherst: University of Massachusetts Press, 2004), 275, as "which ancestor is the most inspirational in his identity quest?"

3. Komozi Woodard, *A Nation within a Nation: Amiri Baraka (Le Roi Jones) and Black Power Politics* (Chapel Hill: University of North Carolina Press, 1999).

4. Wright, "Blueprint," 102.

5. Wright, "Blueprint," 105.

6. Wright, "Blueprint," 105.

7. Wright, "Blueprint," 104–5.

8. Frantz Fanon, *The Wretched of the Earth* (New York: Grove Press [1961] 2004), "On National Culture."

9. Fanon.

10. Fanon, 45.

11. Baldwin, "Smaller Than Life," 577–78.

12. See Christel N. Temple, "Malcolm X and Black Cultural Mythology," *International Journal of Africana Studies* 12, no. 2 (2006): 213–21; Temple, "Molefi Kete Asante's Prediction of Black Cultural Mythology," in *Essays on an Intellectual Warrior*, ed. Ama Mazama (Paris: Menaibuc, 2007); and Temple, "The Documentary Form of Paul Robeson's *Here I Stand* as Black Cultural Mythology," in *Transcendence and the Africana Literary Enterprise* (New York: Lexington Books, 2017).

13. Gates and McKay, *Norton Anthology of African American Literature*.

14. For a comprehensive introduction to worldview, see Karanja Keita Carroll's "A Genealogical Review of the Worldview Concept and Framework in Africana Studies-Related Theory and Research" in *African American Consciousness: Past and Present, Africana Studies, Volume 4*, ed. James L. Conyers Jr. (New Brunswick, NJ: Transaction Publishers, 2011), 23–46.

15. See Sterling Stuckey, *Going through the Storm: The Influence of African American Art in History* (New York: Oxford University Press, 1994).

16. This definition is adapted from Karanja Keita Carroll's discussion in "A Genealogical Review of the Worldview Concept and Framework in Africana Studies-Related Theory and Research" (35), which merges ideas from Wade Nobles, Jacob Carruthers, and Vernon Dixon.

17. See a model of this in Christel N. Temple's chapter "Autobiography and Documentary Forms of *Here I Stand* as Black Cultural Mythology," in *Transcendence and the Africana Literary Enterprise* (New York: Lexington Books, 2017), 59–74.

18. This is the generation of writers from 1934 to 1960 that literary scholar Lawrence P. Jackson describes as "the indignant generation" in his work *The Indignant Generation: A Narrative History of African American Writers and Critics, 1934–1960* (Princeton: Princeton University Press, 2011).

19. Charles Johnson also penned several compelling short stories that bring to life American and African American legendary icons such as Phillis Wheatley and Richard Allen in *Soulcatcher and Other Stories: Twelve Powerful Tales about Slavery* (1998) that serves as a companion to the landmark documentary and historical volume *Africans in America*.

20. Evelyn Jaffe Schreiber, "Personal and Cultural Memory in *A Mercy*," in *Toni Morrison: Memory and Meaning*, ed. Adrienne Lanier Seward and Justine Tally (Jackson: University Press of Mississippi, 2014), 80.

21. Charles Johnson, *Dreamer: A Novel* (New York: Scribner, 1998), 13. Some of the text in *Dreamer* was in italic. For readability, however, this has been changed to roman type.

22. Johnson, *Dreamer*, 14.

23. Johnson, *Dreamer*, 14.

24. Johnson, *Dreamer*, 14.

25. Johnson, *Dreamer*, 14.

26. Johnson, *Dreamer*, 15.

27. Johnson, *Dreamer*, 17.

28. Johnson, *Dreamer*, 17.

29. Johnson, *Dreamer*, 20.

30. Johnson, *Dreamer*, 18.

31. Joseph Darda, "MLK and the LA Riots: Civil Rights, Memory, and Neoliberalism in Charles Johnson's *Dreamer*," *Twentieth Century Literature* 60, no. 2 (2014): 197.

32. Darda, "MLK," 198.

33. Johnson, *Dreamer*, 26.

34. Johnson, *Dreamer*, 29, 31, 30.

35. Johnson, *Dreamer*, 32.

36. Johnson, *Dreamer*, 33.

37. Johnson, *Dreamer*, 33.

38. Johnson, *Dreamer*, 34.

39. Johnson, *Dreamer*, 35.

40. Johnson, *Dreamer*, 38.

41. Johnson, *Dreamer*, 38.

42. Johnson, *Dreamer*, 41–42.

43. Johnson, *Dreamer*, 43.

44. Johnson, *Dreamer*, 59.

45. Johnson, *Dreamer*, 45, 44.

46. Johnson, *Dreamer*, 47.

47. Johnson, *Dreamer*, 48.

48. Johnson, *Dreamer*, 91.

49. Johnson, *Dreamer*, 92.

50. Johnson, *Dreamer*, 142.

51. Johnson, *Dreamer*, 155.

52. See Patrice Rankine's *Ulysses in Black: Ralph Ellison, Classicism, and African American Literature* (Madison: University of Wisconsin Press, 2006), quoted in Éva Tettenborn, "'A Mountain Full of Ghosts': Mourning African-American Masculinities

in Colson Whitehead's *John Henry Days*," *African American Review* 46, nos. 2–3 (2013): 272.

53. Rankine, 272.

54. Colson Whitehead, *John Henry Days: A Novel* (New York: Doubleday, 2001), 161.

55. Whitehead, *John Henry Days*, 261.

56. Sylvie Bauer, "Voix en suspens dans *John Henry Days* de Colson Whitehead," *Revue française d'études américaines* 121, no. 3 (2009): 50.

57. Scott Reynolds Nelson, *Steel Drivin' Man: John Henry, the Untold Story of an American Legend* (Oxford: Oxford University Press, 2006).

58. Michael K. Walonen, "'This Making of Truth Is Violence Too, Out of Which Facts Are Formed': Colson Whitehead's Secret History of Post-Reconstruction America in *John Henry Days*," *Literature and History* 23, no. 2 (2014): 70.

59. Whitehead, *John Henry Days*, 34.

60. Whitehead, 34.

61. Whitehead, 34.

62. Whitehead, 48.

63. Whitehead, 66.

64. Whitehead, 67.

65. Whitehead, 67.

66. Whitehead, 35.

67. Whitehead, 49.

68. Peter Collins, "The Ghosts of Economics Past: *John Henry Days* and the Production of History," *African American Review* 46, nos. 2–3 (2013): 285.

69. Whitehead, *John Henry Days*, 42.

70. Whitehead, 42.

71. Whitehead, 378.

72. Whitehead, 58.

73. Whitehead, 59.

74. Collins, "Ghosts," 286.

75. Whitehead, *John Henry Days*, 65.

76. Whitehead, 15.

77. Whitehead, 50.

78. Whitehead, 114.

79. Whitehead, 114.

80. Whitehead, 44.

81. Whitehead, 45.

82. Whitehead, 114.

83. Whitehead, 114, 189.

84. Whitehead, 115.

85. Whitehead, 116.

86. Whitehead, 116.
87. Whitehead, 320.
88. Whitehead, 321.
89. Whitehead, 378.
90. Whitehead, 382.
91. Whitehead, 383.
92. Whitehead, 382.
93. Whitehead, 322.
94. Whitehead, 322.
95. Jaya Shrivastava, "Recollection and Self-Assessment in Colson Whitehead's *John Henry Days*," *ANQ: A Quarterly Journal of Short Articles, Notes, and Reviews* 30, no. 1 (2017): 59.
96. Shrivastava, 58.
97. Robert O'Hara, *Insurrection: Holding History*, in *The Fire This Time: African American Plays for the 21st Century*, ed. Harry J. Elam Jr. and Robert Alexander (New York: Theatre Communications Group, 2004).
98. O'Hara, *Insurrection*; see "Author's Statement."
99. Rebecca Balon, "Kinless or Queer: The Unthinkable Queer Slave in Toni Morrison's *Beloved* and Robert O'Hara's *Insurrection: Holding History*," *African American Review* 48, nos. 1–2 (2015): 141.
100. Faedra Chatard Carpenter, "Robert O'Hara's *Insurrection*: 'Que(e)rying' History," *Text and Performance Quarterly* 23, no. 2 (2003): 187.
101. Carpenter, "Robert O'Hara's Insurrection," 187. Carpenter's discussion is profoundly historical, and her specific references to history, recollection, and consciousness make room for new discussions on mythology, in addition to her objective to query queerness.
102. O'Hara, *Insurrection*, 261.
103. O'Hara, 271.
104. O'Hara, 318.
105. O'Hara, 271.
106. Carpenter, "Que(e)rying," 187.
107. O'Hara, 289.
108. O'Hara, 301.
109. O'Hara, 301.
110. O'Hara, 306.
111. O'Hara, 321.
112. O'Hara, 321–22.
113. O'Hara, 307–8.
114. O'Hara, 299.
115. O'Hara, 274.
116. O'Hara, 276.

117. O'Hara, 282.
118. Jill Scott, "Wake Up Baby," *The Original Jill Scott from the Vault, Volume I*, Hidden Beach Records (2011).
119. O'Hara, 277, 280.
120. O'Hara, 330.
121. Carpenter, "Que(e)rying," 191.
122. O'Hara, 335.
123. Laini Mataka, "freedom's divas should always be luv'd," in *Restoring the Queen* (Baltimore: Black Classic Press, 1994), 59–61.
124. Felix Boateng, "African Traditional Education: A Tool for Intergenerational Communication," in *African Culture: Rhythms of Unity*, ed. Molefi Kete Asante and Kariamu Welsh Asante (Trenton, NJ: Africa World Press, 1996), 109.
125. Boateng introduces and defines these features of the "oral tradition" as well as secret societies, ceremonies, and gender specific peer/cohort instructional and transitional age groups.

Conclusion

1. Michael Rothberg, *Multidirectional Memory: Remembering the Holocaust in the Age of Decolonization* (Stanford: Stanford University Press, 2009).
2. These often begin with Joseph Campbell, whose prologue to *The Hero with a Thousand Faces* (Princeton: Princeton University Press, 1949) begins with a derogatory reference to "the dreamlike mumbo jumbo of some red-eyed witch doctor of the Congo" (3).
3. Cilas Kemadjiv in "Postcolonial Mythologies" (2004) considers Jean Metellus's *L'Année Dessalines* (1986), plus five other works by Metellus; Aimé Césaire's *A Season in the Congo* (1966), about Patrice Lumumba; Boubacar Boris Diop's *Les Tamboures de la Mémoire* (1987); and Maryse Condé's *Segou* (1987) as possibilities of charismatic memory, even though not all of the authors' protagonists are actual historical figures.
4. Christina Sharpe, "Black Studies: In the Wake," *Black Scholar* 44, no. 2 (2014): 60.
5. Sharpe, 60, 59.
6. Celeste-Marie Bernier, *Characters of Blood: Black Heroism in the Transatlantic Imagination* (Charlottesville: University of Virginia Press, 2012).
7. Maulana Karenga, *Introduction to Black Studies* (Los Angeles: Kawaida Publications, 1982), 36.

Bibliography

"Actual Date First Africans Arrived in English North America Revealed." Accessed September 27, 2017. http://www.project1619.org/index.html.
Adler, David A. *A Picture Book of Harriet Tubman*. New York: Scholastic, 1992.
"African Landing Day." Accessed August 15, 2019. http://box5485.temp.domains/~rojecwf4/events/african-landing-day/
Alkalimat, Abdul. "Rethinking Malcolm Means First Learning How to Think: What Was Marable Thinking? And How?" June 2011. http://brothermalcolm.net/marable/pdf/alkalimat.pdf.
"American Evolution: Virginia to America, 1619–2019." Accessed October 29, 2017. https://catalog.hathitrust.org/Record/100105441.
Angelou, Maya. *All God's Children Need Traveling Shoes*. New York: Vintage, [1986] 2010.
Araujo, Ana Lucia. *African Heritage and Memories of Slavery in Brazil and the South Atlantic*. Amherst, NY: Cambria Press, 2015.
Araujo, Ana Lucia. *Living History: Encountering Memory*. Newcastle upon Tyne, UK: Cambridge Scholars Press, 2009.
Araujo, Ana Lucia. *Politics of Memory: Making Slavery Visible in Public Space*. New York: Routledge, 2012.
Araujo, Ana Lucia. *Public Memory of Slavery: Victims and Perpetrators in the South Atlantic*. Amherst, NY: Cambria Press, 2010.
Araujo, Ana Lucia. *Shadows of the Slave Past: Memory, Heritage, and Slavery*. New York: Routledge, 2014.
Araujo, Ana Lucia. "Welcome the Diaspora: Slave Trade Heritage Tourism and the Public Memory of Slavery." *Ethnologies* 32, no. 2 (2010): 145–91.
"Arrival of the First Africans in Colonial America." Accessed October 21, 2015. http://project1619.org/10.html.
Asante, Molefi Kete. "African Betrayals and Recovery for a New Future." In *Africa in the 21st Century: Toward a New Future*, edited by Ama Mazama, 71–78. New York: Routledge, 2007.
Asante, Molefi Kete. *The Afrocentric Idea*. Philadelphia: Temple University Press, 1987.

Asante, Molefi Kete. *Afrocentricity*. Trenton, NJ: Africa World Press, 1988.
Asante, Molefi Kete. *An Afrocentric Manifesto: Toward an African Renaissance*. Malden, MA: Polity Press, 2008.
Asante, Molefi Kete. "The Ideological Significance of Afrocentricity in Intercultural Communication." *Journal of Black Studies* 14, no. 1 (1983): 3–19.
Asante, Molefi Kete. *Kemet, Afrocentricity, and Knowledge*. Trenton, NJ: Africa World Press, 1990.
Asante, Molefi Kete [Arthur L. Smith]. *Language, Communication, and Rhetoric in Black America*. New York: Harper and Row, 1972.
Asante, Molefi Kete. "Location Theory and African Aesthetics." In *African Aesthetics: Keeper of the Tradition*, edited by Kariamu Welsh-Asante, 53–62. New York: Praeger, 1994.
Asante, Molefi Kete. *Malcolm X as Cultural Hero and Other Afrocentric Essays*. Trenton, NJ: Africa World Press, 1994.
Asante, Molefi Kete. *Maulana Karenga: An Intellectual Portrait*. Cambridge, UK: Polity, 2009.
Asante, Molefi Kete. *Race, Rhetoric, and Identity: The Architection of Soul*. Amherst, NY: Humanity Books, 2005.
Asante, Molefi Kete [Arthur L. Smith]. *Rhetoric of Black Revolution*. Boston: Allyn and Bacon, 1969.
Asante, Molefi Kete. "Television's Impact on Black Children's Language." In *Contemporary Black Thought: Alternative Analyses in Social and Behavioral Science*, edited by Molefi Kete Asante and Abdulai S. Vandi, 181–94. Beverly Hills, CA: Sage, 1980.
Asante, Molefi Kete, and Peter A. Anderson. "Transracial Communication and the Changing Image of Black Americans." *Journal of Black Studies* 4, no. 1 (1973): 69–83.
Asante, Molefi Kete, and Stephen Robb. *The Voice of Black Rhetoric: Selections*. Boston: Allyn and Bacon, 1971.
Asante, Molefi Kete, and Abdulai S. Vandi. *Contemporary Black Thought: Alternative Analyses in Social and Behavioral Science*. Beverly Hills, CA: Sage, 1980.
Asante, Molefi Kete, and Kariamu Welsh. "Myth: The Communication Dimension to the African American Mind." *Journal of Black Studies* 11 (1981): 387–95.
Assman, Jan. "Communicative and Cultural Memory." In *A Companion to Cultural Memory Studies*, edited by Astrid Erll and Ansgar Nünning, 109–17. New York: Walter de Gruyer, 2010.
Associated Press. "Rededicating Historical Marker for Arrival of First Africans." August 20, 2105. http://www.newsplex.com/home/headlines/Rededicating-Historical-Marker-for-Arrival-of-First-Africans-322430332.html.
Avenati, Alesso, Angela Sirigu, and Salvatore M. Aglioti. "Racial Bias Reduces Empathic Sensorimotor Resonance with Other-Race Pain." *Current Biology* 20, no. 11 (2010): 1018–22.

Baker, Houston A. *Long Black Song: Essays in Black American Literature and Culture*. Charlottesville: University of Virginia Press, [1972] 1990.
Baker, Houston A., Jr. "Theoretical Returns." In *African American Literary Criticism: A Reader*, ed. Winston Napier. New York: New York University Press, 2000.
Baldwin, James *The Fire Next Time*. New York: Vintage International, [1963] 1992.
Baldwin, James. *Notes of a Native Son. James Baldwin: Collected Essays*. New York: Literary Classics of the United States, [1949] 1998.
Baldwin, James. "Smaller Than Life." Book review of *There Once Was a Slave: The Heroic Story of Frederick Douglass, Nation*, July 19, 1947. In *Baldwin: Collected Essays*, 577–78. New York: Library of America, 1998.
Ball, Jared, and Todd Steven Burroughs. *A Lie of Reinvention: Correcting Manning Marable's Malcolm X*. Baltimore: Black Classic Press, 2015.
Balon, Rebecca. "Kinless or Queer: The Unthinkable Queer Slave in Toni Morrison's *Beloved* and Robert O'Hara's *Insurrection: Holding History*." *African American Review* 48, nos. 1–2 (2015): 141–55.
Baraka, Amiri. "Amiri Baraka Reviews Manning Marable's Malcolm X." Review of *Malcolm X: A Life of Reinvention* by Manning Marable. May 10, 2011. http://www.theblacklistpub.ning.com/profiles/blogs/amiri-baraka-reviews-manning.
Baraka, Amiri. *The Black Mass*. New York: Marion Boyars, 2000.
Baraka, Amiri, and Larry Neal, eds. *Black Fire: An Anthology of Afro-American Writing*. New York: Morrow, 1968.
Barashango, Ishakamusa. *Afrikan People and European Holidays: A Mental Genocide, Book One*. Baltimore: Afrikan World Books, 2001.
Barashango, Ishakamusa. *Afrikan People and European Holidays: A Mental Genocide, Book Two*. Baltimore: Afrikan World Books, 2001.
Barnett, Ashley. "*1619: The Making of America*." *Early American Literature* 49, no. 2 (2014): 607–11.
Bauer, Sylvie. "Voix en suspens dans *John Henry Days* de Colson Whitehead." *Revue française d'études américaines* 121, no. 3 (2009): 50–60.
Beavers, Herman. "Bondage as Discipline: Pedagogy as Discomfort in *The Sorcerer's Apprentice*." In *Charles Johnson: The Novelist as Philosopher*, edited by William R. Nash and Marc C. Connor, 40–56. Jackson: University Press of Mississippi, 2007.
Bell, Bernard. The Contemporary *African American Novel: Its Folk Roots and Modern Literary Branches*. Amherst: University of Massachusetts Press, 2004.
Bell, Derrick. "An American Fairy Tale: The Income-Related Neutralization of Race Law Precedent." In *The Derrick Bell Reader*, edited by Richard Delgado and Jean Stefancic, 117–22. New York: New York University Press, 2005.
Bernier, Celeste-Marie. *Characters of Blood: Black Heroism in the Transatlantic Imagination*. Charlottesville: University of Virginia Press, 2012.
Biko, Steve. "Black Consciousness and the Quest for a True Humanity." *Ufahamu* 11, no. 1 (1981): 17.

Black Panther. 2018. Directed by Ryan Coogler, screenplay by Coogler and Joe Robert Cole, starring Chadwick Boseman, Michael B. Jordan, Lupita Nyong'o, Danai Gurira, Martin Freeman, Daniel Kaluuya, Letitia Wright, Winston Duke, Angela Bassett, and Forest Whitaker.

Blight, David W. *Beyond the Battlefield: Race, Memory, and the American Civil War*. Amherst: University of Massachusetts Press, 2002.

Boateng, Felix. "African Traditional Education: A Tool for Intergenerational Communication." In *African Culture: Rhythms of Unity*, edited by Molefi Kete Asante and Kariamu Welsh Asante, 109–22. Trenton, NJ: Africa World Press, 1996.

Bobo, Jacqueline. "The Color Purple: Black Women as Cultural Readers." In *The Black Studies Reader*, edited by Jacqueline Bobo, Cynthia Hudley, and Claudine Mitchell, 177–92. New York: Routledge, 2004.

Bontemps, Arna. *Black Thunder: Gabriel's Revolt: Virginia, 1800*. New York: Beacon, [1936] 1992.

Bontemps, Arna. *Drums at Dusk*. Baton Rouge: Louisiana State University Press, [1939] 2009.

Boyd, Herb, and Ron Daniels, eds. *By Any Means Necessary: Malcolm X: Real, Not Reinvented: Critical Conversations on Manning Marable's Biography of Malcolm X*. Chicago: Third World Press, 2012.

Braxton, Joanne M., and Maria I. Diedrich, eds. *Monuments of the Black Atlantic: Slavery and Memory*. New Brunswick, NJ: Transaction Publishers, 2004.

Butler, Octavia. *Kindred*. New York: Beacon, [1979] 2003.

Butler, Octavia. *Wild Seed*. New York: Popular Library, [1980] 1988.

Butler, Robert. *Native Son: The Emergence of a New Black Hero*. Boston: Twayne, 1991.

Calhoun, John F. Introduction to *Flying Home and Other Stories*, by Ralph Ellison. Edited by John F. Calhoun. New York: Random House, 1969.

"Calvin Pearson." Accessed October 21, 2015. http://project1619.org/8.html.

Carlacio, Jami L. "In Their Own Words: The Rhetorical Practices of Maria Stewart and Sarah Grimke." PhD diss., University of Wisconsin, Milwaukee, 2001.

Carroll, Karanja Keita. "A Genealogical Review of the Worldview Concept and Framework in Africana Studies-Related Theory and Research." In *African American Consciousness: Past and Present, Africana Studies, Volume 4*, edited by James L. Conyers Jr., 23–46. New Brunswick, NJ: Transaction Publishers, 2011.

"Carolyn Gage." Accessed December 19, 2017. https://carolyngage.weebly.com/bio-and-vitae.html.

Carpenter, Faedra Chatard. "Robert O'Hara's *Insurrection*: 'Que(e)rying' History." *Text and Performance Quarterly* 23, no. 2 (2003): 186–204.

Carpentier, Alejo. *The Kingdom of the World: A Novel*. New York: Farrar, Straus and Giroux, [1957] 2017.

Carruthers, Jacob. *The Irritated Genie: An Essay on the Haitian Revolution*. Chicago: Kemetic Institute, 1985.

Césaire, Aimé. *Toussaint Louverture*. Paris: Presence Africaine, [1961] 2000.
Chen, Wilson C. "Figures of Flight and Entrapment in Edwidge Danticat's *Krik? Krak!*" *Rocky Mountain Review* 65, no. 1 (2011): 36–55.
Childress, Alice. *Like One of the Family: Conversations from a Domestic's Life*. Brooklyn: Independence Publishers, 1956.
Clark, Kathleen Ann. *Defining Moments: African American Commemoration and Political Culture in the South, 1863–1913*. Chapel Hill: University of North Carolina Press, 2005.
Cleage, Albert. "Myths about Malcolm." Originally published in 1969. In *Malcolm X: The Man and His Times*, edited by John Henrik Clarke, 13–26. Trenton, NJ: Africa World Press, 1990.
Cliff, Michelle. *Free Enterprise: A Novel of Mary Ellen Pleasant*. New York: Dutton, 1993.
Clinton, Catherine. *Harriet Tubman: The Road to Freedom*. New York: Little, Brown, 2003.
Cobb, William Jelani. "Malcolm X: The Man, The Myth, the Mystery." Review of *Malcolm X: A Life of Reinvention* by Manning Marable. *Crisis Forum* (2011): 25.
Collins, Peter. "The Ghosts of Economics Past: *John Henry Days* and the Production of History." *African American Review* 46, nos. 2–3 (2013): 285–300.
Condé, Maryse. *Heremakhonon*. Washington, DC: Three Continents Press, 1982.
Conyers, James L., Jr., and Andrew P. Smallwood, eds. *Malcolm X: A Historical Reader*. Durham, NC: Carolina Academic Press, 2008.
Cooper, Anna Julia. *The Voice of Anna Julia Cooper*. Edited by Charles Lemert and Esme Bhan. New York: Rowman and Littlefield, 1998.
Creed. 2015. Warner Brothers. Directed by Ryan Coogler, screenplay by Coogler and Aaron Covington, starring Michael B. Jordan, Sylvester Stallone, Tessa Thompson, Phylicia Rashad, Tony Bellew and Graham McTavish.
Creed II. 2018. Warner Brothers. Directed by Steven Caple Jr., screenplay by Juel Taylor and Sylvester Stallone, starring Michael B. Jordan, Sylvester Stallone, Tessa Thompson, Wood Harris, Phylicia Rashad, and Dolph Lundgren.
Crosley, Hilary. "Crazy Talk: Slavery Was a Blessing in Disguise." *The Root*, October 6, 2012. https://www.theroot.com/crazy-talk-slavery-was-blessing-in-disguise-1790893592.
Dagbovie, Pero. *The Early Black History Movement, Carter G. Woodson and Lorenzo Johnston Greene*. Urbana: University of Illinois Press, 2007.
Danticat, Edwidge. *Krik? Krak!* New York: Vintage Contemporaries, [1991] 1995.
Darda, Joseph. "MLK and the LA Riots: Civil Rights, Memory, and Neoliberalism in Charles Johnson's *Dreamer*." *Twentieth Century Literature* 60, no. 2 (2014): 197–221.
Dash, Michael J. *Haiti and the U.S.: National Stereotypes and the Literary Imagination*. New York: St. Martin's Press, 1997.

Daut, Marlene L. *Tropics of Haiti: Race and the Literary History of the Haitian Revolution in the Atlantic World, 1789 to 1865*. Liverpool: Liverpool University Press, 2015.
"Do African Americans Feel Lucky That Their Ancestors Were Slaves?" *Yahoo Answers*, August 1, 2014. https://answers.yahoo.com/question/index?qid=20140801202215AANF7o1.
Douglass, Frederick. *The Heroic Slave*. New Haven: Yale University Press, [1852] 2015.
Du Bois, Shirley Graham. *Du Bois: Pictorial Biography*. Chicago: Johnson Publishing Company, 1978.
Du Bois, Shirley Graham. *Gamal Abdel Nasser, Son of the Nile: A Biography*. New York: Third World Press, 1972.
Du Bois, Shirley Graham. *His Day Is Marching On: A Memoir of W. E. B. Du Bois*. Philadelphia: Lippincott, 1971.
Du Bois, Shirley Graham. *Julius Nyerere: Teacher of Africa*. New York: Julian Messner, 1975.
Du Bois, Shirley Graham, and Selden Rodman. *Haiti; The Black Republic*. New York: Devin-Adair, 1955.
Du Bois, W. E. B. *The Education of Black People: Ten Critiques, 1906–1960*. Amherst: University of Massachusetts Press, 1973.
Dyson, Michael Eric. *Making Malcolm: The Myth and Meaning of Malcolm X*. New York: Oxford University Press, 1995.
Elliott, Alyce. Preface. *King Commemorations: A Book of Activities*. N.p.: Create Space Independent Platform Publishing, 2009.
Ellison, Ralph. *Flying Home and Other Stories*. Edited by John F. Calhoun. New York: Random House, 1969.
Ellison, Ralph. "Mister Toussan: A Short Story." *New Masses* (November 4, 1941), 19–20.
Erll, Astrid, and Ansgar Nünning, eds. *A Companion to Cultural Memory Studies*. New York: De Gruyter, 2010.
Eyerman, Ron. *Cultural Trauma: Slavery and the Foundation of African American Identity*. New York: Cambridge University Press, 2001.
Fabre, Geneviève, and Robert O'Meally, eds. *History and Memory in African-American Culture*. New York: Oxford University Press, 1994.
Fabre, Michel. *The World of Richard Wright*. Jackson: University Press of Mississippi, 1985.
Fanon, Frantz. *The Wretched of the Earth*. New York: Grove Press, [1961] 2004.
"The First Africans." *Jamestown Rediscovery*. Accessed October 16, 2017. http://historicjamestowne.org/history/the-first-africans/.
Floyd-Thomas, Stacey M., and Anthony B. Pinn, eds. *Liberation Theologies in the United States*. Cambridge: Cambridge University Press, 2004.
Franklin, John Hope. *George Washington Williams: A Biography*. Durham, NC: Duke University Press, 1998.

Freeman, Mack. "Peterson, Nancy G., *Against Amnesia: Contemporary Women Writers and the Crises of Historical Memory*." *Biography: An Interdisciplinary Quarterly* 25, no. 4 (2002): 701–7.
Fuller, Charles H., Jr. "Black Art is Socio-Creative Art." Originally published in 1967. In *Modern American Poetry: Documents from the Black Arts Movement*. Accessed January 1, 2019. http://www.english.illinois.edu/maps/blackarts/documents.htm.
Gage, Carolyn. *Harriet Tubman Visits a Therapist*. First performed in 1996. In *Under Thirty: Plays for a New Generation*, edited by Eric Lane and Nina Shengold, 441–56. New York: Vintage Books, 2004.
Gates, Henry Louis, and Nellie Y. McKay, eds. *The Norton Anthology of African American Literature, 2nd Edition*. New York: W. W. Norton, 2004.
Gauthier, Marni. *Amnesia and Redress in Contemporary African American Fiction: Counterhistory*. New York: Palgrave Macmillan, 2011.
Gayle, Addison. *The Black Aesthetic*. New York: Doubleday, 1972.
Gayle, Addison. "Blueprint for Black Criticism." *First World* 1, no. 1 (1977): 41–45.
Glass, Kathy L. *Courting Communities: Black Female Nationalism and "Syncre-Nationalism" in the Nineteenth-Century North*. New York: Routledge, 2006.
Glissant, Edouard. *Monsieur Toussaint: A Play*. Translated by J. Michael Dash and Edouard Glissant. Boulder: Lynne Rienner, [1961] 2005.
Graham, Shirley. *Booker T. Washington*. New York: Julian Messner, 1955.
Graham, Shirley. *Dr. George Washington Carver, Scientist*. 1944. New York: Julian Messner, 1964.
Graham, Shirley. *Jean Baptist Pointe de Sable: Founder of Chicago*. Julian Messner, 1953.
Graham, Shirley. *Paul Robeson: Citizen of the World*. Westport, CT: Negro Universities Press, [1946] 1971.
Graham, Shirley. *Pocahontas*. New York: Grosset and Dunlap, 1953.
Graham, Shirley. *The Story of Phillis Wheatley*. New York: Julian Messner, 1949.
Graham, Shirley. *There Once Was a Slave: The Heroic Story of Frederick Douglass*. Julian Messner, 1947.
Graham, Shirley. *Your Most Humble Servant: Benjamin Banneker*. New York: Julian Messner, 1949.
Gray, Thomas Ruffin. *Confessions of Nat Turner*. Baltimore: Lucas and Deaver, 1831.
Guasco, Michael. "The Fallacy of 1619: Rethinking the History of Africans in Early America." *Black Perspectives*, African American Intellectual History Society blog, September 4, 2017. http://www.aaihs.org/the-fallacy-of-1619-rethinking-the-history-of-africans-in-early-america/.
Hagan, Joe. "Michael B. Jordan's Technicolor Dreams." *Vanity Fair*, November 2018. https://www.vanityfair.com/hollywood/2018/10/michael-b-jordan-cover-story.
Hakutani, Yoshinobu, and Robert L. Tener. Afterword to *HAIKU: This Other World* by Richard Wright. New York: Arcade Publishing, 1998.
Halbwachs, Maurice. *The Collective Memory*. New York: Harper and Row, [1968] 1980.

Haley, Alex. *Roots: The Saga of an American Family*. Boston: Da Capo Press, [1976] 2016.

Hamer, Fanny Lou. *To Praise Our Bridges: An Autobiography*. Taped and edited by Julius Lester and Mary Varela. Jackson, MS: KIPCO, 1967.

Hansberry, Lorraine, and Robert Nemiroff. *To Be Young, Gifted, and Black*. New York: New American Library, 1969.

Harbawi, Semia. "Writing Memory: Edwidge Danticat's Limbo Inscriptions." *Journal of West Indian Literature* 16, no. 1 (2007): 37–58.

Harper, Frances Ellen Watkins. *A Brighter Coming Day: A Frances Ellen Watkins Harper Reader*. Edited by Frances Smith Foster. New York: Feminist Press, 1990.

Harper, Frances Ellen Watkins. *Iola Leroy, Or, Shadows Uplifted*. Mineola, NY: Dover [1893] 2010.

Harriet Tubman and Her Escape to Freedom. DVD. Bristol, CT: Mazzarella Media, 2009.

Harris, Helen Webb. *Genefride: Negro History in Thirteen Plays*. Edited by Willis Richardson and May Miller. Washington, DC: Associated Publishers, 1935.

Harris, Trudier. *Martin Luther King Jr., Heroism, and African American Literature*. Tuscaloosa: University of Alabama Press, 2014.

Hartman, Saidiya V. *Lose Your Mother: A Journey along the Atlantic Slave Route*. New York: Farrar, Straus and Giroux, 2007.

Hartman, Saidiya V. *Scenes of Subjection: Terror, Slavery, and Self-Making in Nineteenth Century America*. New York: Oxford University Press, 1997.

Hawthorne, Walter. Review of *Crossing Memories: Slavery and African Diaspora*, edited by Ana Lucia Araujo, Mariana P. Candido, and Paul E. Lovejoy. *New West India Guide* 88, nos. 1–2 (2014): 110–12.

Haynes, Elizabeth Ross. *Unsung Heroes*. New York: DuBois and Hill, 1921.

Henry, Paget. *Caliban's Reason: Introducing Afro-Caribbean Philosophy*. New York: Routledge, 2000.

Herbes-Sommers, Christine, Llewellyn Smith, and Kelly Thomson. *American Denial*. Vital Pictures, 2013.

Higginbotham, A. Leon. *In the Matter of Color: Race and the American Legal Process: The Colonial Period*. New York: Oxford University Press, [1978] 1980.

Hill, Errol. Introduction to *Black Heroes: 7 Plays*. New York: Applause Theatre Book Publishers, 1989.

Hill, Leslie Pinckney. *Toussaint L'Ouverture: A Dramatic History*. Boston, MA: Christopher, 1928.

Hill, Patricia Liggins, and Bernard Bell. *Call and Response: The Riverside Anthology of the African American Literary Tradition*. New York: Houghton Mifflin, 1998.

Hopkinson, Nalo. *Midnight Robber*. 2000. New York: Grand Central Publishing, 2012.

Horne, Gerald. "'Myth' and the Making of 'Malcolm X.'" *American Historical Review* 98, no. 2 (1992): 440–50.

Horne, Gerald. *Race Woman: The Lives of Shirley Graham Du Bois*. New York: New York University Press, 2000.

Hubbard, Jon Michael. *Letters to the Editor: Confessions of a Frustrated Conservative.* Bloomington, IN: iUniverse, 2009. http://www.theroot.com/articles/culture/2012/10/crazy_talk_slavery_was_blessing_in_disguise_says_jon_hubbard.html.

Huggins, Nathan. "Integrating Afro-American History into American History." In *The State of Afro-American History: Past, Present, Future*, edited by Darlene Clark Hine, 157–68. Baton Rouge: Louisiana State University Press, 1989.

Hughes, Langston. *Emperor of Haiti.* New York: Applause, 2001.

Humez, Jean M. *Harriet Tubman: The Life and the Life Stories.* Madison: University of Wisconsin Press, 2003.

Hunt, Albert N. *Haiti's Influence on Antebellum America: Slumbering Volcano in the Caribbean.* Baton Rouge: Louisiana State University Press, 1988.

Igede, Ode S. "Context, Form, and Poetic Expression in Igede Funeral Dirges." *Africa* 65, no. 1 (1995): 79–96.

Jackson, Lawrence P. *The Indignant Generation: A Narrative History of African American Writers and Critics, 1934–1960.* Princeton: Princeton University Press, 2011.

James, C. L. R. *The Black Jacobins: Toussaint L'Ouverture and the San Domingo Revolution.* New York: Vintage, [1938] 1989.

James, C. L. R. *A History of Pan-African Revolt.* Chicago: C. H. Kerr, [1969] 1995.

James, C. L. R. *Toussaint Louverture: The Story of the Only Successful Slave Revolt in History: A Play in Three Acts.* Durham: Duke University Press, [1934] 2012.

Jarrett, Gene Andrew. *A Companion to African American Literature.* Hoboken, NJ: Wiley-Blackwell, 2013.

Jefferson, Thomas. *Notes on the State of Virginia.* Philadelphia: Matthew Carey, 1794.

Jenkins, Robert L., ed. *The Malcolm X Encyclopedia.* Westport, CT: Greenwood Press, 2002.

Johnson, Charles. *Dreamer: A Novel.* New York: Scribner, 1998.

Johnson, Charles. *I Call Myself an Artist: Writings by and about Charles Johnson.* Bloomington: Indiana University Press, 1999.

Johnson, Charles. *Soulcatcher and Other Stories: Twelve Powerful Tales about Slavery.* New York: Harcourt, 1998.

Johnson, Helene. "Sonnet to a Negro in Harlem." In *Norton Anthology of African American Literature*, edited by Henry Louis Gates Jr. and Nellie Y. McKay, 1353. New York: W. W. Norton, 2004.

Jones, Gayle. *Corregidora.* New York: Beacon, 1987.

Jones, Gayle. *Song for Anninho.* New York: Beacon, 2000.

Jones, LeRoi [Amiri Baraka], and Larry Neal. *Black Fire: An Anthology of Afro-American Writing.* Baltimore: Black Classic Press, [1968] 2007.

Kachun, Mitch. *Festivals of Freedom: Memory and Meaning in African American Emancipation Celebrations, 1808–1915.* Amherst: University of Massachusetts Press, 2003.

Kaisary, Philip. *The Haitian Revolution in the Literary Imagination: Radical Horizons, Conservative Constraints.* Charlottesville: University of Virginia Press, 2014.

Kammen, Michael. *Mystic Chords of Memory: The Transformation of Tradition in American Culture*. New York: Vintage, 1993.

Kanneh, Kadiatu. *African Identities: Race, Nation, and Culture in African Ethnography, Pan-Africanism, and Black Literature*. New York: Routledge, 1998.

Kaplan, Carla, ed. *A Life in Letters*. New York: Anchor Books, 2005.

Karenga, Maulana. *Introduction to Black Studies*. Los Angeles: Kawaida Publications, 1982.

Karenga, Maulana. *Introduction to Black Studies*. Los Angeles: University of Sankore Press, 1993.

Karenga, Maulana. *Kawaida and Questions of Life and Struggle: African American, Pan-African, and Global Issues*. Los Angeles: University of Sankore Press, 2008.

Karenga, Maulana. *Kawaida Theory: An Introductory Outline*. Inglewood, CA: Kawaida Publications, 1980.

Karenga, Maulana. *Maat, the Moral Ideal in Ancient Egypt: A Study in Classical African Ethics*. New York: Routledge, 2006.

Karenga, Maulana. *Odu Ifa: The Ethical Teachings*. Los Angeles: Kawaida Publications, 1999.

Karenga, Ron [Maulana Karenga]. "On Black Art." *Black Theatre* 3 (1968): 9–10.

Karenga, Maulana. "Overturning Ourselves: From Mystification to Meaningful Struggle." In *Essays on Struggle: Position and Analysis*, 25–26. Los Angeles: University of Sankore Press, 2016.

Karenga, Maulana. "Reinventing Malcolm with Marable: Pursuing Pathology by Another Name." Review of *Malcolm X: A Life of Reinvention* by Manning Marable. *Los Angeles Sentinel*, April 21, 2011, A7.

Keiley, Charles Russel, ed. *The Official Book of the Jamestown Ter-centennial Exposition, A.D. 1907. The Only Authorized History of the Celebration*. Norfolk, VA: Colonial Publishing Company, 1909.

Kemadjiv, Cilas "Postcolonial Mythologies: Jean Metellus and the Writing of Charismatic Memory." Translated by R. H. Mitsch. *Research in African Literatures* 35, no. 2 (2004): 91–113.

Kennedy, Randall. "Imagining Malcolm X." Review of *Malcolm X: A Life of Reinvention*. *American Prospect* 22, no. 6 (2011): 56.

Killens, John Oliver. "A Symposium: Black Power: Its Meaning and Measure: John O. Killens." *Negro Digest* 16, no. 1 (1966): 31–37.

King, Martin Luther, Jr. *Why We Can't Wait*. New York: Penguin Books, 1964.

Lachmann, Renate. "Mnemonic and Intertextual Aspects of Literature." In *A Companion to Cultural Memory Studies*, edited by Astrid Erll and Ansgar Nünning, 301–10. New York: Walter de Gruyter, 2010.

Lang, Clarence. "Manning Marable and Malcolm X: The Power of Biography." Review of *Malcolm X: A Life of Reinvention* by Manning Marable. *Solidarity*. Accessed February 25, 2012. http://www.solidarity-us.org/node/3358.

Logan, Shirley Wilson. *"We Are Coming": The Persuasive Discourse of Nineteenth-Century Black Women*. Carbondale: Southern Illinois University Press, 1999.

Lorde, Audre. *Zami: A New Spelling of My Name*. Berkeley: Crossing Press, 1982.
Lowry, Beverly. *Harriet Tubman: Imagining a Life*. New York: Doubleday, 2007.
Makinde, Adeyinka. "Manning Marable's Malcolm X—a Life of Reinvention." Review of *Malcolm X: A Life of Reinvention* by Manning Marable. *Daily Independent* (Lagos), June 25, 2011.
Malcolm X and Alex Haley. *Autobiography of Malcolm X*. New York: Ballantine, 1992.
Marable, Manning. *Living Black History: How Reimagining the African-American Past Can Remake America's Racial Future*. New York: Basic Books, 2006.
Marable, Manning. *Malcolm X: A Life of Reinvention*. New York: Penguin Books, 2011.
Marsh-Lockett, Carol P., and Elizabeth West, eds. *Literary Expressions of African Spirituality*. New York: Lexington Books, 2013.
Mataka, Laini. *Restoring the Queen*. Baltimore: Black Classic Press, 1994.
Mayes, Keith A. *Kwanzaa: Black Power and the Making of the African-American Holiday Tradition*. New York: Routledge, 2009.
McCartney, Martha. "Virginia's First Africans." *Encyclopedia Virginia*. Accessed October 16, 2017. http://www.encyclopediavirginia.org/virginia_s_first_africans#start_entry.
McDougal, Serie. *Research Methods in Africana Studies*. New York: Peter Lang, 2014.
McFadden, Alesia E. "The Artistry and Activism of Shirley Graham Du Bois: A Twentieth Century African American Torchbearer." PhD diss., University of Massachusetts, Amherst, 2009.
McLoome, Margo. *Harriet Tubman: A Photo-Illustrated Biography*. Mankato, MN: Bridgestone Books, 1997.
Mickenberg, Julia. "Civil Rights, History, and the Left: Inventing the Juvenile Black Biography." *MELUS: The Journal of the Society for the Study of Multi-Ethnic Literatures* 27, no. 2 (2002): 65–93.
Mihailescu, Dana, Roxana Oltean, and Mihaela Precup. *Mapping Generations of Traumatic Memory in American Narratives*. Newcastle upon Tyne, UK: Cambridge Scholars Press, 2014.
Miller, Eugene. *Voice of a Native Son: The Poetics of Richard Wright*. Jackson: University Press of Mississippi, 1990.
Miller, May. *Christophe's Daughters*. In *Negro History in Thirteen Plays*, edited by Willis Richardson and May Miller, 241–64. Washington, DC: Associated Publishers, 1935.
Miller, May. *Harriet Tubman*. In *Black Heroes: 7 Plays*, edited by Errol Hill, 102–21. New York: Applause Theatre Book Publishers, 1989.
Miller, May. Preface to *Negro History in Thirteen Plays*. Edited by Willis Richardson and May Miller. Washington, DC: Associated Publishers, 1935.
"Mission." Hampton Virginia 2019 Commemorative Commission. Accessed October 29, 2017. http://hamptonva2019.com/about/mission/.
Moore, Alison. "Historicizing Historical Theory's History of Cultural Historiography." *Cosmos and History: The Journal of Natural and Social Philosophy* 12.1 (2016): 257–91.

Moore, Wes. *The Other Wes Moore: One Name, Two Fates*. New York: Spiegel and Grau, 2010.
Mootry, Maria K. "Wright's Male Heroes and Female Characters Are Archetypes." In *Readings on Native Son*, edited by Hayley R. Mitchell. San Diego: Greenhaven, 2000.
Morris, Burnis R. *History, the Black Press, and Public Relations*. Jackson: University Press of Mississippi, 2017.
Morrison, Toni. *Beloved*. New York: Vintage, [1987] 2004.
Morrison, Toni. *Paradise*. New York: Vintage, 1997.
Morrison, Toni. "Rootedness: The Ancestor as Foundation." In *The Norton Anthology of African American Literature, 2nd Edition*, edited by Henry Louis Gates Jr. and Nellie Y. McKay, 2286–90. New York: W. W. Norton, 2007.
Morrison, Toni. "The Site of Memory." In *Inventing the Truth: The Art and Craft of Memoir*, edited by William Zinsser, 83–102. New York: Houghton Mifflin, 1995.
Morrison, Toni. *Song of Solomon*. New York: Vintage, [1977] 2004.
Mortenson, Lori. *Hero of the Underground Railroad*. North Mankato, MN: Picture Window Books, 2007.
Moses, William Jeremiah. *Afrotopia: The Roots of Afro-American Popular History*. New York: Cambridge University Press, 1998.
Murray, Albert. *The Seven League Boots*. New York: Vintage International, 1997.
Muwakkil, Salim. "Malcolm's X-Factor." Review of *Malcolm X: A Life of Reinvention* by Manning Marable. *Culture* 25, no. 7 (2011): 28.
Nat Turner and Thomas C. Gray. *Confessions of Nat Turner; Leader of the Late Insurrection in Southampton, VA*. Miami: Mnemosyne Publishers, [1831] 1969.
Neal, Larry. "The Black Arts Movement." In *Visions of a Liberated Future: Black Arts Movement Writings by Larry Neal*, edited by Michael Schwartz, 62–80. New York: Thunder's Mouth Press, 1989. The essay first appeared in *Drama Review* 12 (1968): 29–39.
Neal, Larry. "And Shine Swam On." Afterword to *Black Fire: An Anthology of Afro-American Writing*, edited by LeRoi Jones and Larry Neal. New York: William Morrow and Company, 1968.
Neal, Larry. "Some Reflections on the Black Aesthetic." In *The Black Aesthetic*, edited by Addison Gayle, 12–15. New York: Doubleday, 1971.
Neal, Larry. *Visions of a Liberated Future: Black Arts Movement Writings by Larry Neal*. Edited by Michael Schwartz. New York: Thunder's Mouth Press, 1989.
Nelson, Scott Reynolds. *Steel Drivin' Man: John Henry, the Untold Story of an American Legend*. New York: Oxford University Press, 2006.
Ngugi, Thiong'o wa. *Something Torn and New: An African Renaissance*. New York: Basic/Civitas Books, 2009.
Nora, Pierre. "Between Memory and History: Les Lieux de Mémoire." In *History and Memory in African-American Culture*, edited by Geneviève Fabre and Robert O'Meally, 284–300. New York: Oxford University Press, 1994.

Obasi, Ezemenari, Lisa Flores, and Linda James Myers. "Construction and Initial Validation of the Worldview Analysis Scale." *Journal of Black Studies* 39, no. 6 (2009): 937–61.
Ogunleye, Tolagbe. "African American Folklore: Its Role in Reconstructing African American History." *Journal of Black Studies* 27, no. 4 (1997): 435–55.
O'Hara, Robert. *Insurrection: Holding History*. In *The Fire This Time: African American Plays for the 21st Century*, edited by Harry J. Elam Jr. and Robert Alexander. New York: Theatre Communications Group, 2004.
Olick, Jeffery K. "From Collective Memory to the Sociology of Mnemonic Practices and Protocols." In *A Companion to Cultural Memory Studies*, edited by Astrid Erll and Ansgar Nünning, 151–61. New York: Walter de Gruyter, 2010.
Pace, Lorenzo. *Harriet Tubman and My Grandmother's Quilts*. New York: Windmill Books, 2015.
Painter, Nell. *Sojourner Truth: A Life, a Symbol*. New York: W. W. Norton, 1997.
Parker, Nate. *The Birth of a Nation*. 20th Century Fox. 2017.
Parks, Suzan-Lori. *The America Play and Other Works*. New York: Theatre Communications Group, 1995.
Parks, Suzan-Lori. *Venus*. New York: Dramatists Play Service, 1993.
PBS Online. *Africans in America: America's Journey through Slavery*. Boston: WGBH Interactive, 2003.
Peterson, Nancy. *Against Amnesia: Contemporary Women Writers and the Crises of Historical Memory*. Philadelphia: University of Pennsylvania Press, 2001.
"Pilgrimage to Point Comfort August 20, 2016." Accessed September 27, 2017. http://www.project1619.org/index.html.
"Project 1619: Arrival of the First Africans in Colonial America." Accessed September 26, 2017. http://www.project1619.org/10.html.
"Project 1619, Inc." Accessed September 27, 2017. http://www.project1619.org/index.html.
Rana, Aziz. "The World House." Review of *Malcolm X: A Life of Reinvention* by Manning Marable. *Nation*, October 11, 2011, 35.
Randall, Dudley, and Margaret G. Burroughs. *For Malcolm X: Poems on the Life and Death of Malcolm X*. Detroit: Broadside Press, 1969.
Rankine, Patrice. *Ulysses in Black: Ralph Ellison, Classicism, and African American Literature*. Madison: University of Wisconsin Press, 2006.
Reilly, John. Afterword to *Native Son* by Richard Wright. New York: Harper and Row, 1989.
Rich, Richard. *Inspiring Animated Heroes: Harriet Tubman*. DVD. NEST Family Entertainment, 2005.
Richards, Dona [Marimba Ani]. "European Mythology: The Ideology of 'Progress.'" In *Contemporary Black Thought: Alternative Analyses in Social and Behavioral Science*, edited by Molefi Kete Asante and Abdulai S. Vandi, 59–79. Beverly Hills, CA: Sage Publications, 1980.

Richardson, Jennifer, and Richard J. Nussbaum. "The Impact of Multiculturalism versus Colorblindness on Racial Bias." *Experimental Psychology* 40, no. 3 (2004): 417–23.
Richardson, Marilyn. *Maria W. Stewart, America's First Black Woman Political Writer: Essays and Speeches*. Bloomington: Indiana University Press, 1987.
Riggs, Marcia. *Can I Get a Witness? Prophetic Religious Voices of African American Women*. Maryknoll, NY: Orbis Books, 1997.
Ringgold, Faith. *Dinner at Aunt Connie's House*. Afterword. New York: Hyperion Books for Children, 1993.
Robeson, Paul. *Here I Stand*. Boston: Beacon Press, [1958] 1988.
Rothberg, Michael. *Multidirectional Memory: Remembering the Holocaust in the Age of Decolonization*. Stanford: Stanford University Press, 2009.
Russell, Heather. *Legba's Crossing: Narratology in the African Atlantic*. Athens: University of Georgia Press, 2009.
Ryan, Judylyn S. *Spirituality as Ideology in Black Women's Film and Literature*. Charlottesville: University of Virginia Press, 2005.
Rycenga, Jennifer. "A Greater Awakening: Women's Intellect as a Factor in Early Abolitionist Development, 1824–1834." *Journal of Feminist Studies in Religion* 21, no. 2 (2005): 31–59.
Schoelcher, Victor. *Vie de Toussaint Louverture*. Paris: Karthala, 1982.
Schreiber, Evelyn Jaffe. "Personal and Cultural Memory in *A Mercy*." In *Toni Morrison: Memory and Meaning*, edited by Adrienne Lanier Seward and Justine Tally, 80–92. Jackson: University Press of Mississippi, 2014.
Schroeder, Alan, and Jerry Pinckney. *Minty: A Story of Young Harriet Tubman*. New York: Dial Books for Young Readers, 1996.
Scott, Jill. "Wake Up Baby." *The Original Jill Scott from the Vault, Volume I*. Hidden Beach Records, 2011.
Scott-Heron, Gil. *So Far, So Good*. Chicago: Third World Press, 1990.
Sernett, Milton C. *Harriet Tubman: Myth, Memory, and History*. Durham, NC: Duke University Press, 2007.
Seward, Adrienne Lanier, and Justin Talley. *Toni Morrison: Memory and Meaning*. Jackson: University Press of Mississippi, 2014.
Shange, Ntozake. *for colored girls who have considered suicide / when the rainbow is enuf*. New York: Scribner Poetry, 1977.
Shannon, Sandra G. "Audience and Africanisms in August Wilson's Dramaturgy: A Case Study." In *African American Performance and Theater History: A Critical Reader*, edited by Harry J. Elam and David Krisner, 149–68. New York: Oxford University Press, 2001.
Sharpe, Christina. "Black Studies: In the Wake." *Black Scholar* 44, no. 2 (2014): 59–69.
Shrivastava, Jaya. "Recollection and Self-Assessment in Colson Whitehead's *John Henry Days*." *ANQ: A Quarterly Journal of Short Articles, Notes, and Reviews* 30, no. 1 (2017): 58–62.

Soyinka, Wole. "The African World and the Ethno-Cultural Debate." In *African Culture: Rhythms of Unity*, edited by Molefi Kete Asante and Kariamu Welsh Asante, 13–38. Trenton, NJ: Africa World Press, 1990.

Soyinka, Wole. *Myth, Literature, and the African World*. New York: Cambridge University Press, 1976.

Spaulding, A. Timothy. *Re-Forming the Past: History, the Fantastic, and the Postmodern Slave Narrative*. Columbus: Ohio State University Press, 2005.

Stewart, Maria W. "An Address Delivered at the African Masonic Hall." In *Maria W. Stewart, America's First Black Woman Political Writer: Essays and Speeches*, edited by Marilyn Richardson, 45–49. Bloomington: Indiana University Press, 1987.

Stewart, Maria W. "An Address Delivered before the Afric-American Female Intelligence Society of America." In *Maria W. Stewart, America's First Black Woman Political Writer: Essays and Speeches*, edited by Marilyn Richardson, 50–55. Bloomington: Indiana University Press, 1987.

Stewart, Maria W. "Farewell Address to Her Friends in the City of Boston." In *Maria W. Stewart, America's First Black Woman Political Writer, Essays and Speeches*, edited by Marilyn Richardson, 65–74. Bloomington: Indiana University Press, 1987.

Stewart, Maria W. "Religion and the Pure Principles of Morality, the Sure Foundation on Which We Must Build." In *Maria W. Stewart, America's First Black Woman Political Writer: Essays and Speeches*, edited by Marilyn Richardson, 28–42. Bloomington: Indiana University Press, 1987.

Stuckey, Sterling. *Going through the Storm: The Influence of African American Art in History*. New York: Oxford University Press, 1994.

Teague, Hilary. "Liberia: Its Struggles and Its Promises." Speech delivered in 1846. In *Masterpieces of Negro Eloquence: The Best Speeches Delivered by the Negro from the Days of Slavery to the Present Time*, edited by Alice Dunbar Nelson, 15–20. Mineola, NY: Dover, [1914] 2000.

Temple, Christel. "The Cosmology of Afrocentric Womanism." *Western Journal of Black Studies* 36, no. 1 (2012): 23–32.

Temple, Christel N. "Literary Malcolm X: The Making of an African American Ancestor." In *Malcolm X: A Historical Reader*, edited by James L. Conyers Jr. and Andrew P. Smallwood, 167–186. Durham, NC: Carolina Academic Press, 2008.

Temple, Christel N. *Literary Spaces: Introduction to Comparative Black Literature*. Durham, NC: Carolina Academic Press, 2007.

Temple, Christel N. "Malcolm X and Black Cultural Mythology." *International Journal of Africana Studies* 12, no. 2 (2006): 213–21.

Temple, Christel N. "Molefi Kete Asante's Prediction of Black Cultural Mythology." In *Essays on an Intellectual Warrior*, edited by Ama Mazama, 191–226. Paris: Menaibuc, 2007.

Temple, Christel N. *Transcendence and the Africana Literary Enterprise*. New York: Lexington Books, 2017.

Terrill, Robert E., ed. *The Cambridge Companion to Malcolm X*. Cambridge: Cambridge University Press, 2010.
Tettenborn, Éva. "'A Mountain Full of Ghosts': Mourning African-American Masculinities in Colson Whitehead's *John Henry Days*." *African American Review* 46, nos. 2–3 (2013): 271–84.
Thompson, Robert Dee, Jr. "A Socio-biography of Shirley Graham Du Bois: A Life in the Struggle." PhD diss., University of California, Santa Cruz, 1997.
Tillet, Salamishah. *Sites of Slavery: Citizenship and Racial Democracy in the Post–Civil Rights Imagination*. Durham, NC: Duke University Press, 2012.
Touré. "Criminal, Minister, Humanist, Martyr." Review of *Malcolm X: A Life of Reinvention* by Manning Marable. *New York Times Book Review* (June 19, 2011), BR18.
"Trip Down Memory Lane." Blog. Accessed October 24, 2017. https://kwekudee-trip-downmemorylane.blogspot.com/2013/06/mbundu-ambundu-people-angolas.html.
Trotman, C. James, ed. *Richard Wright: Myths and Realities*. New York: Garland, 1988.
Turner, Glennette Tilley. *An Apple for Harriet Tubman*. Morton Grove, IL: Albert Whitman and Company, 2006.
Utley, Ebony A. "A Woman Made of Words: The Rhetorical Invention of Maria W. Stewart." In *Black Women's Intellectual Traditions: Speaking Their Minds*, edited by Kristin Waters and Carol B. Conaway, 55–70. Burlington: University of Vermont Press, 2007.
Valade, Roger M. *The Essential Black Literature Guide*. Canton Charter Township, MI: Visible Ink Press, 1995.
Valdun, Marjorie. "Mandela and the Black Diaspora." *Colorlines*, December 8, 2013. https://www.colorlines.com/articles/mandela-and-black-diaspora.
Van Der Horn-Gibson, Jodi. "Dismantling Americana: Sambo, Shirley Graham, and African Nationalism." *Americana: The Journal of American Popular Culture, 1900 to Present* 7, no. 1 (2008): 4.
Van Sertima, Ivan. *They Came before Columbus: The African Presence in Ancient America*. New York: Random House, [1976] 2003.
Walcott, Derek. *The Haitian Trilogy: Plays: Henri Christophe, Drums and Colours, and The Haytian Earth*. New York: Farrar, Straus and Giroux, 2002.
Walcott, Derek. Preface to *The Haitian Trilogy: Henri Christophe, Drums and Colours, and The Haitian Earth: Plays*. New York: Farrar, Straus and Giroux, 2002.
Walcott, Derek. *Walker and the Ghost Dance: Plays*. New York: Farrar, Straus and Giroux, 2002.
Walker, David. *An Appeal to the Colored Citizens of the World*. New York: Hill and Wang, [1829] 1995.
Walonen, Michael K. "'This Making of Truth Is Violence Too, Out of Which Facts Are Formed': Colson Whitehead's Secret History of Post-Reconstruction America in *John Henry Days*." *Literature and History* 23, no. 2 (2014): 67–80.

Wellington, Darryl Lorenzo. "A Man for Many Seasons." Review of *Malcolm X: A Life of Reinvention* by Manning Marable. *Dissent* (September 9, 2011): 100–103.
West, Cornel. "Philosophy and the Afro-American Experience." In *A Companion to African American Philosophy*, edited by Tommy Lott and John Pittman, 7–32. Malden, MA: Wiley-Blackwell, 2006.
Whitehead, Colson. *John Henry Days: A Novel*. New York: Doubleday, 2001.
Whitehead, Colson, and Donna Seaman. "The Carnegie Interview: Colson Whitehead." June 21, 2017. American Library Association Book Club Central. http://www.bookclubcentral.org/2017/06/21/the-carnegie-interview-colson-whitehead/.
"The White Side of the Black Story." *Quora*. Accessed July 17, 2018. https://www.quora.com/The-White-Side-of-the-Black-Story-BUCHANAN-TO-OBAMA-By-Patrick-J-Buchanan-What-is-your-opinion-of-Mr-Buchanans-take-on-this-issue-I-am-not-saying-I-agree-with-him-nor-have-I-verified-his-statistics-I-want-to-know-your-opinion-of-what-he-wrote.
Wiggins, William H., Jr. *O Freedom! Afro-American Emancipation Celebrations*. Knoxville: University of Tennessee Press, 1987.
Williams, Sherley Anne. *Dessa Rose*. New York: William Morrow, 1986.
Williams, Yohuru. "Malcolm X: A Life of Reinvention." Review of *Malcolm X: A Life of Reinvention* by Manning Marable. *Race & Class* 53, no. 2 (2011): 94–110.
Wilson, Amos N. *The Developmental Psychology of the Black Child*. New York: Africana Research Publications, 1987.
Wilson, August, and Sandra Shannon. "August Wilson Explains His Dramatic Vision: An Interview." In *Conversations with August Wilson*, edited by Jackson R. Bryer and Mary C. Hartig, 118–54. Jackson: University Press of Mississippi, 1991.
The Wire: Season 1. 2008. HBO Video. Executive producers: David Simon, Robert Colesbury, and Nina Kostroff-Noble. Starring Dominic West, Idris Elba, Frankie Faison, Lawrence Gilliard Jr., Wood Harris, Deirdre Lovejoy, Wendell Pierce, Lance Reddick, Andre Royo, and Sonja Sohn.
Woodson, Carter G. *African Heroes and Heroines*. Washington, DC: Associated Publishers, [1939] 1944.
Woodson, Carter G. *African Myths and Folktales*. Mineola, NY: Dover Publications, 1928.
Woodson, Carter G. Introduction to *Negro History in Thirteen Plays*, edited by Willis Richardson and May Miller, iii–v. Washington, DC: Associated Publishers, 1935.
Woolfork, Lisa. *Embodying American Slavery in Contemporary Culture*. Champaign: University of Illinois Press, 2008.
Wright, Richard. "Blueprint for Negro Writing." In *The Richard Wright Reader*, edited by Ellen Wright and Michele Fabre, 36–49. New York: Harper and Row, 1978.
Wright, Richard. Foreword to *Blues Fell This Morning: The Meaning of the Blues* by Paul Oliver. New York: Oxford University Press, [1963] 1990.
Wright, Richard. "How Bigger Was Born." In *Native Son*. New York: Harper and Row, [1940] 1989.

Wright, Richard. *Native Son*. New York: Harper and Row, [1940] 1989.
Wright, Richard. *Pagan Spain*. New York: HarperCollins, 1957.
Wright, Richard. *Twelve Million Black Voices*. New York: Thunder's Mouth Press, [1941] 2002.
Wright, Richard. *White Man Listen*! Garden City, NY: Doubleday, 1964.
Yancy, George. *What White Looks Like: African American Philosophers on the Whiteness Question*. New York: Routledge, 2004.
Yellin, Jean Fagan. *Women and Sisters: The Antislavery Feminists in American Culture*. New Haven: Yale University Press, 1992.
Young, Ida. "Keeping Truth on My Side: Maria Stewart." In *Black Lives: Essays on African American Biography*, edited by James Conyers, 117–28. Armonk, NY: M. E. Sharpe, 1999.
Youngblood, Shay. *Black Girl in Paris*. New York: Riverhead Books, 2000.

Index

1619 and arrival of first kidnapped African captives, ix–x, 83, 92, 130; before 1619, 112–13, 114, 115; after 1619, 112, 116, 118–19, 125, 126, 135, 250; commemoration models post 1619, 118–19; as a commemorative reference point, 103–18; events leading to, 104, 111–12, 113–14, 115, 121–22; geographies of, 121–22; importance of, 109; landing at Point Comfort, not Jamestown, 107; meaning of, 111–12, 116–17; memorial practices and commemorations related to, xviii, xxiv, 20, 92, 98, 100, 103–18, 120, 126, 127, 130; questions that need to be asked about, 115–17, 121–22; seen by some as a "godsend" for Africans, 125–26. *See also* Angolans as first Africans sold into enslavement in 1619; Hampton, Virginia; Point Comfort (in colony of Virginia) (now Fort Monroe); Project 1619; quadricentennial celebrations (1619–2019)

"1619: The Making of America" conference, 115–16; "From 1619 to Trayvon Martin" panel at, 116

1660 Virginia Act XXII, 125–26

1808, January 1 law prohibiting international enslavement trade, 95

1834, August 1 law abolishing slavery in British colonies, 95

1863 and abolishment of slavery. *See* Emancipation Proclamation (1863)

1888 Emancipation Law (Brazil), 79

1915 semicentennial of emancipation, 95

1963 and rise of African nations from colonial bondage, 121

abolishment of slavery in US in 1863. *See* Emancipation Proclamation (1863)

abolition and abolitionists, 17, 27, 149, 181, 222; David Walker as an abolitionist, 31–32, 220, 221; Maria W. Stewart as an abolitionist, 20, 25, 26, 27, 29, 33, 221

activism, xiv, xv, 72, 121, 128, 148, 150, 165, 196, 216, 222, 250; commemorative activism, 103, 106–107, 109; cultural activism, xvi, 71, 256; of Giles Jackson, 100; hyperheroic activism, 224; legacy activism, 105; literaray movement activism, 155; of Maria W. Stewart, 26, 27–28, 29–30, 33; scholarly activism, xiii; of Toussaint Louverture, 155, 178

315

"Address Delivered at the African Masonic Hall, An" (Stewart), 32
"Address Delivered before the African-American Female Intelligence Society of America, An" (Stewart), 30
aesthetic memorialization, 116, 219, 239; as an attribute in Black cultural mythology framework, xvii, 23, 84, 89, 156; and Harriet Tubman, 137–53, 219, 233; in *Insurrection: Holding History* (O'Hara), 244; in *John Henry Days* (Whitehead), 239; and the legacy transmission process, 203; maintaining of, 122–23; Shirley Graham Du Bois on, 38, 39; of Toussaint Louverture in "Mister Toussan" (Ellison), 168, 171. *See also* memorialization
Africana Cultural Memory Studies, xvi, 2, 10, 12, 15, 19, 74, 80, 83, 84, 85, 86, 118, 134, 213; Ana Lucia Araujo on, 132, 134; and Haiti's value, 155; historiography of, 54; and historiography of commemoration, 94; introducing as a course, 253–62; in *John Henry Days* (Whitehead), 238; linked to Emancipation, 143; literary practices, 219, 222; Maulana Karenga on, 50, 52, 54; practices in 1619 commemoration, 106; and processes of memory and memorialization, 238; radial chart for (fig. 1.1), 84; specificity of, 142; traditions of, 152; universities offering courses, 259; and William Wiggins, 95
African Aesthetic, The: Keeper of the Traditions (Asante), 48
Africana memory, ix
African American Freedom Day, 96. *See also* Emancipation Proclamation (1863)

African American Heritage Jazz Concert, 105
African American press (Black press), xiv, 14, 97, 218–19. *See also* media
Africana mythology, ix–xi, 77, 133, 164, 221, 239, 255
Africana worldviews. *See* worldviews
African-centered worldview, xvi, xvii, 23, 104, 255
African Heritage and Memories of Slavery in Brazil and the South Atlantic World (Araujo), 257
African Heroes and Heroines (Woodson), 13–14, 112
African Holocaust Day, 103
African Landing Day (Hampton, Virginia) (aka African Arrival Day). *See* Hampton, Virginia
African Methodist Episcopal Church, 99–100
African Myths and Folktales (Woodson), 13
Africans in America (PBS film series), 176
African Tourism Diaspora (organization), 107
Afrikan People and European Holidays: A Mental Genocide (Barashango), 101
Afrocentric Idea, The (Asante), 60, 64, 70
Afrocentricity: The Theory of Social Change (Asante), 64, 65, 66–67
Afrocentrism, Molefi Kete Asante on, 60, 64–65, 66, 68, 70, 72, 73
Afrotopia (Moses), 83
Against Amnesia: Contemporary Women Writers and the Crises of Historical Memory (Peterson), 4, 257
Alkalimat, Abdul, 210, 211, 212, 213
Allen, Richard, 97, 100

All God's Children Need Traveling Shoes (Angelou), 134
Almeyda (in *Song for Anninho)*), 79
AME (African Methodist Episcopal Church), 99–100
American Denial (film), 105
AMERICAN EVOLUTION project, 109–10, 111
American Play and Other Works, The (Parks), 81, 225
amnesia, xvi, 2, 4, 5, 19, 28, 203
Amnesia and Redress in Contemporary African American Fiction: Counterhistory (Gauthier), 5, 257
Amy (in *Dreamer*), 231
ancestor acknowledgment, 54, 71, 141, 178, 233, 258; Amos Wilson on, 58; as an attribute in Black cultural mythology conceptual framework, xvii, 1, 23, 84, 85, 105, 106, 108, 116, 129, 142, 156, 222; in *for colored girls who have considered suicide/when the rainbow is enuf* (Shange), 170; and commemoration, 40, 92; in cultural identity and cultural memory, 28, 37, 50; in *Dinner at Aunt Connie's House* (Ringgold), 144; elements of, 42; as heritage behavior, 106; and hero dynamics, 116, 125; and immortalization, 86; in *John Henry Days* (Whitehead), 244; in *Krik? Krak!* (Danticat), 172; and Malcolm X, 206; meditations on not calendar based, 102; in Richard Wright's work, 188, 191; seeing Toussaint Louverture as a revered ancestor, 177–82; seen in Toni Morrison's works, 76, 77–78
Ancestor Honor Day, 103
ancestral ghosts, 44–45, 46, 159, 160, 171, 177

Andersen, Peter, 64
Angelou, Maya, 134
Angolans as first Africans sold into enslavement in 1619, 109, 113–14, 114, 116, 125–26, 245
Ani, Marimba (born Dona Richards), 48, 83
antiheroics, 18, 33, 106, 114, 116, 132, 186, 196, 260; "1619: The Making of America" conference on, 116; in Amos Wilson's works, 56–57; anti-Black antiheroics, 89; antiheroic force in Tubman's story, 145, 148, 152; as an attribute in Black cultural mythology framework, xvii, 1, 24, 84, 89–90, 223; in "Bicentennial Blues" (Scott-Heron), 126–27; Calvin Pearson's work in opposition to, 107; in *Christophe's Daughters* (Miller), 161; in David Walker's works, 24, 184; in *Dreamer* (Johnson), 226–27, 228, 230, 232; in Edwidge Danticat's writing, 174; in Errol Hill's works, 165; heroics vs. antiheroics, 161–62, 190, 193; in *John Henry Days* (Whitehead), 234–35, 237, 239, 241; Kathleen Clark on, 98–99; and Malcolm X, 204, 205, 206, 211; in Molefi Kete Asante's works, 184; myth that first Africans brought to Jamestown as example of, 107; in Ntozake Shange's work, 170; in Richard Wright's work, xviii, 20, 183–97, 258; Shirley Graham Du Bois on, 37; in Suzan-Lori Parks's works, 225–26; white power structure as antiheroic, 99
Antoine, Guy, 181
Antony (Angolan sold as slave in 1619), 108, 114, 245

Appeal to the Coloured Citizens of the World, but in particular, and very expressly, to those of THE UNITED STATES OF AMERICA (Walker), 21, 24, 31–32, 184, 192, 220, 221
Apple for Harriet Tubman, An (Turner), 145, 146, 147
Araujo, Ana Lucia, 19, 64, 107, 112, 130–33, 134, 256–57
arrival of first kidnapped African captives (1619). *See* 1619 and arrival of first kidnapped African captives
Asante, Molefi Kete, x, 20, 24, 118, 258; on African American myth, 29, 31, 59–75, 77, 96, 141, 193, 261; on Afrocentrism, 60, 64–65, 66, 68, 70, 72, 73; and "beginning again," 2–3, 47, 69, 97; on Harriet Tubman, 137, 141; on location theory, 48; on Malcolm X, 201; and Maria W. Stewart on hero dynamics, 29, 31; on Maulana Karenga, 51–52, 53; on power of Black oratory, 96; and strategy of vilification, 183–84; writing with Kariamu Welsh, 29, 31, 60, 68, 77, 141
Ashanti people, 187
Assman, Jan, 6, 71
Attucks, Crispus, 97
Aunt Connie (in *Dinner at Aunt Connie's House*), 144–45
autobiographies. *See* biographies/autobiographies/memoirs as a genre
Autobiography of Malcolm X, The (Malcom X and Haley), xviii, 205, 208
Avengers (superheroes), 237

Baker, Houston A., 15, 188, 190–91
Baldwin, James, x, 20, 223–24; on commemoration, 119, 120, 122–25, 130; review of *There Once Was a Slave* by Shirley Graham Du Bois, 40, 218
"Ballad of John Henry, The" (song), 237
Balon, Rebecca, 243
Banneker, Benjamin, 36, 41
Baraka, Amiri, 44, 46, 65, 209–10, 213, 223
Barashango, Ishakamusa, 101, 102
Bauer, Sylvie, 234
Bearden, Romare, 144, 256
Beavers, Herman, 8
"beginning again," 104, 114, 142, 183; Haitian Revolution as an episode of, 156; Molefi Kete Asante on, 2–3, 47, 69, 97
Belafonte, Harry, 231
Bell, Derrick, 20, 119, 120, 127–29, 130
Beloved (Morrison), 79, 226
Benny (in *John Henry Days*), 236
Bernier, Celeste-Marie, 257
Bessie (*John Henry Days*), 193, 195
Bethune, Mary McLeod, 55
"Bicentennial Blues" (Scott-Heron), 126–27
Bigger Thomas (in *Native Son*), 185–86, 188, 189, 190, 191–96, 216, 226; death of, 186, 192, 193, 194, 196
biographies/autobiographies/memoirs as a genre, xviii, 10, 218–19, 222; biographical fiction, 40, 42, 210, 226; biomythography, 80; and Harriet Tubman, 138, 139, 140, 141, 142, 144, 151; heroic biographies, 13, 15, 83; historical-biographical approach to literary analysis, 123, 185, 227–28; managing myth and history in Marable's *Malcolm X*, 20, 199–214,

216, 235; Maria W. Stewart's use of, 26, 28, 32–33, 218; Molefi Kete Asante on, 62; and myths, 13, 24, 138; tasks of a biographer, 207; Tony Morrison on autobiography, 76; and Toussaint Louverture, 159, 166, 169–70

Biography Project of Shirley Graham Du Bois, xv, 36–43, 60

Birth of a Nation (Parker), 242

Bishop, Matthew (in *Dreamer*), 229

Black Aesthetic, The (Gayle, ed.), 47

Black Aesthetic Movement, 24, 43–56, 207, 209, 222, 224

Black Arts Movement, xvii, xix, 24, 43–56, 220, 222, 224; and Amiri Baraka, 44, 46; and Charles Fuller, 44, 46; goals of, 46; Karenga and Neal as spokesmen for, 209; and Larry Neal, 21, 44, 48, 51, 77, 209, 261; and Maulana Karenga, 48–49, 54, 77, 209, 261

"Black Arts Movement, The" (Neal), 44, 51

"Black Arts: Mute Matter Given Force and Function" (Karenga), 48–49

Black consciousness, 24, 56, 75

Black cultural mythology: attributes in Black cultural mythology framework. *See* aesthetic memorialization; ancestor acknowledgment; antiheroics; commemoration philosophy; epic intuitive conduct; hero dynamics; historical reenactment of worldview; hyper-heroic acts; immortalization philosophy; mythological structure; reconciliation and renewal; resistance-based cognitive survival; ritual remembrance; sacred observance; sacrificial inheritance (sacred inheritance) and commemorations, 91–135; courses in African Cultural Memory, 259; and Haiti's diaspora-wide mythology, 155–82; and Harriet Tubman, 137–53; in the literary tradition, 215–52. *See also* names of specific works and Manning Marable's Malcolm X, 199–214; philosophical framework for, 23–90; psychological dimensions of, 56–59; and Richard Wright's antihero, 183–97

Black Fire! (Baraka and Neal), 46–47

Black Girl in Paris (Youngblood), 225

Black Heroes: 7 Plays (Hill), 147, 164

Black history movement, 12–13, 14

Black Jacobins, The (James), 159, 176

Black literature: Black cultural mythology concepts applied to, 215–52; Black fiction, 4, 5–6, 8, 37, 77, 159, 176, 183, 195, 213; Black poetry, 45–46, 48, 49, 79, 125, 150, 151, 219, 220, 222–23; cultural function of, 253; juvenile literature, 38, 138, 218. *See also* Biography Project of Shirley Graham Du Bois, Larry Neal on, 43–45; literary traditions, 220–26; Molefi Kete Asante on role of myth in, 69–70; social-behavioral language in, 57; Suzan-Lori Parks on, 81; Toni Morrison on, 77–78. *See also* biographies/autobiographies/memoirs as a genre; literary criticism; writing

Black Lives Matter movement, xiv

Black Love Day, 103

Black martyrs, xiv, xv, 34, 226, 230–31, 238; of Haitian Revolution, 160, 180, 181; Malcolm X as, 53, 206, 209

Black Mass, The (Baraka), 44

Black nationalism, 25, 27, 29, 30, 106, 192–93, 199, 222

Black No More (Schuyler), 223
Black Panther (film), xiii–xiv, xv, 216
Black Panther Party, xv
Black Power, 54, 56, 102, 103
Black press. *See* African American press (Black press)
Black protest calendar, 53, 102
Black Scholar (journal), 49
Black social media, xiv
Black Solidarity Day, 103
Black Studies: and the Kawaida Theory, 50; subject areas in, 51
Black Thunder (Bontemps), 69, 219
Black women's experiences, xiv, xv, 39, 144, 170, 224, 225, 226; activism of, 150; early Black women, 26, 33, 34; Maria W. Stewart on, 29–30; and mythological structure, xiv, 152; Shirley Graham Du Bois on, 38
"Black Writing Is Socio-creative Art" (Fuller), 47
Bland, Sandra, xiv, 196
Blight, David W., 11
"Blueprint for Negro Writing" (Wright), 186
blues (music), 47, 48, 65, 127, 187–88, 230, 233, 256
Boateng, Felix, 251
Bogle, Robert, 231
Bontemps, Arna, 69, 164, 176, 219, 223
Booker T. Washington (Graham Du Bois), 36
Boukman, Dutty, 160, 171–74
Branch, William, 39
Braxton, Joanne M., 133–34, 138
Brown, John, 34, 35, 75, 97
Brown, Michael, 196
Brownies' Book, The (Du Bois), 39, 219
Brown v. Board of Education, 101, 118, 127, 170

"Buchanan to Obama" (article by Pat Buchanan), 91–92
Bunche, Ralph, 223
Burroughs, Margaret C., 260
Buster (in "Mister Toussan"), 167, 168–69, 170, 173, 174
Butler, Octavia, 5, 80, 148–49, 194, 225, 246
Butler, Robert, 188

Cage, Luke (Black superhero), 237
Calhoun, John F., 167
Caliban's Reason: Introducing Afro-Caribbean Philosophy (Henry), 80
Call & Response: The Riverside Anthology of the African American Literary Tradition (Hill, ed.), 44
Cambridge Companion to Malcolm X, The (Terrill, ed.), 202
Candido, Mariana P., 19, 257
Can I Get a Witness? Prophetic Religious Voices of African American Women (Riggs), 27
Carlacio, Jami, 27
Carpenter, Faedra Chatard, 243, 249
Carpentier, Alejo, 172, 176
Carruthers, Jacob, 158, 161–62, 163, 169, 178–79, 180–81
Carver, George Washington, 36, 38, 39–41, 42, 43
celebrations. *See* commemoration philosophy; heritage practices
Césaire, Aimé, 159, 256
Ceteshwayo (Zulu king), 52
Chappelle, Dave, 256
Characters of Blood: Black Heroism in the Transatlantic (Bernier), 257
Charleston, South Carolina revolt of 1822, 25. *See also* Vesey, Denmark
Chaym (in *Dreamer*), 227–32
Chen, Wilson C., 172, 174

Chicago Negro Unit, 37
child development and Black cultural mythology, 56–57, 58, 59, 67–68, 200; child's developmental worldview, 145; and the *mfundalai* rite, 69–70
Childress, Alice, 223–24
Choke, the Theater of, 242–43
Christophe, Henri, 161, 169
Christophe's Daughters (Miller), 161, 163
Cinque, Joseph, 62
civic myths, 2
Civil Rights Act, 127
Clark, Kathleen Ann, 98–100, 101, 102, 110
Clarke, John Henrik, ix
Cleage, Albert, 200–201
Cleaver, Eldridge, 62
Cliff, Michelle, 225
Clinton, Catherine, 140, 141, 142–43, 146
cognitive survival, 18, 82, 88, 89, 106, 137, 166, 243, 250, 261; as an attribute in Black cultural mythology framework, 84, 85–86, 142, 222. *See also* resistance-based cognitive survival; survival strategies
collective memory, 2, 4, 5, 6, 7, 10, 73, 96, 97, 201, 250
Collective Memory, The (Halbwachs), 2
Collins, Peter, 237, 238
Colored Americans (Hopkins), 83
Columbus, Christopher, 184, 209
commemoration philosophy, 20, 23, 110, 111, 143; adding 1619 to the historiography as a commemorative reference point, 103–18. *See also* Hampton, VirginiaAfrican Methodist Episcopal Church as an institutional model of, 99–100; Amos Wilson on, 58; as an attribute in Black cultural mythology framework, 84, 87; black protest calendar, 102, 103; Catherine Clinton on, 143; as a ceremonious remembrance or celebration, 92; commemoration and memorialization of enslavement, 15, 114, 115, 130–35, 256; commemoration intervention, 91–135; commemoration models post 1619, 118–19; commemoration nationalism, 52; commemoration tourism, 127; deconstruction of commemoration, 119–22; Derrick Bell on, 127–28; difference between festival and commemoration, 235; differences between Emanicipation and civil rights-era commemorations, 142; festivals providing sense of identity, 105; Gil Scott-Heron on, 127; and the Haitian Revolution, 155, 181–82; historiography of African American commemoration, 94–103; in *Insurrection: Holding History* (O'Hara), 244; James Baldwin as a model of, 123; in *John Henry Days* (Whitehead), 234, 238, 239; lamentation as commemoration, 92; Martin Luther King Jr.'s approach to, 119–22; role of postage stamps, 235, 236; studies of African American celebration history, 94–103; ways used to memorialize Toussaint Louverture, 177–82. *See also* memorialization
"Commemorative Postage Stamp" in *Malcolm X Encyclopedia, The* (Jenkins, ed.), 202
commodification in language of slavery, 131

Companion to African American Literature, A (Jarrett), 164
Companion to Cultural Memory Studies, A (Erll and Nünning), 6, 8, 254
Condé, Maryse, 215, 256
Confessions of Nat Turner (Gray), 244–45
"congregate-educate-agitate" (Kachun), 96, 105
constellations, metaphor of, 14
"Constitution of Toussaint, The: Another Origin of African American Literature" (Drexler and White), 164
Conyers, James L., Jr., 202
Cooper, Anna Julia, 35, 36, 55, 99
Corregidora (Jones), 79
courting communities, 28
Crandall, Prudence, 33
"Crazy Talk: 'Slavery Was a Blessing in Disguise'" (Crosley), 91
Creed and *Creed II* (films), xiv
Creole (ship), 24–25
Crisis (magazine), 39, 219
Crosley, Hillary, 91
Crossing Memories: Slavery and African Diaspora (Araujo, Candido, and Lovejoy, eds.), 19, 257
cultural criticism, xv, 16, 20, 200, 219, 220
cultural heroics, 4, 6, 35–36, 71, 93, 150, 176, 180, 219, 249–50; cultural heroic storytelling, 145; legendary cultural heroics, 72, 78
cultural inheritance, xv, 35, 71
cultural memory studies, 2, 253–54; Amos Wilson on, 58; Ana Lucia Araujo on diaspora approaches to, 131; black cultural mythology as a stabilizer, 23; and Black fiction, 5–6; commemoration models post 1619, 118–19; and cultural historiography, 15; defining the history of cultural memory, 6; introducing Africana Cultural Memory Studies as a course, 253–62; relationship between rhetoric and symbolism, 68–69; relationship of cultural mythology and cultural memory, 87–88; seen in *Insurrection: Holding History* (O'Hara), 242–49; seen in *John Henry Days* (Whitehead), 233–42; seen in Toni Morrison's works, 76; and studies on trauma, 4, 5; Trudier Harris on, 10; views in *History and Memory in African-American Culture* (Fabre and O'Meally), 12; ways to approach, 19–20; William Wiggins's book as a text for Africana cultural memory studies, 95; as worldview that determines what is sacred, 92
cultural nationalism/national culture, 201, 215–16, 217–18
cultural remembrance, xiii, 20, 55, 201, 238
Cultural Trauma: Slavery and the Formation of African American Identity (Eyerman), 4, 257
culture: and the development of a mythological structure, 59; Maulana Karenga's views on, 44; seven criteria of, 54. *See also* folk traditions/folk culture
Culture (journal), 209

Dagbovie, Pero, 12–13, 14
Daily Worker (newspaper), 36
Dana (in *Kindred*), 80, 148–49, 194, 244, 246
dan Fodio, Usman, 16
Danticat, Edwidge, xv, 21, 164, 171–74, 225
Darda, Joseph, 228–29
Dash, Michael, 161, 180
Daut, Marlene, 164

Davis, Thulani, 39
Dean, Phillip Hayes, 39
death and memorial, 172, 174, 196, 226; Bigger Thomas's death, 186, 192, 193, 194, 196; in *Insurrection: Holding History* (O'Hara), 247–48; in *John Henry Days* (Whitehead), 233, 236–37, 238–39, 240, 241; Malcolm X's death, 201–202, 205, 206, 224, 260. *See also* mourning and funeral rites
Decoration Day, 96
Defining Moments: African American Commemoration and Political Culture in the South, 1863–1913 (Clark), 98–100, 101
Delany, Lucille (in *Iola Leroy*), 34
Delany, Martin, 44, 74, 191
Delany, Samuel, 5
Dessaline, Jean-Jacques, 160–62, 165–68, 169, 171, 175, 176, 178, 179, 180–81, 256
Dessalines (Easton), 166
Dessa Rose (Williams), 83
Developmental Psychology of the Black Child, The (Wilson), 56, 58, 67–68, 143, 200, 261
"Dhabihu" (Swahili for "sacrifice" in recognition of Malcolm X legacy), 53
diaspora, xvi, 51; African and African diaspora worldviews, 17–18, 76, 183; Ana Lucia Araujo on diaspora approaches to cultural memory, 131; and creation of a new culture, 3; diaspora literature, 156–57; diaspora tourism, 132–33; forces responsible for diasporan survival, 16; Haitian Revolution as first diaspora-wide mythology, 83, 155–82; and heritage practices, 181; and memory, xvi; and sacrificial inheritance, xiii, xv, 52; and survival, 16, 254. *See also* engraving identity, process of, on a new soil
Diedrich, Maria I., 133–34, 138
Dingiswayo (African chief), 52
Dinner at Aunt Connie's House (Ringgold), 144–45, 248
"Dinner Quilt, The" (Ringgold), 143
Diop, Boubacar Boris, 256
disremembering, 17, 81, 228
diversity, 72, 89, 109, 110, 115, 129, 138, 236, 242; white supremacist version of, 71
Dixler, Elsa Jane, 36
documentary films, 26, 223, 251
Dougherty, Robin, 140
Douglass, Frederick, x, 24, 44, 55, 75, 82, 97, 143, 149, 158, 191, 224; Molefi Kete Asante on, 61, 62, 74; poetry about, 73, 223; on relevance of the Fourth of July, 102, 126; Shirley Graham Du Bois's biography of, 36, 40, 41, 218, 251
Dreamer: A Novel (Johnson), 21, 69, 78, 79, 219, 224, 226–33
Drexler, Michael J., 164
Dr. George Washington Carver, Scientist (Graham Du Bois), 36, 40
Drums and Colours (Walcott), 177, 221
Drums at Dusk (Bontemps), 164, 176, 219
Du Bois, David, 36
Du Bois, Robert, 38
Du Bois, Shirley Graham, ix, x, xv, 20, 24, 74, 118, 225, 251, 258; Biography Project, 36–43, 60; James Baldwin's review of *There Once Was a Slave*, 218
Du Bois, W. E. B., x, 17, 36, 39, 61, 64, 66, 72, 120, 142, 178; versus Booker T. Washington, 232;

Du Bois, W. E. B. *(continued)*
  caricature of, 223; use of ideas of to serve Holocaust studies, 254–55
Dunbar, Alice, 82–83
Dunbar, Paul Laurence, 65, 219
Durkheim, Émile, 7
Dyson, Michael Eric, 201, 202

Early Black History Movement, The: Carter G. Woodson and Lorrenzo Johnston Greene (Dagbovie), 12
Easton, William Edgar, 162, 166
Ebonic use of heroes, 28, 31, 33, 35
eclectic resistance strategies, 28
Edmunds, Randolph, 39
education ignoring African heritage in curriculum, 61
ego strengthening, 58–59, 207
Eight Men (Wright), 188
Ekgbe Chiefs of Cameroon, 105
Elijah Muhammad, 55, 64, 66
Elliott, Alyce, 128
Ellison, Ralph, x, 21, 39, 164, 223; and "Mister Toussan," 167–69, 171, 173, 174, 251
Emancipation Law (Brazil, 1888), 79
Emancipation Proclamation (1863), xviii, 109, 122, 127–28, 142, 143; celebrations and commemorations of, 20, 94, 94–96, 95, 96, 97, 98, 100, 101, 104, 118, 119, 120; James Baldwin on the hundredth anniversary, 122–25; as a marker of "beginning again," 142; numbers of Africans in US at time of, 146; post-Emancipation, 98; and remembrance, 143; worldviews on, 125–30
Embodying American Slavery in Contemporary Culture (Woolfork), 256
emotional history, 45

Emperor of Haiti (Hughes), 160, 164, 165, 166
engraving identity, process of, xvi, 2, 75, 83, 131; and the African diaspora, 19, 59, 87, 216; Larry Neal on, 48; on a new soil, xvi, 3, 24, 37, 77, 104, 110, 133, 183, 216, 223, 261; as revitalization, 48; Robert O'Hara on, 249. *See also* identity
enslavement: abolishment of slavery in US in 1863, 109; African identity before enslavement, 110, 219; codifying of in Virginia Act XXII (1660), 125–26; commemoration and memorialization of, 15, 114, 115, 130–35, 256; comparison of US and Brazil, 133; effects of on identity, 2; enslavement memory, xvi, 15, 20, 96, 107, 132, 134, 248, 254, 256; enslavement sexuality, 243; psychological deconstruction caused by, 18; revolutions against, xv. *See also* Charleston, South Carolina revolt of 1822; Haitian Revolution (1791–1804); Harpers Ferry, Virginia 1859 revolt; Richmond, Virgina revolt of 1800; Southhampton, Virginia revolt of 1831as trauma, 4, 6; treatment of in juvenile literature, 143; West African heritage of the enslaved, 16. *See also* Angolans as first Africans sold into enslavement in 1619
epic intuitive conduct, 99, 155, 225, 227, 250; as an attribute in Black cultural mythology framework, xvii, 23, 84, 86, 102, 129, 190, 222; and Harriet Tubman, 137, 147; meditations on not calendar based, 102
Erll, Astrid, 6, 254

Essential Black Literature Guide, The (Schomburg Center), 163
Ethiopianism, 31
Ethridge, Mary, 140
Eurocentrism, 31, 56, 59, 69, 74, 114, 116, 130, 184
Evers, Medgar, 224
Eyerman, Ron, 4, 6, 257

Fabre, Geneviève, 12
Fabre, Michel, 188–89
"Factor in Human Progress, A" (Harper), 34
Fanon, Frantz, x, 44, 55, 64, 217–18
"Farewell Address to Her Friends in the City of Boston" (Stewart), 31
Fauset, Jessie Redmon, 39
"fellowship-worship-entertainment" (Wiggins), 87, 95, 97, 105, 248
FESTAC 77, 131
festivals: difference between festival and commemoration, 235; providing sense of identity, 105
Festivals of Freedom: Memory and Meaning in African American Emancipation Celebrations, 1818–1915 (Kachun), 95–98, 100
fiction, poems, and plays. See Black literature
Fire Next Time, The (Baldwin), 122, 124
"First Africans in Virginia" historical marker, 108–9
Flick, Hank, 202
Florence, Franklin, 62
Flores, Lisa, 142
Flying Home and Other Stories (Calhoun, ed.), 167
folk traditions/folk culture, xv, 11, 139, 206, 235–36, 237, 258; Amos Wilson on, 58; Black cultural mythology as part of, 221, 222, 226; folk life of African Americans, 233–34; folkloric African American hero dynamics, 242; Larry Neal on, 47; Richard Wright on, 183, 185, 188, 189, 190, 190–91, 192, 193; William Wiggins on, 99, 101. See also cultural memory studies; culture
Foner, Eric, 140
for colored girls who have considered suicide/when the rainbow is enuf (Shange), 160, 163–64, 169–71
For Malcolm X: Poems on the Life and Death of Malcolm X (Randall and Burroughs, eds.), 260
Fort de Joux in France, 177, 179, 181
fortitude as a force for diasporan survival, 16
Fort Monroe tourism commission, 105
Fortune, T. Thomas, 97
Fourteenth Amendment, commemoration of, 118
Fourth of July celebrations, 97, 101, 102–103, 126
Franco, Marielle, xiv
Freedom Day, 96
"freedom's divas should always be luv'd" (Mataka), 147, 149–51, 152, 251
freedom's traps, 142
Free Enterprise: A Novel of Mary Ellen Pleasant (Cliff), 225
Freeman, John, 140
Freeman, Mack, 4–5
"From 1619 to Trayvon Martin" panel at "1619: The Making of America" conference, 116
Fuller, Charles, 44, 46–47

Gage, Carolyn, 147, 151–52
Gamal Abdel Nasser (Graham Du Bois), 36
Garner, Margaret (as basis for *Beloved*), 79, 226

Garnet, Henry Highland, 62
Garvey, Marcus, x, 44, 55, 61, 64, 66, 74, 120–21, 223
Gauthier, Marni, 5, 257
Gayle, Addison, 83
Genefride (Harris), 160, 163
Ghost Dance (Walcott), 221
Glass, Kathy L., 28, 30
Glissant, Edouard, 21, 39, 157, 159–60, 177
Gomez, Jewelle, 5
Gordon-Reed, Annette, 140
Graham, Shirley. *See* Du Bois, Shirley Graham
Gray, Thomas Ruffin, 244
Greene, Lorenzo Johnson, x, 12, 14, 219
Grossman, Lev, 140
Guasco, Michael, 116–17
Gullah people, 146
Guy Jr. (in "A Wall of Fire Rising"), 172–73

HAIKU: This Other World (Wright), 187
Haiti, xviii, 258; as diaspora-wide mythology, 83, 155–82; transnational value of, 216
Haitian Earth, The (Walcott), 221
Haitian Revolution (1791–1804), xv, xvi, 20, 25, 42, 78, 155–82; heroics of, 219; literature related to, 39, 78, 156–57, 158, 159–61, 163–77, 219, 224; media coverage of, 180; as a prominent commemoration, 118
Haitian Revolution in the Literary Imagination, The: Radical Horizons, Conservative Constraints (Kaisary), 164
Haitian Trilogy, The: Plays (Walcott), 157, 176–77, 221

Haiti's Influence on Antebellum America (Hunt), 164
Hakutani, Yoshinobu, 187
Halbwachs, Maurice, 2, 7
Haley, Alex, xviii, 42, 205, 208
Hamer, Fannie Lou, 55, 82, 118, 224
Hampton, Fred, xv
Hampton, Virginia, 105; African Landing Day (aka African Arrival Day), 98, 105, 106–8, 108; recognizing importance and sacredness of arrival of Africans in 1619, 108; as a sacred location, 104. *See also* 1619 and arrival of first kidnapped African captives; Point Comfort (in colony of Virginia) (now Fort Monroe); Project 1619
Hampton 2019 Commemorative Commission, 106, 107–8
Hansberry, Lorraine, 164, 223–24
Harlem Renaissance, 44, 123, 155
Harper, Frances Ellen Watkins, 34, 35, 36, 99
Harpers Ferry, Virginia 1859 revolt, 34
"Harriet" (play by Miller), 147–48
Harriet Tubman: Imagining a Life (Lowry), 141
Harriet Tubman: Myth, Memory, and History (Sernett), 10–12, 141
Harriet Tubman: The Life and the Life Stories (Humez), 141
Harriet Tubman: The Road to Freedom (Clinton), 141, 142–43, 146
Harriet Tubman Visits a Therapist: A Play in One Act (Gage), 147, 151–52
Harrington, Ollie, 231
Harris, Charles "Teenie," 250
Harris, Helen Webb, 39, 160, 163
Harris, Trudier, 8–10, 65
Hartman, Saidiya, 3, 257
Hatshepsut (Egyptian queen), 138

Hawthorne, Walter, 19
Haynes, Elizabeth Ross, 39
Henri Christophe (Walcott), 221
Henry, Paget, 80–81
Herbes-Sommers, Christine, 105
Heremakhonon (Condé), 215
heritage practices, 1, 13, 37, 76, 83, 88, 97, 116, 142, 231, 258, 261; African cultural heritage, 15, 16, 56, 63, 122, 124, 223; Amos Wilson on, 58; Ana Lucia Araujo on, 130–33; celebrating heritage practices, 97, 103–4, 106, 107, 109, 116, 118, 251; and diaspora, xvi, 51, 181; Edwidge Danticat on, 172, 174; heritage behavior, 89, 219; heritage hero dynamics, 167, 250; heritage memory, 93, 251, 253; heritage of resistance, 141; heritage tourism/sacred participatory tourism, 131, 132, 134–35; humanizing African American agency in, 100; and immortalization, 106; inclusion in curriculums, 13, 61; in *Insurrection: Holding History* (O'Hara), 244, 248; intergenerational heritage, 183; in *John Henry Days* (Whitehead), 234, 235–36; Kathleen Clark on, 98, 100; Martin Luther King Jr. on, 120, 121; Mitch Kachun on, 97, 100, 103; Molefi Kete Asante on, 61–64, 66–67, 70, 74; and mythology, 111, 224; reforming heritage practices, 82; Richard Wright on, 187, 188, 191; sacred heritage, 2, 11; Shirley Graham Du Bois on, 40, 42; UNESCO-supported heritage sites, 131; W. E. B. Du Bois on, 142. *See also* commemoration philosophy; ritual remembrance

hero dynamics, x–xi, xiii, 1, 23, 83, 85, 116, 143, 213, 224, 261; African-centered philosophy of heroism, 18; African world heroics, 218–19; Amos Wilson on, 58; as an attribute in Black cultural mythology framework, xvii, 23, 28, 47, 58, 84, 85, 102, 190, 222; Black nationalist antihero/Black antinationalist hero, 193; Christian heroic (describing King in *Dreamer*), 227; community of heroics, 248; creating a heroic self, 185; cultural memory, 6, 123; documentary films as a genre for, 223; in *Dreamer* (Johnson), 226, 230, 231; Ebonic use of heroes, 28, 31, 33, 35; elements of Africana heroic, 183; enhanced language of, 155; Errol Hill on, 164–66; Faith Ringgold on, 145; folkloric African American hero dynamics, 242; in Haiti, 155, 161, 162, 167, 168, 175, 176, 181, 241; and Harriet Tubman, 78, 141, 147, 149, 150–51, 152; heroes and activists since enslavement, 160; heroes paralleling everyday folk, 235; heroic dysfunction, 232; heroic heritage through the naming of a child, 64; heroic identity, 44, 71, 168; heroic impulses, 258; heroic literature, 15, 158; heroic policy as a collective demonstration of Black citizenship, 98–99; heroic storytelling, 38, 59, 143, 145, 203, 222; in *Insurrection: Holding History* (O'Hara), 243, 244, 248; intellectual heroes, x; James Baldwin on, 125, 218; in *John Henry Days* (Whitehead), 233, 235, 236, 237, 238, 239, 241; language of, 155; and Malcolm X, 201–202,

hero dynamics *(continued)*
208–14; of Maria W. Stewart, 28, 30–33; Marvel Comic Black heroes, 237; meditations on not calendar based, 102; Molefi Kete Asante on, 60, 63, 69; mythification of postcolonial heroism, 16; as not gender-based, 99; philosophy of heroism, xvii; responding to legacies of the culture's heroes, 54; Richard Wright on, 185, 188, 191; study of, xvi; theorizations of heroics in the US and the Caribbean, 260–61; Toni Morrison on, 76; Trudier Harris on, 8–10; use of heroics in Garnet's speeches, 62; womanist heroics, xiii–xiv, xv. *See also* antiheroics; cultual heroics; hyperheroic acts

Heroic Slave, The (Douglass), 24

Higginbotham, A. Leon, 20, 119, 120, 125, 126

Hill, Errol, 147, 164–66

Hill, Lesley Pinckney, 166–67

Hinton, West Virginia (town in *John Henry Days*), 235, 236

historical reenactment of worldview: as an attribute in Black cultural mythology framework, xvii, 23, 84, 85, 105, 106, 108, 116, 142, 144, 156, 207; embodied in *Dinner at Aunt Connie's House* (Ringgold), 144; and Haiti, 156, 175; Houston Baker on, 191; literary example of, 225; Shirley Graham Du Bois on, 38

historiography: adding 1619 to the historiography, 103–18; of African American commemoration, 94–103; defining language of, 101

History, the Black Press, and Public Relations (Morris), 14

History and Memory in African-American Culture (Fabre and O'Meally), 12

Holly, James Theo, 161

Holston, Joseph, 145, 250, 256

Hopkins, Pauline, 83

Hopkinson, Nalo, 225

Horne, Gerald, 36, 37–38, 39, 40–41, 42–43, 202

Howard University, 239

"How Come We here Lord" (song), 116

Hubbard, Jon, 91

Hubert, David, 140

Huggins, Nathan, x, 92–93

Hughes, Langston, 21, 39, 65, 160, 164, 165, 166–67, 223

humanizing mythology through *Dreamers* (Johnson), 226–33

Humez, Jean M., 140, 141

Humphrey, Hubert, 184

Hunt, Albert, 164

Hurston, Zora Neale, 17, 76, 139

hyperheroic acts, 23, 224, 235; as an attribute in Black cultural mythology framework, xvii, 84, 86, 102, 258; Charles Johnson on, 227; in Haiti, 156, 166, 168, 170, 173; and Harriet Tubman, 137, 138, 141–42, 147, 152, 216; hyperheroic survival, 2, 3, 32, 82, 111, 251–52; Kathleen Clark on, 99; and Malcolm X, 211; in *Native Son* (Wright), 194; Shirley Graham Du Bois on, 37

identity, 6, 57, 72, 83, 88, 118, 132, 139, 199, 262; Africana identity as seen by Molefi Kete Asante, 60; African identity before enslavement, 110; and Black cultural heritage, 61, 66, 124; collective identity, 250;

cultural identity, 4, 28, 40, 59, 88, 114, 122, 131, 141, 143, 260; defining Black cultural mythology in framework of African American identity, 220; effects of enslavement on, 2; ethnocentric identity, 134; and festivals, 105; and the Haitian Revolution, 156, 159, 168, 181; and Harriet Tubman, 141, 142, 150, 151, 219; heroic identity, 44, 71, 168; identity-driven decisions, 92; identity survival, 73; influences on, 15; in *John Henry Days* (Whitehead), 234, 236; and Malcolm X, 202, 206; mythic national identity, 92–93, 93. *See also* engraving identity on a new soil

imagination, role of memory in, 76

immortalization philosophy, 24, 73, 117, 219, 262; Amos Wilson on, 58; Ana Lucia Araujo on, 132; Asante and Welsh on, 77; as an attribute in Black cultural mythology framework, xvii, 19, 23, 83, 84, 86, 106, 116, 142, 144, 156, 181, 222, 258; and commemoration, 118, 128; Faith Ringgold on, 144; and Harriet Tubman, 138, 143–44, 153; and heritage practices, 106; and immortalization, 25–34, 35, 60, 63, 162; in *Insurrection: Holding History* (O'Hara), 244; James Baldwin on, 125; in *John Henry Days* (Whitehead), 235; and Malcolm X, 206; male and female models of, 250; Maria W. Stewart on, 25–34, 26, 36, 60, 96–97, 98, 162, 184, 218–19, 221, 230; meditations on not calendar based, 102; in *Native Son* (Wright), 194, 195; Ntozake Shange on, 170, 173; related to heritage tourism, 132; self-immortalization, 32; Shirley Graham Du Bois on, 144; *Song for Anninho* (Jones) on, 79; and storytelling, 143; *Venus* (Parks) exemplifying, 225

Indigenisme/Indigenist movement (Haiti), 155

inheritance, 23, 88, 121, 222; in *Appeal* (Walker), 24; cultural inheritance, xv, 35, 71; and diaspora, 52; in *Insurrection: Holding History* (O'Hara), 243, 247; in *John Henry Days* (Whitehead), 233, 236, 238, 240; Maulana Karenga on, 54; Molefi Kete Asante on, 53, 64, 71, 73; in *Native Son* (Wright), 185, 194; of resistance, 191; survivalist inheritance, 64. *See also* sacrificial inheritance (sacred inheritance)

Insurrection: Holding History (O'Hara), 5, 21, 78, 79, 217, 219, 225, 237, 242–49

intellectual traditions of Black cultural mythology, xvii, xviii, 19, 20, 23–90, 118, 182, 212, 255–56, 260

intercultural mythology and *John Henry Days* (Whitehead), 233–42

intergenerations: and the impetus of mythology, 59; intergenerational empowerment, 57; intergenerational survivalist and resistance tendencies, 58; intergenerational future cultural existence, 244

In the Matter of Color: Race and the American Legal Process: The Colonial Period (Higginbotham), 125

Introduction to Black Studies (Karenga), 50–51, 258–59

Iola Leroy, Or, Shadows Uplifted (Harper), 34

330 Index

Irritated Genie, The (Carruthers), 161, 162, 178
Isabel (Princess Imperial of Brazil), 79, 133
Isabell (Angolan sold as slave in 1619), 108, 114, 245
Isandlwana, Battle of, 52

Jackson, Blyden, 188
Jackson, Giles B., 100
James, C. L. R., x, 158, 159, 176
James-Myers, Linda, 142
Jamestown, Virginia, 65, 107, 113, 115, 130
Jamestown Tercentennial, 100
Jarrett, Gene Andrew, 164
Jasper, John, 68
Jean Baptiste Pointe de Sable: Founder of Chicago (Graham Du Bois), 36
Jefferson, Thomas, 175, 176
Jenkins, Robert L., 202
"jihadist reinvention," 207
Jim Crowism, 102, 196, 197
John Henry, 68, 186, 226
John Henry Days (Whitehead), 8, 21, 78, 79, 219, 224–25; and intercultural mythology, 233–42
Johnson, Adonis (in *Creed* and *Creed II*), xiv
Johnson, Charles, xix, 5, 8, 21, 39, 69, 78, 219, 224, 226–33, 242; on the Haitian Revolution, 164, 174–76
Johnson, Guy (in "A Wall of Fire Rising"), 233
Johnson, Helene, 123–24
Johnson, Lorenzo, x
Jones, Edward, 5
Jones, Gayl, xv, 79, 225
Jones, Toussaint (in *for colored girls*), 170–71
Jordan, Michael B., xiv–xv, 50

Jordan, Winthrop, 117
Jubilee celebrations, 101, 118, 132, 142, 143
Julian Messner Publishers, 38
Julius Nyerere: Teacher of Africa (Graham Du Bois), 36
July Fifth as a Black holiday, 102, 103
Juneteenth celebrations, 95, 96, 101, 104, 105, 118
juvenile literature. *See* Black literature

Kachun, Mitch, 95–98, 100, 101, 103, 105, 110
Kaisary, Philip, 164
Kammen, Michael, 11
Kanneh, Kadiatu, 112
Karenga, Maulana, 20, 24, 43, 48–56, 64, 65, 118; and the Black Arts Movement, 48–49, 54, 77, 209, 261; on cultural mythology, 44, 60, 66, 74–75, 103, 200, 201, 220, 258, 261; on culture, 44; on inheritance, 54; on Malcolm X, 53–54, 71, 205, 208, 209–10, 213; Molefi Kete Asante on, 51–52, 53, 66, 73; on religion, 73; on "scavenger history," 213; on self-determination, 56
"Kawaida on Mythology" (Karenga), 49
Kawaida theory, 49, 50, 51, 54
Kawaida Theory: An Introductory Outline (Karenga), 49
Keeter, Susan, 145
Kemadjiv, Cilas, 16, 256
Kevin (fictional character), 148–49
Killens, John Oliver, 75, 76
Killmonger, Erik B. (in *Black Panther*, movie), xiv, 216
Kimbundu-speaking people, 113, 114
Kindred (Butler), 80, 148–49, 194, 225, 246

King, Martin Luther, Jr., x, xv, 20, 61, 65, 66, 69, 74, 178, 210, 242; approach to commemoration, 119–22, 130; celebrations in honor of, 101, 118, 128–29; death of, 224; heroic nature of, 8–10; as main character in *Dreamer* (Johnson), 78, 224, 226–33; versus Malcolm X, 232; on Marcus Garvey, 120–21; poetry about, 73, 223

King Commemorations: A Collection of Activities (Elliott), 128

Kingdom of This World, The (Carpentier), 176

King Memorial (Washington, DC), 10

Knight, Etheridge, 44

Krik? Krak! (Danticat), 164, 171–74

"Kuzaliwa" (Swahili name for Malcolm X's birthday remembrance), 53

Kwanzaa (holiday tradition), 52, 94

Kwanzaa: Black Power and the Making of the African-American Holiday Tradition (Mayes), 101–103

Lachmann, Renate, 8

lady in brown (in *for colored girls*), 169, 170–71

lamentation, 87, 92, 105, 117, 192, 237

Lamousé-Smith, Willie Bediako, ix–xi

Lang, Clarence, 210, 211–12

Langston, John Mercer, 97

language, 146, 208; Amos Wilson on, 57; body language, 110, 151; commodification in language of slavery, 131; defining language of historiography, 101; Ebonic use of heroes, 28, 31, 33, 35; of immortalization, 28, 36, 97; Maulana Karenga on, 50, 54; of memory, 79, 96, 204; Molefi Kete Asante on, 60, 61–63, 72; mythologies creating vocabularies, 59; shared linguistic practices, 251; of "slavery cultural heritage," 130–31; social-behavioral language, 57; use of to degrade others, 183–84

Language, Communication, and Rhetoric in Black America (Asante), 62

Larry Neal Writers Conference (Second Annual in 1983), 46

Larsen, Kate Clifford, 138

Lawrence, Jacob, 145, 231, 250, 256

legacy tools, xvi, 1, 14, 37, 58, 83, 89, 188, 194, 250; legacy of resistance, 192

Legba's Crossing: Narratology in the African Atlantic (Russell), 80

legend and myth, 204–5; in *John Henry Days* (Whitehead), 233–34, 235–36

"'Let Children's Children Never Forget': Remembrance and Amnesia, 1870–1910" (Kachun), 96

Letters to the Editor: Confessions of a Frustrated Conservative (Hubbard), 91

"Letter to My Nephew" (Baldwin). *See* "My Dungeon Shook: Letter to My Nephew on the Eve of the Anniversary of the Emancipation Proclamation" (Baldwin)

letter-writing as a literary form, 123, 175

Lewis, Edmonia, 35

Liberator, The (abolitionist journal), 25, 26, 33

Library of Congress, 41, 42

"Life beyond the Legend" (Marable), 204

Life of Reinvention, A (Marable). *See Malcolm X: A Life of Reinvention* (Marable)

Like One of the Family (Childress), 224

Lili (in "A Wall of Fire Rising"), 172–73, 174
Lincoln, Abraham, 100, 133
literary criticism, xv, xviii, 47, 75, 214; and Black cultural mythology, xix, 21, 46–47, 79, 215–17, 257; on Haitian heroics, 156; inaugural models of, 79, 215–52. See also *Dreamer: A Novel* (Johnson); *Insurrection: Holding History* (O'Hara); *John Henry Days* (Whitehead)and reviews of *Malcolm X: A Life of Reinvention* (Marable), 207–14; of Richard Wright's work, 188. See also Black literature
Literary Spaces: Introduction to Comparative Black Literature (Temple), 220, 260
"Literature of Slavery and Freedom, The" in *Norton Anthology of African American Literature*, 221
Little Guy (in "A Wall of Fire Rising"), 172, 174
Little/Shabazz family infighting over Malcolm X, 206
"Living Black history" (Marable's methodology), 203–4
Living Black History: How Reimagining the African-American Past Can Remake America's Racial Future (Marable), 202, 203, 204, 205
Living History: Encountering the Memory and History of the Heirs of Slavery (Araujo), 257
Locke, Alain, 39–40
Logan, Shirley Wilson, 30
Loiseaux brothers, 35
Long Black Song: Essays in Black American Literature and Culture (Baker), 188
Lorde, Audre, 20, 80–81

Lose Your Mother: A Journey along the Atlantic Slave Route (Hartman), 257
Louis, Joe, 231
Louisiana Native Guards, 35
Louverture, Toussaint, x, xv, 62, 193, 223, 257; comparing to Napoleon, 160; literature about, 157, 159, 160–61, 163–77, 175; status of a transnational Louverture, 177–82; "Sweet Papa Toussan." See "Mister Toussan" (Ellison), transnational ancestor status of, 156
Lovejoy, Paul E., 19, 257
love memory, 46
Lowry, Beverly, 141
Lumumba, Patrice, 223, 224

Maat, the Moral Ideal in Ancient Egypt: A Study in Classical African Ethics (Karenga), 52
Mackandal, François, 160
Making Malcolm: The Myth and Meaning of Malcolm X (Dyson), 201
Malcolm X, x, xv, xviii, 20, 44, 55, 64, 66, 68, 74, 178, 206; celebrations in honor of, 118; as a cultural hero, 201–202; death of and responses to, 201–202, 205, 206, 224, 260; documentary films on, 223; Larry Neal on, 45–46; legacy and memorialization of, 83, 212; versus Martin Luther King Jr., 232; Maulana Karenga on, 53–54, 71; Molefi Kete Asante on, 61; as a mythoform (mythological structure of), 200, 235; poetry about, 73, 223; reinvention of, 207; resilience of his epic status, 258; as seen by Manning Marable, 199–214; socio-religious concept of resurrection, 52

Malcolm X: A Historical Reader (Conyers and Smallwood, eds.), 202
Malcolm X: A Life of Reinvention (Marable), xviii, xxiii–xxiv, 199, 199–214, 200, 218, 235; reviews of, 208–14
Malcolm X as Cultural Hero and Other Afrocentric Essays (Asante), 61, 73, 201
Malcolm X Encyclopedia, The (Jenkins, ed.), 202
"Malcolm X's Life-After-Death: The Dispossession of a Legacy" (Marable), 203, 206
Mandela, Nelson as subject of "Mandela and the Black Diaspora" (Valbrun), 179–80
Mansa Musa (emperor of Mali), xv
"Man Who Lived Underground, The" (Wright), 188
Mapping Generations of Traumatic Memory in American Narratives (Mihailescu, Oltean, and Precup, eds.), 257
Marable, Manning, xviii, 20, 199–214, 216, 218, 235
Maria W. Stewart, America's First Black Woman Political Writer: Essays and Speeches (Richardson, ed.), 25
Marsh-Lockett, Carol P., 3
Martin, Trayvon, xiv, 196
Martin Luther King Jr. Day, 101, 103
Martin Luther King Jr., Heroism, and African American Literature (Harris), 8
Marvel Comic Black heroes, 237
Mary (in *Native Son*), 189
Maryland Historical Society, 41
Masterpieces of Negro Eloquence (Dunbar), 82–83

Mataka, Laini, xv, 21, 39, 147, 149–51, 152, 225, 251
Maulana Karenga: An Intellectual Portrait (Asante), 51–52
Max, Boris (fictional character), 191, 195
Mayes, Keith, 52–53, 55–56, 101, 102–103, 205
Mbundu people, x, 122
McFadden, Alesia E., 37, 39, 42, 43
Mchawi, Basir, 102
McKay, Claude, 231
Meaning of the Blues, The (Oliver), 187
media, 72, 93, 103, 180, 194, 219, 242; documentary films, 26, 223, 251; and Haiti, 158, 216; impact of on children, 223–24; in *John Henry Days* (Whitehead), 234, 236, 238; legacy use of, 29; role and power of, 67, 234; social media, xiv; television in Black cultural mythology, 67–68. See also African American press (Black press)
Meditations From the Pen of Mrs. Maria W. Stewart (Stewart), 32
Melody (in *Dinner at Aunt Connie's House*), 144–45
memoirs. See biographies/autobiographies/memoirs as a genre
memorialization, xiii, xvi, 51, 111, 250; Ana Lucia Araujo on, 64, 131, 133; Christina Sharpe on, 256; commemoration and memorialization of enslavement, 92, 114, 115, 130–35. See also 1619 and arrival of first kidnapped African captivesconcept of a memorialized leader, 248; Errol Hill on, 165; examples in Black literature, 177, 236, 238, 243; and Harriet Tubman, 150, 151;

memorialization *(continued)*
lamentation and memorialization, 117; legacy and memorialization of Malcolm X, 45, 83, 212, 260; Maulana Karenga on, 50, 53, 55; memory and memorialization, ix, 55, 115, 238; Molefi Kete Asante on, 64–65; narrative memorial, 2; ways used to memorialize Toussaint Louverture, 177–82. *See also* aesthetic memorialization; commemoration philosophy; death and memorial; mourning and funeral rites; ritual remembrance

Memorial of the Great Jubilee of 2000 (in Benin), 132

memory: Africana memory, ix; African American approach, 93–94; collective memory, 2, 4, 5, 6, 7, 10, 73, 96, 97, 201, 250; of a culture's heritage, 253; empowerment through, 4; enslavement memory, xvi, 15, 20, 96, 107, 132, 134, 248, 254, 256; environment shaping, 93; as a force for diasporan survival, 16; importance of to James Baldwin, 125; in *John Henry Days* (Whitehead), 234; memory practices on valuing resistance, 184; Michael Guasco on, 117; mythology and the challenge of heroic memory of Malcolm X, 208–14; need to discuss African identity before enslavement, 219; "plural memories of slavery," 131; political memory, 156; public memory, 131; reconstuctive memory projects, 114; relationship between memory and decolonization, 69; Richard Wright on, 187; rituals to enact grief and memory, 256; role of memory in imagination, 76; sacred remembrance and sacred memory, 2, 23, 87, 110, 118, 171, 181–82, 216, 239, 262; selective memory, 1, 11; as a "social construction," 11, 71; social memory, 7, 79, 177; study of Emancipation celebration history, 95–98; Toni Morrison on, 5, 24, 76–78, 79. *See also* remembrance

Metellus, Jean, 256
mfundalai rite, 69–70
Mickenberg, Julia, 37
Middle Passage, x, 1, 16, 47, 85, 104, 112, 130; and survivalism, 2, 3, 18
Midnight Robber (Hopkinson), 225
Mihailescu, Dana, 257
Miller, Eugene, 189
Miller, May, xv, 21, 39, 147–48, 151–52, 161, 163, 223, 225
Miller, Ron, 39
"Mister Toussan" (Ellison), 164, 167–69, 171, 173, 174, 251
Monsieur Toussaint (Glissant), 157, 159–60, 177
Monuments of the Black Atlantic: Slavery and Memory (Braxton and Diedrich, eds.), 133–34, 138
Moore, Alison, 15–16
Morris, Burnis R., 14
Morrison, Toni, ix, x, xv, 4, 8, 20, 225, 226; on memory, 5, 24, 76–79
Moses (songwriter in *John Henry Days*), 233–34
Moses, Wilson, 83
mourning and funeral rites, 17–18, 87, 213, 238, 256; funeral dirges, xxii, 18, 23, 33, 260. *See also* death and memorial
Moyse, Hyacinthe, 160
Muhammad, Wallace, 206
Multidirectional Memory: Remembering the Holocaust in the Age of Decolonization (Rothberg), 254
Murray, Albert, 215

music and Black cultural mythology, 18, 47, 50, 64, 72, 77, 89, 105, 134, 143, 147, 169, 206, 241, 250, 255–56; diasporic music, 47; in *John Henry Days* (Whitehead), 233–34; in "Mister Toussan" (Ellison), 168; Toni Morrison on the novel and music, 77

"My Dungeon Shook: Letter to My Nephew on the Eve of the Anniversary of the Emancipation Proclamation" (Baldwin), 119, 122

Mystic Chords of Memory: The Transformation of Tradition in American Culture (Kammen), 11

"'Myth' and the Making of 'Malcom X'" (Horne), 202

mythification (mythication), 16, 62, 255

mythoforms (Molefi Kete Asante concept), 60–61, 64, 70, 71, 72, 255; applied to Harriet Tubman, 137, 141; applied to Malcolm X, 200

mythological structure, xvii, 6, 14, 23, 129, 133, 193, 207, 208, 213, 220–21, 251; Amos Wilson on, 53, 57, 62, 70, 194, 194–95, 200, 207, 261; as an attribute in Black cultural mythology framework, 23, 84, 87–88, 136; and Black nationalism, 222; and Black women, xiv, 152; and diasporans, 131, 132; in *Dreamer* (Johnson), 231; in Haiti, xviii, xxvi, 156, 164, 167, 168, 171, 172, 181–82; and Harriet Tubman, 140, 141, 142, 152; in *Insurrection: Holding History* (O'Hara), 244; intellectual foundations of, 23–90; in *John Henry Days* (Whitehead), 239–40; and Malcolm X, 200, 202, 204–205, 206, 207, 209, 235; negative mythological structures,

56–57. *See also* Black cultural mythology, conceptual framework of

mythology: Africana mythology, ix–xi, 77, 133, 164, 221, 239, 255; Biblical mythology, 227; biography as a form of, 204; as a category in culture's conceptual vocabulary, 261; and the challenge of heroic memory of Malcolm X, 208–14; Colson Whitehead's use of term, 236; conceptual mythological status of survival, 253; defining, 1–2; distinction between myth and mythology, 203, 207; distinguishing American and African American worldviews on, 240; humanizing mythology through *Dreamers* (Johnson), 226–33; intercultural mythology, 233–42; Maulana Karenga on, 49–50, 51, 52, 73; post-colonial mythologies, 256; private mythology, 45; sacred mythology, 49, 65; snares of civic myths, 2; survivalist mythology, 10, 183; sustaining cultural memory, 253

"Myths about Malcom X" (Cleage), 200

"Myth: The Communication Dimension to the African American Mind" (Asante and Welsh), 60, 68, 77

Napoleon Bonaparte, 160, 168, 177
narrative memorial, 2
Nasser, Gamal Abdel, 36, 41, 42
nationalism, 60, 115, 118; Black nationalism, xiii, 25, 27, 29, 30, 106, 192, 193, 199, 222; Black nationalist vision, 221; commemoration nationalism, 52; cultural nationalism/national

nationalism *(continued)*
  culture, 201, 215–16; mythic national identity, 92–93; patriotic nationalism, 87; syncre-nationalism, 28; transnationalism, 96, 228; White/Euro-American nationalism, 101
National Juneteenth Observance Foundation, 105
National Parks Service, 105
Nation of Islam, 61, 206
Native Son (Wright), xviii, 20, 183, 185, 188, 189–97
Native Son: The Emergence of a New Black Hero (Butler), 188
Ndongo (kingdom of), 113
Neal, Larry, 20, 24, 43–49, 50, 56, 60, 74, 118, 258, 261; as a Black Arts/Black Power figure, 51, 77, 103, 209; defining Black cultural mythology as a literary tradition, 21, 220
Négritude movement (French African and Caribbean), 155
Negro Election Day events, 96
Negro Historical and Industrial Exposition (Richmond, Virginia in 1915), 100
Negro History in Thirteen Plays (Richardson and Miller, eds.), 147, 163
"Negro Revolution, The" (King), 119
Negro World (magazine), 219
Nell, William C., 97
Nelson, Scott, 235
New Masses (magazine), 167
New Negro movement, 155, 218–19, 222, 223; post–New Negro period, 219
Ngugi, Thiong'o wa, 17–18, 69, 133
Njia: The Way, 70

Nkrumah, Kwame, 64
NOI. *See* Nation of Islam
Nora, Pierre, 12
Norton Anthology of African American Literature (Gates and McKay, eds.), 43, 48–49, 163, 221, 225
Notes of a Native Son (Baldwin), 124
Notes on the State of Virginia (Jefferson), 175
Nünning, Ansgar, 6, 254
Nussbaum, Richard J., 128–29
Nyerere, Julius, 36, 41, 42, 55
Nzingha (queen of Angola), 116, 138

Obama, Barack, 91–92
Obasi, Ezemenari, 142
Odu Ifa: The Ethical Teaching (Karenga), 52, 55
O Freedom! Afro-American Emancipation Celebrations (Wiggins), 94–95, 97, 106, 238
Ogunleye, Tolagbe, 139
O'Hara, Robert, xix, 5, 21, 78, 217, 219, 225, 237, 242–49
Okpewho, Isidore, 16
Olamina, Lauren (in *Parable of the Sower*), 149
Olick, Jeffrey K., 7
Oliver, Paul, 187
Oltean, Roxana, 257
O'Meally, Robert, 12
"On Black Art" (Karenga), 48
Open Door Community Center (Brooklyn, New York), 38
oratory. *See* rhetoric and oratory
Organization for the Promotion of Traditional Medicine (in Senegal), 132
Other Wes Moore, The: One Name, Two Fates (Moore), 227
Ouidah 92 (celebration in Benin), 131

"Overturning Ourselves: From Mystification to Meaningful Struggle" (Karenga), 49
Oxford Companion to African American Literature (Andrews, et al., eds.), 163

Pagan Spain (Wright), 189
Palmares (Brazilian maroon settlement), 79
Pan-Africanism, xiii, 42, 106, 122, 158
Parable of the Sower (Butler), 149
Paradise (Morrison), 5
Parker, Nate, 242
Parks, Gordon, 250
Parks, Rosa, 73, 118, 140, 144, 170
Parks, Suzan-Lori, 8, 39, 81, 225
Patsilelis, Chris, 140
Paul Robeson: Citizen of the World (Graham Du Bois), 36
Pearson, Calvin, 107
Peterson, Nancy, 4–5, 257
Phillis Wheatley (Graham Du Bois), 36
Pilgrimage Prayer, 105, 106
Pinkster Festival, 96
Pocahontas (Graham Du Bois), 36, 42
poetry as a genre. *See* Black literature
Point Comfort (in colony of Virginia) (now Fort Monroe), ix–x, 103, 104, 105, 106, 107, 108–9, 113–14, 115, 127. *See also* 1619 and arrival of first kidnapped African captives; Hampton, Virginia
Pointe de Sable, Jean Baptiste, 36, 42, 231
"Politics of Memory, The" conference, 254
Politics of Memory: Making Slavery Visible in Public Space (Araujo), 257
Porter, Dorothy B., 26

Porter, Ron (in *Insurrection*), 237, 244–45, 246–48, 249
"Possession" (Parks), 81
Powell, Adam Clayton, 62
Precup, Mihaela, 257
private mythology, 45
problem solving, 57, 78, 85, 120, 139, 166
Progressive (magazine), 122
Project 1619, 105, 106, 107, 108, 111, 115. *See also* 1619 and arrival of first kidnapped African captives
Prosser, Gabriel, xv, 25, 69, 118, 190, 193, 207, 223, 248
Public Memory of Slavery: Victims and Perpetrators in the South Atlantic (Araujo), 257
Publishers Weekly (magazine), 140

Quotable Karenga, The (Karenga), 49

Rana, Aziz, 212
Randall, Dudley, 260
Randolph, A. Philip, 223
Rankine, Patrice, 233
reconciliation and renewal, 106, 116, 170; as an attribute in Black cultural mythology framework, xvii, 23, 84, 89, 108, 194, 223, 246
Reed, Ishmael, 5
Re-Forming the Past: History, the Fantastic, and the Postmodern Slave Narrative (Spaulding), 5, 257
Reilly, John, 190
Reinvention. *See Malcolm X: A Life of Reinvention* (Marable)
religion, 184, 187, 192, 193; and Maria W. Stewart, 30, 31, 59; Maulana Karenga on, 49–50, 51, 52, 73; Molefi Kete Asante on, 65, 73; voodoo as a religion, 175

"Religion and the Pure Principles of Morality, the Sure Foundation on Which We Must Build" (Stewart), 30
re-membering (re-remembering), 17, 81
remembrance, 111; cultural remembrance, xiii, 20, 55, 201, 238; definition of, 92; diasporic African remembrance, 17; and disremembering, 17; and Emancipation, 143; Hampton, Virginia celebration as, 105; ritual remembrance, 134; sacred remembrance and sacred memory, 2, 23, 87, 110, 118, 171, 181–82, 216, 239, 262; as seen by Edwidge Danticat, 174; as survivalist mythology, 10; testimony of, 3. *See also* memory; ritual remembrance
rememory, xvi
Remond, Charles Lenox, 61, 62
renewal and reconciliation. *See* reconciliation and renewal
"Report from St. Domingue, A" (Johnson), 174–76
Republic of Haiti. *See* Haiti
resistance-based cognitive survival, xvii, 3, 32, 37, 225, 227; as an attribute in Black cultural mythology framework, 23, 84, 85; in Haiti, 155, 156, 168, 170; and Harriet Tubman, 147, 152. *See also* cognitive survival; survival strategies
Restoring the Queen (Mataka), 149
revivification, 52, 54, 255
Revolutionists, The (Graham Du Bois and Rodman), 42
"Rhetoric and Myth" (Asante), 60
rhetoric and oratory, 17, 27, 48, 86, 88, 120, 220; linkage between oratory and myth, 63, 64; and Malcolm X, 53; and Maria W. Stewart, 27, 28, 29, 31, 33; Molefi Kete Asante on, 61–62, 63, 64, 68–69, 70, 193; power of Black oratory, 96–97; relationship between rhetoric and symbolism, 68–69, 70; and Toussaint Louverture, 180. *See also* speeches and speech delivery devices
Rhetoric of Black Revolution (Asante), 61, 62, 64, 183–84
Rice, Condoleeza, 184
Richards, Dona (now Marimba Ani), 48, 83
Richardson, Jennifer, 128–29
Richardson, Marilyn, 25–26, 27, 29, 32
Richardson, Willis, 163
Richard Wright: Myths and Realities (Trotman, ed.), 189
Richmond, Virginia revolt of 1800, 25. *See also* Prosser, Gabriel
Riggs, Marcia, 27
Riley (in "Mister Toussan"), 167, 168–69, 170, 173, 174
Ringgold, Faith, 144–45, 217, 225, 248
ritual remembrance, 256; as an attribute in Black cultural mythology framework, xvii, 23, 84, 86–87, 108, 116, 144, 156, 222; Braxton and Diedrich on, 134; communal rituals, 251; dysfunctional ritual remembrance, 239–40; as heritage behavior, 106; in *Insurrection: Holding History* (O'Hara), 246; in *Krik? Krak!* (Danticat), 173; related to heritage tourism, 132. *See also* commemoration philosophy; death and memorial; memorialization;

Index 339

memory; mourning and funeral rites; remembrance
Robb, Stephen, 61
Robeson, Paul, 36, 38, 82, 220, 223, 231, 241
Rocky (films), xiv
Rodman, Selden, 42
Ron. *See* Porter, Ron (in *Insurrection*)
"Rootedness: The Ancestor as Foundation" (Morrison), 76, 77
Root Magazine, 91
Roots (Haley), 42
Roots to Glory Tours, 105
Rose, Ernestine, 33
Rothberg, Michael, 254–55
Russell, Heather, 80–81
Ryan, Judylyn S., 27–28
Rycenga, Jennifer, 27, 31, 33

sacred meditation, 55
sacred memory. *See* sacred remembrance and sacred memory
sacred mythology, 49, 65
sacredness of survival. *See* survival strategies
sacred observance (sacred observation): as an attribute in Black cultural mythology framework, xvii, 23, 84, 86–87, 105, 156; and commemoration of 1619, 108, 116; death and memorial, 196; as heritage behavior, 106; in *Insurrection: Holding History* (O'Hara), 243, 246
sacred remembrance and sacred memory, 2, 23, 87, 110, 118, 171, 181–82, 216, 239, 262
sacrificial inheritance (sacred inheritance), xvii, 23, 111, 130; as an attribute in Black cultural mythology framework, xvii, 49, 84,

88–89, 102, 108, 129, 190, 196, 222, 228, 244, 246, 250, 258; and diaspora, xiii, xv, 52; Edwidge Danticat on, 172; and the Haitian Revolution, 157, 166; and Harriet Tubman, 142, 150; meditations on not calendar based, 102; Molefi Kete Asante on, 65; mourning and funeral rites, 18. *See also* inheritance
Sanderson, Jeremiah B., 97
"scavenger history," 213
Scenes of Subjection: Terror, Slavery, and Self-Making in Nineteenth-Century America (Hartman), 257
Schoelcher, Victor, 159
Schuyler, George Samuel, 223
Scott, Jill, 249
Scott-Heron, Gil, 20, 119, 120, 126–27, 129, 130
Seale, Bobby, 62
selective memory, 1
self-awareness, 1, 8, 253
self-definition, 3–4, 37, 67
self-determination, 2, 106, 140, 179, 184, 192–93, 195, 211, 216, 222; Maulana Karenga on, 55–56
self-immortalization, 32
self-preservation, 61
Semple, Jesse B., 223
Sernett, Milton C., 10–12, 140, 141, 152–53
Seven League Boots (Murray), 215
Seward, Adrienne Lanier, 78–79
Shadows of the Slave Past: Memory, Heritage, and Slavery (Araujo), 112, 132–33, 257
Shaka (Zulu chief), 52
Shange, Ntozake, ix, x, 21, 39, 160, 163–64, 169–71, 174, 225
Shannon, Sandra G., 83
Sharpe, Christina, 256

Shrivastava, Jaya, 241
"Site of Memory, The" (Morrison), 76, 77
Sites of Slavery: Citizenship and Racial Democracy in the Post–Civil Rights Imagination (Tillet), 257
Sitting Bull, 75, 221
Slavery Abolition Act for the British Colonies (1834), 95
Smallwood, Andrew P., 202
Smith, Chaym. *See* Chaym (fictional character)
Smith, Llewellyn, 105
social memory, 7, 79, 177
Sojourner Truth, 65, 74, 75
Something Torn and New: An African Renaissance (Ngugi), 17, 69, 133
Song for Anninho (Jones), 79
Song of Solomon (Morrison), 4
"Sonnet to a Negro in Harlem" (Johnson), 123
Soulcatcher and Other Stories: Twelve Powerful Tales about Slavery (Johnson), 164, 174–76
Southampton, Virginia revolt of 1831, 25, 149, 244. See also *Insurrection: Holding History* (O'Hara); Turner, Nat
Southern Christian Leadership Conference, 229, 231
Souza, Francisco Feliz de, 132
Soyinka, Wole, 65, 134
Spaulding, A. Timothy, 5–6, 257
speeches and speech delivery devices, 29, 33, 82–83; Molefi Kete Asante on, 61, 62–63. *See also* rhetoric and oratory
Stackolee (aka Stagolee, Stagger Lee), 68, 188, 207
Steel Drivin' Man (Nelson), 235
Stewart, Maria W., ix, 24, 39, 55, 74, 118, 162, 225, 258; as an

abolitionist, 20, 25, 26, 27, 29, 33, 221; and activist heroics, xv, 36, 63, 218; and antiheroic elements, 99, 184; on Black nationalism, 192; on David Walker, 32; and immortalization, 25–34, 26, 35, 36, 60, 63, 96–97, 98, 162, 184, 218–19, 221, 230; and religion, 30, 31, 59
storytelling, 8, 193, 202, 223, 225, 230, 232, 260; about Haitian Revolution, 157–58, 163, 168–69; about negative experiences, 111; cyclic storytelling, 86, 144, 145, 216, 218–19, 253; emancipatory style, 145; and embellishments, 157, 219, 250, 251, 253; gender-balancing storytelling, xv; and Harriet Tubman, 139, 140, 141–42, 144, 219; heroic storytelling, 38, 59, 143, 145, 203, 222; in *John Henry Days* (Whitehead), 233, 235, 239, 241; mythological storytelling, xv, 157, 171, 217, 235; orality of, 163; outcomes of, 217; and remembrance, 89, 138; of Shirley Graham Du Bois, 36–37, 38, 39, 41–42; and symbolism, 1, 39
Street, Mr. (in *John Henry Days*), 238–40, 241
Street, Pamela (in *John Henry Days*), 237, 238–40, 241
Stuckey, Sterling, 221
"Sufferings During the War" (Stewart), 26
"Summer After Malcolm, The" (Neal), 45–46
Sundiata of Mali, 16
survival strategies, xv, 251; Africana survivalism, 15, 23–25, 183, 255; cognitive survival, 85, 86; collective survival, 250; consciousness and

subconsciousness of, 258; cultural survival, xiii, 110–11, 129, 158, 194, 206, 231, 243, 244, 249, 254; and diaspora Africans, 16, 254; and Harriet Tubman, 141–42; having a conceptual mythological status, 253; identity survival, 73; in *Insurrection: Holding History* (O'Hara), 245, 246–47; intergenerational survivalist and resistance tendencies, 58; James Baldwin on, 125; for living in a dramatically different worldview, 93; and the Middle Passage, 2, 3, 18; Paul Robeson on survival as a hyperheroic act, 82; philosophy of survival, xvii, 51; and ritual remembrance, 134; sacredness of survival, 82, 258; survival mythology, 10, 183; survival plus memory, 3. *See also* cognitive survival; resistance-based cognitive survival
Sutter, J. (in *John Henry Days*), 234, 236–38, 240, 241
"Sword That Heals, The" (King), 120
symbols, 6, 7, 207, 217, 256; Amos Wilson on, 57; freedom symbols, 127; in *Insurrection: Holding History* (O'Hara), 243, 244; in juvenile literature, 146; Larry Neal on, 44, 45; Malcolm X as a symbol, 45, 207; Molefi Kete Asante on, 64, 67, 69; in *Native Son* (Wright), 195; relationship between rhetoric and symbolism, 68–69, 70; "white" cultural symbols, 64, 128, 191
syncre-nationalism, 28

Talcott, West Virginia (town in *John Henry Days*), 235, 236, 237
Talley, Justin, 79
Tanner, Benjamin, 96–97

T'Challa (in *Black Panther*, movie), xiv
Teague, Hilary, 82–83
television's role in Black cultural mythology. *See* media
Tener, Robert L., 187
Terrill, Robert E., 202
Tettenborn, Éva, 233
Thébaud, Léon, 181
There Once Was a Slave: Frederick Douglass (Graham Du Bois), 36, 40, 218
They Came before Columbus (Van Sertima), 112
Thomas, Clarence, 184
Thompson, Robert Dee., Jr., 37
Thomson, Kelly, 105
Till, Emmett, xiv, 43, 170, 223, 226
Tillet, Salamishah, 2, 257
time travel: in *Insurrection: Holding History* (O'Hara), 245–46, 249; in *Kindred* (Butler), 80, 148, 244
T.J. (in *Insurrection*), 244, 245, 246–48, 249
To Be Young, Gifted, and Black (Hansberry and Nemiroff), 164
Toni Morrison: Memory and Meaning (Seward and Talley), 78–79
Touré (journalist), 210–11
Toure, Sekou (president of Guinea), 55
tourism: commemoration tourism, 127; diaspora tourism, 132–33; heritage tourism/sacred participatory tourism, 131, 132, 134–35; "roots tourism," 131
Toussaint (Hill), 166
"Toussaint" (unfinished play by Hansberry), 164
Toussaint Louverture (Césaire), 159
Toussaint Louverture: A Play in Three Acts (James), 159
trauma, 4–5, 5, 6, 8, 18, 88, 110, 114, 152, 172, 253; enslavement as,

trauma *(continued)*
  4, 6, 60, 244, 254; in *John Henry Days* (Whitehead), 237, 240; Martin Luther King Jr.'s assasination as, 10
"Tree of Life" (spiritual), 125
Tropics of Haiti: Race and Literary History of the Haitian Revolution in the Atlantic World, 1789 to 1865 (Daut), 164
Trotman, C. James, 189
Trotter, (James) Monroe, 44
Tubman, Harriet, x, xiii, xv, 59, 74, 78, 83, 97, 224, 257; and aesthetic memorialization, 137–53, 233; death of, 140; fiction, poems, and plays about, 73, 147–52, 223; as a hero, 140, 143, 145, 251; hypervisibility of, 258; in juvenile literature, 143–47, 152, 216, 248; as a mythoform, 137, 141; as prototype for African American myth, 67, 68; self-emancipation of, 25; treatment of in storytelling, 141–42, 143; and US paper currency, xiii, xviii, 20, 137–38, 152
Tubman, Henry (brother), 148
Tucker, Chris, 122
Tucker, William (recorded as firstborn child to Angolans sold as slaves in Virginia in 1619), 108, 114, 116, 126, 245
Tupac Shakur, 207
Turner, Glennette Tilley, 145, 146
Turner, Nat, x, 44, 143, 149, 191, 207; as a Black hero, 62, 75, 97, 188, 226, 257; documentary films on, 223; Harriet Tubman's reverence for, 152; *Insurrection: Holding History* (O'Hara) as a play about, 78, 219, 225, 242–49; leader of 1831 revolt against slavery, xv, 25, 65, 118, 152, 190. *See also* Southampton, Virginia revolt of 1831

Tuskegee Institute (now Tuskegee University), 34, 41, 239
Twelve Million Black Voices (Wright), 186–87, 189

Ulysses in Black (Rankine), 233
Umoja Karamu (Black Thanksgiving), 103
UNESCO-supported heritage sites, 131
university courses on Africana Cultural Memory, 259
Unsung Heroes (Haynes), 39
US Bicentennial (1776–1976), 20, 80, 112, 126–27, 148, 149
"Us in the Tradition of Our Ancestors: Decades of Daring Distinction" (Karenga), 55
Utley, Ebony A., 27

Valbrun, Marjorie, 179
Van Der Horn-Gibson, Jodi, 37
Vanity Fair (magazine), xiv–xv, 50
Van Sertima, Ivan, 112
Vasconcelos, Luis Mendes de, 113
Venus (Parks), 225
"Vernacular Tradition, The" in *Norton Anthology of African American Literature*, 221
Vesey, Denmark, xv, 25, 62, 75, 190, 248
victimization, xviii, 4, 114, 132, 226; in *Native Son* (Wright), 192, 194, 197
Vie de Toussaint Louverture (Schoelcher), 159
vilification, 183–84
Virginia Act XXII (1660), 125–26
Virginia Wesleyan College, 106–107
Visions of a Liberated Future (Neal), 46

Vodun Festival and ceremonies, 131, 132
Voice of a Native Son (Miller), 189
Voice of Black Rhetoric, The (Asante and Robb), 61
voodoo, 189
Voting Rights Act passage, 118

Wakanda (comic book world of), xiii
"Wake Up Baby" (song), 249
Walcott, Derek, ix, 21, 39, 157, 176–77, 221
Walker, Alice, 213
Walker, C. J., 223, 231
Walker, David, 21, 24, 126, 161, 184, 192; as an abolitionist, 31–32, 220, 221; Houston Baker on, 191; as a mentor to Maria W. Stewart, 31–32; Molefi Kete Asante on, 61, 74
Walker and Ghost Dance: Plays (Walcott), 221
Wallace (fictional character), xiv
"Wall of Fire Rising, A" (Danticat), 164, 171–74
Walonen, Michael K., 235
Washington, Booker, T., x, 35, 36, 44, 66, 120, 178, 232
Washington, Isaiah, 122
Washington, Madison, 24–25, 62
"We Are Coming": The Persuasive Discourse of Nineteenth-Century Black Women (Logan), 30
W. E. B. Du Bois: Pictorial Biography (Graham Du Bois), 36
Wedgwood, Theobald (in "A Report from St. Domingue"), 174–76
Wellington, Darryl Lorenzo, 208, 210, 212
Wells-Barnett, Ida B., 55, 223
Welsh, Kariamu, 29, 31, 60, 68, 70, 77, 141
Welsing, Frances Cress, 149–52

West, Elizabeth, 3
Weylin, Rufus (in *Kindred*), 148–49
"What Are We Worth?" (Cooper), 35
Wheatley, Phillis, 35, 36, 42, 97
White, Edgar (playwright), 39
White, Ed (literary critic), 164
Whitehead, Colson, xix, 8, 21, 39, 78, 219, 224, 233–42
White Lion (English pirate ship), 104
White Man Listen! (Wright), 187
white nationalism and celebration of holidays, 101
White over Black (Jordan), 117
"Whither Now and Why?" (Du Bois), 142
Why We Can't Wait (King), 119–22
Wiggins, William H., Jr., 94–95, 97, 99, 100, 101, 105, 106, 238; "fellowship-worship-entertainment," 87, 95, 97, 105, 248
Wild Seed (Butler), 225
Williams, George Washington, 97, 219
Williams, Sherley Anne, 83
Williams, Yohuru, 211
Williamsburg, Virginia, 109, 111
"William Tucker Cemetery Dedication," 108
Wilson, Amos N., 20, 24, 64, 74, 118, 213, 258; on the development of the Black child, 56, 58–59, 67–68, 143, 174, 200, 227, 261; on mythological structure, 53, 57, 62, 70, 194–95, 204, 207, 261; psychological dimensions of cultural mythology, 56–59, 60
Wilson, August, 50, 83
"windowsonhaiti" website, 181
Wire, The (television series), xiv
Wit, Mutha (in *Insurrection*), 248
women. See Black women's experiences
Women and Sisters (Yellin), 33
Woodard, Komozi, 215–16

Woodson, Carter G., x, 12–15, 58, 112, 163, 219, 261
Woodson, George, 13–14
Woolfork, Lisa, 256
worldviews: African American, 75, 98, 121, 126, 167, 240; Africana worldviews, 23, 100, 104, 111, 112, 156, 168, 217, 222, 240, 254, 255; African-centered worldview, xvi, xvii, 1; child's developmental worldview, 145; cultural memory determining what is sacred, 92; of cultural wholeness, 89; defining, 221; demographic sampling of, 240; diasporan worldview, 17–18, 76, 183; distinguishing Amerian and African American worldviews on mythology, 240; on emancipation and bicentennial commemoration of, 125–30; restoring healthy centered worldviews, 216; survival strategies, 93, 255; white American, 75; Worldview Analysis Scale, 142. *See also* historical reenactment of worldview
Wright, Fanny, 33
Wright, Jeremiah, 92
Wright, Richard, x, xviii, 226; and the antihero, 20, 183–97, 223, 258. *See also* Bigger Thomas (in *Native Son*) as author of first best-selling African American novel, 83; on Black cultural mythology's power, 81–82, 217; on writing, 186, 216–17
writing, 47, 76, 156, 253; African American structured writings, 21; and Black women, 34, 224; letter-writing as epistolary form of, 123, 175; of Maria W. Stewart, 26, 27, 28, 30, 31, 33; Richard Wright on, 186, 216–17; of Shirley Graham Du Bois, 37, 38, 39, 40; writer's motives, 9

Yaa Asantewaa (Ashanti queen mother), 16, 138
Yahoo! Answers (internet forum), 91
Yancy, George, 83
Yellin, Jean, 33
Yette, Sam, 261
Young, Charles, 43
Young, Ida, 28
Youngblood, Shay, 225
Your Most Humble Servant: Benjamin Banneker (Graham Du Bois), 36

Zami: A New Spelling of My Name (Lorde), 80
Zulu people, 52, 54

www.ingramcontent.com/pod-product-compliance
Lightning Source LLC
Chambersburg PA
CBHW020226240426
43672CB00006B/433